A HISTOR
KITCHEN
GARDENING

A HISTORY OF
KITCHEN
GARDENING

SUSAN CAMPBELL

FRANCES LINCOLN

To my second grandchild,
Freddy Robert Campbell

Frances Lincoln Ltd
4 Torriano Mews
Torriano Avenue
London NW5 2RZ
www.franceslincoln.com

A History of Kitchen Gardening
Copyright © Frances Lincoln Limited 2005
Text and drawings copyright © Susan Campbell 2005

British Library Cataloguing in Publication data
A catalogue record for this book is available from the British Library

First Frances Lincoln edition 2005

ISBN 0 7112 2565 6

Printed and bound in Singapore

9 8 7 6 5 4 3 2 1

Commissioned and edited by Jane Crawley
Designed by Becky Clarke

CONTENTS

PREFACE
TO THE NEW EDITION

The kitchen garden at the centre of this book first appeared with the name of 'Charleston Kedding'. The garden was not only given a fictitious name; it was also an amalgamation of two or three kitchen gardens that I had come to know particularly well since 1980, when I first began my research on the history of the walled kitchen garden. I disguised the true identity of the garden, its owners and their gardeners because I wished (mistakenly as it has since turned out) to protect their privacy.

In a book that was otherwise as historically accurate as possible, several critics (and many readers) found the fabrication of the house, gardens and estate, and the lives of its inmates, both irritating and puzzling. It irritated my editors at Frances Lincoln too, to such an extent that the publication of a new edition was conditional on my replacing all my invented material with the truth.

It is nine years since the first edition of this book was published, and since then the general interest in old walled kitchen gardens has most gratifyingly increased. I have therefore taken the trouble to rectify an omission which seemed unimportant at the time, which was to provide the page numbers of all my references. I hope I have thereby made the book more useful to serious students.

I have also added a small amount of new material, some of which has been gleaned only recently, and I have corrected a number of errors, which the diligent reader will be able to spot by comparing the first with this second, more muscular edition.

S.C. 2005

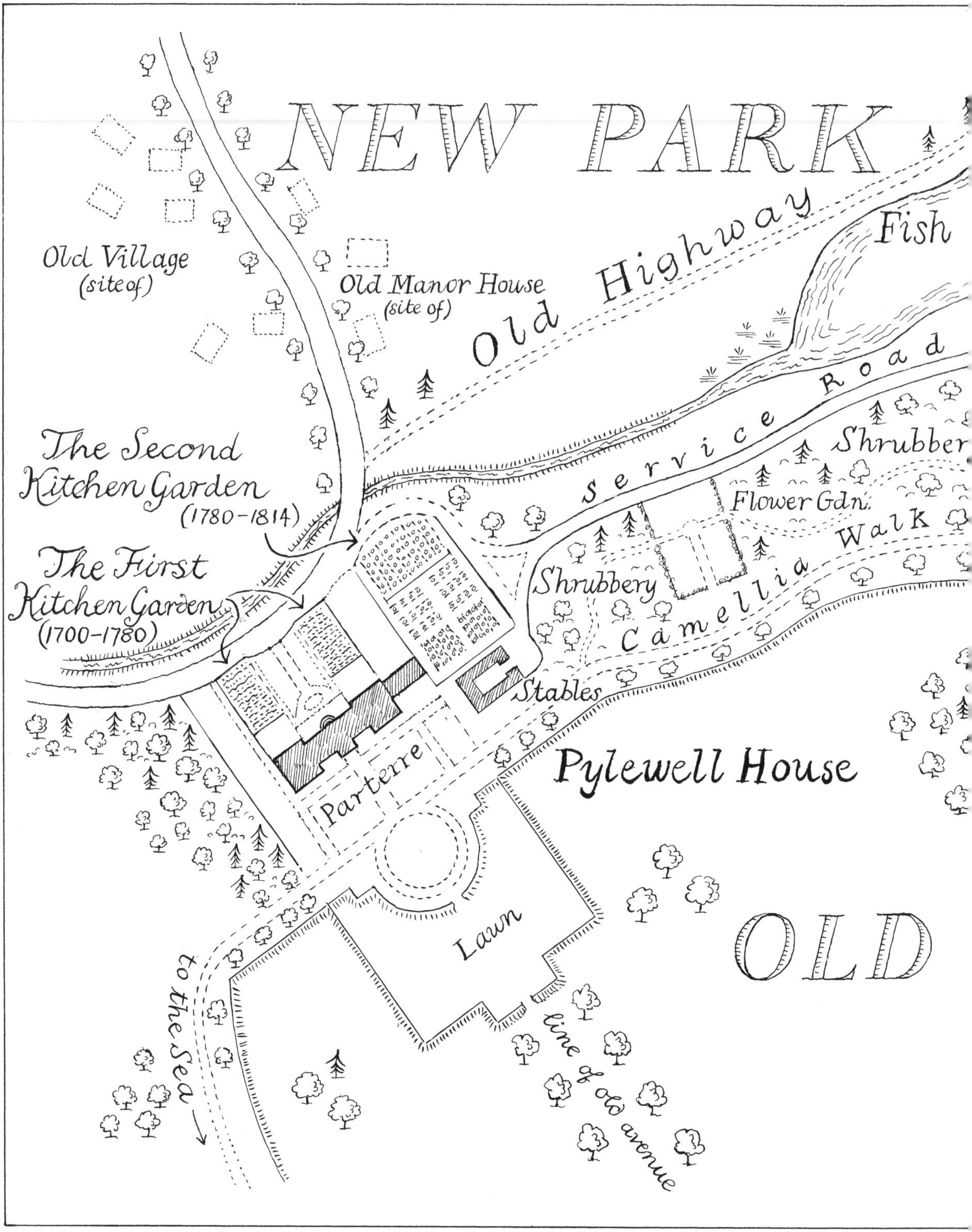

NEW PARK

Old Village
(site of)

Old Manor House
(site of)

Old Highway

Fish

service Road

Shrubber

The Second
Kitchen Garden
(1780–1814)

The First
Kitchen Garden
(1700–1780)

Flower Gdn.

Shrubbery

Camellia Walk

Stables

Parterre

Pylewell House

to the Sea →

Lawn

line of old avenue

OLD

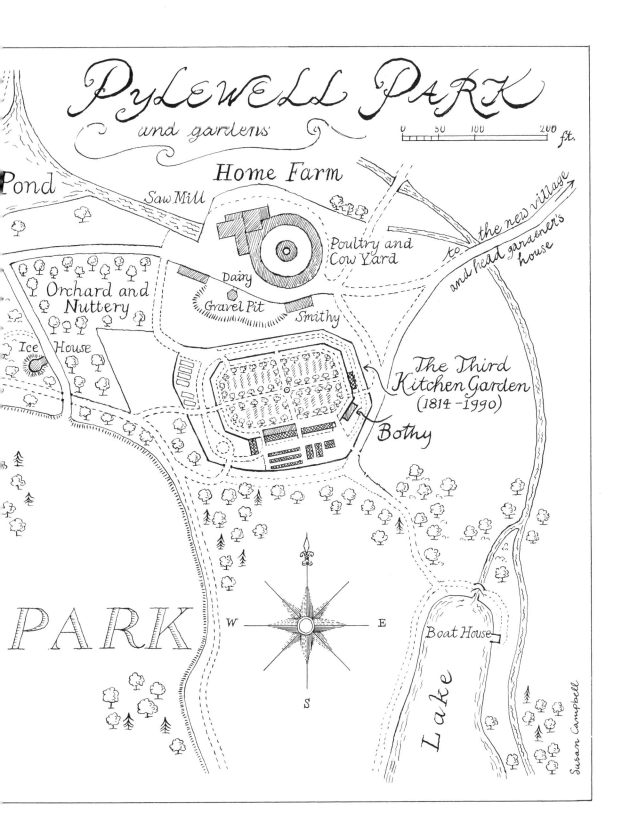

TWO NINETEENTH-CENTURY PLANS

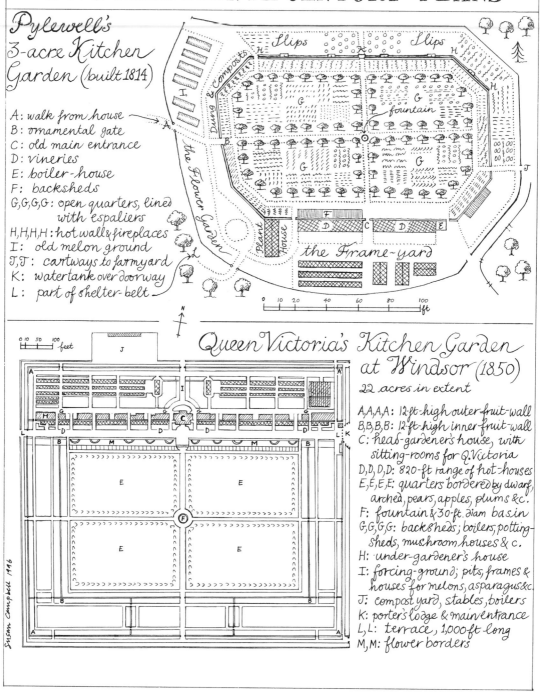

Pylewell's 3-acre Kitchen Garden (built 1814)

A: walk from house
B: ornamental gate
C: old main entrance
D: vineries
E: boiler-house
F: backsheds
G,G,G,G: open quarters, lined with espaliers
H,H,H,H: hot wall & fireplaces
I: old melon ground
J,J: cartways to farmyard
K: watertank over doorway
L: part of shelter-belt

Queen Victoria's Kitchen Garden at Windsor (1850)

22 acres in extent

A,A,A: 12-ft-high outer fruit-wall
B,B,B: 12-ft-high inner fruit-wall
C: head-gardener's house, with sitting-rooms for Q. Victoria
D,D,D: 820-ft range of hot-houses
E,E,E: quarters bordered by dwarf, arched, pears, apples, plums &c.
F: fountain & 30-ft. diam basin
G,G,G: backsheds; boilers, potting-sheds, mushroom houses &c.
H: under-gardener's house
I: forcing-ground; pits, frames & houses for melons, asparagus &c.
J: compost yard, stables, boilers
K: porter's lodge & main entrance
L,L: terrace, 1,000 ft long
M,M: flower borders

Susan Campbell 1996

INTRODUCTION

This book takes the form of a conducted tour around an old walled kitchen garden in the south of England. The garden, which I disguised in the first edition of this book as 'Charleston Kedding' (an anagram of 'old kitchen gardens') is at Pylewell Park, near Lymington in Hampshire. There are hundreds of old kitchen gardens like it throughout the British Isles. Most of them are now disused and in ruins, but within living memory, and for several centuries before that, the cooks in the kitchens they supplied never had to buy anything from a greengrocer, except citrus fruits and pine-apples – and even these luxuries were grown in such gardens, once upon a time. My purpose is to discover how these old kitchen gardens were capable of such sophisticated productivity, and thus relate their history.

When I began to write this book, in the early 1980s, I talked to several members of the Whitaker family, who owned the estate, and to two old estate workers, a woodman-cum-factotum named Willie Woodford and a gardener-cum-carter named Percy Gregory, both of whom remembered Pylewell in its heyday.

Percy was then in his eighties. When he began work here just after the First World War he had been one of a team of between twelve and sixteen men, under a head gardener named Mr Hamilton. Hamilton had

worked at Pylewell all his life, finally retiring as head gardener in the early forties, having first come here as a pot-washing garden boy in 1905. I also talked to Mrs Newstead, a lady then in her nineties, who as 'Mrs' Holmes had been the cook at Pylewell for many years. This was in the days of the second William Ingham Whitaker (known as 'Ingham'), son of the first William Ingham Whitaker (known as 'Willie'), who had bought the estate in 1874. All of these people were disguised as fictitious characters in the first edition of this book and have since died; in now writing without the need for fiction, I have had to resort to talking to their children, whose memories of pre-war days are, sadly, as distant as my own, and as little concerned with the running of a large country house kitchen garden as mine would have been. Nevertheless, I have been able to build on what I had already found out, and Pylewell's kitchen garden remains the central focus of the story.

The present kitchen garden was built in 1814. It is moderately large, occupying about three acres. One and a half acres are enclosed by high walls and the rest is taken up by the forcing houses, frames, back sheds, and slip gardens that lie outside the walls.

The head gardener's cottage stands at one of the four entries to the 200 acre park, where it doubles as an entrance lodge; it is about

300 yards from the kitchen garden. Its position here is not typical, as head gardeners liked to be as near to the centre of operations as possible; however, there was also a small bothy by the kitchen garden, and the Home Farm with its saw mill, dairy and smithy was close by. The mansion itself, which the kitchen garden was designed to serve, is a further one third of a mile away and is surrounded by twenty to thirty acres of shrubberies, woodland gardens and formal gardens, which in turn are set in a large area of parkland.

EARLY HISTORY OF PYLEWELL

The park is situated two miles east of Lymington, facing the Isle of Wight on the north-western shore of the Solent. It is also on the south-western boundary of the New Forest. The earliest recorded building at Pylewell was a house, or more probably a hunting lodge, which

appears as 'Pie House' on Norden's map of 1595. It stands in a deer park in the manor of Badgeley, also known as Badsley or South Badsley (and now a hamlet known as South Baddesley). The manor of Badsley can be traced back to the time of Edward the Confessor. [1]

THE WORSLEYS

In 1617 a 'capital messuage' and ninety acres of land at South Badsley were bought by Richard Worsley (1588-1621), who already owned property at 'Pylewell ground'.[2] Worsley was a member of one of the leading families on the Isle of Wight and was created First Baronet of Appuldurcomb in 1611. His great grandson James (1645-95) inherited Pylewell in 1676 and in 1688 married and moved in. Seven years later he died, leaving the property to his five-year-old son, also James. Young James married in 1714, but it is probable that the enlargement and improvement of the old hunting lodge and the laying out of its gardens had been begun by his father, to be continued by the son at the time of his marriage.

The date of the original house is unknown, but it would have had splendid views across the deer park, southwards towards the sea. An anonymous, undated, bird's-eye view engraving of *circa* 1700 shows Pylewell's north front, with just such a view (see page 22). This front is in the William and Mary style, with a pair of Elizabethan pepper-pot towers (for viewing deer?) just visible on either wing, and some fairly ancient-looking stables and a farmyard attached to its east side. A modest kitchen garden and orchard lie to the north of the farmyard. The kitchen garden is rectangular, with the longest axis running north-south. The plot is contained on three sides by low walls (one of which forms the boundary of the main highway from Lymington to Beaulieu). On the fourth side there is a narrow canal backed by a high, thin hedge. The hedge screens the kitchen garden from the house and the formal approach to the north front – a gravelled forecourt ornamented by topiaried shrubs and grass plats.

The kitchen garden is balanced symmetrically by a soft-fruit garden on the other side of the forecourt; this too is screened from view from the house by a tall hedge (technically known as a palisade) and bounded by another canal (an ornamental strip of water, rather than a canal in the modern sense). Its other boundaries are formed by a continuation of the wall beside the main highway, and by a tall fence of flat palings. A small terrace or parterre (a carpet-like design of turf, gravel or clipped shrubs) lies between the kitchen gardens and the mansion.

The palisades, canals, parterre and topiaried trees are typical of the geometrical, late baroque period of garden design which was fashionable from the end of the seventeenth to the early eighteenth centuries. The print of 1700 shows even more elaborate formal gardens to the south of the mansion. A central vista is created by

a lengthy avenue running due south to the sea, while the mansion is faced by a semicircular lawn, bounded by more palisades, which screen a maze-like 'wilderness' containing arbours, topiaried trees, arches and *allées* or alleys.

A later print, published in 1739 in *Britannia Illustrata*, shows the same view, and virtually the same garden layout. There are a few changes; the towers are now castellated turrets, and the kitchen garden has switched places with the fruit garden on the west of the forecourt, enabling it to double in size. Its original site is now all orchard.

It is highly likely that these gardens, and possibly even the house at Pylewell, were designed by John James of Greenwich (*circa* 1672-1746). He was an architect and garden designer and the translator, in 1712, of d'Argenville's *Theory and Practice of Gardening*. He was also a follower of George London and Henry Wise (at that time the leading exponents of garden design). The possibility that he might have worked at Pylewell is supported by two slim pieces of evidence: although the work was never completed, John James was employed between 1701 and 1710 by Sir James's cousin Robert Worsley (the fourth baronet, born in 1669) to rebuild Appuldurcomb on the Isle of Wight[3] and two of the subscribers to the d'Argenville translation were Sir James himself and his cousin Henry.

In 1747 Robert Worsley died without a direct heir, and Sir James became the fifth baronet and inherited Appuldurcomb, but he continued to live at Pylewell. He was M.P. for Newtown on the Isle of Wight in nine parliaments and a historian of the Isle of Wight. In 1750 he let Pylewell as a summer residence for Frederick, Prince of Wales and his family, who came here for the sea bathing. (There was a small pavilion or bath house on the shore at the end of the long avenue.)

Sir James died in 1756, and his son Thomas, then aged twenty-eight, inherited Pylewell. He was colonel-in-chief in the South Hants Militia and, according to his captain, the young Edward Gibbon, he was 'a man of fashion and entertainment' and 'an easy good-humoured man fond of the table and his bed'. He was also given to 'the daily practise of hard and excessive drinking'.[4] His mark on Pylewell was negligible as he spent much of his time abroad. He died in 1768 and was succeeded by his son Richard, then aged only seventeen.

Sir Richard Worsley, rather than make his home at Pylewell, chose to return to Appuldurcomb, where he employed Lancelot 'Capability' Brown to landscape the grounds. Pylewell was meanwhile let, in 1777, to the current Sheriff of Hampshire, a wealthy man who had made his fortune in India, named Ascanius William Senior (?1730-89).

ASCANIUS SENIOR AND THOMAS ROBBINS

In 1781 Senior bought Pylewell and the nearby manors of Pilley and Warborne from Worsley for £22,000. A pen and wash drawing done in the 1784 by Thomas Rowlandson, of the south front of Pylewell, shows that the turrets on the east and west wings of the house are now pavilions, and the garden has been swept clear of all the old clipped hedges and matching parterres.[5] Lancelot Brown was not only working at Appuldurcomb at this time, but also at the nearby estates of Cadland and Highcliffe; do the drastic changes at Pylewell suggest his influence reached this corner of Hampshire as well?

There is no direct evidence that Senior was responsible for the radical changes to Pylewell's grounds, but these changes, apparent in the Rowlandson drawing, are more fully described by Richard Warner in his *Topographical Remarks relating to the South Western parts of Hampshire . . .* This was published in 1793, six years after Senior had sold his by now considerably enlarged estate to a Thomas Robbins. Warner remarks that:

the grounds around it are laid out with great simplicity; an extensive lawn, belted by a shady walk, with occasional openings, stretches from the house to the seaside. This disposition of them is extremely different and highly improved from what it was about fifty years ago, as appears from a print I have of Pile-well at that time. [i.e. the *Britannia Illustrata* print of 1739.]

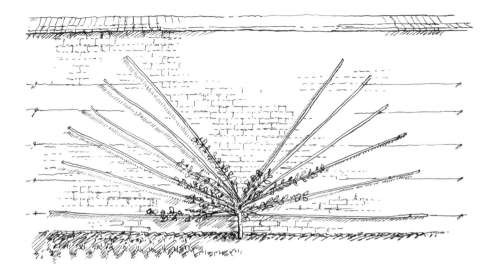

Neither this, nor some comments published by William Gilpin,[6] mention the kitchen garden, but if it was Brown who was the influence here, the grounds to the north of the house would have had the same treatment as those to the south, and the orchard and kitchen garden would most certainly have been moved to a place where they would be hidden both from the mansion and the sight of the best parts of the park or gardens. A full-scale survey of the entire estate proves this to be the case.[7] The survey was made in 1803 by Henry de Bruyn for Thomas Weld of Lulworth, who purchased Pylewell from Robbins. It is with this survey, by the way, that the spelling becomes 'Pylewell'.

By sweeping away the formal drive, its bordering lawns, canals and hedges, as well as the kitchen gardens, the view to the north of the house has been replaced by one similar to that to the south; it is of pleasure grounds and parkland in keeping with the romantic, picturesque and natural style of the time.

The north front of Pylewell is now approached from the old highroad by a sweeping carriageway. The parterres, mazes and topiaried walks to the south of the house have been replaced by the 'extensive' lawn described by Gilpin, which has done away with the northern end of the avenue of fine oaks, half a mile long and a hundred years old, leading from the south front to the sea. The old deer park now appears to merge with the lawns, thanks to the ha-has or invisible ditches which have been dug about 100 yards from the north and south fronts. A small flower garden has appeared to the east of the mansion.

A new kitchen garden has been made to the north of the old farmyard and stables, and east of the original seventeenth-century site. It occupies just over one acre and has a semicircular south-facing fruit wall. Another wall divides it across, possibly to provide more walls facing south, as the longest axis of this new kitchen garden still runs inconveniently north-south.

JOSEPH WELD

In 1802 Thomas Weld (1750–1810), a wealthy Roman Catholic landowner of Lulworth in the neighbouring county of Dorset, bought the Pylewell estate as a wedding present for his second son Joseph (1777-1863). Joseph Weld was both an agriculturalist and a keen yachtsman – he was to have seven racing yachts built for him on Pylewell's own 'hard' or beach between 1821 and 1857, one of which was the famous 248 ton schooner, *Alarm.*

As had happened before when Pylewell acquired a new owner, the house, gardens, park and farms were to undergo improvements. In 1810, on the death of Senior's brother-in-law, the rights of the old manor house, the village, its water-driven corn mill and all the land to the north of the house on the far side of the highway reverted to Joseph Weld. Now he could enhance the views in that direction and enlarge his park.

Over the next ten years he swept the ancient hamlet of Baddesley from its original site and demolished the equally ancient manor house, rehousing his tenants in seven new cottages beyond the park boundaries. He razed the village chapel and built a new one by the new cottages. He made a Roman Catholic chapel for the family in a wing of the mansion. He realigned the highway so that it skirted the new park. He created a fifteen acre lake in a marshy part of the pleasure grounds, firming the clay bottom by driving herds of sheep to and fro across the site; the clay excavated for the lake was taken to kilns on the estate to make bricks for several new buildings.

Half a mile to the east of the house he built a new mill house for the miller. In 1814 he began to build a model farming complex with a new farmhouse, a water-powered saw-mill, a carpenter's house, a smithy, an ornamental dairy, a slaughter house, new barns, wagon lodges, piggeries, stables and a circular cow yard 250 feet in diameter, with a circular poultry yard and chicken houses in the centre (see pages 8–9).[8]

And naturally he had to have a new kitchen garden. Weld was, as well as an agriculturalist, an ardent horticulturist; letters from his gardener, Abernathy,[9] show that the old garden was quite productive – 250 sticks of 'sparrowgrass' (asparagus) were sent 'by caravan' to Lulworth in April 1809, along with two brace of cucumbers, potatoes, radishes and kidney beans, which means that some sort of forcing was being done – but he would have been far from satisfied with the kitchen garden built (possibly) by Senior, which, apart from the inconvenience of its north-south orientation and its position (for it now protruded into the new parkland), was situated on damp ground, sloped downwards to the north and was far too small for Weld's large family. Moreover, it would have had inadequate work sheds and storage houses, a glasshouse that was by now very out of date, and inadequate accommodation for the head gardener and the garden boys.

In 1814 Weld built the kitchen garden we see today, on three acres of ground to the south of the new farmyard. The site is ideal, embodying all the requirements for a productive fruit and vegetable garden. It lies on a little rise to the south of the farm, mill and mill pond, thus avoiding the boggy soil and damp, freezing fogs which put the previous garden at a disadvantage. The belief persisted well into the nineteenth century that 'mill-dew' or 'infectious mist' was the cause of blight on fruit trees (see Chapter 15). The orientation of the main axis is east-west, with a slight inclination to east of south, so that the longest walls receive the most sunshine late in the day (see page 10).

The inner garden, quartered by paths meeting at the centre by a little iron fountain, was enclosed by high walls. It occupies about one and a half acres; outside these walls Weld had another one and a half acres of cultivated ground, technically known as 'the slip gardens'. Joseph Weld also planted a nuttery and an orchard just beyond the slip garden. He continued to make improvements at Pylewell until 1837, when his older brother Thomas, the famous Cardinal Weld, died. Thomas had inherited Lulworth in 1810 and on entering the church had passed it on to Joseph in 1828, but eventually the extravagance of running two estates (as well as his racing yachts) proved too much of a financial strain, and in 1850 Joseph Weld sold the 1,288 acre manor and estate of Pylewell to a barrister, George Peacocke.

The sale particulars of 1850 describe:

A CAPITAL KITCHEN GARDEN, Walled in on three sides [this is an estate agent's error, it was walled on four sides], very productive, partly laid out in Pleasure Gardens. In this garden is a Vinery, 40-ft long, with choice Vines in prime bearing. *Second Garden*, a Vinery and Green House, same dimensions. An Orangery, a 12-light Pine Pit, at the back a range of Buildings for Tools, Stoke Holes, Mushroom Houses, Potting Houses, Melon Ground, with brick-built Pit for 18 lights. A Turf House and Fuel Store. [10]

Three years later Pylewell was sold again, to William Peere Williams-Freeman, who, during his twenty years of ownership, built a new village school and enlarged the church built for the villagers by Weld.[11] He also bought more land, made a new parterre in front of the mansion, a bowling green beside it and a boathouse on the lake. He died in 1873 and a year later Pylewell Park, with its mansion, sundry houses and cottages, brick fields, farms, corn and saw-mills, was bought by 'Willie', the first William Ingham Whitaker, for £72,000.

THE WHITAKERS, 1874 TO THE PRESENT DAY

The Whitaker fortune was made in Sicily, with Ingham's Marsala wine. Willie made his move to England from Palermo in 1875, with a young son of ten and an ailing wife, in the hope of the climate improving her health, but she died only a year after coming to Pylewell. Both Weld and Williams-Freeman had enormous households, but on his purchase of the mansion Whitaker made major alterations: it already had at least a dozen bedrooms, five reception rooms, a library and a chapel but he added another storey and a conservatory.

He also demolished the circular cow yard and moved the home farm to a farm in the village (where he built a village hall opposite Freeman's school), but he made few changes to the park and gardens. Apart from modernizing the heating systems in the greenhouses, he made even fewer changes to the kitchen garden. It was in his son Ingham's ownership of Pylewell – from 1893 to 1936 – that the gardens reached their heyday. (Ingham also built even more

additions to the mansion, but removed the conservatory as his wife said it was damp and unhealthy.)

Ingham Whitaker married in 1903, eleven years after inheriting Pylewell, and had five children. With the Whitakers themselves, one or two nannies and a governess, two or three ladies' maids, a housekeeper, butler and cook, two kitchen maids, a scullery maid, two footmen, five housemaids, a hall boy and an odd man living in the house, there were never less than twenty-five people to provide with fruit and vegetables. The kitchen gardens and glasshouses were at full stretch, with at least four men working full-time in the hot houses, four in the kitchen garden and another eight in the pleasure grounds. There were also several woodmen, seven gamekeepers and a dairyman who made fourteen pounds of butter a week in the dairy by the water-mill below the kitchen garden.

Ingham's passion was for Japanese plants and rhododendrons; in the 1890s he planted Kansan flowering cherries in the wild garden and in 1912, with the help of Mr Hamilton and thirty labourers from Lymington, he created an enormous lily pond – virtually another lake – with a Japanese bridge, just below the kitchen garden. His collection of rare Himalayan rhododendrons was formed from seeds found by plant-hunting expeditions in the 1920s, and with plants from Hamilton's friends, who were head gardeners in many well-known gardens all over the country, including Bodnant, Exbury and Kew. The wives of two of the gardeners were employed for six weeks in the late summer and autumn to dead-head the rhododendrons every afternoon; as the daughter-in-law of one of them told me: 'It helped to pay for our holidays'. Ingham renewed most of the glasshouses, pits, forcing houses and frames in the kitchen garden's old melon ground in the 1930s, but apart from that the kitchen garden changed very little in appearance; it still looked much the same as when Joseph Weld built it in 1814.

The two youngest children, Penelope and Jean, still remember how the kitchen garden looked in the thirties, with its herbaceous borders and apple trees on either side of gravel paths, espaliered peaches, apples, pears, morellos, plums and figs on the walls and raspberries, currants and strawberries in cages. There were grapes, nectarines and more peaches in the lean-to greenhouses. Strawberries were forced there too, for their father's birthday every year, on April 3. In their mother's rooms there were always posies of Malfitano violets, brought from great aunt Tina's villa in Palermo and here grown in frames. There was a rose garden and beds of flowers for cutting for the house in the outer garden or 'slip'. The pigs and chickens that provided bacon and eggs for their breakfasts were nurtured, like the cows which provided all the butter, milk and cream, at the Home Farm, one of the eight farms that comprised the estate.

Ingham Whitaker died in 1936; his widow moved to London. Her son, the third William Ingham Whitaker ('Billy'), inherited the estate and found that he had to make economies; half the house was shut down and most of the servants and gardeners had to go. Moreover, World War Two was looming; head gardener Hamilton went into semi-retirement, knowing that many of his younger gardeners would be called up to serve in the Forces.

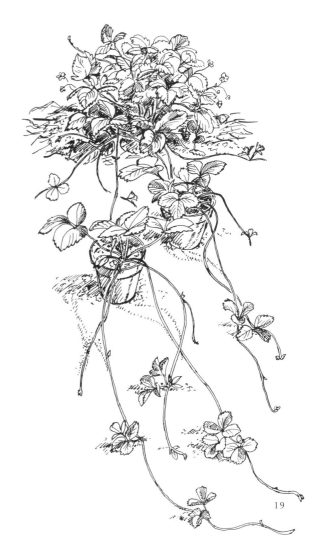

The mansion was requisitioned for use, first for the Northumberland Fusiliers and then for the London Fusiliers; the park and gardens were used as an assault course and battle school, and were rather damaged as a result. The next military occupants were Americans, who, with their exotic supplies of food and nylon stockings, were very popular in the neighbourhood. Finally it was inhabited by Italian prisoners of war. Mrs Whitaker meanwhile lived at the Home Farm, with her three younger children serving in the war, as did many of the men and women who had worked at Pylewell as servants. The green-houses were used to raise tomatoes and the kitchen garden was let to a market-cum-nursery gardener. As part of the war effort he raised fruit and vege-tables for a green-grocery in Lymington. Mr Hamilton came out of retirement for the duration of the war and acted as a gardens supervisor.

Even after the war ended in 1945, the house was still requi-sitioned, now as an army convalescent home. It was not derequisitioned for another five years. Neither Billy nor his sister Penelope had married; when Pylewell was finally restored to them they found both it and its gardens in a sorry state. Billy pulled down two wings of the mansion (one containing the chapel; the other the ballroom) and the bedding-out in the gardens was simplified to suit post-war austerity. With only four gardeners now to keep all the twenty to thirty acres of garden going, the kitchen garden was still producing plants for sale, as well as a few fruits and vegetables for Billy's relatively small household; his indoor peaches and nectarines were raised with the minimum amount of heat, and the plant house, with its exotic blooms for the mansion, was kept warm with portable heaters. In 1958 half the kitchen garden was turned over to the production of Christmas trees.

I first saw the kitchen garden at Pylewell in 1968, invited there by Billy, the third William Ingham Whitaker. He still kept the house, gardens and estate in a fairly grand style – not as grand as his father and grandfather before him, but grand enough to keep a butler-cum-chauffeur, a cook, two maids and four gardeners as well as a carpenter-cum-woodman and a gamekeeper.

Billy gave wonderful dinner parties. His guests were served with fish fresh from the sea that formed the southern boundary of the estate, and with game from his coverts, fields and ponds. These delights were accompanied by the freshest, most delicate salads, herbs and vegetables from the kitchen garden. The meal would end with plums and pears from the garden walls; apples and nuts from the orchard; peaches, figs and grapes from the glasshouses; strawberries from the cold frames; or sorbets and fools made from the raspberries, gooseberries and currants in the fruit cage.

And the house itself was full of flowers. In the principal rooms planters and jardinières were filled all the year round, according to season, with forced bulbs, azaleas, orchids, mimosa, gardenias, pelargoniums and lilies. Weekend guests would find their bedside tables adorned with posies made from camellias picked in the shrubberies, carnations from one of the glasshouses, or flowers grown purely for cutting – all still available in the kitchen garden.

But by the end of the 1970s Billy could see that economies must be made if he was to leave enough money for his heir, a nephew with ten children, to run the place. Once again he had to cut down, letting out the home farm and the shooting, dispensing with his flat in London and keeping only two gardeners. He died in 1988, a year after the terrible hurricane that wrecked the park and the rhododendron woods.

Since then, the tidying up of the park has taken place, the kitchen garden is now a wholesale nursery for herbaceous plants, and the lawns and paths are kept tidy.

I have been visiting old kitchen gardens and glasshouses for twenty years now in my quest to discover the secrets of that branch of gardening. Some of them go right back to the time when kitchen gardening began. This book is about these secrets. Pylewell's was the first of some four hundred kitchen gardens which I have since recorded, and as such it forms the template for this history.

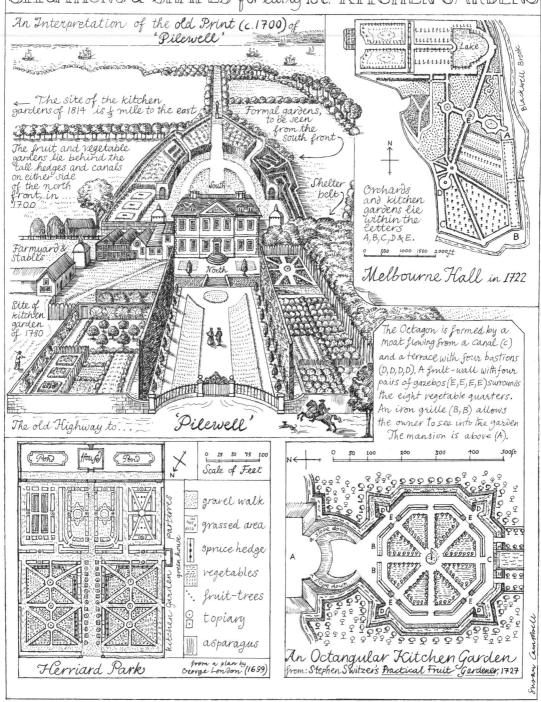

SITUATIONS & SHAPES for early 18th c. KITCHEN GARDENS

An Interpretation of the old Print (c.1700) of 'Pilewell'

← The site of the kitchen gardens of 1814 is ⅓ mile to the east

The fruit and vegetable gardens lie behind the tall hedges and canals on either side of the north front, in ... 1700

Formal gardens, to be seen from the south front →

Shelter belt

South

North

Farmyard & stables

Site of kitchen garden of 1780

The old Highway to... 'Pilewell'

Melbourne Hall in 1722

Lake

Blackwell Brook

N

Orchards and kitchen gardens lie within the letters A, B, C, D & E.

0   500   1000 1500   2000ft

The Octagon is formed by a moat flowing from a canal (c) and a terrace with four bastions (D, D, D, D). A fruit-wall with four pairs of gazebos (E, E, E, E) surrounds the eight vegetable quarters. An iron grille (B, B) allows the owner to see into the garden. The mansion is above (A).

Herriard Park

Pond   House   Pond

N

kitchen garden parterres   green house

0   25   50   75   100
Scale of Feet

☐ gravel walk
▦ grassed area
▮ spruce hedge
⋮ vegetables
∴ fruit-trees
⊙ topiary
▥ asparagus

from a plan by George London (1699)

An Octangular Kitchen Garden

from: Stephen Switzer's Practical Fruit Gardener, 1727

N ←

0   50   100   200   300   400   500ft

slope down

Susan Campbell

CHAPTER ONE

LOCATION

I had visited Billy in his house at Pylewell many times before I found out where the kitchen garden was. It cannot be seen from the long ilex avenue which runs from the north lodge at the main gates to the north front of the house, nor from the house itself, nor from any parts of the garden surrounding the house, nor from any vantage point in the 200 acre park surrounding the pleasure grounds. The few places from which it can be seen are all on the service road. This runs past the kitchen garden and the mill, connecting the stables beside the mansion to the little thatched lodge which was once the head gardener's cottage. This concealment is quite deliberate. The kitchen garden was moved to its present secluded position by Joseph Weld because the walls of Ascanius Senior's eighteenth-century kitchen garden, like those of countless others across the country, were not only so high as to be unsightly but also obstructed views from the house.

There was also the constant to-ing and fro-ing of gardeners, the picking and cutting of crops, the digging of the open ground or 'quarters', the stirring of composts, the manuring of hotbeds and the smells arising from those departments, which mingled with the occasional but hefty scents of decaying cabbage leaves and bruised, wind-brushed celery or onion. None of this was welcome at close hand, and none of it made for the ornamental or restful place that a garden is supposed to be.

Seventeenth-century kitchen gardens – Pylewell's amongst them – were situated, not necessarily right under the windows of the best rooms, but as close to the house as possible, and on the best soil available, with a handy supply of water. Other considerations were an open aspect, with shelter from the worst of wind and weather.

Kitchen gardens were not thought wholly unsightly until they began to increase in size, to become almost industrial in character and to loom large in a landscape that, throughout the eighteenth and well into the nineteenth century, was changing from formal to 'natural'

door to the kitchen garden

– an English landscape in which there was no place for straight lines. Everything straight had to go; straight paths, straight beds, straight hedges, straight ornamental canals, straight avenues and, above all, straight walls. Kitchen gardens spoiled the impression of Arcadia that 'artist gardeners' were now creating with carefully planned haystacks and watering places, boathouses, bridges, temples, mausoleums, hermits' cottages and grottoes. Any of these made desirable eye-catchers; on the other hand, vast brick or stone boxes formed by fifteen-foot-high walls, enclosing dung heaps, frameyards, work sheds, bothies and primitive glasshouses (each one accompanied by a smoking chimney), did not.

In 1728, Batty Langley, landscape gardener, architect and author, directed 'That all gardens be grand, beautiful and natural', and that the main front of the house should lie open to:

An elegant Lawn or Plain of Grass, adorn'd with beautiful Statues . . . That grand Avenues be planted from such large open Plains, . . . That Views be as extensive as possible. That such Walks, whose Views cannot be extended, terminate in Woods, Forests, misshapen Rocks, strange Precipices, Mountains, old Ruins, grand Buildings &c. [1]

If these picturesque features could not be contrived naturally, they must be put there by art – painted on canvas and placed as screens at the end of a vista that might otherwise end in a squalid bothy or greenhouse. If it were impossible for kitchen gardens to be put out of sight, they would be concealed with shrubs or belts of trees, or they might be built a little way off, with circular or oval walls and a shrubbery planted outside, so that the whole department would look like a clump of trees or a little wood within the park.

By the mid nineteenth century, when large kitchen gardens were required (as at Pylewell), the offices, workshops, storerooms and yards of the entire garden workforce were usually placed within the precincts of the kitchen garden department, and these precincts were functional rather than ornamental. A large kitchen garden complex and all its working parts should, therefore, preferably not be visible from the house.

The first kitchen garden at Pylewell was just outside the kitchens of the Worsleys' old hunting lodge, and there it remained when the new house was built at the end of the seventeenth century. It looks as if it was Ascanius Senior who took it a step or two to the east of the original site in the 1780s, and finally, in 1814, just one year before the battle of Waterloo, Joseph Weld moved it to its present position about a quarter of a mile further to the east of the house. The kitchen garden is so well hidden that without the guidance of its owner I might never have found it. A walk round the park and pleasure grounds proves that it is well and truly screened by strategic clumps, by the lie of the land and, closer to its tall brick walls, by shrubs and a shelterbelt of large trees.

On my first visit I approached the kitchen garden from the lawn below the south front of the house, as would any of the guests of the Welds or the Whitakers in the old days.

THE APPROACH

The nineteenth-century kitchen gardens of very large establishments such as Windsor Castle in Berkshire, Welbeck Abbey in Nottinghamshire or Chatsworth in Derby-shire might be a mile or more from the houses they served. If they were to be visited by their owners a longish walk would be necessary; the ladies would go by pony-chaise along a specially made carriage drive. However, for most owners, like the Welds, the kitchen garden was within easy walking distance.

The walk itself had to be enjoyable too. And Pylewell's is delightful: we walk through the pleasure grounds along a wide, level gravel path, lined with camellias and ancient oaks, which leads us from the lawns and parterres on the south side of the house. A swimming bath, shrubberies and the remains of a flower garden lie to the left of the path, and on our right the park stretches almost a mile south-wards, until it reaches the sparkling sea.

Our path, which is known as the Camellia Walk was planted by Billy and leads eventually to the wild garden and an arboretum beside the lake, but an inviting fork to the left takes us to an opening between two brick pillars. Through it we can, at last, see the kitchen-garden walls, with a wrought-iron gate directly ahead. The gate, which replaces the wooden door that was originally here, was a gift from Billy and his four sisters to celebrate their parents' silver wedding in 1923. Although the Whitakers prefer to use this gate, it was not Joseph Weld's original entrance to the kitchen garden. To find that, we must continue to the right, along a walk bordered until recently by wide herbaceous beds. A further turn to the left brings us to the hothouses which stand in front of and against the south face of the kitchen-garden wall. This wall is almost entirely taken up with two forty-foot vineries; the space in front of them is occupied by four more glasshouses, some with frames attached.

doorway between vineries

Weld's entrance to the kitchen garden stands between the vineries, in the centre of the wall. This is exactly as it should be, for a northern approach, via the service road, would have led visitors through the farm, and their first view of the garden would have been of the offices and workshops at the back of the vineries. The visitor was never allowed to make the mistake of approaching the kitchen garden from behind, an approach that was even more inappropriate in gardens where the hothouses were sited on the south side of the north wall. The workers, on the other hand, always approached the garden from the service road, because gardeners, like kitchen gardens, were supposed to be invisible.

THE SERVICE ROAD

Until recently the Camellia Walk was never under any circumstances used by the gardeners and garden boys. All the produce that went to the kitchens, the conservatory and the flower-arranging room had to be taken along the service road in carts, wheelbarrows and handbarrows – stretcher-like boards used especially for pot plants, baskets of fruit and bunches of cut flowers. Head gardeners would insist on hand-barrows for the more delicate produce; it was liable to be jolted and bruised if it went by cart or wheelbarrow.

The service road leads from the back of the kitchen gardens to the kitchens and stables which still occupy the eastern end of the house, and parallel to, but at a distance from, our walk. This road – really no more than a lane – is sufficiently secluded for it to run openly into the kitchen yard, but there are several examples – including Claremont in Surrey and Farnborough Hall in Warwickshire – where the kitchen approach takes the form of a tunnel, so objectionable to the sight of the stiffer type of family was any member of the gardening fraternity, other than the head gardener.

THE SLIP GARDENS

At Pylewell the hothouses and frames stand in a portion of land lying outside, and encircling, the kitchen garden walls. This piece of land is known as 'the slip' or 'slip garden' (see page 11). Slip gardens were originally created in the mid eighteenth century to take advantage of the outer sides of kitchen garden walls (especially those facing east, west and south) and of the ground below and beyond. The space encompassed was usually about thirty feet wide – as it is here – and it was used for growing hardy fruits and vegetables that needed space, but not much shelter or cosseting. In smaller gardens the slip would be planted with a mixture of ornamental shrubs and hardy fruit trees.

Mr Hamilton grew cherries, plums and late pears on north and east-facing walls, and decorative climbers on west-facing ones. Rhubarb, currants and gooseberries grew in beds in the northern part of the slip. The north-western portion accommodated the compost and fuel yards, and in the south-western part there had always been a flower garden. The southern slip was once a melon ground and a reserve, or nursery garden. In the 1920s Billy's mother turned the flower garden into a little rose garden, which is still there though very overgrown. It lies to the left of the wrought-iron gate leading into the kitchen garden.

Two borders were made in the slips; one against the walls, the other against the 'ring' or outer fence. A broad path made a circuit of the slips, between the borders. The path was wide enough for a horse and cart, so that dung, fuel and other bulky materials could be delivered to smaller doorways in the kitchen-garden walls and wheeled from there to where they were needed. The horse and cart entered at the north-west corner, the one most convenient for access to the stables, the farmyard and the mill-pond.

The slip gardens are now invisible (and impenetrable) under a tangle of brambles and nettles. Above the tangle, here and there, we can see the strangled remains of some old soft-fruit bushes, a wayward fig tree and a few enormous, leaning, unpruned cherry trees.

Beyond the western and northern slips are the nuttery and an orchard, both replanted several times since Weld first laid them out. To the east lie the garden boys' bothy and the head gardener's cottage. The bothy has not been occupied since the last war, but Hamilton lived in the gardener's cottage until he finally retired.

THE LIE OF THE LAND
The vineries and glasshouses are in a slightly unusual position in relation to the rest of the kitchen garden. Vineries were usually built on the south-facing wall within the garden, so that the work sheds and furnaces - the back sheds behind them - lay inside the slips to the north. But much of the ground between the farm and this kitchen garden is on the site of an old gravel pit, and the rest was taken up by farm buildings, so the land to the south was used instead. Nevertheless, Joseph Weld chose a good place for his kitchen garden. Apart from its seclusion, this site offers all the attributes that the kitchen garden planner would look for. The garden's aspect, its shape, size, drainage and soil, and its proximity to supplies of dung and water, can be appreciated by walking round the outside of the walls.

The advantages of a slope in a kitchen garden had long been recognized, for, especially in colder climates, better crops were achieved if the ground lay open to the sun. The garden at Pylewell is at the top of quite a steep slope, high above the farm and mill-pond, but once inside the walls it seems almost flat; this is deceptive as the incline towards the south is so gentle as to be hardly noticeable.

Apart from the fact that a south-facing slope gives a boost to growth and ripening, it also helps to dispel frost. In some gardens, to prevent the creation of a frost pocket and to help frost escape, the boundary at the bottom of the slope consisted of an open fence or a hedge, rather than a wall. If there were a wall it might have *clair-voyées* cut into it, which as their name implies, allowed a view from the garden into the park or gardens beyond, as well as letting the frost out.

To a classical, Mediterranean gardener a slope acted primarily as an aid to drainage, but it must not be too steep. Stephen Switzer, the eighteenth-century landscape gardener and horticultural writer, advocated a fall of not more than six inches in ten feet, though a fall of as little as two or three inches in ten feet would do. A steep slope of more than one foot in ten was bad: it would mean 'A constant Uneasiness in being always ascending and descending', and would also cause the topsoil to wash off in the rain. A terraced slope, though beautiful, was expensive both to lay out and to maintain, but if terracing could be had, it should be on three levels. The lowest level would be the dampest and coolest, with the richest soil; it would therefore be best suited for moisture-loving things such as cauliflowers and cabbages, late peas and beans, quince stocks and anything that the gardener wished to retard in summer (the shade cast by the south wall was useful here); the middle level was best for plants needing lighter soil, like asparagus; the upper level, airy and 'most perflatile', with the lightest, warmest soil, was best for root crops and early peas and beans. [2]

SHELTERBELTS

The only disadvantage of an open slope on a rise is that it is vulnerable to the wind. The prevailing winds at Pylewell are strong, sometimes tempestuous, salty sou'westerlies, breezing in straight off the sea. Biting frosts and chill winds come from the opposite side of the compass; the kitchen garden here is therefore protected by two stout shelterbelts of trees, mainly tall conifers and oaks, which were planted when Weld first put the kitchen garden on its present site. Storms have recently taken their toll, but several fine oaks, Scots pines and ilexes still stand guard.

Unless the lie of the land provided natural protection, a screen of forest trees (usually a mixture of deciduous and evergreen) was planted to shelter the kitchen garden. It would lie some 50 to 100 yards to the windward of the most exposed walls; not too close, or the trees' roots would rob the garden crops of nourishment and their leaves would fall on the beds. A 'wood or skreen of shrubs enveloping the whole', [3] and productive trees such as crab and cider apples, perry pears and wild cherries (which would, it was hoped, attract the birds

away from the better fruits in the kitchen garden), were also planted outside the slips which encircled the walls, to provide shelter and secluded walks as well as acting as screens against any unsightly view of the walls. These too, are still to be seen at Pylewell, although they are somewhat overgrown and ragged now.

CONVENTIONAL SHAPES

Apart from its productiveness (which included a supply of herbs for medicinal, household, brewery and kitchen use) and a supply of water, the chief requirement of a medieval, Elizabethan or even Caroline kitchen garden was that it should be sited conveniently near the house, preferably closer to the kitchens and the stables than to the best rooms. Its shape was not so important. Its soil and situation were taken into account, but (possibly because the plants grown then were less demanding than the tender, introduced salads, vegetables and fruits of later gardens) these considerations were of less consequence then than they were to become from the end of the seventeenth century onwards.

From the evidence of old estate maps and views, it can be seen that until about the end of the seventeenth century, a kitchen garden was square, as often as not. If it were rectangular, this tended to be because the space dictated it, with little or no regard to the direction of the sun's rays. By the beginning of the eighteenth century, with the realization that the warmth of the sun was an advantage, especially for growing fruit, new kitchen gardens usually had the longer axis running more or less east and

damson 'Merryweather'

west, so that the south-facing walls were the longest. There was also a vogue for separate fruit gardens, which came from France. (The Worsleys' twin fruit and vegetable gardens in front of the house were very *à la mode.*) The kitchen garden made by Ascanius Senior combined fruit and vegetables, and had one innovatory feature: a semicircular 'projection' on the north side. According to Charles M'Intosh, a mid-nineteenth century gardener and writer, this type of curved, south-facing fruit wall, was added by Walter Nicol (a slightly earlier gardener and writer) to most of the gardens he designed. [4] It was supposed to take maximum advantage of the sun and is found in many kitchen gardens of the period.

The present Pylewell garden appears rectangular, but this is deceptive; it is actually more of a parallelogram, with each of the four corners snipped off, giving it eight sides in all: two long, two middling and four short. Once again, the object was to provide as much sun-warmed wall space as possible for fruit;

indeed, the open, south-facing walls within the garden here were once devoted entirely to peaches and nectarines.

ADAPTABLE SIZES

I have to admit that the first time I saw the one and a half acres enclosed by the walls at Pylewell, I wondered how any household could need a kitchen garden so large. But as we have already seen, the Whitakers had large families; so did Williams-Freeman and the Welds; the census of 1841 shows that the Welds' household consisted of thirty-four people. This figure included a resident priest, Wood the steward, and twenty-two servants.

With the slip gardens, the cultivated ground is doubled to three acres; it was calculated that one acre of intensively cropped kitchen garden would do for a family of twelve, provided that potatoes, cabbages and roots were grown elsewhere. At Pylewell, a ten to twelve acre field was dedicated to these crops.

By Georgian or Victorian standards one and a half acres was an average size for a kitchen garden; larger families might need four or five acres and ducal or royal palaces would have gardens of from ten to twenty-five acres. The size of the workforce could be calculated by the size of the kitchen garden; one acre of open kitchen garden needed a man and a very hardworking boy to keep it cultivated; more gardeners would be employed to look after the glasshouses, if any; a total of six gardeners for three acres of kitchen garden, slip garden, frameyard and glasshouses was not unusual.

Kitchen gardens were much smaller before the mid seventeenth century, when the art of kitchen gardening was less sophisticated. It should also be remembered that from the earliest times pulses, onions, roots and brassicas were usually grown as field crops, while apples and pears, which were used mainly for perry and cider, were grown in orchards. Other fruits such as wild strawberries and gooseberries were collected from woods and hedgerows.

SOIL AND DRAINAGE

One of the most important factors affecting the choice of site for the kitchen garden was the quality of the soil and its subsoil. The subsequent effect on fertility and moisture were considerations frequently overlooked in even the grandest kitchen gardens. At the beginning of the eighteenth century the royal kitchen gardens were the source of repeated grief on this account to the gardeners responsible for supplying the royal tables in London. The kitchen gardens at Kensington Palace were sited on poor soil on, and adjacent to, an old gravel pit. Henry Wise and Joseph

Carpenter, gardeners to George I, found that, through no fault of their own, they were having to supplement the royal gardens with produce bought in from market gardens as well as with stuff grown in their own 100 acre gardens and nurseries at Brompton Park, just over the road. [5]

However, Wise himself (with his then partner, George London) was responsible for the position of the kitchen gardens at Longleat in Wiltshire, laid out between 1685 and 1711. Here the situation was different: the gardens were made in a valley, on 'tenacious Clay and spewy Gravel', with the result that by 1731, Switzer reported that '. . . notwithstanding all the Cost and Pains that has been laid out, there is no such thing as a good Peach, Apricock, or any thing else; though the Garden Part of that noble Seat, is said to have cost forty thousand pounds.' [6]

The cure for 'spewy Land' was to drain it. The simplest and cheapest form of drainage was to dig ditches, but unless these took an ornamental form they were not considered convenient or sightly in kitchen gardens. Next in cheapness came the covered drain, a V-shaped trench which could be either turfed over in such a way as to leave a space at the bottom for the water to flow, or filled first with rubble or pebbles and then with faggots, ferns or brambles to form a permeable watercourse. Neither of these, however, was as good as more expensive drains made with stones, bricks, tiles or pipes. From the end of the eighteenth century, the drainage system would also incorporate the overflow from rainwater tanks in the greenhouses and, where the lie of the

land was suitable, they could supplement the garden's water supply by feeding water into dipping ponds, as at West Dean in Sussex, or into a canal, as at Crichel in Dorset.

The best soil for fruit trees is good, sound, slightly calcareous loam; vegetables do better on sandy loam judiciously enriched with humus and lime. In both cases the ideal kitchen garden has rich, light, friable earth reaching down to a depth of about three feet, soil which Philip Miller, gardener, writer and curator of the Apothecaries' Garden in Chelsea from 1722 until his death in 1771, described as 'not too wet, nor over-dry, but of a middling Quality; nor . . . too strong or stubborn, but of a pliable Nature, and easy to work'. [7]

If the site and aspect were suitable, and the subsoil good but the topsoil thin, more soil would be brought in from further afield, sometimes at considerable expense. (Soil from the new railways was taken to Kensington Palace for this purpose early in the nineteenth century.) If the subsoil were bad, and in particular if iron were present, it would need to be drained and dressed with lime or chalk.

At Pylewell the subsoil is of gravel lying over clay and poses no drainage problems. The topsoil is of fibrous loam lying over gravelly loam and is rather light, but the proximity of both the farm and the mill-pond meant that there were always ample supplies of manure and water. After many years of working and enrichment with composts and manures, the soil in a kitchen garden becomes dark, rich and deep. It seems wicked to allow it to be overrun with couch grass.

WATER

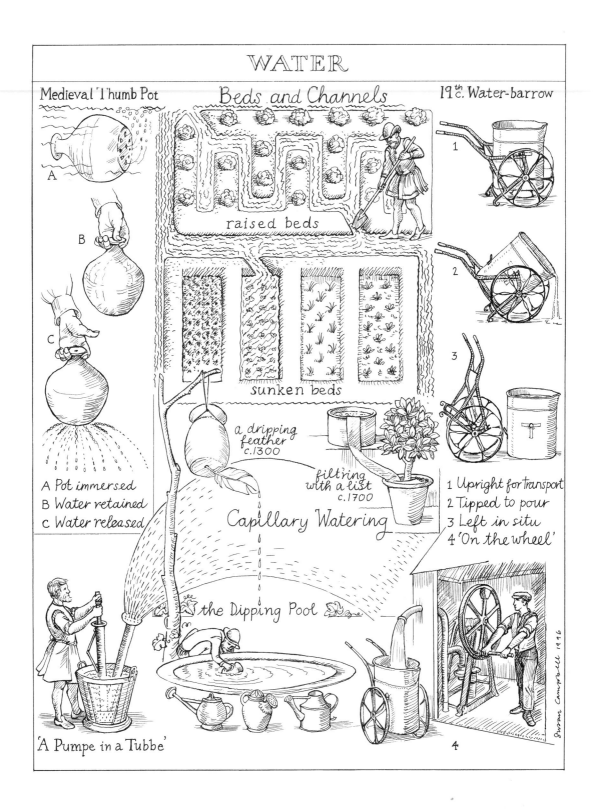

Medieval Thumb Pot

A

B

C

A Pot immersed
B Water retained
C Water released

Beds and Channels

raised beds

sunken beds

a dripping
feather
c.1300

filtring
with a list
c.1700

Capillary Watering

the Dipping Pool

'A Pumpe in a Tubbe'

19th c. Water-barrow

1

2

3

1 Upright for transport
2 Tipped to pour
3 Left in situ
4 'On the wheel'

4

CHAPTER TWO

WATER

Under one of the ilexes in the shrubberies beside the kitchen garden, there is an old galvanized water-barrow. Its wheels are awry, but it can still be tipped to and fro. It was one of several barrows like it that were used at Pylewell in hot summers, when the gardeners spent mornings and evenings, weekdays and weekends, wheeling the things from one bed to another, tipping the contents into large watering cans, for Mr Hamilton would have insisted on the use of a watering can, rather than a hosepipe, to water his more delicate crops.

Water is as crucial to a kitchen garden as shelter and good soil, but in most cases it needs to be applied gently. We may complain about the drudgery of watering as we turn on the tap and direct our light, plastic hoses and sprinklers wherever we wish, but the flexible gutta-percha garden hose of which they are the successors was not invented until 1845. Before then, hoses were made of leather or tarred canvas and were huge, heavy and cumbersome, being some three or four inches in diameter. They were also very powerful. A brass rose could be screwed to the end to diffuse the water, but these hoses were mainly used in gardens to water lawns or paths, to fill up water containers or to wash down fruit trees. Fruit trees were

regularly and vigorously syringed with water to rid them of bugs, caterpillars, dust, insect eggs, larvae and cobwebs.

Gardeners therefore had the arduous task of carrying and carting water from one part of the garden to another, when gentler watering was required. They filled cans, pots and water-barrows from strategically placed ponds, dipping pools, stand-pipes, wells and rainwater tanks. In places where a pump had to be primed by turning a wheel, the job was done by the garden boy. The wheel, usually about four feet in diameter, was housed in a shed above a well. The wheelhouse walls at Kilworth, a garden in the Midlands, are covered with the autographs of garden boys who had been obliged to 'go on the wheel' first thing every morning. Twenty-two turns were enough to start the water flowing, and

then the boy would fill all the water carts and water barrows for the gardens, including the lawn-watering barrow and the boiler-house cisterns, wheeling some of the barrows himself, until sufficient water had been drawn for the day.

'Spot' watering was applied with watering cans wherever and whenever it was needed. Hotbeds, plants in pots and tubs, seedlings in boxes and seedlings newly transplanted, greenhouse plants, plants under cloches, plants in pits and in frames, and thirsty plants such as celery and cauliflowers – all needed careful, regular, individual watering by hand, sprinkling rather than dousing. No wonder that watering was so often skimped by lazy gardeners. Even with rubber hoses, gardeners still found it a tedious job; when Percy Gregory was a boy he had to give the twenty peach trees along the south wall at Pylewell ten minutes each of water, daily, in the summer, soaking the mulch that extended six by three feet around each tree.

Mr Hamilton knew at once if he had given them short measure.

EARLY WATER SYSTEMS

Unless there is a permanent, natural water supply, or some artificial means of supplying water, only the most primitive kind of gardening can be achieved. Without water, vegetables and salads will grow only during the rainy season, but the writers of the earliest husbandries were Greeks, Arabs and Romans who lived and gardened in the Mediterranean – in places with long, dry summers. Their kitchen gardening was far from primitive; it depended on water stored in tanks and carried by man-made channels.

Roman and Arab gardens were sited ideally on or near a permanently flowing stream; alternatively they had wells and reservoirs supplied with water via pipes, conduits or aqueducts. Water was raised from a well with a bucket, a pulley and a rope; a *shaduf* or swing beam was used to take water from a river; the Roman gardeners also made use of pumps, water wheels, windmills and Archimedean screws.

Once the water reached the garden it was sent into an irrigation system which ensured that every bed had its share. This system can still be seen in the kitchen gardens of warmer countries today. It works best if the garden is laid out on a grid as well as on a slope, with square or rectangular beds and straight paths, which double as water channels, running between them. Banks of earth on either side of the paths control the water's route; it can be stopped or diverted with one thrust of a boot or a spade.

The Romans of the first century AD thought the Britons knew nothing about gardening; the haphazardly planted compounds cultivated by the natives looked so unlike their own, orderly kitchen gardens. But it was only the need to be sure of a water supply that led the classical gardener to devise a regimented, irrigated garden – a measure that was scarcely necessary in a country as damp as Britain. Wells were almost certainly introduced to Britain by the Romans. With improved water supplies the classical, grid-like kitchen garden, with a pool or well either at its centre or to one side, followed close behind. [1]

RAISED BEDS AND
WATER CHANNELS

The classical garden was divided, depending on its size, into two, four, six or eight compartments or 'quarters', then sub-divided into narrow beds which were usually raised above the alleys or trenches that ran between them, though – depending on the type of crop and the situation – they were sometimes made level and sometimes lower. In that case each plot or bed was edged with sloping, rounded banks. The beds were never more than four or five feet wide, as the gardener needed to reach comfortably to the middle from either side in order to thin, weed and gather the crops without treading on them (treading on the beds would compact the soil). The beds had to be

short enough to be walked round without inconvenience. Raised beds were also known as 'ados'; the sides were sometimes supported by boards laid lengthwise, or even by low edgings of wattle.

The trenches that surrounded each bed doubled as irrigation furrows and paths. The water was directed by the gardener to this bed or that, by damming up or breaching the sides of the trenches. This system of irrigation channels is still used in southern Europe and in most hot countries, especially where hoses are not to be found. And because the alleys act as drains, raised beds are also seen in damp climates, for example in Scotland and Ireland, where they are known as 'lazy beds' (see page 32).

The source of water was placed either at the highest point above the garden or in the centre of it. It follows that a slight slope was advantageous in distributing the water, and that if the garden lay on a steep slope, some sort of terracing was helpful. The dung heap, too, stood on a slope above the garden, so that the moisture oozing from it could be diverted into the water channels.

The earliest references to the raised bed system are Roman, but the technique was doubtless practised by civilizations older than theirs; it was also adopted by the Moors of southern Spain and the earliest monastic gardeners. Long, level rows on wide, flat quarters, such as we see now in most northern European gardens, were a development of the early eighteenth century. The patterns created by Roman, Arab, medieval and Tudor garden beds changed with the seasons, although their size and shape were always governed by the restrictions about stepping on them once they were sown or planted, and by the need to keep the channels both straight and slightly inclined.

MEDIEVAL WATER SYSTEMS

Medieval monastic kitchen gardens used the grid-like layout with beds divided by water channels for reasons of tradition – the monks followed the classical methods of husbandry closely – but also because the bed-and-channel system was both an invaluable aid to watering and a help with drainage.

Monasteries – like castles and palaces – were invariably sited close to a good source of water, for water was essential to the well-being and efficiency of their communities. The water supply to the gardens would have been part of a complex system of conduits, wells, reservoirs, tanks, canals and aqueducts. Water was needed for drinking, bathing, washing, cooking, lavatories, fishponds and mills as well as bakeries, brewhouses, tanneries and other workshops. Drains and sewers, while essential to town life, were also adapted to the kitchen garden complex so that valuable night-soil could be recycled.

Capillary watering was practised too, especially on melons, gourds and pumpkins, which needed particular care to ensure that the water reached the roots and avoided the leaves. As early as 1385, Friar Henry Daniel, a Dominican physician, herbalist, gardener and botanist, gave instructions to punch a small hole in an earthenware pot and hang it, full of water, from a crooked stick over a gourd, letting the water drip from it very gently down a feather stuck in the hole.[2] Similar advice appears in later gardening treatises, using shreds of cloth or wisps of straw in place of the feather (see page 32).

CLIMATE AND ITS EFFECT ON WATERING

The need for irrigation is largely governed by rainfall, or rather the lack of it. However, the British climate has not always had a preponderance of damp days. Between AD 750 and 1215 it is thought to have been slightly warmer and drier; the vines planted here by the Romans would have continued to flourish. There is a legend that Thomas à Becket planted 500 fig trees at an orchard in West Tarring, near Worthing in Sussex, in 1145. (A fig orchard was recorded there in 1745; it was still renowned for its figs in the nineteenth and earlier parts of the twentieth century, and one hundred standard fig trees, said to be grown from the roots and suckers of the original trees, were still flourishing there in 1985.) [3]

The adoption of the classical kitchen garden layout by northern gardeners in the early Middle Ages was therefore not unreasonable; the bed and water channel system was probably fairly widespread until at least the fourteenth century. The weather in Britain, then as now, had periods of extreme cold and wet alternating with periods of heat and drought. At the time of the Norman Conquest, it is thought to have been warmer than it is now, thereby encouraging the cultivation of vines, but it was cold enough to wipe them out in the first half of the fifteenth century. The period between 1420 and 1850 is known as 'The Little Ice Age', with the lowest temperatures occurring between 1600 and 1720. On 24 January 1684, the diarist and horticultural writer John Evelyn recorded that the sea and the Thames at London were frozen, with 'The Fowls, fish and birds and all our exotic plants and greens universally perishing'.

The sixteenth-century writings of the English horticulturist Thomas Hill suggested

pumpkin
'Crown Prince'

that Tudor kitchen gardens should be laid out entirely on the raised bed system. Jean-Baptiste de la Quintinye, gardener to Louis XIV and creator in 1687 of 'Le Potager du Roy' at Versailles, described his 'ados' or raised beds as having two forms, either as a type of sloping bank against a sunny wall for forwarding peas, beans or artichokes, or as double-ridged or furrowed banks made back-to-back in damp or marshy ground. [4]

In 1717 the nurseryman Joseph Carpenter complained that after heavy rains the alleys between raised beds became too muddy and miry to walk along and suggested that the whole garden ought to be level. Moreover, he thought that beds raised higher than the alleys were unsightly.[5] Plants needing copious amounts of water, such as cauliflowers and cucumbers, were then grown in rows with alleys between them, so that, as his contemporary, Richard Bradley, wrote, they 'should be floated, that is, the Alleys between the Rows should be damm'd up at each End, and filled with Water; and one of these Floatings will do more good than six Waterings close to their stems.'[6]

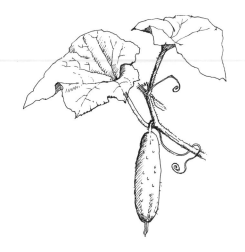

In practice, as English gardeners discovered, an alley that doubles as a drain or water channel becomes inconvenient as a path, even if it is only for gardeners to walk on, unless it can dry out rapidly.

Today, Britain's increasingly frequent hot, dry weather has helped to popularize once more the use of raised beds separated by water channels or alleys. It is claimed that they are more economical of space than beds on level ground. More plants can be grown on a raised bed than on long, widely spaced rows with paths between them; the plants can be grown closer together than on an open bed, thus producing smaller vegetables (an advantage to small households), discouraging the growth of weeds and creating an advantageous microclimate. Because it is never trodden on, the lighter, less compacted soil is easy to weed; because it is carefully manured and compost-rich, the beds promote root growth and warm up more quickly in the spring, giving seedlings a head start. Lastly, the raised bed system allows the gardener to build fertile beds on sites otherwise endowed with poor soil.

DIPPING PONDS

Kitchen garden ponds may well go back to the fourteenth or fifteenth centuries; the Renaissance gardener would have appreciated their ornamental value as well as their usefulness. These ponds were quite shallow, with a thick lining of tempered clay protected by a layer of stones and gravel. They were placed close to, or even inside, the kitchen garden, where they would be given decorative shapes – round, oval, octagonal or square – according to taste. The cast-iron fountain in the centre of the kitchen garden at Pylewell was all that was left of the dipping pond which once encircled it. Special ponds were made for northern gardens so that the ice-cold water that had been pumped or drawn from deep wells or reservoirs could be allowed to lose some of its chill and become what Cobbett called 'softened by the air' before being used in a watering pot or can[7].

In spite of the advances in hydraulic technology which led to their gradual

replacement, dipping ponds still formed the central feature of many a nineteenth-century kitchen garden. They often took the overflows from greenhouse rainwater tanks and their soft water was appreciated. They should have a place in the modern kitchen garden, acting as useful standbys in droughts, when the use of hoses is banned.

TUDOR SYSTEMS

A little dung could be added to sun-warmed water to procure 'a proper nourishment to the tender plants and yoong hearbes comming up', according to Thomas Hill. He also mentioned irrigation troughs, watering pots, pumps and syringes but made no reference to any kind of hose, despite the fact that by his time leather hoses with pumps had long been used on ships. And he stressed that beds should be gently sprinkled with water so that the plants were not 'cloyed' by over-watering.[8]

Watering pots were usually made of earthenware, with holes at the base (see page 32). Although inconvenient, they were

still in use a hundred years later, made of tin and painted with a mixture of linseed oil and red lead to stop them rusting.[9] According to Hill, a copper pot more like the modern watering can had, however, just begun to make its appearance in 1577. It was big bellied with a narrow neck, and had two handles, one fastened to the belly and the top, the other 'fastened Artly to the lips of the pot' to help with the sprinkling. The water came from 'a long pipe full of little holes on the head' that reached to the bottom of the pot. Hill's gardeners could also sprinkle their plants with syringes, which he called 'great Squirts made of Tin'. These caused water to fall like rain, if the gardener 'squirted upwarde' (see page 32).

Hill's book has two illustrations of a garden being watered. One shows the channels or 'troughes' between the beds being filled with water from a pump by means of a long funnel; the other shows a pump standing in a tub of water. It resembles a stirrup pump with a long spout pointing upwards; the top of this spout is covered

with a perforated plate. This machine and its tub were carried from one part of the garden to another until the watering was completed. It would seem to be the precursor of the wheeled 'garden engines' of the seventeenth and eighteenth centuries, which were in fact the very same as the fire engines kept in great mansions in case of emergency.[10]

LATER SYSTEMS

Fire engines, equipped with leather hoses by the 1720s, were particularly useful for washing caterpillars out of fruit trees – a job done two or three times a week during the summer. A large engine drawn by a pony could be taken into big gardens, as long as the paths were wide enough. By the eighteenth century these engines could be filled with water by hand pumps and horse pumps, by wind or water wheels, or even by steam. Water was also stored in reservoirs above or below ground and filled via vaulted and ventilated aqueducts of stone, brick, lead or earthenware. Pipes made of wood, iron, pottery and lead took water, again underground, from reservoir to pool or stopcock. Although no one remembers its

being used in the kitchen garden for watering, the fire engine at Pylewell, which was drawn by a small carthorse, was until recently kept by the mill pond in case of emergency and used in the pleasure gardens for watering during droughts.

Hydraulic rams or ram-pumps were invented in 1792, but did not come into general use until the 1860s. Both rams and water wheels were commonly used in the nineteenth century to raise water from artesian wells and boreholes as well as from rivers to water towers and large brick, cement-lined reservoirs, tanks or cisterns. As long as the reservoir was situated higher than the garden, a sufficient head of water would be available to feed fountains and waterfalls, as well as providing pressure for

the flow of water to stand-pipes placed conveniently about the garden. Stand-pipes were fitted with short flexible tubes, to which hoses could be attached.

Later in the nineteenth century, reservoirs and water towers began to be supplied with mains water (as the garden at Pylewell has been since the 1970s), but there is no evidence that there was any sort of raised tank or reservoir above the kitchen garden at Pylewell as early as 1814. Joseph Weld's new kitchen garden could have been kept supplied with water only by pumping or carting it from the mill pond.

A ram-pump and tank were possibly installed in or before 1868 by Williams-Freeman, for the Ordnance Survey map of that date shows a pond and fountain, which would otherwise have been difficult to maintain, in the centre of the garden. A hydraulic ram was certainly installed by 1874, as it is mentioned in the sale catalogue of that date. The remains of this ram, which was eventually replaced by a petrol driven pump, could still be seen by the mill pond in the 1980s, and two brick piers on either side of a door in the centre of the north wall support a large galvanized iron tank. Pipes from it fed various stopcocks in the kitchen garden quarters, the dipping pool and fountain, and the boilers in the green-houses. Other sources of water would have come from the rainwater tanks that were installed beneath various drainpipes running off the roofs of the greenhouses, sheds and bothies.

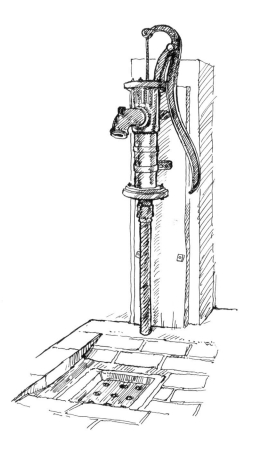

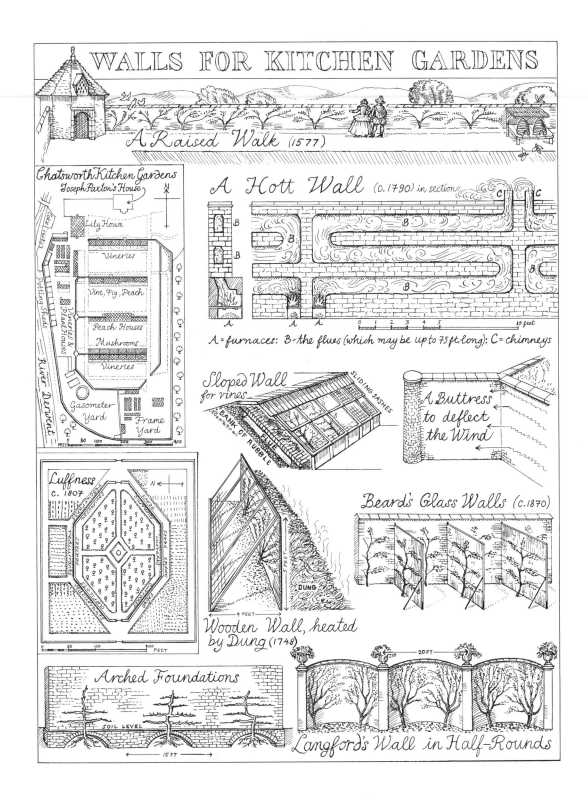

WALLS FOR KITCHEN GARDENS

A Raised Walk (1577)

Chatsworth Kitchen Gardens
Joseph Paxton's House

N

Lily House

Vineries

Vine, Fig, Peach

Peach Houses

Mushrooms

Vineries

Vineries & Planthouses

Potting Sheds

River Derwent

Gasometer Yard

Frame Yard

0 30 100 200 300 400 FEET

A Hott Wall (c.1790) in section

A = furnaces: B = the flues (which may be up to 75 ft. long): C = chimneys

0 1 2 3 4 5 10 feet

Sloped Wall for vines

SLIDING SASHES

BANK OF RUBBLE

FLUE

A Buttress to deflect the Wind

Luffness
c. 1807

N

Beard's Glass Walls (c.1870)

Wooden Wall, heated by Dung (1748)

4 FEET

5 FEET

DUNG

Arched Foundations

SOIL LEVEL

15 FT

Langford's Wall in Half-Rounds

20 FT

CHAPTER THREE

WALLS FOR PROTECTION

The ideal old-fashioned kitchen garden of our imaginations is always, surely, a walled garden. A kitchen garden with a boundary of hedges or palings is not unusual, but without walls the kitchen gardener is deprived of a great asset. Walls give security; they support a variety of glass and other structures; above all, they are invaluable for the production of first-class fruit.

The inner kitchen garden at Pylewell is completely enclosed by huge brick walls, twelve feet high in places; though in summer, from the outside at least, they are almost invisible under a thicket of fig and ivy leaves, interspersed here and there with undisciplined saplings of damson and wild cherry, mature suckers sprouting from the stocks to which finer fruits were once grafted. Here and there some of the original fruit trees have survived, but it is years since they were last pruned and nailed correctly and they have become gnarled, wayward things, ranging freely above and away from the walls to which they were once so strictly trained.

High walls announce that the kitchen garden is here. Seen from the back lane it looks like an enormous brick box or a fortress; from a distance, across the park, it is invisible, screened discreetly by shrubberies and tall trees. Nowhere else on the estate are there

walls like this, four-square and windowless, with few exits or entrances; nowhere else on the estate is there such an air of inviolability and secrecy. From outside, there are very few signs of what goes on within; the occasional glimpse of a glasshouse roof or the sight of a waving, unpruned branch, laden with blossom or fruit, appear at first to be the only clues.

And yet the walls themselves, both inside and out, are full of information. They do more than announce: 'This is the kitchen garden'; they do more than delineate its shape and extent. By studying their alignment, width and

Lutyens doorway

height, by looking at their construction, from the foundations to the copings, we can tell if a wall was cheap or dear to build; we can guess at its date and discover evidence of long-forgotten horticultural techniques. Even without a map or compass, sun or stars, we can gather enough clues from the walls of an old kitchen garden to tell north from south. Even where there is literally nothing left but the walls, something of the gardens they enclosed can be discovered by studying the surviving masonry.

At Pylewell, as in many other old kitchen gardens, gnarled stumps at the foot of a wall, with suckers of bullace, or crab apple and quince sprouting from them, tell us that plums, apricots or peaches were once grafted on the one, and that dessert apples and pears grew on the other. Even a naked wall, especially one punctuated with rusting nails and curious attachments, may indicate what sort of fruit grew there, and how it was trained, while patches of flaking plaster or whitewash and bits of old flashing reveal the previous existence of lean-to glasshouses. The very styles and positions of doors and gateways tell us more; they show the directions we should take to find the mansion, the stables or the farmyard.

DOORWAYS AND GATEWAYS

In many ways an old kitchen garden resembled a theatre, with a grand front entrance for the owner, his family and friends, and humbler access at the rear for the people who actually ran the show. At Pylewell, if I was on business, or one of the gardeners, I would have entered the gardens through the back door, but as a respectable visitor, or as 'family' of the Welds and early Whitakers, I would have used the southern doorway, between the vineries – the 'best' entrance to the kitchen garden – and this is where I am now standing.

The view from the south door runs straight through the centre of the garden. It is punctuated halfway along by the little cast-iron fountain, now rusting and defunct; beyond is the north doorway with the old tank on top. Today the vineries are not a pretty sight, with their empty sashes, dangling rafters, peeling paint and rusting iron supports, but in 1814, when the garden was first made, they sparkled, their glass reflecting the blue of the sky, their paintwork gleaming white, and they created a grand framework for the vista beyond.

This vista was the first that an outsider would have seen of what lay within the fortress. In Pylewell's heyday it was truly theatrical. The southern doorway revealed an auditorium of well-ordered cultivation bisected by a central aisle. I can imagine a weedless pathway of smooth hoggin leading, not to an old tank, but to a doorway under an arch of roses. The path, swept daily, was bordered by low, clipped box; wide herbaceous beds lay on either side and they, in turn, were backed by low fences of neat, espaliered pears and apples. Beyond these, like an audience ranked in its seats, were rows of vegetables.

It is true that this layout is atypical of a nineteenth-century kitchen garden, where the hothouse range would form the focal point after one had entered the garden, but the site at Pylewell was better suited to hothouses placed in front of the garden rather than within it.

The family and its friends would wander towards the playing fountain, and rest perhaps on the seats encircling it, before continuing their walk round the garden. Care was taken to distract the eye from half-dug beds of naked earth or partially cropped rows of cabbages and celery; from a branch of gardening, in short, that had less aesthetic appeal than the parterre, the flowerbed or the ornamental shrubbery. Thanks to the espalier screens and the skilful stage-management of the approaches, visitors were unaware that they had entered a place devoted almost exclusively to the production of culinary plants.

In the seventeenth and eighteenth centuries, the main entrance of a grand kitchen garden was most likely to be situated on the shortest side of the garden (usually but not invariably, in those days, in the east or west wall), in order to give the longest view of the garden. This would give prominence to a stately alley that traversed and divided it into two equal parts. As in the nineteenth century, each of these parts was subdivided into squares of vegetables, soft fruit, herbs, dwarf fruit trees and so forth. Then too, a central pool or fountain, or perhaps an urn, occupied the centre of the garden where the principal walks intersected each other. A hundred years later, when cheap fountains and sundials were made of cast iron and artificial stone, kitchen gardens, like the pleasure gardens outside, were still allowed their decorations, as long as they were 'of a useful description'.[1]

The main entrance began to appear in the southern wall in the early nineteenth century. By that time significant advances had been made in the design, construction and heating of glasshouses. They had become quite handsome, especially in places where the owner had recently been spending money on the kitchen gardens. This led naturally to the feeling that the main approaches and family entrances should be managed in such a way that the first thing to strike the visitor's eye was the glasshouse range. With a southern approach it would be seen at once in all its glory, standing as the culmination of a floral and fruit-trained vista which, for visual impact, could compare with the first sight of the mansion itself, a skilfully planted clump

Doorway at Osborne

of trees, or a strategically placed monument in the park beyond.

The main, or visitors', entrances to kitchen gardens were in many cases a reflection of the grandeur, or otherwise, of the properties in which they stood. They ranged in style from a modest, latticed door, a wrought-iron gate or Pylewell's original small brick portal, to massive stone porticoes such as those at Blenheim Palace in Oxfordshire, built by the architect Sir John Vanbrugh in 1704 to link the Duke of Marlborough's bastion garden to his eight acre kitchen garden. As if to commemorate recent victories over the French, it became fashionable in Queen Anne's time to lay out gardens in a military style, with regiments of trees in blocks and straight lines, look-outs shaped like bastions and archways ornamented with martial trophies. Tall walls were built round increasingly large kitchen gardens in keeping with this fashionable, fortress-like look. Grandeur is also seen at Osborne, Queen

Victoria's summer retreat on the Isle of Wight, where in 1850 Prince Albert raised the garden walls and reused the front porch from the old mansion as the entrance to his kitchen garden. Fantasy could be brought to these gateways too: a German diarist and traveller, Prince Pückler-Muskau, visiting a Gothic villa in rural Stanmore, Middlesex in 1832, noted that, 'Even the doors in the walls surrounding the kitchen garden were adorned with windows of coloured glass at the top, which had a singular and beautiful effect among the foliage.'[2]

In most kitchen gardens the exits and entrances were furnished with plain, painted wooden doors, set as close to the corners of the walls as the shape of the garden would allow, in order to give maximum space to the wall fruit. At Pylewell there are several of these doors, in addition to the wrought-iron gate that lines up with the cross paths. There is also a double doorway, which gave fuel-carts access to the boilers; it is set in the south-east corner. All the doors have rounded tops to fit the segmental arches in the brickwork and are wide enough to allow a man to pass through comfortably with a laden handbarrow. They are made of solid oak but it is years since they were last painted. This paint, always blue-grey, and manufactured by the painters in their own workshop, identified every cottage, workshop and farm building on the estate; it was also applied regularly to all their woodwork. Like the gardeners, the painters are long gone.

SECURITY FROM THEFT

Fruit and vegetables are labour-intensive and very tempting to thieves, both animal and human. Every door and gateway leading to the best kitchen gardens was fitted with padlocks and chains or locks and bolts. Pylewell was no exception.

The oldest husbandries all stress the need for secure enclosures. The Romans – with one eye, as always, on the cost – recommended as the cheapest forms of defence quickthorn or bramble hedges, and fences with banks and ditches. Stone or brick walls, they believed, were more durable, but more expensive; fired brick was preferable to sun-dried bricks or to walls moulded from mud (both of which are destroyed by rain). Even today, Egyptian gardens have mud-brick walls, just like the kitchen gardens of biblical times. Best of all though, in the opinion of the gardeners of the antique world, was a stone wall, daubed with clay to keep insects out of the crevices; their view is still held by Continental gardeners, especially in France.

But a wall, of whatever material, was not just built round a kitchen garden as a form of defence; it had two sides, both of which could be usefully furnished with fruit trees. The fruit growing on the outer side of a wall was protected from thieving animals and village boys by a ditch and a thorn hedge. The space created between the ditch and the garden wall was that useful area of ground later known as 'the slip'. Alternatively, the slip might be enclosed by a ha-ha or by a paling to which was nailed a vicious *cheval de frise* – a wooden

beam pierced with long nails so that the points projected on either side - or, more expensively, by yet more walls in the top of which iron spikes or broken glass would be embedded. The trees as well as the fruit might be at risk; John Claudius Loudon reported in his *Encyclopaedia of Gardening* that when he visited a peach grower of Montreuil near Paris in 1819, he saw the younger trees fastened to the walls by hooks to protect them from theft.

PROTECTION FROM BAD WEATHER

Walls also protect plants from the worst of the elements; and according to their orientation, they either reflect heat or cast shade on to the borders beneath, thus providing suitable conditions for forcing or retarding crops. Late nineteenth-century research into the amount of heat reflected to a distance of about seven inches from a sunny, south-facing wall showed it to equal the temperature of a garden at seven degrees latitude to the south; therefore a peach growing on a wall in southern England might enjoy a temperature similar to that of the south of France, while a fruit wall in Edinburgh could be as warm as a garden in Paris.[3]

Large kitchen gardens on exposed sites might be divided by more walls or, to lessen

the damaging effects of blasting winds, rain, hail and frost, by cross hedges of yew, holly, beech, bay, privet or box. Very high walls can create a destructive, scurrying movement of the winds blowing along them. These blasts may be softened on the outer sides (the slip sides) by placing huge wings or buttresses at the most strategic points, on the corners (see page 42). This type of buttress, which might project some sixteen or seventeen feet from the wall, is most usually seen in the north of England and in Scotland.

VARIATIONS IN HEIGHT

The kitchen garden walls at Pylewell are of various heights. As I shall explain, each wall varies in height for a number of reasons. As in all kitchen gardens, wall heights are influenced by the garden's orientation, by the need for security and by the materials from which the walls were built. In addition, both the height and the length of a new wall were controlled by the depth of the owner's pocket as well as by the type of fruit trees that were to be grown on it.

A kitchen garden wall need not be very high. If it is intended solely to keep out stock, four to five feet will do, but if it is to offer privacy or protection from the weather it needs to be higher, say seven or eight feet. Five or six feet is reckoned high enough for peaches, cherries, vines and figs, but plums, apricots and pears need more. Low walls are also suitable for fruit trees trained as espaliers on dwarfing rootstocks, but when horticultural fashion called for larger fruit trees, as it did progressively throughout the eighteenth century, kitchen and fruit garden walls of fifteen or eighteen feet were not uncommon.

Tudor gardens were walled in order to combine privacy with beauty and utility. A decorative touch might be found at each corner in the form of a gazebo or a little garden house that could be used as a look-out, fruit store, tool house, banqueting room, dovecot, bee house or bothy. From the outside the walls might look high enough for wall fruit, but ramparts were often built all round the inside, forming a raised walk just below the top of the wall. This walk would give the garden's owners and their visitors a view of the surrounding parkland or countryside (see page 42). They could stroll along it, admiring the landscape beyond or the kitchen flower-fruit-and-herb garden within, but the inside wall space was greatly reduced.

If there were no raised walk, and the wall were high enough, a vine covered lean-to arbour or a more solid lean-to, for over-wintering citrus trees in pots – known as an orangery – might be built against it, inside the garden, but the training of fruit trees and the construction of heated, glazed greenhouses were relative novelties in sixteenth-century Britain. Later, when wall fruit and lean-to greenhouses were wanted, the height of a medieval or Tudor garden wall would be raised by building a few courses of brick or stone on top, although this might call for buttressing, or strengthening by piers. Walls that show signs of such additions are often those of an ancient garden; some, such as a wall at Harrington Hall in Lincolnshire, even have raised walks, or the remnants of them, left against their inner sides.

In almost every kitchen garden, including the one at Pylewell, the south-facing wall was higher than either of the west or east-facing walls and considerably higher than the north-facing wall. A kitchen-cum-fruit-garden like this, built in the first half of the nineteenth century, enclosing say one or two acres, could have a north wall as much as sixteen feet high, east and west walls of fourteen feet and a south wall of twelve feet.

In kitchen gardens with a glasshouse range on the north wall, the differences in height between each wall were accounted for as follows: the back or north wall was the highest, firstly to protect the garden from the cold north winds and secondly to provide plenty of height for the best fruit and glasshouses. The height of this wall was critical, too, in deciding the width and the angle of the roofs both of the glasshouses and the backsheds behind them. The shadow of the south wall fell into the garden, and for this reason it was dispensed with altogether in some gardens. The side walls split the

difference in height, mainly in order to create an effect pleasing to the eye. Larger gardens had proportionately higher walls but they were rarely more than eighteen feet high; otherwise the trees might become inaccessible for pruning, washing and fruit gathering.

The relation between the height of a wall and the space it enclosed was also a consideration. Even in the utilitarian kitchen garden the proportions had to be pleasing: the gloomy, prison-yard effect of high walls enclosing too small a space was avoided if possible.

ORIENTATION

In keeping with other kitchen gardens of the day, Pylewell is not laid out on a dead north-

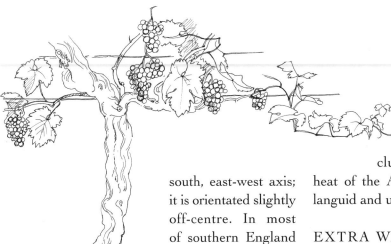

south, east-west axis; it is orientated slightly off-centre. In most of southern England and in other, warmer parts of the country such as those influenced by the Gulf Stream, kitchen gardens faced a little to the east of south, so that the warmest wall received the full sun an hour or more before noon. In colder places it faced a little to the west of south, so that it received the sun an hour or more after noon. The afternoon sun, besides being warmer than the morning sun, would also leave the south-west facing walls well stored with heat for the night. Another advantage of a west-of-south orientation was that blossom was less at risk from a sudden thaw.

Ever since the early eighteenth century there has been a good deal of discussion about this arrangement. Stephen Switzer observed that 'The Morning air is purer'; he thought 'a South wall declining about 20 degrees to the East' was probably best; it would be sunny from early in the morning till about two in the afternoon. The sun 'Meets with the Dew while it is yet fresh upon Plants, reviving them after a long Rest and (as it were) refreshing Sleep'. Although a south-west aspect meant greater

heat later in the day ('The Sun shines stronger in the Afternoon, because it continues to act on Air already warmed'), he concluded that 'The extraordinary heat of the Afternoon Sun . . . is generally languid and unhealthy.'[4]

EXTRA WALLS

As at Pylewell, a good fruit and vegetable garden would be given as many sunny walls as possible. At Luffness, in Scotland, a six-sided *jardin clos* for fruit was created inside a rectangular vegetable garden (see page 42). There was a tradition in France not only for separate fruit gardens but also for one enclosure to act as a fruit garden inside another; in 1690 de la Quintinye had recommended 'smaller walls within the outer ones'. Large gardens might consist of a series of walled enclosures, or be subdivided by one or more south-facing walls to increase the number of glass lean-tos and thus the amount of fruit. This idea was adopted by Joseph Paxton when in the 1830s he redesigned the kitchen gardens at Chatsworth in Derbyshire, where he was head gardener. He ended up with a number of walled enclosures, in a style that was to become typical of the larger kitchen garden. This ducal garden, sited two and a half miles from the house, was enormous; it occupied thirteen and a half acres in all (see page 42).

Alternatively, the enclosure might have several detached fruit walls, all running east and west, with fruit trained on both sides; George London and Henry Wise (royal gardeners and partners at the great nursery at Brompton Park from 1687 to 1714) designed a kitchen garden like this for Sir Thomas Coke at Melbourne Hall in 1704. The north sides would have been planted with late fruiting varieties of pears and plums, or midsummer fruits with high acidity, such as morello cherries, gooseberries and currants; the south sides would have supported the best kinds of apples, pears and plums as well as figs and vines, peaches, apricots and nectarines – all fruits then in demand as fashionable desserts.

ALTERNATIVE SHAPES

The layout of the Melbourne Hall garden might seem a little eccentric (see page 22), but eccentrically shaped gardens, as well as those with a military tinge, are typical of the early eighteenth century. These gardens appear to have been designed as much for entertainment and show as for an increased fruit crop.

In 1727 Stephen Switzer published a design for an octagonal kitchen garden measuring almost 350 feet across, subdivided to provide a total of thirty-two fruit walls and eight compartments for 'kitchen stuff'. It was intended to be seen from the house, which stood on a rise. In the centre of the garden stood a fountain; four pairs of pavilions acted as fruit rooms, with tool stores and banqueting rooms below. The outer walls were surrounded by a walk with bastions from which the visitor could look down into a moat and view the park beyond. It is not known if

this garden was ever built for any of Switzer's clients, but it is very like the bastion garden at Grimsthorpe in Lincolnshire, which he designed for the Second Duke of Ancaster some time after 1711 (see page 22).

Humphry Repton was particularly fond of six or seven-sided kitchen gardens; he built several of these in the 1790s, with hexagonal dairies and fruit houses to match. The kitchen gardens at Herriard in Hampshire, Tyringham in Buckinghamshire and Grovelands in Middlesex are all examples of this style.

In spite of de la Quintinye's observation, in 1690, that triangular, pentagonal and hexagonal gardens, though suitable for the planting of wall trees, were expensive to make and both inconvenient and perplexing for the gardeners, 'Who are thereby hindred from forming any sightly squares in their kitchen-gardens',[5] fruit and kitchen gardens continued to be designed as rhomboids and trapezoids, or as ovals and circles. The two latter forms were the least popular, as their shapes made it difficult to create regular beds and greenhouses, or straight paths for the wheeling and carrying of crops and manures. Squalling, entrapped winds were also more likely to occur in gardens with round or oval walls, thereby causing injury to the plants within; but as late as 1853 a Mr Arbuthnot of Mavis Bank, Lasswade, is said to have had a kitchen garden made to exactly the same size and shape as the Colosseum at Rome, with an Italianate villa to match.[6]

In 1898 William Robinson, one of the foremost writers on gardening in the late

*Flemish bond
(single brick)*

*Flemish bond
(brick & a half)*

nineteenth and early twentieth centuries, chose an oval plan for his new kitchen garden at Gravetye Manor in Sussex. He said it suited the slope of the ground: 'The usual rectangular plan would have led us into awkward angles and levels.' He built the wall with dressed stone taken from his own quarry for, like the French gardeners whom he so much admired, he preferred stone to brick, 'Both for its colour, endurance and fewer interstices for harbouring insects'.[7]

BRICK WALLS

Where fruit is the prime consideration, brick walls are preferred to stone walls by almost everyone with an opinion on the subject

(William Robinson appears to be the exception). The consensus is that brick walls act as strong, durable, dry, heat-retentive and beautiful supports for fruit trees. The cavities created inside brick walls by certain types of construction are an asset too, helping to keep the wall warm, dry, ventilated and, in some cases, heated.

Pylewell was rich in bricks, as they were made on the estate, but elsewhere brick walls were comparatively expensive to build. The largest part of the expense was often the cost of transporting the bricks. To economize, especially in stone-bearing areas, the outside of a kitchen garden wall was sometimes built of stone, with a brick face on the inside only. Brick walls are also expensive to maintain, especially when fruit trees are trained against them, as constant nailing and re-nailing of the branches destroys both bricks and mortar.

The introduction of a Brick Tax in 1784 led to an increase in the thickness of English bricks; thicker bricks meant that fewer were needed. Another way of economizing on bricks and thereby lessening the tax on them was to build walls with the bricks on edge. However, as can be seen by the numerous buttresses against the walls of the garden at Longstock Park in Hampshire, walls built in this way tended to be rather unstable. In 1828 Caleb Hitch, of Ware in Hertfordshire, patented a brick that could be used on edge with greater safety (see page 58). A wall made with Hitch's bricks can be seen at Hampton Court in Middlesex. The Brick Tax was repealed in 1850.

Like the mansion and most of the cottages in the village, the walls at Pylewell are made of bricks manufactured on the estate. The bricks were originally pale yellow, due to the chalk that was mixed with the clay; they have aged and lichened to a beautiful pinky, greyish yellow, similar in colour to the peaches that once grew on them.

Ideally, a kitchen garden wall should be made of the darkest red, most highly fired and therefore hardest bricks available; these absorb most heat and stand up best to the weather. Cheap, soft bricks were used only for parts of the walls to be covered by glass or backsheds. If the protective covering structure is removed, cheap bricks soon deteriorate – in many an abandoned kitchen garden a clue, like old plaster or limewash on a wall, to the one-time presence of a lean-to greenhouse or outbuilding.

The best tone for a wall – dark or light – was a question which was answered by an elaborate nineteenth-century experiment, referred to on page 47. A fruit tree had the wall behind it painted half black and half white. It was known that dark-coloured walls absorbed more heat on sunny days than pale walls. However, although the blossom broke sooner on the dark half, it was then more susceptible to a check in colder weather; moreover the fruit on the dark half ripened no faster than the fruit on the white half. Finally, as the black looked so gloomy and the white was so dazzling, it was decided that the best colour was the natural colour of the brick, whatever that might be. However, the back wall of a glasshouse was always painted with white lime, firstly to compensate for light lost by the absorbency of rather primitive glass and secondly to keep insects at bay.

STONE WALLS

Stone walls, if well built and made of regular dressed stone laid in courses, have the advantage of being more durable than brick; moreover, stone for garden walls can be cut at the quarry to any size. Narrow courses, built with long, thin blocks, make nailing and training easier, particularly if the necessary fixtures are placed in the wall at the time of its construction. The stone most favoured for garden walls in the nineteenth century was dark whinstone, a form of basalt commonly found in the north of England. Being close-grained, it absorbed less moisture than other types of stone. In Scotland, where the native building material is stone, the preferred type was Caithness pavement stone, cut four inches thick.

Objections to using stone for fruit walls were based on its chilliness and dampness compared to brick, the difficulty of nailing it once it was built, and the width of the crevices between less than perfectly jointed stones, which made hiding places for pests such as snails, earwigs and woodlice (nuisances that could be avoided only by plastering the wall or pointing the cracks with mortar or cement).

COB, MUD AND CHALK WALLS

Where brick is difficult or too costly to obtain, fruit and kitchen garden walls can be made of local materials such as boulders, flint or cob, which is based on mud or chalk. Cob walls are found in gardens the world over; in Britain cottages and gardens walled with cob or chalk are still to be found wherever there are belts of those materials, most particularly in Northamptonshire, Wiltshire, Hampshire, Dorset and Devonshire. They are good-looking, warm, cheap, simple to make and durable too, as long as they are given 'A good hat and a good pair of shoes' – a waterproof coping and solid foundations.

Their method of construction is ancient – it is described by Pliny, the Roman encyclopaedist and natural historian. Cob or mud walls are made from the most basic materials: a quantity of wet marly earth, which is a naturally occurring mixture of clay or chalk, into which a choice of short straw, old

hay, horsehair, pigs' bristle and cow dung is mixed. The foundations, sufficiently deep and two or three feet high, can be of brick, stone, chalk blocks or, if it is a modern cob wall, of concrete. The mixture is rammed, in six inch layers at a time, on top of the foundations, between two boards. As it sets the boards are raised until the required height is reached. The face of the wall is daubed with clay, lime and hair mortar or plaster to finish it. Copings are made of stone, tile or brick, secured with mortar, but the most traditional coping is of thatch, which is frequently replaced nowadays with corrugated iron – unsightly, but better than nothing, as without a coping a mud wall is soon destroyed by rain and frost.

If the wall is to have fruit trained on it, suitable fastenings to which the branches may be tied are placed in the wall as its construction proceeds. Long nails, iron hooks or spikes, wooden pegs, lathes, lattices and vertical wooden slips for the insertion of wall-eyes have all been recommended; if the wall is good and strong it will take more nailing after it has been built, but pegs are more suitable if it has become weak with age or weathering. To encourage bees, William Lawson recommended that dry earth walls, well-coped with 'Glooe and Mortar', should be sown with wallflower seed at Michaelmas. [8]

GLASS, REED AND WOOD

In the late nineteenth century inexpensive walls were made with walls of solid cement or even of glass. Patent-glass walls were made between 1850 and 1870 by Beard's of Bury St

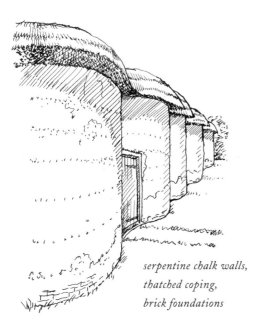

serpentine chalk walls,
thatched coping,
brick foundations

Edmunds; these consisted of thick sheets of rough plate glass bolted to iron frames which could either be mounted on permanent foundations or simply driven into the ground. They were designed for use in smaller gardens and had the advantages of cheapness, economy of space, portability, and flexibility of arrangement, as they could be erected in lines, blocks, herringbones or zigzags (see page 42).

Even cheaper fruit walls were made of reeds or wood. Stephen Switzer, comparing the price of a reed wall with one of brick, concluded that reed was forty per cent cheaper. He particularly liked reed walls for ripening peaches; they were used for this purpose, apparently, in the royal kitchen gardens at Hampton Court. They lasted no more than ten or twelve years, but that, as Switzer pointed out, was no longer than the useful life of a peach tree. To make a reed wall or 'hedge', a line of posts and rails was made, six or seven feet high, with lathes of deal every eighteen inches; the reeds were nailed between the lathes and fixed with wire; the tree-side was plastered with lime and hair, leaving the lathes visible for nailing. Wooden fruit walls, according to Switzer, cost half as much as brick, lasted well and were easily nailed. They could be made of deal boards, but he preferred oak, 'Pitch'd and tarr'd over to make them hold the longer'. Even better were tarred boards from old ships.[9]

Free-standing walls constructed of deal planks were used as an economical and early form of heated wall; the source of heat was the

Bee-wall, Heligan

same as that of a hotbed - namely a pile of fermenting dung (see Chapter 8). Dung heat was first suggested for use in conjunction with brick walls by the Reverend John Laurence, a keen amateur gardener and horticultural author, in 1718.[10] Its first recorded use with wooden walls comes from Switzer in 1731; he had seen it practised by Mr Millet, a market gardener near Hammersmith (then a village to the west of London), to force cherries.[11]

The dung-heated wooden wall was described in detail by Benjamin Whitmill, a nurseryman of Hoxton (then a village to the east of London), for forcing peaches, apricots, nectarines, cherries, currants, gooseberries and grapevines as well as strawberries, salads, early peas and beans, roses and flowering bulbs. Perhaps it should be more correctly described as a forcing frame, and not a hot wall, but as a form of fruit wall its ingenuity earns it a place in this chapter.

Whitmill's wall was apparently capable of ripening green gooseberries 'fit for tarts' by

zigzag wall

January, cherries by February, ripe gooseberries and currants by March, apricots by early April and early peaches, nectarines and 'forward plums' by late April. The wall was made of inch-thick planks twelve feet long, laid horizontally to a height of five feet, and kept upright by stakes six feet apart. Glass lights were leant over it against the top of the wall, to form a long, tall frame, and doors were made at each end. A border four feet wide was dug on the south side, and wall fruit trees, seven or eight years old, were planted in the border in the summer, four or five feet apart and close to the wall. They were pruned just before forcing was begun, towards the end of November.

The heat was supplied to Whitmill's wall by dung, just as in hotbeds, only in this case the plants were grown not on top of the heat but in front of it. Fresh dung was heaped against the back of the wall, sloping up to the top of the wall in the same manner as the glass on the other side – four feet wide at the base, sloping to two feet across at the top. After about six weeks, when it had sunk to a height of three feet, fresh dung was applied. It was reapplied at monthly intervals until the fruit was ripe (see page 42).[12]

SERPENTINE, ZIGZAG AND NICHED WALLS

A tall straight wall will not stand up unless it is given good solid foundations to a depth of two or three feet and is either built to the necessary thickness in relation to its height, or given support from piers or buttresses, which are not always desirable on a fruit wall. The 1784 Brick Tax may have contributed to the popularity, at the turn of the century, of serpentine and zigzag walls, which were also known as 'ribbon' or 'crinkle-crankle' walls. They saved one third of the amount of bricks needed for a straight wall as they could be built half as thick; their strength lay in their own curves or angles. Another advantage was their extra length over an equal distance. Serpentine walls need not necessarily be built of brick; they may also be made of cob, as at Shrewton in Wiltshire.

The popular legend attached to serpentine or ribbon walls is almost everywhere the same – that (like the garden at Luffness) they were built by Napoleonic prisoners of war. The inference, therefore, is that these walls are of French design and that they were built between 1796 and 1814. They were certainly built in profusion at about that time, and prisoners of war might well have been used as cheap labour, but serpentine walls are not found in France. It is more probable that they originated in the Netherlands, where they are relatively common and are known as *slangenmuren* or snake walls.

Walls like these are found in several counties in England, though they are particularly numerous in Suffolk and Norfolk, which adds strength to the probability that their design originates in the Netherlands. There were, at a recent count, at least thirteen serpentine walls in the town gardens of Lymington itself, where Dutch troops and French prisoners were housed during the Peninsular Wars; they are also commonly found in Warwickshire, particularly in the neighbourhood of Pershore, which was well known for its fruit growing industry. The oldest existing serpentine wall in England pre-dates the Napoleonic wars by at least sixty years; it is at West Horsley Place, Surrey.[13] Serpentine walls were popular with the late Victorians too; to make use of both sides, the Scottish horticultural journalist, David Taylor Fish, suggested building a peach wall 'in waving or curved lines', giving it 'bold curves of 10 or 12 feet on the southern side, with curves half the size on the north'. To increase the 'protective powers' of the wall, a cordon pear was planted at the extremities of each curve.[14]

serpentine wall

The protectiveness of serpentine walls was debatable; the pretty curves acted as sun traps for the fruit, but their detractors claimed that they caused the wind to eddy, thus injuring the trees. An earlier, but similar type of structure, consisting of a series of half-rounds or alcoves linked by flat pillars, was described in 1681 by Thomas Langford. This design appears to have originated in Italy, as a wall for raising melons. Each semicircle was south-facing and eighteen feet in diameter; the curve was therefore large enough to take two trees. The pillars between each curve were two feet wide. They could have tall flowerpots on top, or a vine running up them, 'which every summer you may let spread it self a little into the half-rounds on each side of it' (see page 42).[15]

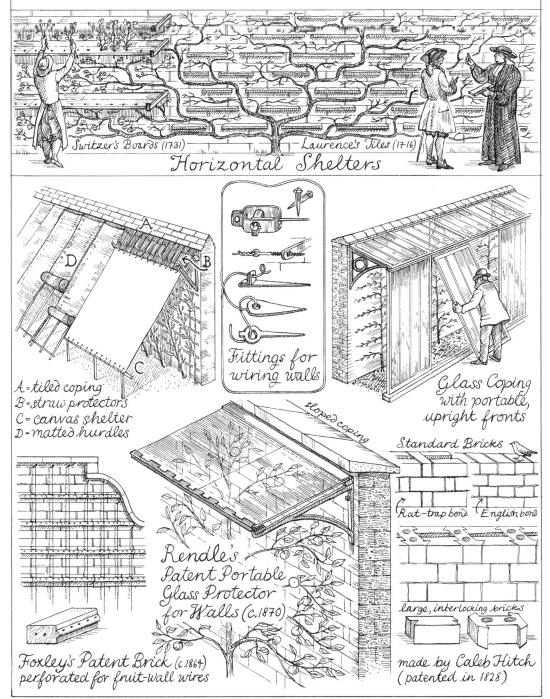

COPINGS & FIXTURES

Switzer's Boards (1731) — Laurence's Tiles (1716)

Horizontal Shelters

A = tiled coping
B = straw protectors
C = canvas shelter
D = matted hurdles

Fittings for wiring walls

Glass Coping with portable, upright fronts

sloped coping

Rendle's Patent Portable Glass Protector for Walls (c.1870)

Standard Bricks

Rat-trap bond — English bond

large, interlocking bricks

Foxley's Patent Brick (c.1864) perforated for fruit-wall wires

made by Caleb Hitch (patented in 1828)

CHAPTER FOUR

HEATED WALLS AND OTHER EMBELLISHMENTS

Concave, niched, or alcoved, sun-entrapping fruit walls are mentioned in a book on gardening by Sir Hugh Platt, knighted in 1605 for his services to science. The book was published posthumously in 1608, and some of the ideas and experiments described in it, of which the alcoved walls are but one, are advanced indeed. One of Platt's ideas was to grow vines on a sloping bank, 'backed with boords, or lead, for reflexion, that so your trees wold prosper and beare most excellent fruit'.

The use of walls to forward fruit was still in its infancy in the sixteenth century, but Platt was already several jumps ahead. He suggested lining concave walls with lead or tin plates, or pieces of glass, which would reflect the sun's heat back on to the fruit trees. He also considered growing fruit against walls warmed by kitchen chimneys.[1]

The chimneys of a Tudor house served a central hearth, which meant that until now a domestic chimney against an end wall was something of a rarity. It was about to become less so, thanks not only to the increase of the use of sea coal rather than wood for fuel (the coal smoke was intolerable in an open hearth), but also because the kitchen, which had previously been situated outside the larger type of dwelling, was by the end of Platt's lifetime beginning to occupy one end of the house, with a wide fireplace for long logs and spits and a good brick chimney to draw up the smoke.

Platt, the son of a brewer, was also familiar with industrial boilers and furnaces and had noticed the indirect, horticultural benefits of the heat they generated. However, there is no record of a garden with a wall heated solely for the benefit of the plants grown against it, or of a garden wall that was not only heated, but also sloped, for at least another hundred years. Then, in the early eighteenth century, a sloping wall was built at Belvoir Castle for John Manners, the Second Duke of Rutland (see page 42). This wall was the inspiration of one Nicholas Faccio de Duillier, a Swiss mathematician, religious fanatic, author, in 1699, of a book entitled *'Fruit-walls improved by inclining them to the Horizon'* and one-time tutor to the Duke's eldest son. Some time before 1718, small stoves were installed behind the wall, which lay at an angle of 45 degrees to the sun and supported vines. The wall was heated by the flues carrying hot air and smoke from the stoves, which burned constantly from Lady Day (25 March) to Michaelmas (29 September). The Duke was rewarded with 'The largest Grapes, and even the best Frontignacs' as early as July.[2]

There were other advantages: a sloping wall built against a bank of earth, using bricks with their widest face outwards, was cheap to construct; moreover, it had no foundations to impede the tree roots. However, stoves were found necessary to counter the dampness from the soil behind the wall, which spoiled the fruit. The wall had further disadvantages: the forced blossom was damaged by early frosts and the trees themselves were badly harmed by lying open to rain and hail. As well as that, mice had unimpeded access to the grapes.

It turned out that the disadvantages of the sloping wall at Belvoir outweighed the advantages, and flues had to be built not only behind the wall but also under the border, to heat both the branches and the roots of the ducal vines. To ensure success, glass casements (similar to those used in stove houses at that time) were put in front of the vines. The casements could be opened and closed at will.

Eighteenth-century theories relating to heated walls were exactly the same as those propounded by Platt: that the heat from a kitchen chimney (or any chimney from a fireplace on an outside wall) would warm the outer side of that wall to the great advantage of anything growing against it; and that with the assistance of this heat, trees would be forced to blossom earlier and therefore bear fruit earlier. Gardeners soon discovered, however, that the heat was not that easy to manage. It was difficult to keep it constant, gentle and spread equally over the whole wall. Nevertheless, the flued, heated, fruit wall was henceforward considered to be a desirable addition to the kitchen garden.

In the 1820s the problem of erratic and unequally distributed heat was alleviated by the introduction of hot-water pipes instead of hot-air flues. Both of these heating systems continued to be used in old-fashioned places until well into the twentieth century, but it is doubtful if hot walls were built much later than the mid-nineteenth century. By the 1880s the more avant-garde horticulturalists considered them to be 'nearly or quite obsolete'.[3]

The designers of the earliest heated walls attempted, at first, to combine artificial heat (as supplied by stoves behind the walls sending smoke and hot air up angled flues) with the debatable advantages of niched or alcoved walls and sloping walls. As at Belvoir, they placed movable glass casements in front of the fruit for good measure, but by the mid-eighteenth century the 'hott wall' or 'fire-wall', as it was now known, had become relatively simplified. It was built tall and straight, with stoves, ovens or fireplaces placed, usually in pairs but sometimes singly, in little sheds or 'fire-houses' at the back (see page 42).

The fireplaces were tiny, no bigger than those in housemaids' bedrooms, but they could burn any type of fuel: coal, peat or billets of wood. The fuel was stored alongside the fires in the little sheds which housed them. The under gardeners had to fuel the fires for as long as the head gardener deemed necessary, nights and weekends included. This might mean attention once in every four hours to anything up to twenty or thirty fires.

Stoves also had to have the ashes raked and the dampers adjusted, and from time to time the flues had to be cleaned. In some gardens these flues were large enough to be swept by children; the hot-wall flues built in 1780 at Fonthill in Wiltshire by the writer William Beckford were cleaned out by his Jamaican dwarfs, or so the story goes.[4]

Hot walls were usually built of brick, as brickwork lent itself more readily than stone to the construction of a flued wall. However, as we have already seen, brick walls were also built with cavities as an economy. It follows that not all cavities are flues; moreover, not all flued walls are hot walls – they could be the hot-air flues of an old greenhouse. How then can a hot wall be detected? There is no evidence of a hot wall at Pylewell, but I have discovered them at

many gardens all over the country. To find them it is usually necessary to hack your way through the nettles, laurels and brambles that form thickets of dank greenery on the outer, northern side of a south-facing wall; if you discover tiny, bricked-up archways, often in pairs, low down or even silted up with earth or rubble, then you have found the fireplaces of a hot wall.

A closer examination of the wall might next reveal, higher up at regular intervals, rectangular patches of newer brickwork – blocked-up openings which once allowed access to the flues for cleaning. I have seen entrances to flues made from stone blocks, with rings inserted in them, so that they could be pulled out, but most flues were covered with small iron shutters, which have usually rusted away. There may be more clues; the outlines of a series of pitched roofs may be just visible on the brickwork where little sheds sheltered the fireplaces. There would have been three or four steps down to the fireplaces but these, like the sheds themselves, have usually been dismantled long ago.

A hot wall is also far wider than any of the other walls in a kitchen garden – at least two feet thick from front to back. On some walls the brickwork can be 'read', by the trained eye, to show where the flues run. If the wall has collapsed, the flues will reveal themselves as cavities black with soot – further evidence that this is a hot wall – though at Audley End, in Essex, the flues are as pristine as the day they were made, suggesting that this hot wall was made, but never used as such. In some places, such as Tatton Park in Cheshire, and Croxteth, near Liverpool, the chimney pots are still in place, in pairs, but usually they have been removed. A climb to the top of a wall may reveal the old holes for chimney pots, but these, like the fireplaces, might well have been covered by flat coping-stones similar to the rest of the coping on the wall, to keep out vermin and damp. The copings on a hot wall are wide enough to walk along quite comfortably.

The construction of a hot wall was quite subtle; in some walls the tops and bottoms of the flues were made simply by using extra long bricks as headers; in others, we might find stone slabs or specially made tiles. The front of the wall, where the fruit trees grew, was built only one brick thick to allow the heat to penetrate, while the back might be three bricks thick, to provide the necessary support. The flues themselves were deeper in the lower courses than at the top, to allow for the decrease in heat as it reached the chimney. They were also well-plastered inside, so that the smoke was confined to the flue. The structure as a whole needed to be well built if it were to withstand the constant attentions of the gardeners; iron plates at the back of the fires protected the brickwork from being beaten out by the poker; the plaster in the flues also helped to strengthen the joints, weakened by continual nailing and the gases in the smoke.[5]

Towards the end of the eighteenth century, dampers were introduced to regulate the heat of a stove, but there was still some danger of scorching the fruit trees on a hot wall, especially in the springtime, when the shoots were new. Victorian gardeners therefore tended not to light their fires until the trees were 'vegetating' of their own accord. They also grew their trees – the lowest parts of them, if not the whole – against trellises which could be positioned a few inches from the wall. This is why raised lines of brick may sometimes be seen on the lower parts of a hot wall.

Hot walls were eventually used solely for ripening the wood and the fruit. The blossom and young shoots were now protected from spring frosts, as on unheated walls, by screens of glass or canvas (which, as we shall see, were fixed to the wall with a variety of ingenious gadgets). Fires in some gardens might not be lit until August, and even then, the walls would never be allowed to become 'warmer than the hand after having been kept a few minutes in the bosom'.[6]

COPINGS

The coping on a wall protects the structure from the effects of rain, snow or frost and gives it a good appearance. Pylewell's flat stone flags, which project a couple of inches on each side, are the simplest, most practical and most efficient form of coping for a kitchen garden wall. They are subtly designed to conserve heat rising from the face of the wall and to throw the rain to the north or east side – the worst side, from the fruit-growing point of view. Coping stones are laid

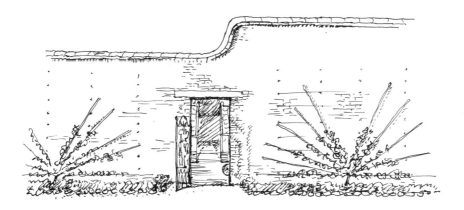

with a slight slant towards the north or east, or are cut sloping. The best edge is also 'throated' beneath, with a narrow groove to stop water making its way back against the face of the wall.

More elaborate copings, either temporary or permanent, have also been designed to defend both blossom and fruit from birds and the weather. Below the stone copings of the peach wall at Pylewell there were still, when I first saw the garden, a number of glass panes on brackets, with hooks, struts and pulleys - the remnants of an elaborate system by which nets, casements and blinds were once placed over the Whitakers' best wall-fruit.

LAURENCE'S HORIZONTAL SHELTERS

Horizontal shelters have a strange history; they were the subject, in the eighteenth century, of a surprisingly vehement, long-drawn-out horticultural wrangle. The ferocity of the controversy is almost comical, given that one of the main protagonists was a clergyman, the Reverend John Laurence

MA, rector of Yelvertoft in North-amptonshire from 1703 to 1721 and author, between 1714 and 1726, of four books on fruit growing and agriculture.

Laurence's first act on moving to the rectory at Yelvertoft was to pull down part of the mud wall that enclosed a miserable, weed-infested garden, and build a brick wall, nine feet high, for fruit. As an advocate of horizontal training, he disliked the new fashion for building walls fourteen to sixteen feet high, thinking that the upper parts of the trees would be blasted by winds; that the gardener would be tempted to train branches vertically, to cover the wall quickly; that high walls were expensive and that the security they offered could equally well be achieved by the threat of a man-trap (ordered by him, and left hanging in the smith's shop as a warning).

Laurence had been at Yelvertoft some twelve years when he decided that the best defence against the fruit gardener's other 'great Evil and dangerous Enemy' – namely frost – did not lie in the common and ancient practices of covering the blossom and young fruit with lean-to hurdles, or poking large leaves, conifer branches, pea haulms and brushwood in among the branches, or fixing bass mats, palliasses, canvases or other hangings over the trees. The gardener could be caught unprepared by a late frost, and in a high wind these contrivances might damage the fruits they were supposed to protect.

Better by far was a remedy suggested to him by the experiments of an unnamed but 'very ingenious Gentleman and worthy Friend, himself a great Lover and Improver of Vegetable Nature'. The theory was that as frosts 'fell perpendicularly', horizontal projections would act as perfect shelters. To test the validity of this idea, his friend had fixed tiles or thin boards between every two or three courses of brick, dipping down slightly to 'throw off the wet' and jutting out about one and a half inches. Staggered gaps were left between these projections so that the trees could only be trained horizontally. 'Indeed the Gardiner must have a very unhappy Genius, if he can in these Cases prune a fruit tree amiss.'[7]

He published an illustration of his 'horizontal shelters' with this account (see page 58) in 1716, and was rewarded shortly afterwards with a visit from a Mr Samuel Collins and a clergyman friend. Little is known about Collins, save that he also lived in Northamptonshire, and that he was a gardener of twenty-three years' experience. Collins published his own account of his visit to Laurence in 1717.[8] Collins was most suspicious of Laurence's shelters. He thought

the whole idea 'Chimerical'; he also wondered how these tiles would keep off perpendicular frosts and mists. Moreover, on seeing the wall, Collins was shocked to find that Laurence had stuck the tiles into his own wall only the day before. In fact, Laurence does not make it all that clear that this scheme is purely experimental, and Collins makes some valid points. Laurence subsequently amended his original ideas. In his next book, *The Fruit-Garden Kalendar*, published only a year after Collins's visit, he calls his jutting tiles 'Occasional shelters'.

In 1724 Philip Miller, by then the gardener at the Apothecaries' Garden in Chelsea, joined the debate. He approved of Laurence's theory, but thought it would be difficult to train trees between the tiled projections, which might also harbour vermin. He suggested that boards should be fixed to the tops of the walls 'to keep off Rain, Dews and Morning Frosts'.[9] Laurence elaborated on Miller's suggestion. In 1726 he came up with a plan to fix rows of movable deal-boards on permanent supports of oak, designed to project about ten or twelve inches from the wall. The boards needed to be in place only during March, April and part of May. He also recommended leaning 'matted Hurdles' (which he had previously disliked) against the walls.[10]

Stephen Switzer gave directions for something very similar to Laurence's revised idea. Sloping boards were to be placed on projecting brackets at heights of three feet from the ground, then every two or three feet up the wall, the boards to be kept in place until the fruit was the size of a very large pea. Switzer also suggested making gimlet holes along the edges of the planks to take green-leaved branches of oak, as extra frost-protection.[11]

The controversy appears to have died down in the 1730s, and a reasonable method of keeping wall fruit safe from frost evolved, using rollers, pulleys and brackets at the top of the wall to hang double or treble thicknesses of fishing nets, fine canvas made more durable by oiling, painting or dipping in a tanner's bath, cloth, reed or straw matting or even, suspended from a coping of boards, a curtain made of 'old ships' flags, which may be bought by the hundredweight'.[12]

In 1805, two devoted ladies of Perthshire made a net for their brother's fruit trees out of thickly woven, coarse woollen yarn, big enough, when fully stretched, to cover a wall at least 100 yards long and twelve feet high. It was so closely meshed that a finger could hardly poke through it and made yet denser by 'the bristliness of the material and its constant tendency to contract'. The blossom was 'wonderfully safe, and very snug indeed'.[13]

Alternatively, as at Pylewell, high brackets supported panes of glass. The old safeguards of shading the blossoms by sticking sprigs of bracken or greenery between the branches were still considered by some to be satisfactory, provided they were firmly fixed, as were the leaning, matted hurdles with which two men could cover forty to fifty

trees in an hour, according to Switzer (though both foliage and mats reduced the benefits of sunshine).[14]

The use of Laurence's horizontal boards continued at least until 1830; they were now eighteen inches wide and any convenient length, and were laid on projecting iron pins, like shelves, about the middle and top of a wall. Towards the end of the century, elaborate patent structures began to be manufactured; by the turn of the century the garden wall could be turned almost into a miniature greenhouse by means of these temporary shelters.

TREE FASTENINGS

The peach wall at Pylewell had cared-for peach trees on it until only a few years ago. Now it is bare, save for the occasional metal name-tag tied to one of the thousands of rusty nails that once helped to hold the trees to the wall. On a sunless day the nails are

hothouse peaches

*cordon pear
at West Dean*

when fingers are numb and the days short. For another, the ties have to be firm enough to withstand the tugging of a blustery wind, but soft and loose enough not to damage the young wood. All the previous year's ties have to be undone so that the tree stands completely free from the wall; then, when the branches have been pruned and realigned, they are fastened with new ties to supports that will not chafe the tree, that will remain firmly attached to the wall and that may need repositioning as well.

Although almost every kitchen garden we see today has walls pierced like pincushions with old, rusty nails - some of them quite handsome, ancient, handmade floor-nails - these are not the best fastenings. They may be the cheapest and easiest fixings to work with but they weaken the mortar and injure the branches. Moreover, where they are removed to make way for new nails, they leave holes for insects to creep into. At Pylewell both the bricks and mortar are full of holes; it is many years since the walls were repointed.

Cast-iron nails intended for fruit tree ties were specially treated to stop them rusting and make them easier to remove from the walls; they were made red-hot, then thrown into cold linseed oil. This gave them a varnished surface and prevented the mortar sticking to them.[15] In some gardens nails were driven into walls in a regular quincunx pattern. A gardening magazine of the 1840s instructed that nails be placed eight or nine inches apart in every course for fan-trained

almost invisible; they have been so much eaten away by rust they are hardly thicker than darning needles. But when the sun shines aslant, each nail casts a sloping shadow so that the downy, yellowish-grey surface of the wall appears to be covered in thousands of dashes as if it had just been splashed by rain. An expert eye can tell from the positions of these old nails exactly where each tree stood, and how it was trained – espalier, fan or cordon. The odd remaining name-tags tell which varieties were grown.

For a professional gardener, the business of tying and training fruit trees to walls is, like so much else in kitchen gardening, never as simple as an amateur might imagine. For one thing, it is a job that has to be done at pruning time – in the chilliest months of the year, trees, and in every other course for horizontally trained trees. De la Quintinye preferred sheepshanks as fixtures – smooth round bones which could be incorporated in the wall, quincunx-fashion, as it was built. About four or five inches of the bone went into the wall, leaving only one inch sticking out. Switzer recommended wooden pegs, to be used in a similar manner to the sheepshanks.

The best ties for these bones or pegs were 'lists' – shreds or strips of cloth, sheepskin or chammy leather, half an inch wide and a finger length long, though they also had the disadvantage of making attractive hiding places for insects. Cloth was preferred to leather, as leather shrinks. Black, scarlet and reddish-brown lists were preferred by the most stylish gardeners, 'as contrasting well with vegetation'.[16] Alternatively and even more cheaply, strips of bast, osier, withy, bulrushes and Spanish broom were recommended. These made less constricting, weaker ties, with the advantage (to the tree) that they gave way as the branches grew. Brass or iron wires, painted to make them last, could be stretched between flat-headed nails, lengthwise, diagonally, or crosswise for cheapness; but again, wires might chafe the branches.

In areas of Britain where walls were more usually made of stone, gardeners preferred painted lattices made of poles or laths, supported about one inch from the wall on iron hooks or on the bones of horses or oxen. Like the sheepshanks, these were fixed in the wall as it was built. Trellis was more popular in France and Holland. English gardeners approved of trellises on heated walls – indeed they prevented the trees from getting scorched – but they were thought to be less useful on an unheated wall; the wind could get behind the trellis and damage the fruit, and the radiant heat from bricks warmed by the sun would be less immediate.

William Robinson encouraged English gardeners to use horizontal wires for wall fruit fastening, as they did in France; in 1868 he pointed out that wires, once fixed, were permanent, 'whereas nails had to be bought, and shreds cut, annually.'[17] Moreover, wires did not damage the wall, and were simpler to work with. He recommended fixing them to eyed nails, built into the wall in horizontal lines, so that the wires could be kept taut with a special ratchet.

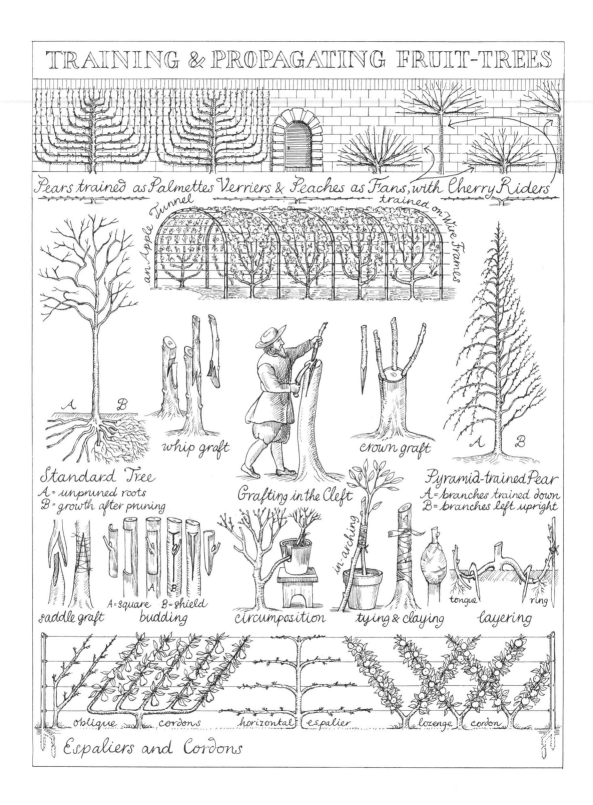

TRAINING & PROPAGATING FRUIT-TREES

Pears trained as Palmettes Verriers & Peaches as Fans, with Cherry Riders

an Apple Tunnel

trained on Wire Frames

whip graft

crown graft

Grafting in the Cleft

Standard Tree
A = unpruned roots
B = growth after pruning

Pyramid-trained Pear
A = branches trained down
B = branches left upright

saddle graft

budding
A = square   B = shield

circumposition

in-arching

tying & claying

layering
tongue   ring

oblique   cordons   horizontal   espalier   lozenge   cordon

Espaliers and Cordons

CHAPTER FIVE

WALLS FOR FRUIT

Figs and mulberries were known in Britain before the sixteenth century, and Henry VIII's gardener, Richard Harris, introduced new varieties of apples, pears and sweet cherries to England from Flanders and France. At the same time, improved varieties of apricots, peaches and almonds were introduced from the Continent. The desire to grow foreign, tender dessert fruits increased considerably in the second half of the sixteenth century, during the reign of Elizabeth I, and so the advantages of a fruit wall became apparent.

French gardeners were the acknowledged masters of this type of gardening and France was the chief source of new fruit trees. It may be a coincidence that so many of the emissaries sent by Elizabeth to Paris on matters of state – men such as Francis Walsingham, William Cecil (Lord Burghley) and Francis Carew, or members of their entourages – were also keen gardeners; they certainly took advantage of their missions abroad by bringing home stones, pips, seeds, cuttings and even young trees such as oranges, lemons, myrtles and other exotics, from nurseries specializing in orchard fruits and greenhouse plants.

Until then, English apples and pears were grown chiefly for the making of cider and perry. Other native fruits - plums and cherries, gooseberries and currants, medlars and quinces - were tough enough to withstand frosty winters and to ripen their fruits in the open, even in cool summers. The new introductions tended to flower early, well before the dangers of frost were past, and to need considerable warmth to ripen their fruit. They would have had no hope of flourishing in the open, in a British orchard or field, like our indigenous fruit. As it happened, though, the French raised fruit trees that were small enough to be closely planted and protected, when necessary, by canvas tents or other coverings; they also had methods of training fruit trees against walls or rails and poles, thus forming screen-like 'pole-hedges' or 'espaliers' (see opposite).

These small Continental fruit trees were known as 'dwarfs'. They were created in two ways, either by pruning and 'heading down' ordinary trees (lopping them drastically to reduce

Quince 'Vranja'

their height) or by grafting a chosen variety of fruit (the scion) on to a rooted stem (the rootstock) of a kind that was of low stature. The scion was usually that of a cultivated tree and the rootstock often that of a wild one, or a seedling.

GRAFTING

Grafting is an ancient art, known to the earliest Mesopotamians, to the Chinese 2,000 years before Christ, to the Greeks and to the Romans. Jews were forbidden to practise it because by grafting one variety of fruit on to another (albeit a compatible variety) they were creating a hybrid, a 'mingled seed', which was contrary to rabbinical law.[1]

The advantages of grafting are twofold: it ensures the reproduction of a desired variety (which is not always the case with seedlings), and produces trees that reach maturity more rapidly than those raised from seedlings or cuttings. The process is simple: the scion is cut in such a way as to fit exactly into a cut made on the rootstock, then bound to it with bands and pasted over (for example with clay, moss and cloth) until the two have grown together. Depending on the characteristics of the scions and rootstocks, the nurseryman or gardener can create trees of any size, habit or vigour. Nurserymen were particularly interested in raising trees that were damp or drought tolerant, were early or late in fruiting and flowering and were capable of bearing fruits prolifically, of any desired size, flavour, colour or shape. In the nursery ground at Pylewell rhododenrons were the subject for

experiment; Mr Hamilton bred a variety there, still available from nurserymen, that was named 'W.F.H.' after him. (The W.F. stood for William Frederick.)

The art of dwarfing was by tradition a speciality of medieval French monasteries and one that was apparently unknown in post-Reformation Britain. There were three dwarfing rootstocks: those of the diminutive, crab-apple-like, shrubby *pomme de Paradis* or Paradise apple; the slightly more vigorous *Doucin* or Sweeting; and the *St Jean* or St John's apple, which was said to be the *melimelium* or honey apple of the Romans. After grafting with suitable scions, dwarf fruit trees would bear large, early, sweet, summer apples on trees that were both prolific and quick to mature. They grew no more than three feet high and, when planted in sheltered borders or in quarters of their own, thrived in England as well as they did on the Continent. Walled gardens made the best shelter, though, and every self-respecting gardener who wanted edible fruit built them, regardless of cost.

HUGUENOT GARDENERS AND THEIR TRAINING

In the sixteenth and seventeenth centuries, thousands of Protestant refugees – Huguenots fleeing from Catholic oppression in France and Flanders – sought sanctuary in Britain. This had an influence on British gardening and especially fruit growing, as many Huguenots were expert market gardeners, especially those from Flanders. They set up fruit and vegetable gardens all over East Anglia, the London area and Kent, bringing with them both espaliers and dwarfs. These techniques had certainly reached Britain by 1600. Sir Hugh Platt, writing in 1608, recommends them, although he does not use the term 'espalier': 'Instead of privie hedges about a Quarter, I commend a fence made with lath or sticks, thinly placed, and after graced with dwarf apple and plomme trees spred abroad upon the stick.'[2]

SEVENTEENTH-CENTURY FRUIT WALLS

Seventeenth-century fruit walls were rarely more than eight or nine feet high, as the trees trained against them were usually 'headed down' or grafted on dwarfing stocks. Horizontal, or espaliered, training was preferred for the more vigorous growers such as pears, apples, plums and some varieties of cherry, not only because it was thought to be more fruitful than fan-training (see page 68), but also because it required less height. Fans had their champions, however, being thought more natural, especially where nectarines, peaches, apricots, almonds and morello cherries were concerned. 'Vertical' training was reserved for quick-growing gap-fillers such as vines, cherries, currants and gooseberries.

THE DUTCH INFLUENCE

Paris was still the source of the more exotic plants – pomegranates, oranges, peaches, figs, myrtles and Muscat vines – but by the early decades of the seventeenth century the Netherlands had become equally famed for their nurseries. In 1610 and 1611 Lord Burghley's son, Robert Cecil, sent his gardener John Tradescant (the Elder) to Holland and Flanders to buy plants, seeds, bulbs and fruit trees. In Delft, Haarlem and Antwerp, Tradescant bought vines, cherries, quinces, pears, apricots, medlars, mulberries, walnuts and currants for his master's newly laid out kitchen garden, vineyard and orchard at the rebuilt palace of Hatfield in Hertfordshire. In Leiden he bought rare roses and shrubs, and admired the university's famous physic garden; at The Hague he visited the Prince of Orange's garden, famed for its covered walks.[3] The arrival and coronation in England in 1689 of the Prince of Orange's son William brought Dutch and English gardeners even closer together and gave a further boost to the art of fruit tree training and dwarfing. By about 1700 gardens of dwarf fruit trees were all the rage.

THE ART OF DWARFING

Apples were dwarfed in England by grafting them no more than five or six inches from the ground, to stocks raised from cuttings of 'the Gennet-moil [a corruption of St John, which was also known as 'Joannine' or *pomme de Jannet*], the Kentish codling and others',[4] as well as by working them on to stocks of the slower growing, smaller, French Paradise apples. Pears and medlars were dwarfed by grafting to quince stocks (preferably the

Portugal quince). Stocks for dwarf cherries and plums came from suckers of 'the common harsh red cherry . . . or any ordinary plum tree'.[5] Apricots, peaches and nectarines were budded, rather than grafted, to damsons, plums and almonds. Root pruning, heading down and double grafting were also practised at this time, to reduce the size of the trees and improve the quality of the fruit. The great novelty to emerge from these techniques was the dwarf fruit tree growing in a pot. Its portability meant that it could be placed in a forcing frame until the fruit was ripe – cherries, for example, could be forced to ripen in March.

Thanks to what a diarist of 1702 called 'The new order of fruit trees',[6] nurserymen did a roaring trade, even selling dwarf fruit trees as decorative plants for parterres. At first they fetched the relatively high price of five shillings each (four times as expensive as an ordinary apple tree); by the 1730s they could be had for one shilling apiece.

FILLING THE WALL SPACE

Young wall trees are slow to grow to their full extent; they leave vast expanses, at first, of empty wall. To combat this, Joseph Carpenter (who succeeded George London as partner to Henry Wise at Brompton Park nurseries in 1714) advocated the French method of planting upright vines or half-standard cherries between the fanned or espaliered dwarfs. The fillers (also known as 'riders') were reduced in size by pruning when the intended trees grew into their allotted space, and were eventually removed (if suitable) to the open quarters (see page 42). Planting distances were increased to suit the wetter climate of England, for Carpenter found that dwarfs grew larger here. He therefore increased the distances recommended by French growers by as much as one third, directing that a wall nine feet high should have dwarf peaches planted at intervals of twelve feet, if they were to have cherries or vines grown between them; if not, they should be nine to ten feet apart.

EIGHTEENTH AND NINETEENTH-CENTURY FRUIT WALLS

This arrangement was adopted by the naturalist Gilbert White in 1761 when he planted his new fruit wall at Selborne, in Hampshire. He placed a passion flower at each end of the wall and alternated his two peaches, three nectarines and an apricot with five vines. English peach walls were still planted in this way as late as 1904, when it was recommended that a twelve foot wall should have three-year-old dwarf fan-trained peaches planted twelve feet apart, with tall standard trees between them to fill the wall quickly.[7]

Although dwarfs remained popular well into the nineteenth century, it appears that they were not as long-lived as trees grown on non-dwarfing stocks. Above all, it seemed logical to suppose that bigger trees – standards and half-standards – would produce more fruit than dwarfs. Taller, wider trees required higher, longer walls. By the end of the eighteenth century, planting distances for peaches had increased from Carpenter's 1717 recommendation of twelve feet apart on a wall nine feet high to as much as fifteen to twenty feet apart on a twelve to fifteen foot wall. Pears, which are generally the largest fruit trees, if grown on pear stocks rather than quince, were given the highest walls and planted as much as twenty-four to thirty feet apart.

REASONS FOR HIGH WALLS

With the development of heated glass, tall walls became an absolute necessity. Lean-to glasshouses were built on the sunny, south-facing sides, while work sheds, bothies and storage places were constructed on the colder, north-facing backs. And gardeners were jealous of their wall space. Doorways were kept to a minimum; bothies, cottages or houses built against the outer slip-side of a fruit wall were never given windows on the inner garden side. The same applied to supporting piers which, if necessary, were placed on the outside, to give an uninterrupted run for the best fruit trees on the 'good' side. (The walls in question might well need support, being anything up to eighteen feet high.)

By training as an espalier rather than a fan, a lower wall could be used, but the seventeenth-century French style of Louis XIV's day (as recommended by his gardener, Jean-Baptiste de la Quintinye), in which walls no higher than seven or eight feet were planted with trees nine to twelve feet apart, was considered old-fashioned by 1837, when Queen Victoria came to the throne.

Espaliers were actually being grubbed up, much to William Cobbett's dismay. In 1833, scornful of 'the new fashioned taste of despising espaliers', he assured a friend that an espalier some twenty feet long would carry more apples than two very large standard trees in the same garden. The friend bet him a hundred to one that he was wrong. Cobbett declined the bet, but was right: the espalier contained half a bushel more than the crop of the two standards combined.[8]

By the 1850s the demand for very large fruit gardens and very high walls was at its peak, as was the quest for more varieties of fruit to cover them, and for fruits which would extend the season by ripening early, ripening late, or keeping well, in order to supply the family with dessert and culinary fruit all the year round. On the grandest estates kitchen gardens had become so large, and their walls so high, that they were no longer considered suitable ornaments for the immediate environs of the house; as at Pylewell, they had to be removed to a more respectful distance.

And yet, contrary to expectations, large trees did not necessarily produce more fruit than dwarfs in proportion to the space they occupied. Their size depended on huge rooting systems, which produced plenty of leaves and branches, but less fruit. They also grew and came into bearing more slowly than dwarfs and, where they were planted as standards in the quarters, they robbed the soil of nutrients and cast inhibiting shade, preventing the cultivation of crops beneath them.

What occurred next was seen at the time as a revolution in fruit culture; in reality it was a return to the methods of dwarfing and training which were first introduced to England in the seventeenth century. The credit for instigating this 'revolution' was generally given to the nurseryman and author Thomas Rivers. It was certainly assisted by his self-advertisement and proselytizing in print. Like Carpenter and

most of the best nurserymen in England, the Rivers of Sawbridgeworth in Suffolk had business connections in France. Basing his theories on what he saw both in his own and in French nurseries, Thomas Rivers began experimenting in the 1840s with dwarfing stocks and root pruning.

Like Carpenter before him, he was quick to see the business potential in dwarfs. These fruit trees, he thought, would be ideal for the smaller gardens which were now being created all over Britain by a burgeoning, prosperous middle class. Not only did dwarfs take up less space, they fruited within a year or two of grafting, were easy to work on when it came to thinning branches or fruit, and needed only a few barrows of manure should the new garden happen to be sited on impoverished land. Also, so that the land-owning classes might not reap all the benefits of their rented properties, these little trees, even after fifteen or twenty years' growth, could easily be dug up and transported to a new home – a boon to tenant gardeners.

Rivers had discovered by chance that dwarfed fruit trees did better after frequent moves in the nursery.[9] The disturbance had the same effect as root pruning, a technique practised less on the Continent because of the drier climate, but which had long been established in Britain. Rivers used it in combination with the traditional French method of dwarfing.

The French still used the three original types of dwarfing rootstocks: the *pomme de Paradis*, the *Doucin* (now also known as 'the

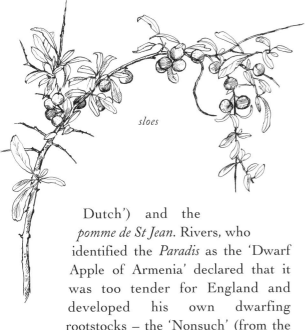

sloes

Dutch') and the *pomme de St Jean*. Rivers, who identified the *Paradis* as the 'Dwarf Apple of Armenia' declared that it was too tender for England and developed his own dwarfing rootstocks – the 'Nonsuch' (from the French *Nonpareil*) and the 'broad-leaved English Paradise'. Both proved more vigorous than the Paradise rootstocks but, as 'Malling 6' and 'Malling 1' respectively, they formed the basis for the modern bush trees raised at the East Malling Research Station in Kent.

The original French stocks were not rejected altogether. A rival nurseryman, John Scott of Merriott in Somerset, preferred them to Rivers's English stocks; he particularly liked the extremely dwarf *pommier de Paradis* which he identified as *Pyrus malus præcox*, a native of Russia, the Caucasus and Siberia. Trees grown on 'Scott's Paradise' could be planted as little as three feet apart.[10]

Problems connected with the longevity of trees worked on Paradise stocks were certainly solved during the 1850s, for specimens planted then were still to be found in England in the 1900s, full of fruit and vigour. And the improved dwarfs were to prove as beneficial to the owners of larger gardens, and even to the market gardener, as they were to the small gardener. Dwarf plums and greengages were created by the old custom of grafting them on sloes; cherries were dwarfed by grafting them on mahalebs (*Prunus mahaleb*, the French *bois de St Lucie*, the English Perfumed Cherry, so-called for its scented wood), and pears were once again dwarfed by grafting them to quince stocks, a form of grafting that had long been rejected by English gardeners in the mistaken belief that it gave the fruit an inferior flavour.

The next step in the search for greater fruitfulness in a smaller space, both on the walls and in the open, was a return to the old French methods of training fruit trees as cordons, vases, bushes and columns. These shapes were achieved with the aid of metal armatures and repressive pruning. Old giants and young trees alike were headed down and turned into neat, fructifying pillars, pyramids and urns. In 1848 Rivers invented the orchard house (see Chapter 13) and reintroduced the cultivation of fruit trees in pots for his 'miniature fruit-gardens'. Scott claimed that orchard houses were less use than a conventional greenhouse, but here there would seem to be more than a touch of professional jealousy.

DELAYING THE RIPENING OF FRUIT

The delaying or retarding of the ripening of a fruit was, in a way, the reverse of forcing.

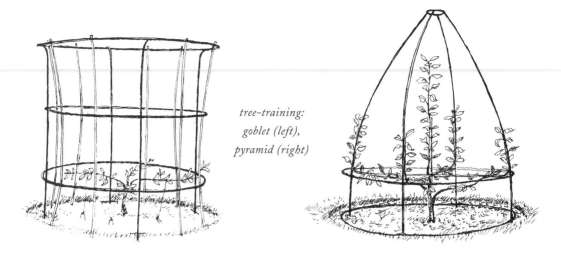

tree-training: goblet (left), pyramid (right)

The reason for doing it, however, was the same: to extend its season. The practice died out after the late nineteenth century, when a wider selection of early and late sorts of fruit became available. Picking fruit before it ripened and storing it in a cold place was one method of retardation; covering the tree (while the fruit was still unripe) with damp canvas or light matting was another.

One of the earliest records of this trick is Hugh Platt's description of how Sir Francis Carew – owner of the famous orangery at Beddington Park (see Chapter 10) – presented Queen Elizabeth I with ripe cherries from a tree in his garden well over a month after they should have been in season. Some time in advance he had covered the tree with canvas and kept it damp, removing it just before the expected visit. 'A few sunny days brought them [the cherries] to their full maturity.' [11]

The ripening of currants, cherries, plums and gooseberries was retarded by their being grown on the north side of a wall; earlier fruit could be expected from fruit on the sunny side, or from bushes in a warm spot. Fruit grown on the north side of a wall was retarded by the lack of sun, but its season could be extended further by placing wattle fencing in front of or around the trees and bushes and covering them, when the weather was dry, with mats, bunting or canvas, in early August. This process was known as 'matting-up' or 'matting-over'. If the damp could be kept out, the fruit remained in perfect condition until October, or even longer, as the mats also protected it from frost. On Saturday 12 November 1796 Parson Woodforde noted in his diary '. . . we gathered some white Currants from a tree in the walled Garden this Day about Noon.'

Fruit trees grown in pots were easily retarded by keeping the pots on the shady side of a wall or building, or by standing them on the sunny side under shades, then removing the shades and letting them have the full benefit of the sun so that they would eventually ripen with vigour. The trees could also be kept in an ice-house (see Chapter 18) from March to September, then gradually brought in to warmer temperatures to ripen their fruit for Christmas. They could then be picked direct from the tree at the table.

PLANTING WALL TREES

The old gardening adage goes: 'Like root – like shoot'. Gardeners had noticed, as long ago as the seventeenth century, that the most fruitful trees were those whose roots, like their branches, were fibrous, short and spreading. These root systems could be obtained, as we have seen, by root pruning and by using dwarfing stocks, but they occurred naturally too, wherever the topsoil was shallow and the subsoil was stony, gravelly, chalky, rocky or otherwise impenetrable. On the other hand, where the subsoil consisted of what Switzer described as 'blewish clay or Iron-mould ground', or was 'barren, sandy, loose' and 'spungy or bad in the Bottom', trees tended to send out long tap-roots, searching for nourishment but finding only 'sterile Juices'. Proof of this was the fact that their branches, though correspondingly lengthy, were either fruitless or else produced misshapen, ill-flavoured fruit, eventually becoming cankered, mossy and 'hidebound'.

To combat these problems Switzer suggested placing a number of small drains in a clayey subsoil, or laying down a bed of chalk at least one foot thick.[12] He also noted another, older solution (first described by the fruit grower Thomas Langford in the second, 1696 edition of his *Plain and Full Instructions. . .*). This was to place large flat stones beneath the roots whenever trees were planted over barren subsoil. Stones like these are still to be found at regular intervals and various depths in the borders below the fruit walls – useful indicators of where to plant new trees – as are the original metal name-tags, now buried, but once attached to the wall itself.

Although roots were thereby discouraged from penetrating the harmful subsoil, they were encouraged to run freely in the more nourishing topsoil. In the 1750s Thomas Hitt proposed that fruit-wall foundations should be built on arches springing from pillars placed at intervals of about fifteen feet, to allow the roots a free run on either side of the wall, thus gaining 'double the quantity of soil to collect the proper juices from'. Each tree was to be planted at the centre of each arch, the tops of the arches being just level with the surface of the border.[13] Arched foundations are sometimes revealed by digging, or by the settling of the border (see page 42).

redcurrant cordon

BORDERS & COMPARTMENTS

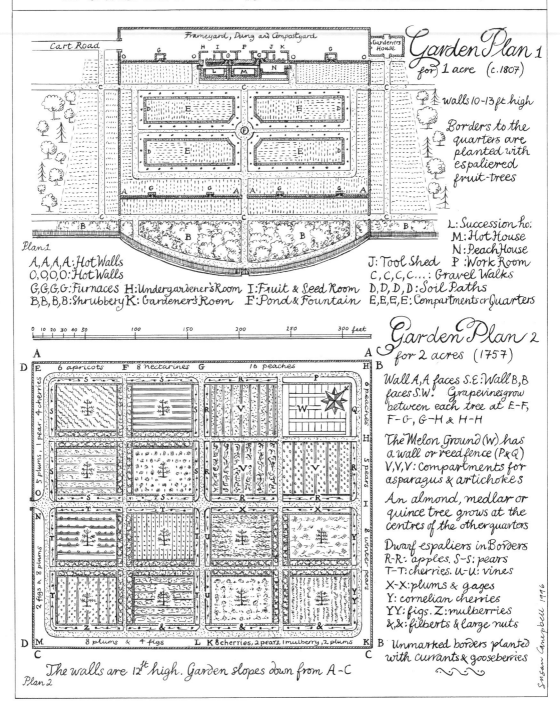

Garden Plan 1
for 1 acre (c. 1807)

Cart Road

Frameyard, Dung and Compostyard

Gardeners House

walls 10-13 ft high

Borders to the quarters are planted with espaliered fruit-trees

L: Succession ho:
M: Hot House
N: Peach House
J: Tool Shed   P: Work Room
C, C, C, C...: Gravel Walks
D, D, D, D: Soil Paths
E, E, E, E: Compartments or Quarters

Plan 1
A, A, A, A: Hot Walls
O, O, O, O: Hot Walls
G, G, G, G: Furnaces   H: Undergardener's Room   I: Fruit & Seed Room
B, B, B, B: Shrubbery   K: Gardener's Room   F: Pond & Fountain

Scale: 0 10 20 30 40 50   100   150   200   250   300 feet

Garden Plan 2
for 2 acres (1757)

6 apricots   8 nectarines   16 peaches

5 plums, 1 pear, 4 cherries

2 figs & 8 plums

8 plums & 4 figs   L K 8 cherries, 2 pears, 1 mulberry, 2 plums

Wall A, A faces S.E: Wall B, B faces S.W. Grapevines grow between each tree at E-F, F-G, G-H & H-H

The Melon Ground (W) has a wall or reed fence (P & Q) V, V, V: Compartments for asparagus & artichokes

An almond, medlar or quince tree grows at the centres of the other quarters

Dwarf espaliers in Borders
R-R: apples. S-S: pears
T-T: cherries. U-U: vines
X-X: plums & gages
Y: cornelian cherries
YY: figs. Z: mulberries
&, &: filberts & large nuts

Unmarked borders planted with currants & gooseberries

The walls are 12 ft high. Garden slopes down from A-C

Plan 2

Susan Campbell 1996

CHAPTER SIX

THE LAYOUT OF BEDS, BORDERS AND PATHS

The most intensively cultivated part of any kitchen garden is the open space enclosed by the fruit walls, the part that gardeners call 'the open ground', or 'the quarters'. When I first visited Pylewell's kitchen garden, most of the open ground, pathways included, was covered in roughly mown grass. It is now a nursery garden, but for 170 years it had provided its owners with vast quantities of fruit, flowers and vegetables (with supplements from the potato field in the home farm, the kitchen-garden slips, the greenhouses and the frames). This chapter looks at what was once the heart of the kitchen garden complex – the part moreover that most resembles the kitchen gardens of antiquity.

Roman villas, medieval manor houses, palaces, castles and monasteries all had gardens enclosed like Pylewell's, with beds and borders divided by straight walks and paths. In similar gardens, Elizabethan gardeners were advised by Thomas Hill to grow their 'herbes, rootes and salletts' according to precepts laid down by Greek and Roman writers on husbandry. They also used these gardens, as the ancients did, as quiet resorts and walking places, for meditation and exercise. The security and shelter of the walls made for peace and privacy: they also made it easier to raise the less robust, as well as the more ordinary, fruit and vegetables. In general, everything grown in this area was of the kind that is hardy enough to grow out of doors, without any assistance other than thinning, weeding, feeding, watering and, where necessary, tying to supports.

Some nineteenth-century kitchen gardens, especially the larger ones, were laid out with no regard to their looks. The kitchen garden at Pylewell, however, was typical of the formal, traditional ideal in which beauty and utility were combined. The more or less rectangular area within the walls was divided into four by two walks. They met in the centre, at the little iron fountain (still there in the 1970s), which once trickled peacefully into the now vanished dipping pool, thus creating the four 'quarters'. Because the walls were slightly askew and the crossing point was not dead centre, the quarters were not exactly equal in size; however, each measured roughly seventy-five by thirty-five feet (see page 10).

As I walked in this garden I had to imagine the wide herbaceous borders, backed by espaliered fruit trees and edged with low box hedges, that once bordered the cross-paths, for they had disappeared in the sixties. Old Percy Gregory had told me of the twice and sometimes thrice yearly clipping of the box. The little hedges' total length was 1,713 yards – just forty-seven yards short of one mile – which was one of the reasons for grubbing them up. Other grubbings-up followed as the number of gardeners diminished: the dipping pond was taken out; the espaliered apples and pears screening the quarters behind the borders became unproductive and cankered, so they went too. In many gardens like Pylewell's first one, then another, and finally all four quarters are grassed over, so that now, as at the royal kitchen gardens at Windsor, the space resembles the field which occupied its site before the garden was made.

THE PRINCIPLES OF LAYOUT

A formal kitchen garden was usually square or rectangular in plan, so that it could be divided easily into workable sections. It needed to be fairly large if it was to provide a useful amount of cultivable space between paths of a comfortable width: the paths were intended for the owner and his friends to walk along, as well as giving the gardeners access to the quarters with their barrows and tools. Herbaceous borders, espaliers and box edgings were necessary too, to enhance the walks and to screen the quarters, with their rows of humble vegetables, from genteel eyes. This arrangement was only practicable, however, in large kitchen gardens attached to houses of some consequence.

The kitchen gardens of more humble places made the best of whatever space was available. These gardens were often small and irregularly shaped, making them relatively primitive and informal. They were (and still are) fitted into odd corners between buildings, squeezed into long, narrow strips beside roads, rivers and city walls, or worked as patches and pockets of fertile soil and leaf mould in the middle of rocky terrain or woodland. Formal kitchen gardens demand order, neatness and the maximum of output and industry, with something of a show for their owners. Primitive gardens, although they can be as much a source of pride, are more private and relaxed; they defy organization and all-out, full-time productivity. Although they are mostly associated with cottages and smallholdings, they do have some relevance to the history of the larger kitchen garden.

THE INFORMAL KITCHEN GARDEN

To appreciate the reasons for laying out a kitchen garden in a formal manner we need only to look at the older cottage gardens in Pylewell's neighbouring New Forest villages. One such garden occupies a roughly triangular area of about one-sixteenth of an acre between the side of the cottage, a paddock and the lane outside. It is fenced and

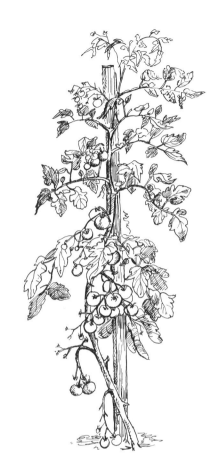

hedged against cattle, sheep, ponies, donkeys, rabbits and passers-by with a variety of materials – old bedsteads, wooden pallets, wire netting and an interwoven, living mixture of hazel, bramble, thorn, dog rose, damson and crab apple.

This garden has a compost heap, beehives, a well, a privy covered with a climbing rose, a chicken run and a toolshed; there was once a pigsty too, but this has been converted into a woodshed. A narrow, well-trodden, grassy path winds through the middle, skirting an old apple tree. Because the garden is such an odd shape, none of the beds lies parallel to another. They run this way and that. Some are long and thin, some are short and wide; others are round, triangular or square. Flowers and herbs, clumps of rhubarb, mint and horseradish are planted wherever they can be fitted in, fighting for space, moisture and light. Raspberry canes, currant and gooseberry bushes are draped with old net curtains to protect the fruit from the birds as it ripens. Strawberries and tomatoes flourish in an assortment of boxes, tins and tubs.

Apart from the gable end of the cottage itself, which has an old pear tree trained on it, there are no fruit walls, no forcing houses, no hothouses, cold frames, storage rooms or hotbeds. Not only is there no space for such refinements, there is no call for them. Out-of-season delicacies are therefore unknown in this garden, but its owners are happy enough, as the seasons come and go, to eat whatever is ready; they have a choice of cabbages, carrots, onions, lettuces, leeks, potatoes, peas and beans. Nor is there any room for land-greedy perennials such as asparagus, though there are a few globe artichokes in the flowerbeds.

On the other hand, a cottage kitchen garden does not demand attendance round the clock, as Pylewell's did in its heyday. The cottage gardener needs only the weekends and an hour or so in the summer evenings to keep his garden going. It is admittedly rather bare in winter, but in the summer it is highly productive and in the autumn there are gluts of marrows, plums, apples and runner beans. Short of storage space and finding the ready

cash useful, the cottager sells his excess produce at the garden gate, along with the odd bunch of dahlias, pots of honey and some of his wife's home-made jams and pickles.

Basic kitchen gardens and backyards like this one can be seen all over the world. They are characterized by random planting. When the Romans first went to Britain, they claimed that the natives were ignorant of gardening. Faced with small, haphazardly planted compounds, with a patch of peas for drying here, a line of cabbagey greens there, collections of edible weeds and the whole encircled by a hedge of brambles reinforced with hazel, sprouted from wands originally stuck in as fencing, they may have been correct. At home in Italy, similar, but more productive gardens were described by the Roman poet Virgil; he called them orchard-gardens.[1]

Such gardens, often provided with beehives and vine arbours, appear to have been typical of medieval, artisan kitchen gardens in both town and country, in England as well as in the rest of Europe. They are certainly depicted as such in illuminated manuscripts; fenced by wattle or walled with brick, stone or boulders, random in shape, they appear to contain no more than one or two different crops and perhaps a fruit tree.

ANCIENT GARDENS

The formal kitchen garden – the prototype of a garden such as Pylewell's – was the antithesis of gardens like Virgil's and the cottage garden. It was based on the grid-like pattern of the kitchen gardens of the classical husbandries and a four-square pattern that can also be seen in paintings of ancient Egyptian gardens. One of the oldest depictions of an Egyptian garden – a grave inscription of the Third Dynasty, *circa* 3000 BC – is of date palms, figs and trellised vines growing in a walled garden, at the centre of which is a rectangular pond containing waterlilies, bordered by flowerbeds. The four-square design, it should be said, was deliberately ornamental and not exclusive to the kitchen garden. It was used in cloister gardens, pleasure gardens, flower gardens, and fruit gardens too. But the traditional division of a walled garden into four quarters, with a central feature, is almost certainly older than the Christian cloister.

The educated villa gardener, both at home and in the remotest colonies of the Roman Empire, such as Britain, would have been familiar with Greek and Roman treatises on husbandry, botany and medicine, even if the subjugated races were not. The authors were scientists, naturalists and philosophers such as Theophrastus, Pliny, Dioscorides, Galen and Apuleius. Their treatises were greatly respected, and were read and copied by generations of scholars, even as late as the sixteenth century, in England and in the rest of Europe.

It is difficult to describe pre-Roman kitchen gardening in Britain without involving the reader in a tedious amount of guesswork, and it is scarcely easier to work out what went on in the kitchen gardens of Roman Britain, although the Roman occupation of Britain lasted for 400 years. We do know, however, that viticulture – the cultivation of grape vines – which requires similar skills to kitchen gardening, was certainly practised in Britain in the third century. Vines were introduced to Britain by order of the Emperor Probus in about 280 AD; thirty-eight vineyards are mentioned in Domesday (1086), the largest, in Berkshire, was about twelve acres in size. We also know that the Romans introduced several edible plants (see Chapter 7), as well as irrigation systems using aqueducts and wells, so we may at least assume that the villa gardener had a kitchen garden laid out on the grid-like plan dictated by the ancient bed and water-channel system (see Chapter 2).

PREPARING THE GROUND

In most kitchen gardens of all dates, the main walks would never be disturbed, but the disposition of the beds and borders would be altered at least once a year. Regular manuring and digging were necessary to replenish the soil's fertility. Where the bed and channel system was employed this meant digging up both the beds and the trenches. Crop rotation was practised too, from earliest times, with certain sections left fallow, cultivated with a different crop from the previous one, or given a dressing of some kind of manure (see Chapter 9).

In classical Mediterranean gardens, and in European gardens thereafter, the areas which were to be sown and planted with summer salads, vegetables and roots were dug and dunged thoroughly in the autumn, before the frosts set in, then laid out and sown in the spring. The sections which were to be sown in the autumn were dug and manured in the spring, leaving them fallow all summer; either way, digging allowed the benefits of heat and cold, air and moisture to work on the soil. Before each section was formed into beds and planted it would be well dug again, then raked and hoed to get rid of stones and

weeds. Pliny reckoned that it would take eight men a day to dig a Roman acre (two thirds of an English acre) three feet deep, mixing dung as they went and marking it out in plots. The gardener would work out the size, shapes and positions of his beds, plots and borders with a line, treading the channels between them with his feet.

MONASTIC GARDENS

The earliest monastic gardens were no more than tiny, primitive enclosures, capable of supporting hermit-like monks on a vegetarian diet, but as the monasteries developed into self-sustaining communities, their gardens evolved along similar lines to those of the formal, irrigated, enclosed gardens of the Egyptians, Romans and Arabs.

Early Islamic gardens provided green shade, lush foliage, the perfume of flowers, bird song and the music of running water, in soothing contrast to the harsh, dry deserts outside their walls. Gushing or flowing channels of water divided them into halves or quarters. Water,

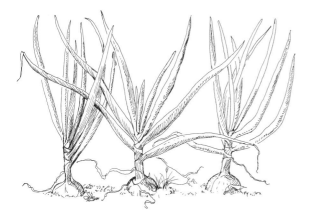

greenery, shade, trees, flowers and fruitfulness are converted, in a monastic garden, into religious symbolism. The enclosed garden, secluded from the outside world, made an ideal retreat for contemplation. Here were tangible manifestations of Christian belief: the assuagement of hunger and thirst; the cycle of life; birth, death, redemption, rebirth, salvation and eternity.

One of the oldest plans for a monastery, with gardens, has survived to this day. It dates from about 820 and was found at the lakeside abbey of St Gall, an early Benedictine abbey in Switzerland. It shows the classic layout of beds and paths in three productive gardens and a cloister-garth within the precincts.[2] (See page 96.)

The largest garden occupies about one-sixth of an acre; it is an orchard-cum-cemetery, largely given over to fourteen burial plots. It contains thirteen well-spaced fruit trees, each bearing a different fruit or nut. Each plot was intended to accommodate seven bodies; seven is a sacred number, while thirteen represents Christ and the twelve apostles. Next in size is the kitchen garden or *hortus*. This is about one-tenth of an acre in size and contains eighteen long, narrow rectangular beds, each twenty feet long and five feet wide, for different esculents. The third garden, the infirmary garden, occupies about one-fortieth of an acre. It contains sixteen beds half as long and half as wide as those in the *hortus*, for what appear to us to be mainly culinary herbs, but they would have had medicinal uses too.

TUDOR LAYOUT OF BEDS

Thomas Hill, writing for English gardeners in the sixteenth century, quoted extensively from the Greek and Roman husbandries, regardless of the fact that they were written one and a half millennia before his time, for Mediterranean gardeners. With his great respect for the words of 'the worthie Antients', Hill ordained that Tudor gardens should be laid out in the same manner as classical gardens. As in the St Gall plan, his beds were long and narrow and, as in Roman gardens, they were separated by well-trodden and gently sloping trenches for carrying water to every bed. He added, possibly from his own experiences of British weather, that the trenches could be supplied with central gutters to help them carry surplus rain into a convenient place at the lowest point of the garden. His gardens were divided into quarters, like a cloister garden.

Hill also gave dimensions. The trenches should be one foot wide between beds of similar types of vegetables and three and a half feet wide where one section needed to be separated from the next. The beds were to be raised one foot or so above the trenches (in damp places they might be as much as two feet high) and made of any length, though for convenience this was rarely more than twelve feet. As in Roman gardens, the width was never to be more than double the length of the gardeners' arms, so that the beds could be reached from either side without being trodden on. The size, shape and disposition of these beds and trenches were also determined by the nature of the crops to be grown in them. Not only were they divided into winter and summer crops, they were also divided by species.[3] (See page 96.)

THE DEVELOPMENT OF ORNAMENTAL KITCHEN GARDENS

The combination of beauty and utility was achieved, in Hill's late sixteenth-century kitchen garden, by surrounding the quarters containing vegetables with a low railing and long, narrow flowerbeds. Marigolds, ox-eye daisies, columbines, primroses, cowslips, 'sweet John' (*Dianthus carthusianorum*), gilly-flowers (an old name for wallflowers, as well as carnations and pinks), irises, peonies and holly-hocks were the Elizabethan favourites. The borders below the enclosing boundary wall or hedge were also planted with flowers or fragrant herbs and, to give an additional touch of decoration, some of the vegetable beds within the

quarters were laid out in circular or diagonal patterns (see page 96).

These gardens were designed for walking in, as well as for produce; they were criss-crossed by alleys and walks, three or four feet wide. To keep the visitors' feet dry, the paths were evenly trodden-out, levelled, and sifted over with sea or river sand. The kitchen garden was also furnished with shady, scented arbours and seats covered in growing camomile, similar to the retreats in medieval pleasure gardens. 'Delectation and jucunditie' were provided by the shade, sight and fragrance of 'upright Archhearbs' (roses, privet, jasmine and rosemary) and 'winding Archhearbs' (vines, cucumbers and melons) climbing over 'Arche herbers' (arbours) made from juniper or willow poles, 'bound togither with Osiers, after a square forme, or in arch maner winded.'[4]

The enclosed, sixteenth-century garden served all purposes – fruit, flowers, medicinal herbs and vegetables grew there together, and it was a place for walking and conversing. By the end of the first quarter of the seventeenth century, when Charles I was on the throne, the separation of flowers, fruit and kitchen-garden produce had begun, and the kitchen garden itself was becoming more compartmentalized, with separate beds for perennial herbs, both culinary and medicinal, and a screened-off area for hotbeds (see Chapter 8).

Those without the time or means to bring their gardens up to date were advised by John Parkinson, apothecary, botanist, friend of Tradescant the Elder and herbalist to James I, to make one garden serve all purposes. Ideally, though, from now on the flower gardens or gardens of pleasure 'of any worthy house' were laid out in ornamental fashion and visible from the best rooms in the house, while the kitchen garden was put out of sight and at a distance.[5]

As we know from the early eighteenth-century engraving of the view of Pylewell (see page 22), the kitchen garden lay on one side of the central approach and the fruit garden lay on the other, with tall hedges hiding them from view. This symmetrical arrangement, with the use of high hedges as screens throughout the garden, is typical of the period.

BEDS, PATHS AND QUARTERS IN THE SEVENTEENTH CENTURY

The late seventeenth-century Scottish writer, John Reid, also liked balance on either side of the main paths within the quarters: 'The order is to make every sort [of vegetable] oppose itself. Example if you plant a Ridge of Artichoacks on the one hand, plant another at the same place on the other . . . In short what ever you have on the one side, you should have the same in every circumstance on the other.'

Reid gave specific measurements for what he called his 'ridges', as well as the borders and beds, and the paths, furrows and walks between them. Each 'level-ridge' was divided into seven beds, six feet wide and ten or twelve feet long, with furrows or paths one and a half feet wide between them. The space, level-ridge or 'compartment' taken up by these beds therefore measured some fifty-four feet across. The compartments were arranged in quarters with three-foot wide service paths between them. The internal beds were given neat edges three inches higher than the furrows or paths that separated them, 'all hansomly clapt up with the Rakehead, by a line'.[6]

Reid's measurements were somewhat smaller than those given by his French contemporary, Jean-Baptiste de la Quintinye; he recommended 'squares' or quarters of ninety to one hundred and twenty feet by forty to forty-five feet, the main walks to be never less than six or seven feet wide, and the service paths two feet wide.

François Gentil, a Carthusian lay brother, for thirty years the gardener to the Charterhouse in Paris, wrote anonymously in 1704 of his own, similarly sized quarters; they were ninety feet long and fifty-eight feet wide, with borders six feet wide round the quarters and beneath the walls. His beds were four feet wide, each one encompassed by a path one foot wide.[7]

TECHNIQUES THAT CHANGED THE LAYOUT

The sixteenth-century kitchen gardener grew all his produce in the open quarters, using the bed and channel system, with little or no assistance from any form of artificial heat until the late 1570s, when the introduction of

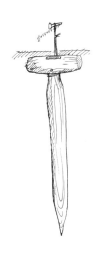

'dibble' or 'dibber'

hotbeds caused the layout and design of kitchen gardens to change. With the help of hotbeds, gardeners were able to make far more use of their gardens during the colder months. As we shall see, the mess created by the necessary dung heaps was hidden to some extent by sheltering walls, screens or hedges, but it was not until the eighteenth century that hotbeds were removed from the quarters and placed in the slips.

The bed and channel system was still used in the seventeenth century, with sunken beds as much in evidence as raised beds. The cultivation of celery or asparagus, for example, which entails earthing-up as the plants progress, led to the practice of starting the plants off in furrows and using earth tipped into the 'Intervalls' beside them to form a raised bed as the season advanced.[8]

The ancient practice of sowing a mixture of seeds of different kinds, broadcast, on beds was retained (see Chapter 8), but by the 1670s gardeners were also beginning to sow large areas of the quarters with seeds of a single kind in rows or, as they were then known, in 'trayles' or 'drills'. The word 'drill' had evolved from the channels made by the farmer's horse-drawn drill, at that time a relatively new invention for the planting of corn, peas and beans in rows, which had lately been taken up by market gardeners. The owners of gardens that were large enough for a horse-drawn implement followed suit, using the resulting 'trenches or gutters' for garden peas and beans. Those with smaller gardens were advised to use the corner of a hoe to make their drills.[9] Alternatively, they could use a line and what Reid called a 'setting stick' to make 'a scratch or little ebb gutter' for the seeds.[10]

With the introduction of the seed drill came the first instructions for the precise distances apart of rows and thinned-out seedlings, with calculations of how much seed was needed for a given area. There were several advantages to sowing seed in drills rather than sowing them broadcast in beds. Economy was one: the gardener used less seed in a drill, and was unlikely to sow the same part twice by mistake. The seedlings were easier to thin from a row, and the rows were easier to weed with a hoe (beds were usually weeded by hand).

FRUIT-WALL BORDERS

The late seventeenth-century gardener now had a variety of methods by which to cultivate his quarters: he had the choice of 'beds or larger quarters' and borders, either below the walls or beside his paths. The borders beneath the new fruit walls were allocated to different crops according to the orientation of the wall: the borders beneath the south and east-facing walls, being the warmest, were formed into banks for early lettuces, peas and early and late plantings of kidney beans, as well as broad beans, and nurseries for strawberries. The borders under the west-facing walls were used as nurseries or seedbeds for the plants that were sown in summer, to stand there all winter and be transplanted to the south border in spring. Under the north-facing walls the border was sown with late strawberries and salads. Nothing deep-rooted was allowed to grow in the wall borders, however, lest it took nourishment from the fruit trees.

WALKS AND BORDERS FROM THE SEVENTEENTH CENTURY

The main walks in seventeenth-century kitchen gardens were made of gravel for comfortable walking, as they were in Tudor gardens. They were raised in the middle, to drain off the wet, and treated with various concoctions of such things as salt, fine shells, tobacco refuse and infusions of walnut leaves to keep them free of slugs, snails and disfiguring worm-casts. Gravel walks were preferred because they reflected heat on to the fruit walls and were hard-wearing; grass possessed neither of those virtues and was therefore considered unsuitable for kitchen gardens. But gravel was difficult to keep clean. Planks had to be laid down if muddy wheelbarrows were to be taken along a gravel walk. In nineteenth-century kitchen gardens boot scrapers were provided at each exit of the quarters to the main walks, and at the entrances to every garden building. Their use was insisted on by the head gardener.

John Reid disliked cross walks, preferring one central walk, with another going round the whole plot parallel to the wall. The width of his main walks depended on their length: a walk 100 feet long, for example, had to be ten feet wide; a walk 1,000 feet long should be thirty feet wide. The walks in Gentil's four acre garden were twenty feet wide near the house; down the centre and along the walls they were fifteen feet wide and the two side walks measured twelve feet across.

Borders beneath the walls looked best if they were as wide as the wall was high, but for ease of pruning, tying and fruit gathering, a small path, wide enough for a barrow, was made about three feet from the wall. The introduction to Britain of dwarf and espaliered fruit trees (see Chapter 5) encouraged the idea of planting them in the borders to the main cross walks so that disruptions to the beds within the quarters could be hidden, but it was important that these living screens should not be so high as to cast shade on the beds. In the most up-to-date gardens of the late seventeenth century, a row of dwarf fruit trees – cut as balls, cups or pyramids – or a line of espaliered fruit trees was planted in the borders along the walks to act as screens for the quarters. The French trained their espaliers against the walls, but the English removed them to the open ground; this form of freestanding espalier was known as the *contre-espalier*.

A triple border, doubling as a screen, was described in detail by John Reid; it was intended to line the paths and surround the open ground of a fairly large Scottish kitchen garden – indeed, his book on gardening was written specifically 'for the Climate of Scotland'. Each of the three borders was six feet wide, with two two-foot paths between them. The border next to the main path was a hedge of holly, the middle border was a row of gooseberries and currants and furthest from the path, at a distance of sixteen feet from the hedge, came a row of dwarf fruit trees. These borders were intended to protect the quarters from wind and weather, make people keep to the paths and conceal the 'ruggedness' of the kitchen beds they enclosed.[11]

EDGINGS

The edges of kitchen-garden borders needed to be 'boxed' in stone or timber, to prevent the soil washing down or falling from the borders on to the walks. 'Hard' or 'dead' edgings were made for Parkinson's early seventeenth-century knot gardens, and possibly for the more decorative kitchen garden too, of one inch oak boards, of half tiles (which had the disadvantage of being fragile), of lead (the lower edge tucked under the gravel and the top cut like battlements), of bones and of stones. Ideally, as in Reid's garden, the top of the boxing and the earth in the border were level with the centre of the walk, which was gently cambered to enable it to remain dry.

Bone edgings were made of sheepshanks, set close together with the knuckle end upwards – a similar edging, of horse's

legbones, was seen by Peter Kalm at the botanist Peter Collinson's garden in Peckham, London, in 1748 – and John Parkinson related that gardeners in the Low Countries used jawbones too, as edgings, but he thought that this was 'gross and base'. Stones, which he noted were the latest fashion, were large, whitish or bluish pebbles, set on the level ground. The use of large stones as edgings to kitchen garden paths was common in stony districts. Specially manufactured tile edgings in a variety of designs came into use towards the 1870s; bricks on edge were also used at this time, if not before (see page 262).

Alternatively, borders beside walks were given 'soft' or 'live' edgings of plants such as box (recommended by all the authorities as the best), juniper and yew (kept small), thyme, lavender, hyssop and rue. In this case the earth in the border was made level with the sides of the walk. The disadvantages of most living edgings, excepting box, is that they die out after a time and the shrubbier plants need clipping to prevent them becoming leggy, which means that they should not be allowed to flower. As if to compensate for this, Reid also suggested low front-edgings of parsley, strawberries, violets, gillyflowers and so on.

Dwarf box (known today as *Buxus sempervirens* var. *suffruticosa*) was used to edge all kinds of garden paths from the seventeenth century onwards. John Parkinson mentions it as early as 1629; he uses it 'to border up a knot, or the long beds in a Garden'. As to its size, Charles M'Intosh, writing in 1847 says: 'box-edging should not be allowed to exceed three inches in height, and two in breadth at the bottom, tapering upwards to a point.' The modern reader must think he means 'feet' rather than 'inches', but I can confirm that he goes on to say: 'Nothing looks worse than misshapen box-edging, particularly when allowed to attain a large size. The only real use of an edging of any kind is to separate the gravel of the walk from the mould in the border, and an edging of the above dimensions is sufficient for that purpose: larger ones only harbour vermin, and give the garden a neglected and careless appearance.'[12]

EIGHTEENTH-CENTURY LAYOUTS

With new, high, fruit walls enclosing the kitchen garden, a greater variety of late and early kinds of vegetables, increasing competence in the art of hotbed management, and the beginnings of hothouse cultivation, the productions of the open ground could be extended throughout the year. The borders beneath the walls, though primarily intended to supply nutrition and moisture to the fruit trees planted in them, were sloped slightly upwards towards the wall and, as in earlier gardens, planted with shallow-rooting plants.

The idea was still in force, in the early eighteenth century, that 'Cabbages, pease, beans and other vegetables [are] in themselves, not the most agreeable, as to prospect nor smell'.[13] Dwarf fruit trees were still used to line the walks, but these were now thought to be less productive than espaliers. The fashion for espaliered borders lasted until the 1830s, was then eclipsed by a preference for dwarfs, standards or fruit trained over low arches (as at the royal kitchen gardens at Windsor), and only found favour again in the 1870s, when borders along the main walks usually consisted of herbaceous flowering plants, backed by espaliers and edged with either low, single cordons, or with box.

The kitchen gardens of the mid eighteenth century retained the earlier tradition of divisions into quarters. These were now less often laid out as beds and channels and more usually sown in rows. In the earlier part of this period, in the gardens of wealthier owners, the quarters were sometimes designed as elegant, but somewhat impractical, shapes to add to the enjoyment of looking at them.

WALKING IN THE KITCHEN GARDEN

Although kitchen gardens and fruit gardens in the eighteenth and nineteenth centuries were always separated from the flower garden, they were still used for walking in. Their high walls or hedges made these kitchen gardens beautifully sheltered, but for them to be included among the sights worth visiting, some kind of softening or ornamentation was still necessary. An enclosure devoted to nothing but regimented rows of peas and lettuces, spinach and runner beans, divided into four equal parts by straight paths and unrelieved by any other sort of planting would be bleak, if not severe, giving the sensitive owner the impression that he had strayed by mistake into a municipal allotment, a market garden or even a ploughed field. However, given firm, dry, clean paths to walk on, borders to those paths of flowers and fragrant herbs, espaliered fruit trees to divide the borders from the quarters, shady seats and arbours for rest and shelter, then the pleasure of a trip to the kitchen garden was enhanced without detracting from its essential purpose, which was to provide the family with esculent plants.

The owner could incorporate other decorative devices. He might add beehouses, aviaries and dovecots, step-over cordons or avenues of dwarf fruit trees, walks shaded by tunnels of ripe and ripening fruit, pergolas, topiaried shrubs in tubs, hedges cut in fantastic shapes, trelliswork, sundials, statues, urns and ornamental fountains. And in winter, a kitchen garden with good glasshouses would still be worth a visit, for they offered both warmth and interest, virtues that were lacking at that time of year in the gardens outside.

Kitchen gardens, in short, could be even more enjoyable, in William Cobbett's opinion, than the pleasure grounds, especially in spring when all the trees were in blossom.[14] For some, the pleasures of walking in a kitchen garden were due as much to its necessary neatness and order as to the knowledge that the place was mainly intended to supply food. In 1828, Harriet, Countess of Granville, wife of the British Ambassador in Paris, while at home in England on a visit, wrote to her sister Georgiana at Castle Howard (with a fervency that only those with a passion for kitchen gardens will understand) of the first glimpse of her friends' kitchen garden at Trentham Park in Staffordshire:

> They [the Earl and Countess of Stafford] were out when we came and I rushed to the *potager* - you know my weakness - and walked up and down between spinach and dahlias in ecstasy. This is in many ways a beautiful place and the tenure, the neatness, the training up of flowers and fruit trees, gates, enclosures, hedges, are what in no other country is; and then there is repose, a *laisser aller*, and a security . . . that no other destiny offers one.[15]

It might be supposed that very large kitchen gardens were unsuitable, perhaps too large and too distant, to act as ornamental *potagers*, or places of recreation. How, for example, could the open quarters of a garden such as that of the banker Henry Drummond, at The Grange, in Hampshire, look decorative? According to an inventory of its contents, dated 19 October 1795, it contained, in stores or on the open ground, 22 poles of spinach, 150 bushels of potatoes,

16 bushels of onions, 30 bushels of carrots, 1200 Savoy cabbages, 700 late cabbages, 2000 early cabbages, 700 purple-sprouting broccoli, 700 cauliflowers, 2200 celery, 660 Brussels sprouts, 1800 lettuces, 2600 endives, 8 beds of asparagus, 8 rows of artichokes, 10 poles of horseradish and 10 perches of strawberries. (The place was being rented at the time to the Prince of Wales.)[16] Yet large gardens like these could be made attractive. Queen Victoria's kitchen gardens at Windsor were outstanding in this respect (see page 10).

QUEEN VICTORIA'S KITCHEN GARDEN

This garden was first laid out (with advice from Prince Albert) in 1844. It occupied a total of thirty-one acres, of which some thirteen acres formed the main quarters, and 150 gardeners were employed in its upkeep. A special gravel drive was made (again under the direction of Prince Albert) from the castle to the kitchen gardens, one and a half miles away, so that Her Majesty, who took the greatest interest in her splendid new garden, could drive there in her pony-carriage. The royal entrance to the kitchen garden (a modest pair of iron gates flanked by a porter's lodge) lay at the eastern end of a line of hothouses which extended for over 1,000 yards. These were so magnificent that, in 1853, there was a proposal to move the main entrance to the south, 'so that the visitor, on entering the walled garden, will have presented to his view the elevation of the finest range of glass in any

garden in Europe'.[17] This proposal was never carried out.

Still in her pony-carriage, the Queen would proceed along the terrace in front of the hothouses, stopping halfway at the head-gardener's cottage. Here she would take tea (with strawberries and cream, or whichever fruits were in season) in an elegant little drawing room specially set aside for the Royal Family's visits.

The terrace in front of the gardener's cottage was twenty feet wide. It was laid out with flowerbeds in front of the glasshouses; on the other side of the drive was a grass verge and more flowerbeds, bounded by a low parapet ornamented with vases. Shallow steps led down to the quarters, which were bisected and bounded on all sides by paths of immaculately swept gravel, wide enough for the passage of the royal pony-carriage or a cartload of manure. In the centre of the garden was a fountain in a circular basin, thirty feet across; the basin was made of polished Peterhead granite (the same stone as that used for the fountain basins in

Trafalgar Square), and pipes leading from it provided water for the whole garden. The Queen could survey her kitchen garden from the terrace without obstruction, for the pear trees planted on either side of the walks were trained over arched trellises only four feet high. The walls surrounding the quarters were twelve feet high and surmounted at the main entrances by massive stone eagles with outstretched wings.

The total cost of this kitchen garden was £50,000, a sum that was raised without any demand on the public purse by selling the land occupied by the royal kitchen gardens at Kensington Palace in London – the same

gardens that were situated on 'the worst land that can be had for that purpose', and were so much disliked by Carpenter and Wise (see Chapter 1). Expensive mansions for the *nouveaux riches* were built on the Kensington site; they are now largely occupied by embassies and millionaires.

THE POTAGER AT VILLANDRY

In the twentieth-century re-creation of a sixteenth-century kitchen garden at Villandry, on the Loire, in France, small arbours of trelliswork adorn the four inside corners of each quarter. There are nine square quarters, each of them forming a differently patterned maze, parterre, or patchwork of brightly coloured, box-edged beds in the form of zigzags, squares and rectangles, coloured entirely by the close planting of 30-40,000 vegetables and flowers. Reds come from ruby chard stems, strawberries, peppers, tomatoes and roses; mauves, blues and purples are supplied by red cabbages, flowering chives, sage and petunias; oranges and yellows shine from ripe pumpkins and gourds, courgette flowers, rudbeckia, calendulas, golden celery and golden lettuce; silvers, greys and whites come from artichoke leaves, white blette (Swiss chard) stems, white cabbages and flowering basil; blacks from aubergines and black pimentos; every shade and texture of green is seen in cushions of parsley, leek fronds, carrot tufts, beets and spinach.

The kitchen garden is based on views of *Les Plus Excellents Bastiments de France,* published in 1576 and 1579 by the architect Jacques Androuet du Cerceau. It was laid out between 1914 and 1918 as an ornamental, 'Renaissance' potager, intended to be walked in and also to be seen from above, either from the windows of the château or from the vine-arcaded, elevated walks which run all round the garden. It is a joy to see, but it is unlikely that a sixteenth-century kitchen garden really looked like this, since like a parterre it relies for the success of its design on intricate blocks of colour. A contemporary of du Cerceau, the royal gardener Claude Mollet, said that beds for vegetables should be made large and simple.[18]

The engravings that inspired the layout of Villandry's potager show kitchen-garden plots that are far less complicated. Ornamental beds such as these, if historically correct, would have relied on low-growing flowers, herbs, grass, clipped shrubs or coloured earths and clays for their colour, rather than on transitory vegetables. What we have here is a work of art rather than an historical reconstruction. Any garden devoted chiefly to raising vegetables for the pot, but planted as decoratively as this, could never have had plants such as cabbages or leeks cropped piecemeal without spoiling the effect. Here the individual beds must be dug, planted and cropped in their entirety, all at one go.

At Villandry we encounter one of the more esoteric philosophies of the twentieth-century kitchen gardener. The garden's *raison d'être* is not to keep the kitchen and medicine cupboard supplied. The vegetables are to be eaten, but the garden is primarily ornamental. Its maintenance, according to François Carvallo, the son of the creator of Villandry, is an aesthetic, intellectual and moral exercise. He planted his vegetables with a painter's eye; their colours will change as they develop:

The green tomato becomes . . . bright red . . . shiny and satiny like a piece of porcelain. The cabbage turns from grey-green to bluish, then sumptuously red: a Veronese red. Celery has surprising shades of empire green. The light green leek darkens with age and finishes like an old tapestry woven with silver thread. The humble beetroot goes from sea-green to the red of Bordeaux wine.[19]

BEDS-AND-CHANNELS

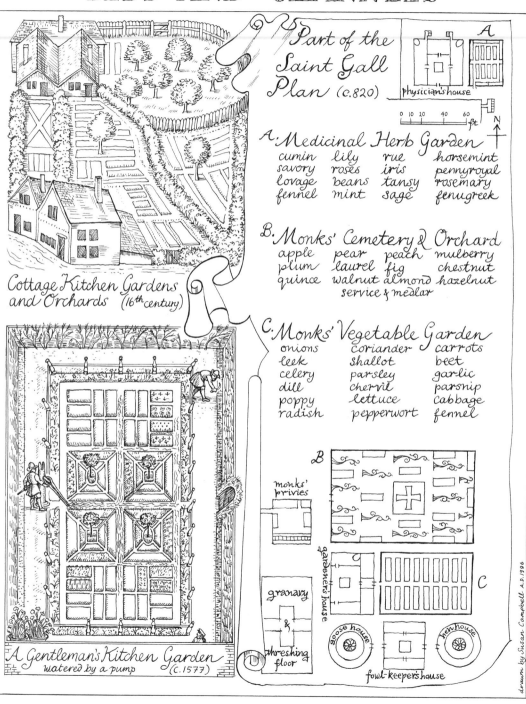

Part of the
Saint Gall
Plan (c.820)

physician's house

A

0 10 20 40 60 ft

N

A. Medicinal Herb Garden

cumin	lily	rue	horsemint
savory	roses	iris	pennyroyal
lovage	beans	tansy	rosemary
fennel	mint	sage	fenugreek

B. Monks' Cemetery & Orchard

apple	pear	peach	mulberry
plum	laurel	fig	chestnut
quince	walnut	almond	hazelnut
	service & medlar		

C. Monks' Vegetable Garden

onions	coriander	carrots
leek	shallot	beet
celery	parsley	garlic
dill	chervil	parsnip
poppy	lettuce	cabbage
radish	pepperwort	fennel

Cottage Kitchen Gardens
and Orchards (16th century)

A Gentleman's Kitchen Garden
watered by a pump (c.1577)

monks'
privies

granary
&
threshing
floor

B

gardener's house

goose house

hen house

fowl-keeper's house

C

drawn by Susan Campbell A.D. 1996

CHAPTER SEVEN

NEW VEGETABLES, OLD TECHNIQUES

It is not my intention to describe, plant by plant, every vegetable that was grown in the open ground throughout the history of the kitchen garden. From time to time, however, introductions were made that caused notable changes not only to our diet, but also to methods of cultivation.

THE IRON-AGE KITCHEN GARDEN

It is difficult to be sure what was grown in British kitchen gardens before the Roman occupation, but according to paleobotanists, the indigenous vegetables of Iron-Age Britain included quite a nourishing selection of plants which were found in the wild or grown in gardens in an 'unimproved' state – alexanders, nettles, mints, cresses, fat-hen, celery, beet, carrot, leafy brassicas and asparagus. The Britons also grew crops of ancient varieties of wheat, barley, peas, vetches (a small species of pea) and horse beans in fields that provided a number of edible weeds; and remains have been found of tasty seeds such as dill, coriander, fennel, poppy and anise, that may have been imported as flavourings. There were also several woodland or hedgerow fruits such as hazelnuts, gooseberries, crab apples, wild pears and strawberries, sloes, bullaces and cherries.

Compared with the vegetables we grow now, the wild ancestors of our kitchen garden crops were often either insipid or bitter in taste. Furthermore, while some were small in size, others tended to be stringy, woody or tough; all were limited in variety and most were only available for short seasons. Fruits and vegetables have been improved by selection, hybridizing, grafting and careful cultivation, and many gardeners throughout history have spent much of their working lives in that department; equally the garden has been enriched by receiving different varieties and new species from friends, neighbours, travellers, even invaders.

THE SPREAD OF CLASSICAL HUSBANDRY

The Romans brought a number of hitherto unknown, flavoursome and succulent vegetables and fruits to Britain. During their 400 years of occupation they introduced onions and mustard, as well as garlic, leeks,

copied too, but less carefully than the words, thereby making it hard to recognize the plants they purported to represent. Only in the twelfth century, when artists began to draw from nature, were their drawings of any help with identification.

MONASTIC KITCHEN GARDENS

A monastic gardener was expected to supply medicinal plants for the pharmacy and infirmary, flowers for church decoration and religious festivals and, above all, fruit and vegetables for communities which at times ate virtually no meat.

We know the layout and plantings of one early ninth-century garden; the monastery plan from the abbey of St Gall (*circa* 820) identifies each bed (see page 96). The plants in the kitchen-garden beds, such as onions, garlic, shallots, leeks, leaf-beet, coleworts, included several items – celery, lettuce, parsnips, carrots and radishes, for example – that were not to become familiar in English gardens for another two or three hundred years. The kitchen garden also had beds for parsley, coriander, dill and chervil. The plants were mostly annuals, but the infirmary garden had a larger proportion of perennials, giving the arrangement of the beds some permanence. The beds were labelled with very few medicinal herbs, but it may be that these were gathered from the wild; there are many that we would think of as purely culinary, as well as roses, irises and a climbing kidney bean (the North African *Dolichos lubia*).

lettuces, parsnips, skirrets, turnips, radishes, walnuts, figs, vines, peaches and improved varieties of apples, pears, plums and cherries. Many of these vanished from gardens during the turbulent period that followed the Roman departure from Britain late in the fourth century, and were not seen in the country again for another three hundred years.

Greek, Roman and Arabic pharmacopoeiae and books on husbandry were copied throughout classical times and later, as Christianity spread and Europe became re-Romanized by monks. Much of the gardening and pharmaceutical expertise was doubtless passed on by word of mouth, but the classical ideal was kept alive throughout the Middle Ages and into the Renaissance by copies and translations of ancient herbals and treatises on gardening, agriculture and farming. The copies were kept in monastic libraries and, as learning and the monastic movement spread, were copied again and again. With the invention of printing, these husbandries began to appear in the libraries of universities, hospitals, churches and landowners. They were still being consulted well into the sixteenth and seventeenth centuries. At first, the illustrations were

There was only one of each species among the trees in the monks' orchard-cemetery: a pear, a fig, a plum, a service tree, a medlar, a laurel, a chestnut, a quince, a peach, a hazelnut, an almond, a mulberry and a walnut. These plantings were possibly symbolic; they can hardly have been part of a practical plan for the feeding of a community calculated to have consisted of 270. A considerable amount of food would therefore have been bought in or grown in outlying fields and orchards.

With the establishment in the eleventh century of a Norman dynasty in England, horticultural expertise spread there from northern France. Once again, the influence of monasticism was important. The Cistercian order was founded in 1098 in Burgundy. Its precepts were based on St Benedict's original 'Rule', by which the monastery had to provide everything the community needed, so that it could survive independently of the outside world. The order was so successful that it became established throughout northern Europe. The Cistercians' development of hydraulic power, metal technology and agriculture led to the creation of an empire based on the most up-to-date industry. Their gardens and orchards were kept in a state of high productiveness. The soil was well tilled, manured and watered; fruit trees were carefully grafted and pruned; nurseries were planted with replacements and trials. Their root stores and fruit rooms were well stocked and their cellars filled with wine, ale

and cider. Their pharmacists were supplied with medicinal plants, and profits were made from the sale of surplus products, crops and seed. The Cistercians are known to have exchanged seed, slips and cuttings of fruit trees with one another, taking them from France as far afield as Germany and Denmark.

The Cistercian monastery at Beaulieu in Hampshire was founded in 1204, and within

*bean
'Dolichos lablab'*

sixty years the abbey had become one of the largest English monasteries of its time, supporting a community of some 120 brethren and 250 hired workers. According to the account books of 1269, the Beaulieu monastery had, as in the St Gall plan, one area known as the *curtilagium* or kitchen garden, one called the *gardinarium* or orchard and another designated as the infirmary garden. In addition there were twelve other cultivated enclosures or 'curtilages' within the abbey precincts, each producing two or three crops for the whole community, and each one associated with either a non-ecclesiastical building or a workshop. It may be that as the abbey at Beaulieu grew, the original spaces allotted for the vegetable garden and orchard proved too small, making it necessary to use these extra plots as well. Whatever the reason, within the riverside precincts of fifty-five acres, these scattered gardens occupied a total of eight or nine acres – far more than the two or three acres of productive gardens in the St Gall plan.[1]

The Beaulieu curtilage keeper had five under gardeners. He was also responsible for all the workshop crops (which included honey and what we would think of as agricultural crops), as well as his own. His curtilage produce, as recorded in the accounts, consisted of beans, leeks, 'olera' (*Brassica oleracea* and vars), wheat, oats, vetches, hemp and honey (crops identical, incidentally, to those produced at Evreux Cathedral, in Normandy, at almost the same date).

The accounts for the yard by the brewhouse listed beans and honey, as well as grapes; the parchment-maker's yard contributed beans, leeks and hemp; and the gatehouse yard provided leeks, onions, hemp and flax. The infirmary garden produced beans, grapes, vetches, honey and pigeons. It may have contained medicinal herbs as well, though they are not mentioned in the accounts. The orchard keeper (the *gardinarius*) produced apples for cider (which, with apples from outlying orchards, amounted to 4,800 gallons a year), as well as rye, oats, vetches and hemp, honey and wax.[2] The accounts obviously only recorded garden produce that was sold, and there are no details as to the varieties of the 'olera' in the *curtilagium* but from other records we know that English gardeners of the thirteenth century grew leafy brassicas, leaf-beet, onions, radishes, celery and possibly lettuces.[3]

MEDIEVAL VEGETABLES

Medieval fruit and vegetable gardens did not, of course, belong exclusively to religious houses and monasteries; there were similar gardens serving royal palaces and aristocratic households, colleges and castles. There were also market gardens on the outskirts of towns, and fruit and vegetable markets in the towns themselves, at which the surpluses of private gardens could be sold.

The other vegetables grown in the medieval kitchen garden were broad beans (also grown as a field crop), coleworts (a form of

rocket

cabbage which is also known as collards, kale or greens), leafy beets (beets were not cultivated for their roots in England until the sixteenth century), mustard (grown for its spicy seed), garlic, chibols (known to us as Welsh or winter onions) and scallions (which may also be taken to mean chibols, or shallots, or any young onion eaten green). These plants were usually made into a kind of soup or 'porray' (pottage or purée), thickened with bread, oatmeal or dried pulses (field-peas, vetches and beans), and enlivened with a choice of cress, mint, parsley, sage, hyssop, dittander and fennel.

The medieval kitchen garden was known either as the 'curtilage' or as the 'leac-garth' or the 'leac-tun' from the Anglo-Saxon 'leac' (leek) and 'garth', 'geard', 'zeard' or 'tun' (yard or enclosure). Americans still call their back gardens backyards, which shows how closely the language of the earliest, Elizabethan colonists was linked to the Anglo-Saxon of their ancestors. The use of the term 'kechyngardyn' or 'kechengardyn' is quite late; it is thought to have first appeared in English in the Bishop of London's account

rolls for the manor of Stepney of 1383-84 and 1395-96.[4]

A late medieval kitchen garden like the Bishop of Stepney's would grow all the preceding plants, plus three or four important additions, all roots, none of them widely eaten in England before 1300 and never as a separate dish, but only in porrays and even then only by the wealthy. These roots were skirrets (mentioned as early as 1275),[5] parsnips, turnips, navews (long-rooted turnips which were grown too for their edible leaves), yellow or purplish-brown carrots and possibly radishes.[6] Other fourteenth-century novelties were lettuces and endive (names which are frequently interchangeable), rocket, 'gourds' (here, possibly meaning cucumbers, maybe pumpkins) and headed cabbages (white, red and green), together with a number of fragrant and medicinal herbs.

beet spinach

There are also frequent mentions of 'spynach', but there is some doubt as to whether the true spinach *(Spinacia oleracea)* was grown here before about 1500; plants previously called 'spinach' in English could have been chicory, orache or orage *(Atriplex hortensis)* and were even more likely to have been fat-hen or Good King Henry *(Chenopodium bonus-henricus)*, or one of the other edible goosefoots. True spinach was introduced to Moorish Spain from Persia and Afghanistan by the Arabs in the eleventh century; it is also associated with the Saracens, who called it *isfanaj*. It may have reached Italy by 1305, as the cultivation, comparisons and description of spinach made by the Italian writer, Pietro de' Crescenzi, tally with the real thing.[7]

THE HERB BED

From early medieval times gardeners had used the word 'herb' to describe all useful plants, whether they were grown as food or flavourings, medicines, narcotics or hallucinogens, disinfectants or pesticides, perfumes, poisons or dyes. It was not until the eighteenth century that plants used mainly as food began to be called 'vegetables', leaving the word 'herb' to describe, as it does today, a multitude of plants that are life-enhancing (and on occasion, deadly) without necessarily being nourishing in any way. By a tradition as old as medicine itself, curative or health-giving properties were ascribed to nearly every plant grown in the kitchen garden. Indeed almost all plants, cultivated and uncultivated, edible and non-edible, were believed to have medicinal virtues and humoral values. (It was believed from ancient times that the four principal elements of the natural world were air, fire, water and earth. These elements had corresponding characteristics – cold, hot, wet and dry. When paired, these characteristics produced the four 'complexions': sanguine (hot and wet), phlegmatic (cold and wet), choleric (hot and dry) and melancholic (cold and dry). Furthermore each complexion had a 'humour', namely blood, phlegm, yellow bile and black bile. Thus an excess of yellow bile, as displayed by the hot and dry temperaments of choler or anger, could be 'qualified' or tempered with a diet of 'phlegmatic' foods – lettuce and other salads for example – which were characterized by their opposing coldness and wetness. Cabbages and onions, being classified as hot and dry, were to be avoided.)

Many plants, of course, were useful in more ways than one. The Romans are believed to have introduced a particularly vicious type of stinging nettle *(Urtica pilulifera*, 'hot and dry'), chiefly to alleviate rheumatism. The cure was a stimulating rub with the uncooked leaves, a remedy which is still part of English country lore. But the Romans also ate the cooked leaves 'to keep disease away all year' and boiled the roots with tough meat to make it tender.[8] Roots of the common nettle *(U. dioica)* were used to make a yellow dye and the fibrous stems were once manufactured into fine cloth and cord. The whole plant, harvested and dried, made fodder for animals and poultry; the seeds were said to give horses sleek coats. The juice acts like rennet on milk and makes a green dye; it was also said to be an antidote to venomous insect stings, the bite of a mad dog and baldness. The plant is still used as a poultice for sciatica and is recommended by homeopaths for its astringent properties, while the gatherers of 'free food' enjoy the leaves as a springtime soup or purée, which can be washed down with nettle beer.

Lettuce was credited with almost as many qualities as the nettle. The legendary symbol of the transitory nature of human life, it was also regarded as the herb of impotence, a diuretic, a purifier of the blood, a promoter of milk in nursing women, a cure for hangovers and a soporific.[9]

Unless there was a specific need for an infirmary garden (as in the St Gall plan) there was no distinction in the earlier kitchen gardens between quarters devoted to food plants and those devoted to herbs. For simplicity of cultivation herb beds were usually planted according to whether the plants to be grown in them were annuals or perennials, tall or short, and suitable or not as edgings. Medieval kitchen herbs were also grown in portable tubs, boxes and pots, making them both ornamental and handy for the cook. Gardeners tended to label certain plants 'pot-herbs', 'chopping herbs', 'sweet herbs' or 'sallet herbs' if they were to go to the kitchen, and 'physic herbs' if they were meant for the medicine cupboard, but the

categories frequently overlapped.

The most important fourteenth-century introduction among the herbs grown for flavouring was rosemary, sent by her mother to Philippa of Hainault in 1338, when she married Edward III. Its reputation as a 'purifier' when burnt made it more desirable, especially during episodes of the Plague. Clary, borage, rue, savory, marjoram, chervil and coriander

borage

were also grown in fourteenth-century gardens, and used to enhance food and drinks.

Both classical and medieval herbalists believed that wild herbs were more efficacious than cultivated herbs. Never-theless, many herbs with medicinal, veterinary, economic and culinary properties were grown, particularly in monastery gardens, where a wide variety of herbs was needed for the hospice, infirmary and pharmacy as well as for the kitchen, brewery, winery, distillery, dyeworks, poultry yard and farmyard. Among the medicinal plants traditionally grown with food plants were mallow, valerian, marigold, agrimony, comfrey, hart's-tongue, southern-wood, camomile and wormwood. Very

poisonous herbs such as nightshade, agrimony, aconite and henbane were rarely mentioned in lists of plants suitable for a domestic garden, which implies that they were either gathered from the wild, or were grown only by the apothecaries.

'Physicke' for ailments ranging from fleas to measles could be bought in towns from the apothecary, but in the country medicines were largely home-made. The housewife concocted tonics, lotions, purges, poultices and salves in her still-room, using specific leaves and flowers, roots and seeds, or whole plants from gardens, hedges and woods. Fresh herbs from your own garden, dried 'in the shadowe ... open towards the South' and kept in leather bags or boxwood chests, were considered to be far better than those bought from the 'Poticaries', who '...hang up the Physicke hearbes in their open shoppes and ware-houses, through

which, the vertue of these not only breathe away, but the hearbs [are] charged and clagged with dust, Copwebs, dung of flies, and much other filth'.[10]

By the sixteenth century the kitchen garden had become quite orderly. One compartment was planted only with medicinal herbs such as the blessed thistle *(Carduus benedictus)*, wormwood, dittander, self-heal, and so on. Strongly scented herbs such as sage, hyssop, marjoram, rosemary, southernwood, lavender, balm, running thyme, costmary, savory and camomile were planted in individual beds. Some of these herbs were grown here and later taken, as slips or seedlings, to make knots and parterres in other parts of the garden. Camomile was used for camomile seats as well as for physic.

The early seventeenth-century gardener John Parkinson proposed that, where convenient, certain perennial herbs such as thyme, sage and hyssop could be grown in beds dedicated to nothing else – a herb garden as distinct from a kitchen garden, for 'Physicall herbes' were still used 'to preserve health' and cure minor ailments.[11]

By 1670 it had become a 'convenient practice tending to handsomness and good order' to put together, as in the St Gall plan, 'in one quarter or in beds by themselves, all such Herbs as are durable, and not to be renewed every year'; these included thyme, winter savory, hyssop, pot marjoram, winter-sweet marjoram, balm, costmary, mints (preferably with their roots contained), bugloss, sorrel and succory. Other bushy perennials such as lavender, sage and rosemary were cut 'smooth and handsome' to act as ornaments to the garden, as well as 'an hedge to lay small cloaths upon to white and dry'.[12]

A century later came the Industrial Revolution, and with it larger towns and villages complete with retail druggists. Old-fashioned country remedies were supplemented by new medicines based on chemicals and exotics. The medical fraternity, eager to promote the latest drugs, discouraged the use of rural 'physicke', which for townspeople had become difficult to obtain. However, the demand for home-grown medicinal herbs increased, if anything. It was now satisfied commercially by market gardeners. Like his forebears, the nineteenth-century kitchen gardener grew these herbs as well, but only for economy and convenience. The virtual exclusion of medicinal herbs from the kitchen garden is relatively recent; it dates from the gradual replacement of home remedies with drugs manufactured for us by the pharmaceutical industry.

THE ARAB INFLUENCE

The Arab influence in European gardening is seen in decorative features such as fountains and arbours, in techniques connected with forcing and in the introduction of new varieties of fruit, flowers and vegetables. Many of these were grown in order to make candied fruits and flowers, and non-alcoholic distillations of plant oils and essences. (The still itself is an Arab invention.)

The Moorish Arabs ruled southern Spain for nearly seven hundred years – from early in the eighth century, and were not expelled from that country altogether until 1609. From Persia, India and beyond they introduced agricultural crops such as rice and sugar cane, and in their Andalusian kitchen gardens they grew, besides spinach, eastern plants such as oranges and other citrus fruits, saffron, red-rooted carrots (early European varieties were either yellow or purple), aubergines (said to be fatal to Christians) and cauliflowers. None of these, with the exception of saffron, which had reached England by the mid fourteenth century, were grown in the rest of Europe until the fifteenth century, when they were

cardoon in flower

105

blanched chicory

introduced into southern France and Italy from the Levant and Spain.

The Moorish Arabs also grew artichokes and cardoons (likewise to become fashionable in Italy in the fifteenth century). The parts of globe artichokes that were eaten – the thistle-like flower buds – were said to have aphrodisiac properties. Cardoons, thought by early botanists to be a wild form of artichoke, are not grown for their flower buds, which are tough and inedible, but for their stems ('cardoon' derives from 'chard' or 'stem'). Both Pliny and Theophrastus said that cardoons grew only in Sicily, and that their stems were edible; but neither mentioned the practice of making those stems more edible by blanching (see below) although both writers were familiar with the technique. Nor was the blanching of cardoon stems mentioned in any Arabic garden treatise; it appears not to have been practised on cardoons

in gardens until the sixteenth or seventeenth century. Even then, cardoons were unknown to English gardeners.

ENCOURAGING TENDER LEAVES

Blanching, or whitening a plant's young leaves, shoots or stems by excluding light, thereby rendering them crisper, whiter, sweeter, taller and more tender, was practised by classical, medieval and Elizabethan gardeners. The term first came to be used in the late eighteenth century; it was probably discovered by noticing the effect on a plant that had been accidentally covered, and the covers then removed. Lettuces, kale, turnip roots, endives and beet-leaves were blanched by covering the growing plant with pots or tiles, heaping earth or sand round it, or tying the leaves together.

The blanching of lettuces, chicory and endives, celery or smallage, sweet parsley and fennel was achieved either by binding the leaves and burying whole rows out of doors in

cut-and-come-again

trenches, covering them with fresh dung to speed up the process and giving them mats to keep out the rain, or by burying them indoors in cellars, covered with sand (the root uppermost, to keep sand out of the leaves 'and you finde it in the dish when they serve it').[13]

Old artichoke plants which were about to be changed after five years' bearing were treated like cardoons – cut down to within six inches of the ground in autumn and then, when the new growth was about three feet high, the gardener should bind it up 'with a wreath of long straw, not too close, and surround with dung to blanch'. At the same time 'bells' of solid earthenware or wicker- work were also used for blanching; the process again was speeded up by heaping fresh horse dung over the covers (see page 262).

The desire for sweet and tender vegetables was satisfied in some cases by allowing leafy plants with a tendency to do so to sprout again after cutting. This technique, now known as cut-and-come-again, was practised by the Greeks and Romans, as well as by gardeners of every age thereafter. It was said (by Theophrastus and repeated by Pliny), that the new leaves tasted sweeter than those that had been cut away. Basil, lettuce and cabbage in particular benefited from this technique.

French gardeners of the fourteenth century applied the same technique to beets, borage, orach, 'greens and porray', raking earth over the tops in summer so that they sprouted again four or five times. The author of a

contemporary gardening book remarked that even if cabbages were eaten by caterpillars 'to the veins' the stumps would bear sprouts again if you stripped off what was left of the leaves, transplanted them and buried them right up to the topmost eye. The stumps left after a cabbage was cut in summer would sprout greens in time for Lent.[14]

TRENCHES AND WEEDING

Kitchen-garden quarters are usually dug extra deeply, or trenched, every four or five years. This is a system of digging with spades that probably predates the agricultural plough; trenching may have been practised by the Romans. John Evelyn simply described it as digging two spits deep, and forming a trench with the first spade's soil underneath the second.[15]

Trenching was usually done by gardeners working in pairs or threes, one or two digging and shovelling, another wheeling and throwing in the manure. Trenching at Pylewell in Mr Hamilton's day had to be three spits deep (one spit is a spade's depth, usually about eleven inches); Percy Gregory had horrible memories of the time when, as a garden boy, he was made to be the front digger; the man behind him would threaten to 'chop off his heels' if he slowed down.

As the spring and summer progressed, the beds, the alleys between them and the main walks began to need weeding. By the seventeenth century, this was done wherever possible with hoes, but 'In beds where hawes cannot go, you must weed with your hands on both sides, sitting in the furrow on a straw cushion.'[16] Spades and iron rakes were used on the paths; hoes, 'scrapples of iron', weeding knives or fingers took care of the beds. The task was best done after a shower of rain. Large gardens were usually weeded by the under gardeners, but in smaller gardens the job was done by the mistress's maids, in which case the mistress was advised 'either to be present herselfe or to teach her maids to know hearbs from weeds'.[17] By the late seventeenth century the job of weeding was almost always done by women. A stone statue of an old 'weeder woman used in the garden' was made by the Duke of Bedford at Woburn Abbey, so lifelike that Celia Fiennes,

on a visit there in 1697, 'tooke it to be a real living body'.[18] By the nineteenth century, a weeding glove, for use by both sexes, had been invented; this was a glove with hard metal tips – 'wedge-like thimbles of steel, kept sharp' – on the thumbs and first fingers.[19]

THE ENGLISHMAN'S ATTITUDE TO VEGETABLES

There is a still an element in the English attitude to food which regards the eating of vegetables as 'sissy'. It certainly existed in the sixteenth century, according to the contemporary historian William Harrison. He claimed that the Englishman's love of meat and rejection of vegetables dated from the previous century, 'so that from Henry the fourth till the latter end of Henry the seventh, and the beginning of Henry the eighth, there was little or no use of them in England, but they remained either unknown, or supposed as food more meet for hogs and savage beasts to feed upon, than mankind'.

However, by 1587, when this account was published, Harrison was able to say that vegetables and fruits were back in favour not only 'among the poor commons', but also 'at the tables of delicate merchants, gentlemen, and the nobility, who make their provision yearly for new seeds out of strange countries'.[20]

In fact it now seems that throughout the fifteenth century the market gardeners of Flanders (a stronghold of the Huguenots) exported choice fruits and young vegetables to this country, where they were bought as luxuries at considerable expense. The fact that they had to be bought does add strength to Harrison's assertion that the art of kitchen and market gardening had become feeble, if not altogether absent at the time in England. However, there is evidence that English kitchen gardens were undergoing a revival much earlier than 1525, when new plants like artichokes came in.[21]

The early sixteenth century saw the break with Rome and dissolution of the monasteries in England, and the beginning of the persecution in France (and later in the Netherlands) of the Huguenots who eventually sought refuge in Britain, in America and in the Protestant countries of Europe. The Huguenots brought with them (among other skills) the art of fruit and vegetable growing. Their arrival in Britain coincided with the publication of some of the earliest treatises in English on gardening, and with the introduction of herbs, plants and fruits from newly discovered parts of the world. Most of these introductions – even the edible ones – made their way, as we shall see, not to the kitchen garden, but to the apothecaries' and botanists' gardens, where they were either examined for their pharmaceutical potential or grown as 'curiosities'.

TUDOR VEGETABLES

Meanwhile, the quarters in the Tudor kitchen garden, still laid out in the classical bed and channel system, had the crops disposed in them according to their nature and season of

broad bean

planting. Thomas Hill thought it best to sow plants in the early autumn that were sown in their own countries in late autumn, and in late spring those normally sown in early spring.[22] Sowing times were further specified; most authorities decreed that all seeds should be sown with a waxing moon.

There was also a desire to have fresh vegetables for as long as possible throughout winter, as well as the pleasure of eating young green leaves in early spring and the religious dictum that forbade meat-eating during Lent. These requirements led to the custom of sowing as many hardy varieties of vegetable as possible in the late summer, thinning them or transplanting them in the autumn and leaving them to grow in sheltered beds and

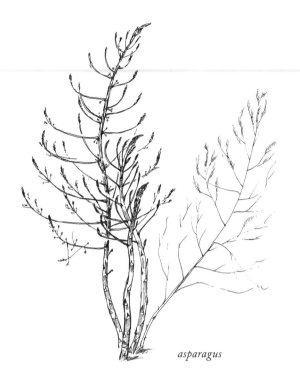

asparagus

wild on seashores, river banks and wastelands, whence it was taken to gardens and 'improved'. By the mid sixteenth century, according to the botanist William Turner, asparagus was found wild only on the Continent: 'in Englande it groweth no where els that I knowe, but in gardines.' [23]

Another section was devoted to nursery beds for cuttings and flower, salad and vegetable seedlings which were transplanted, when large enough, to other beds. There were also individual beds for strongly scented herbs and for medicinal herbs, as well as for onions and their relatives and for melons and cucumbers, which had not yet been banished to the slip garden (see Chapter 8).

borders over winter. Cabbages, beets, spinach, certain varieties of lettuce, endives, turnips and broad beans came into this category; with the advent of the hotbed (see Chapter 8) and glasshouse (see Chapter 10) the range was greatly extended.

The brassicas – coleworts, cabbages, 'navews', turnips and rapes – were placed in one section of the garden, in long, wide beds one foot apart with an alley three feet or more wide dividing them from the next section, which might consist of smaller beds of leafy salad plants and culinary herbs such as orach, spinach (the real kind), rocket, parsley, sorrel, chervil, leaf-beets, dill, mint and fennel. Asparagus, which was cooked and eaten cold as a salad, was also grown in this quarter, and was treated as a perennial. A European native, it is still found growing

MIXED PLANTING: INTERCROPPING, SOWING AND TRANSPLANTING

Hill also recommended sowing fast-maturing salad plants such as radishes, purslane and rocket in the beds at the same time as slower-growing coleworts, onions and leeks, a system that later became known as mixed planting or mixed sowing. The plants that matured first were harvested before the slower crops, which then grew into the vacated space. The bed-and-channel system was also suitable for intercropping: the sides and ends of the beds were sown with 'trayles' of a fast-maturing crop, leaving blocks of slower-growing crops in the middle. Later on, when sowing in drills became more usual, fast crops were sown between rows of slower crops.

If the seed of a single crop were sown thickly, the thinnings were either eaten as salad plants or transplanted to new beds, to grow on into mature vegetables. Transplanting was acknowledged to be necessary if fine, well-developed plants were desired; it usually entailed shortening the seedling roots and smearing them with dung before planting them in prepared beds, in well-spaced holes made with a dibble, then watering well. Transplanting is mentioned in classical books on husbandry, though mixed sowing (except as a form of companion planting) is not; both, however, are described in detail by the fourteenth-century Italian lawyer and writer Pietro de' Crescenzi.

Mixed planting also avoided constant disturbance to the soil in the beds, which was one of John Parkinson's concerns. In John Reid's Scottish gardens too, beds were sown with 'mixtures'. Beat-rave (beetroot) or parsley was sown with onions, and would grow on over winter after the onions had been harvested. Beetroot, skirrets and beans were also planted in the gaps between newly planted artichokes or cabbages, or in the edges of the furrows running between other beds.[24]

Onions, radishes and lettuces could be sown among newly set asparagus, artichokes or liquorice. In the late sixteenth century, English-grown liquorice was found to be sweeter than the foreign kind, which gave rise to the liquorice industry of Pontefract in Yorkshire (home of the eponymous cakes and Liquorice All-Sorts); the plant was also popular in gardens at that time. The juice, rhizomes and roots were used medicinally, particularly as a cure for lung complaints, and also made into gingerbread, comfits (sweets) and a sort of ale.

By the late nineteenth century, inter-cropping had become 'simultaneous cropping'. The technique was particularly favoured where space was at a premium. Suggested combinations included radishes and lettuces or endives sown on the banks thrown up by trenches made for celery (the endives were taken up in autumn for forcing when the celery was earthed up); broad beans ('Dwarf Mazagan') and early potatoes planted in the same row; tall and dwarf peas sown in the same row, the dwarf used first and pulled up when the peas were 'fit', to make room for the taller, later peas; rhubarb and seakale growing in alternate rows, to be forced together, and strawberries and onions, the onions sown in drills two to two and a half feet apart, with strawberry runners planted

between them in July, to grow on after the onions had been cleared off and to crop the following year.[25]

PEAS AND BEANS

Although recorded in monastic accounts as a medieval garden crop, peas are rarely mentioned as kitchen-garden vegetables before the mid sixteenth century, as until that date they were grown mainly in fields or market gardens, to be harvested when fully ripe and dry, for keeping over the winter. The sweeter and more tender varieties of pea, eaten fresh, with or without their pods, when immature and therefore green, were a novelty to the Elizabethans; the habit was introduced from the Continent. Their cultivation in English gardens, like that of tender, young parsnips, turnips, carrots and the cauliflower, was pioneered by immigrant Huguenot gardeners. Earlier, fourteenth-century references to 'green' or 'new' peas do not necessarily mean immature peas; they may equally well mean green-coloured seed (as opposed to white or grey seed), or the season's new crop of dried peas.

The oldest named varieties of pea are the 'Hastyz' and the 'Runcival'. 'Hastyz' peas were large and early, as their name (from the French *hastif*) suggests; this became Anglicized to 'Hastings'. 'Hastyngez' peas (sown in November) were grown in England from the late fifteenth century. 'Runcivals' take their name from the Abbey of Roncesvaulx in Navarre. They were grown in England at the Hospital of St Mary Rounceval (near the present Charing Cross in London) at about the same time; they are distinguished by being excessively tall and needing sticks to support them, unlike the common field pea, which needs no such support. Thomas Tusser, writing in 1557, referred to the grey-seeded 'Runcivall pease' as 'dainties' to be sown in January.[26]

Kidney beans of the genus *Dolichos* or *Vigna* (lablabs and cowpeas of Asian and African origin) were grown in Mediterranean gardens in classical times. Pliny described the cavalance bean (*Vigna sinensis*), a tall, climbing bean of which the pods were eaten green. This should not be confused with the runner bean (known as the climbing kidney bean until the late eighteenth century) which, like the haricot, flageolet and French bean, comes from the Americas and belongs to the genus *Phaseolus*. Field, Celtic and broad beans (all varieties of *Vicia faba*) were the only beans grown in Britain until the arrival of the Phaseolus tribe from the New World. The herbalist John Gerard remarked, as early as 1597, that 'The

Fruit and Cods of Kidney Beans boyled together before they be ripe, and buttered, and so eaten with their Cods, are exceedingly delicate meate, and do not engender Winde as others do.' [27] That kidney beans were a novelty, even when eaten dried, was underlined by John Worlidge, who wrote eighty years later that 'within the memory of Man [they] were a great rarity here in England. Although now a known and common delicate food'.[28]

Even as late as 1677 there were only two named varieties of broad bean on sale to gardeners, the 'Windsor' and the 'Sandwich'.[29] Both were varieties for spring planting, introduced by Huguenot gardeners and given the names of the two English places most noted for their cultivation. Early in the eighteenth century 'Spanish' and 'Lisbon' began to be imported, to be followed shortly by the 'Mazagan', from a Portuguese settlement on the Atlantic coast of Morocco. (The naturalist Gilbert White was one of the first to grow 'Mazagans', in 1755.) These varieties could be planted in late autumn, against a warm fruit wall; the 'Mazagan' retained its popularity until the early years of this century, when it was ousted by improved strains of 'Windsor' and 'Aquadulce'.

The scarlet-flowered runner bean is said to have been collected in Virginia in 1633 by Charles I's gardener, John Tradescant the Younger, and brought to the royal gardens at Oatlands in Surrey the following year. It was favoured solely for its bright red flowers, which were picked for nosegays and garlands.

As a climbing perennial capable of reaching some twelve or fourteen feet, it became popular for covering balconies, arbours 'and any Defects in our Walls'. It continued to be grown purely for decoration in the eighteenth century.[30] The earliest varieties of climbing kidney bean to be grown as food were the Dutch and Battersea beans, both of which had white flowers and seeds. It was not until 1759 that Philip Miller championed the scarlet runner bean as food, declaring that although 'this Sort is chiefly cultivated for the Beauty of its Flowers at present, yet I would recommend it as the best Sort for the Table.' He even found it preferable to 'all the other Kinds yet known'.[31]

SEAKALE AND RHUBARB

Seakale and rhubarb were novelties in the eighteenth-century garden; the former had long been known as a wild seaside plant, which in its natural habitat on the coasts of England is blanched by being covered with shingle. The blanched stems were eaten by the poor and sold in local markets as a seasonal speciality in the spring. Seakale was grown in seaside gardens, but it was not widely known until 1799, when the apothecary and botanist William Curtis published a pamphlet giving detailed instructions (and a packet of seeds) for its cultivation. He wrote that it was as delicate as asparagus and easy to digest; in a later edition he claimed that it was good for preventing the formation of kidney stones as well.[32]

rhubarb

Rhubarb *(Rheum officinalis,* and possibly *R. palmatum)* was described as a laxative in a Chinese herbal of 2700 BC; it was later valued as a purge and a tonic, the root (the only part used) being taken as a powder or an infusion. The dried roots of these medicinal varieties were imported at great expense from their native lands, China, Siberia and the Himalayas. The word 'rhubarb' is said to be derived from 'Rha', the ancient name of the river Volga and 'barabaron', the foreign lands beyond the Roman Empire. In the sixteenth century, a living plant was sent to Britain in the hope that it could be grown there, but it was of little medicinal use, being *R. rhaponticum.* Attempts to cultivate sufficient quantities of the medicinal variety continued into the late eighteenth century. In 1763 a gold medal was offered by the London Society for the Encouragement of Arts, Manufactures and Commerce to the person who could produce the largest number of plants. It was not awarded until 1792; the successful grower, with 300 plants, was one Sir William Fordyce.

Some sixty years earlier, however, it had been discovered that the stems of 'the Siberian Rhubarb', peeled, cut up and baked 'in a crust with sugar and a little cinnamon ... has none of the effects that the roots have. It eats most like gooseberry pie.'[35] Thereafter, rhubarb tarts became a popular dessert. Rhubarb was liked even more when it was discovered, by accident, in 1815 that the stems were sweeter and more tender after being blanched like seakale. To avoid too much disturbance when picking the stems, first of seakale and later of rhubarb, their blanching was facilitated by the use of special pots with removable lids (see page 262).

FURTHER INTRODUCTIONS FROM THE NEW WORLD

Gerard's kidney bean seems to have been the first of the many new edible plants from the New World to reach the table. Potatoes, tomatoes, maize, peppers and yams had been discovered in South America; vegetable marrows and other varieties of pumpkin, Jerusalem artichokes and scarlet runner beans had been found in North America. On their arrival in Europe these new plants were grown at first as botanists' curiosities; some – potatoes for example – were sold at first for high prices, as aphrodisiacs. Their acceptance as food was relatively slow, particularly amongst Englishmen, partly for fear of their being poisonous, partly because gardeners and cooks were not sure how to grow or cook them.

Potatoes were discovered by the conquistadors in Peru in the 1530s, reaching

England as booty in the ships of Sir Francis Drake and Sir Walter Raleigh in the 1580s. One of the stories connected with the potato's early history is that Raleigh's gardener waited until his potato flowers had set their little 'apples' or seeds and sent *them* to the kitchen, thinking they were the edible part. A hundred years later, John Evelyn assured his readers that pickled potato fruits were good eaten as a salad.[34] The confusion is understandable, given that the potato is a *Solanum*, a member of the deadly-nightshade family and closely related to the tomato, a plant that took even longer than the potato to be accepted as food.

Tomatoes were considered purely ornamental fruits when they first came to England in the sixteenth century. They were started on a hotbed, then planted out against a warm wall or an espalier. The earliest introductions included a yellow variety, hence the Italian *pomo d'oro* which in France became *pomme d'amour*, so that, like the artichoke and potato before it, the tomato too gained a reputation as an aphrodisiac. Tomatoes were enjoyed as food in the warmer European countries, and also in the North American colonies, but here it seems

they rarely reached perfection, being 'of a faire pale reddish colour, or somewhat deeper, like unto an Orenge, full of a slimie juice and a waterie pulp.'[35]

Late in the nineteenth century, the Americans encouraged Britons to try tomatoes in sauces and salads, and slowly they caught on, but I can well remember an old nurserywoman telling me how nervous she was, when, as a little girl, she ate her first tomato.

THE QUARTERS FROM THE SEVENTEENTH CENTURY ONWARDS

The disposition of the vegetables within the quarters did not alter much in the century that separated the reigns of James I and Queen Anne, but more use was made of the slip garden and of temporary shelters for plants raised on hotbeds. In a kitchen garden

horseradish

*rocambles
or garlic onions*

of 1700, 'The Herbs [i.e. vegetables], which may serve the Occasions of the Kitchen' were still grown in separate 'Apartments . . . according to their several Uses'. Medicinal plants – 'Physick-Herbs' – if not given a garden to themselves, had provision made for them in every quarter, while 'up and down the beds let there be planted such common Flowers as may serve for Garniture or Shew'.

The first quarter was set aside for 'Odiferous Herbs such as are fit for the Pot, or the Distillatory'. This section still included our own familiar culinary herbs and vegetables such as thyme, savory, fennel and parsley, as well as sorrel, orach, violets, southernwood, comfrey, hyssop, bugloss and 'beets of all sorts'; the onion tribe were included here as well.

The second quarter was devoted to roots; these were carrots, scorzonera, radishes, horseradish, parsnips and skirrets.[36] Potatoes were still regarded with mistrust by most people in the late seventeenth century, in spite of earlier attempts to subsidize plantations of them as food for the poor.[37] Potatoes, together with another introduction from the New World, the North American Jerusalem artichoke, were grown, if at all, in 'common Ground', being 'a wild sort of Fare'. Field peas, beans, cabbages and the like were also grown outside the kitchen garden, being needful of 'more room than what we can allow them in this Place'.

The third quarter was 'assign'd for Sallad-Herbs'; here were lettuces of all sorts (and by now there were at least eleven kinds to choose from), celery, endive, rocket, corn-salad, garden cress (*Lepidium sativum* or pepperwort – the cress of mustard-and-cress), which had to be differentiated from another South American introduction, Indian cress (*Tropaeolum minus*, the dwarf nasturtium), cucumbers, rampions, rocket and spinach as well as alexanders, with flavourings; sweet basil, chervil, salad burnet, garlic, rocambole and shallots.

The fourth quarter held plants needing larger plots; asparagus, cauliflowers and broccoli, globe artichokes and 'the finer sorts of cabbages'.[38]

A portion of the warmest quarter was devoted to hotbeds for tender exotics such as pomegranates, myrtles and dates, and orange and lemon seedlings grown from pips (the young leaves were eaten in salads). It was shared by the now well-established dwarf kidney beans and musk melons – 'musk melon' being the early name for 'true' melons, rather than pumpkins or squashes, which were also known as melons or 'millons'. A reed fence was erected to protect this area, which shortly became known as 'the melonry', forcing ground or frameyard (see Chapter 8).

The walls, of course, were all planted with fruit trees and, to protect this citadel of good things, Nourse advised that the gardeners should have lodges near the walls 'with good Mastiff-Bitches to guard them'.[39]

By the middle of the eighteenth century, the slip garden took the overflow, as it were, of produce for which there was no room in the main quarters; it was also found more convenient to place the soft fruits, the nursery beds, the mushroom beds (see Chapter 16), the melonry and forcing ground in the slips. More attention was paid, too, to the cultivation of the borders beneath the walls, which were now invariably covered with fan-trained or espaliered fruit trees.

With the development of the new, high walls supporting glasshouses, worksheds and fruit, the quarters were left unencumbered. The changeover from beds and channels to large flat areas sown in rows was almost complete by the beginning of the nineteenth century. As at Pylewell, nearly everything in the quarters was grown in long rows, and everything in the borders was grown in blocks, or in shorter rows, with the sunniest portion devoted to culinary herbs from the Mediterranean.

As to what was grown in the quarters, there were few, if any, startling nineteenth-century introductions, but the increase in the varieties of each species grown out of doors was tremendous. This wealth of choice, with the assistance of forcing beds and houses in the winter, enabled gardeners to supply a succession of roots, herbs, greenery and salads throughout the year; they could buy seeds, slips and tubers to suit any season and any soil. By the time of Queen Victoria's death in 1901, virtually every esculent plant that could be grown in an English kitchen garden was to be found growing there.

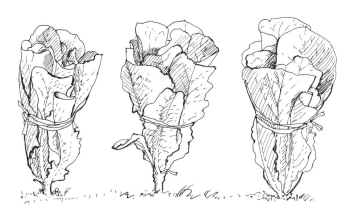

FRAMEYARD

McPhail's Pit
1794

Forcing Pits
designed to maintain heat without
disturbing the crop
D = dung (fresh): S = soil or mould: R = rubble:
◉ = drains: ◎ = hot water pipes: P = planks:
GL = ground level:

West's Pit
c.1820

Thomson's Pit
c.1880

**Hot Bed with Linings
and Frame**

lining

lining

Mitchell's Pit
c.1890

warm vapour

cold air

1

2

3

4

5

6

7

8

A Hot Bed and Various Covers

1 canvas covers
2 oiled paper covers
3 straw matting
4 osier cover

5 bell glass
6 frame with lights
7 matting wigwam
8 hand-light

S.C

CHAPTER EIGHT

THE FRAMEYARD

The frameyard evolved from a fenced-in portion of the open ground set aside originally for growing melons and cucumbers on heated beds. In seventeenth-century France it was known as the *melonière*: this was Anglicized to 'the melonry', 'melon ground', 'melon yard' or 'melon plot'. Later, as heated beds began to be used for forcing a greater variety of plants into early growth and fruiting, the melonry became 'the forcing ground'.

The heat of the beds was prevented from escaping by straw mats supported on wooden frames, or by glass casements (also known as sashes or lights, as they were made in the same way as window sashes) supported by wooden frames. More permanent frames could be made of brick or stone, but many gardeners preferred wooden frames, as they were – and still are – not only cheaper but also portable. The whole structure, bed included, gradually became known as 'a frame', and eventually it gave the forcing ground its final name – 'the frameyard'.

From the Sale Catalogue of 1850 it looks as if Weld's 'Melon Ground' at Pylewell, with an eighteen-light brick pineapple pit, occupied an area behind one of his vineries, but by Williams-Freeman's time (as shown by the First Edition Ordnance Survey map of Pylewell dated 1868), four large and seven smaller pits or frames had been built in the southern slip in front of the two lean-to vineries. By 1932 this area was occupied by Mr Hamilton's four span-roofed green-houses. His frameyard was situated out of sight in the eastern slip garden.

Unlike the quarters, which were designed to be visited, this solely utilitarian yard was, by tradition, devoid of any ornament or decorative planting. The four span-roofed glasshouses have frames attached to their sides and are still in quite good condition, both houses and frames having been used in Billy's time for forcing early and late cucumbers, melons and tomatoes, and for growing pot plants and carnations. But the frameyard has been abandoned and, like most abandoned frameyards, it is so covered in rampant brambles, nettles and self-sown saplings that it is impossible to see if there are any frames still in there, or not.

The restored frameyard at West Dean in Sussex is a good example of how such places once looked. There, some frames and pits have low, wide, double-span roofs, others have half-span roofs. Some are only two or three feet high; and while others appear to be only two or three feet high, they are actually the superstructures of pits dug into the ground, deep enough for a man to stand

melons ripening on tiles

inside. With the assistance of heat they were able to produce out-of-season salads and strawberries, young potatoes, asparagus, peas and French beans, herbs, lilies-of-the-valley and violets and, above all, melons and cucumbers. The paths between the frames were laid with ashes from the boilers and kept scrupulously weed-free. Old frames can still be of use, even without heat, to harden off seedlings or raise slightly earlier crops, but most frameyards are now in varying stages of dereliction. The sashes on a few frames might be still in place, but the glass will be either covered in algae or missing; and while the timbers of some might still bear traces of white paint, the rest will have simply fallen to pieces.

It is probable that some, if not all of Pylewell's frames were heated by the hot-water system supplying the vineries. This was certainly a cleaner and more reliable way of heating frames than the old eighteenth-century method, as can be seen from the fact that the two previous kitchen gardens at Pylewell were situated close enough to the stables to ensure a fresh, and constant supply of horse manure. This was essential, for fermenting manure is what the beds inside its frames and pits relied on for their source of heat.

MELONS, GOURDS AND CUCUMBERS

Our ancestors' love of oranges led to the invention of the seventeenth-century orangery, and their love of pineapples caused the invention of the eighteenth-century bark stove; but before they discovered those pleasures, it was their love of melons and cucumbers that fostered the sixteenth-century hotbed and created the frameyard.

Melons originated in tropical Africa and southern Asia. Classical and medieval botanists describe several varieties, including 'insipid', 'sweet' and 'bitter' kinds. For the ninth-century poet and Abbot of Reichenau, Walafrid Strabo, the sweet variety was:

> . . . the spoil and chief pride
> Of a garden, a choice and delectable feast
> That will tickle your palate, yet not in the least
> Set your teeth upon edge. Down it slips like
>   a dream,
> And refreshes your soul with its icy-cool
>   stream.[1]

The Elizabethans grew 'Pompons, Mellons and Muske Mellons'. The two first may be taken to be varieties of pumpkins and gourds; the third is the sweet, or dessert, melon *(Cucumis melo)*. Some varieties of pumpkin

pumpkin 'Big Cheese'

and gourd could be grown in temperate, northern European gardens without heat. However, dessert melons need a temperature of 18C/65°F to germinate and grow, and 23-6C/75-8°F for the fruit to ripen. It is therefore fairly certain, since no other form of artificial heat existed beforehand, that sweet melons were not grown in England until the hotbed was introduced in the late sixteenth century.

Cucumbers, melons, gourds and water-melons were all grown in the Mediterranean gardens of classical times, for medicinal as well as culinary reasons. Gourds, which have strong, grasping tendrils, are happiest when climbing and made ideal subjects for the cladding of arbours. Melons and cucumbers, with feebler tendrils, tend to do better sprawling over low hills or ridges, the modern, outdoor or 'ridge' cucumber being so called for that very reason.

Thomas Hill, who introduced the art of raising melon seedlings on hotbeds to English gardeners, directed that the young plants should be set in pots below the level of the alleys that doubled as water channels in his garden, in troughs on either side of the beds. He thought they preferred damp soil, but later gardeners found that they did better on beds raised at least eighteen inches above the alleys. Gourds and cucumbers were planted beside a hedge or arbour, so that they had a structure to climb over.

Melons, gourds, pumpkins and cucumbers are closely related botanically and were so confusingly named in the earliest husbandries and gardening treatises that it is often difficult to identify which of them is being referred to. However, two characteristics remained constant, even in the old books on husbandry: directions for cropping invariably stipulated that melons and pumpkins should not be

gathered until they were fully ripe and falling from the plant, while cucumbers were best eaten unripe.

The more obvious characteristics – of opposing tastes and shapes – are not such reliable indicators as they might seem, as they occur in modern melons and cucumbers to a far greater extent than they did in the past. Although a melon was only eaten when ripe, the fragrance, sweetness and lusciousness which we think of as typical of a good specimen seem to be atypical of melons grown by the Romans. This, 'in a country where gourmets were not wanting', suggested to Alphonse de Candolle, the nineteenth-century plant historian, that it was only after the Renaissance, with improved cultivation and the introduction of new varieties from the East, that the melon became a dessert rather than an entrée.[2]

Cucumbers have a particularly ancient history. They were cultivated in India long before they reached Ancient Egypt, Greece or Rome, by which time there were many different varieties – large and small, green and yellow, round and elongated. Most varieties of cucumber and gourd are hardier than melons; both were grown in England long before melons, as early as 1321.[3] The malleability of young gourds and cucumbers and the ease with which they could be trained into 'fantasticall shapes' provided amusement for gardeners from Pliny's time onwards.

Hill explained to his Elizabethan readers that 'Roman letters, strange figures & scutchings or armes imbossed on the green rind' could all be had if moulds of wood, clay or plaster of Paris, made with these devices, were fastened on the young fruit. Cucumbers were also said by Hill to be 'an enemy to lust', owing to their cold nature and habit of growing bent, which was made worse by the presence of oil or thunder. However, they could be encouraged to grow fast and straight if a bowl of water were placed under them.[4]

Gardeners seem to have an obsession with growing straight gourds and cucumbers. Even today, snake gourds are grown in India with stones tied to them to encourage them to hang straight; the Romans trained cucumbers to grow straight inside large, hollow reeds or canes, which were attached as soon as the embryo fruit began to form.[5] Victorian gardeners had the same preoccupation, either because they were dominated by cooks who demanded straight cucumbers, or because of the stipulations laid down by horticultural shows. Some old gardeners used to make do with lamp glasses; others had glass straighteners specially made for the purpose, so in due course a cucumber house would look as if it were hung with green icicles, while the roof of a melon house would be festooned in orange or pale jade globes, each fruit hanging in a net in case it fell at the moment of ripening.

MAKING A HOTBED

Old-fashioned hotbeds had a revival during the Second World War, in gardens where they still wished to forward early crops. Their practitioners claimed that they were saving coal and helping the war effort but really they had little choice: dung was plentiful and fuel was rationed. There are very few gardeners now who still remember how to make a hotbed, but this is how it was done a hundred years ago.

First of all a cartload of fresh dung was shaken, forkful by forkful, into a flat-topped, volcano-shaped heap. After a day bacteria would get to work, and the heap would begin to ferment and to steam. It was left undisturbed for two to three days then re-formed into a similar heap, with the outer parts of the first heap turned innermost. Three days later it was turned again and watered if the weather was dry. Three separate fermentations over a period of nine days helped to spread the bacterial activity more evenly throughout the manure and prolong its heating powers.

Having prepared the manure, the gardener built his hotbed on a level, rectangular piece of ground, facing south to get the benefit of the sun. He defined the shape of the bed, using lines fixed between upright posts at each corner. He could make it any length to suit his purpose, but the width was always about five or six feet across. The height would be four or five feet to start with but the bed would sink as the fermentation progressed. He began making the bed by forking the dung little by little on to the marked-out space, beating it down evenly as he added more fresh dung and keeping the sides perfectly perpendicular. Then he covered the top with a layer of good, well-sifted loam and, as soon as the first, fierce heat had abated, sowed it with seeds or planted it with young plants. He set a protective frame with wooden sides and a glass lid on top of the bed to keep out the cold and conserve the heat created by the fermenting manure.

Hotbeds, like today's heated frames, were used to force all kinds of crops, from salads to strawberries, as well as melons and cucumbers. They made their first appearance in English kitchen gardens in the 1570s, but their history goes back much further than that – Moorish Arab gardeners were using them in Andalusia, in southern Spain, over a thousand years ago.

THE ORIGINS OF THE HOTBED

The use of fermenting dung as a source of heat is almost as old as the kitchen garden itself. Fermentation occurs quite naturally within a heap of any vegetable waste such as grass mowings, dead leaves or even ordinary garden rubbish, as well as farmyard manure. Any of these materials can be used to make a hotbed, but the greatest heat, according to the Arab authorities, was provided by droppings fresh from the stables of horses, mules or donkeys, freed of any earth or 'foreign bodies and dried bits'. Their horses had stables with stone or brick floors, and beds (made up twice a day) of powdered, dried manure, earth or sand. The droppings were cleared as soon as they occurred. The best horses were given a rich diet of barley, beans and alfalfa, which made the most superior manure for heating, being highly nitrogenous.[6]

The Moors used hotbeds primarily as seedbeds; the seedlings were then planted out in the garden as soon as it was warm enough. The advantage of the hotbed was that seeds could be sown on it sooner than in the open ground, thus giving earlier crops. Much later, in northern Europe in the eighteenth and nineteenth centuries, it was found to be useful for forcing roots that would normally be dormant in the winter, such as endive, horseradish, potatoes, seakale, asparagus and rhubarb.

The first reference to hotbeds appears in an agricultural and gardening calendar compiled *circa* 961 at Cordoba.[7] The gardener was instructed to make raised beds of dung – '*min masâtab al-zabal*' – in December, the coldest, darkest time of the year, and to sow them with gourds and aubergines. The seedlings were transplanted in April. The raised beds were indubitably hotbeds; without heat, such seeds would never have germinated at that time of year, especially not in the mountains of Andalusia; they were sown, moreover, two to three months before summer vegetable seeds like these were normally sown out of doors.

The oldest instructions for making hotbeds appear 120 years later, in the gardening section of a Moorish agricultural manual written sometime before 1085. The author was Ibn Bassâl, gardener to al-Ma'mun, the sultan of Toledo. He used hotbeds in winter to force the seedlings of *bâdinjân* (aubergines), *qara* (gourds) and *baqla al-yamâniyá* or *yarbuz* (amaranths or blite). This, more or less word for word, is how Bassâl made what he called his 'beds of manure':

We use soft, slightly dried-out mule or horse dung, free of all foreign bodies. We break it up and mix it well. We make the beds for early fruit in December and January, against the walls of a house facing east. For gourds we make them one cubit [20 inches] high, three cubits [60 inches] wide and whatever length is needed, depending on the quantity of seed. If the dung has gone cold we add pigeons' dung (one-third of pigeons' dung to two-thirds of horse or mule dung).

We make the top of the beds even, then sow the seed, mixed with fine, well-decayed dung. To retain the heat we cover the beds with a canopy of cabbage or cauliflower leaves. We leave it in place until the seedlings show, watering the beds if necessary. The seedlings are transplanted from these nursery beds as soon as they are big enough, from early March to late May.[8]

The origins of the technique of sowing seeds on a hotbed; covering it with temporary shelters during bad weather, or overnight; 'forcing' or accelerating plant growth; extending the season of favourite fruits and vegetables; and growing exotics in climates that could be a great deal cooler than the Arabian deserts are hard to discover, but the desert itself may hold the answer.

According to Aristotle, dung heaps were used by the Egyptians of the Late Dynastic Period as a means of hatching eggs artificially: they were 'hatched spontaneously in the ground, by being buried in dung heaps'.[9] This technique was still being practised in Egypt as late as the nineteenth century.[10] Greek and Arab alchemists were using dung heaps for distillations needing prolonged, slow heat long before the first century AD, when the Arabs invented the distillery heated by fire.

The Romans also practised forcing, but although they had some kind of frame they do not appear to have used true hotbeds. Both Pliny and Columella describe in their works on Roman husbandry how their emperor, Tiberius, was supplied with cucumbers all the year round. Apparently he had 'a remarkable partiality' for cucumbers; to satisfy this appetite his gardeners grew them on portable, wheeled beds. These were kept in the shelter of a building in cold or stormy weather and moved out when the sun shone, even on cold days. On these occasions protective frames holding panes of *lapis speculare* (fine

aubergine 'Long Purple'

sheets of mica, selenite or gypsum) were placed over the cucumbers. The portable beds were made of basketwork. They were filled with well-manured soil, but no mention is made of fresh, fermenting and, therefore, heating dung. When the spring equinox was over (25 March) these baskets were placed, with their cucumber plants, in beds in the open garden.[11]

As the first recorded instance of the use of the truly hot, horticultural dung bed appears in the Cordoban Calendar, it looks as though the hotbed was an Arab, rather than a Roman invention. On the other hand, the

Romans may certainly take the credit for being the first to use a protective, transparent frame, superior, surely, to Bassâl's cauliflower leaves and an artefact which his treatise never mentions. This raises a question to which there seems to be no answer – namely, why did it take so long for this miraculous invention, the hotbed, to be taken up by gardeners in the rest of Europe? Although a Castilian version of Bassâl's treatise was available to Christian Europeans, the usefulness of the hotbed appears not to have spread beyond Moorish Spain for almost three centuries.

THE LATE MEDIEVAL HOTBED

In 1275 the Castilians finally expelled the Moors from Andalusia. Some thirty years later Pietro de' Crescenzi, a retired lawyer in Bologna, wrote a treatise in Latin on agriculture, *Liber Ruralium Commodorum*. Much of it was derived from the classical husbandries, but a good deal of it is original, including a passage which is tucked away in the section dealing with melons and gourds. This contains the first mention of the hotbed outside of Moorish Spain.[12]

Why the hotbed should appear at this point in gardening history is uncertain, but at the time Bologna was the seat of a renowned university and was, with Paris, one of the two most important intellectual centres in Europe, just as Toledo and Cordoba had been in the twelfth and thirteenth centuries. Bolognese academics with scientific and agricultural interests may have had access to

Castilian translations of Bassâl; alternatively, immigrant Moorish gardeners may have introduced the hotbed to gardeners in the environs of Bologna.

Another possibility is that the current passion for magic and alchemy led to experiments at Bologna with plants and seeds and thence to the hotbed. It is known that alchemists attributed special powers to dung heaps ('animal strength' was one); it was even believed that a human being could be 'generated' by putting a substance (unspecified) in a vase and leaving it buried in horse manure for three days.[13]

De' Crescenzi was clearly not very familiar with the hotbed technique. He limited its use only to the raising of gourds and melons. His instructions for growing these 'in the usual way' – that is, without a hotbed – was to sow them in April or early May (training them when they were as high as a man to form arbours for shade). He added, almost as an afterthought:

There is another way of planting melons earlier so as to have the fruit all the sooner. One takes a little well-worked soil and places it on top of a heap of hot dung, fresh from the stable, in March. In this soil one sows gourd or melon seeds, which quickly germinate thanks to the heat of the dung. When the seedlings emerge they must be protected from tempests and chilly nights with some sort of shelter. As soon as the weather is good enough they may be transplanted to wherever is convenient.

De' Crescenzi may have had only the slightest knowledge of hotbeds but his book was to be one of the most widely read treatises of its kind. It deals with orchards, vineyards and winemaking; hunting, fishing and falconry; livestock, agriculture and water supplies as well as pleasure grounds and kitchen gardens. It was translated from its original Latin into Italian in 1350, into French in 1373 and, between the invention of printing in the mid fifteenth century and 1602, it appeared in some sixty editions, in Latin, Italian, French, German and Polish. Information about the hotbed was therefore available to an ever-widening European audience from the beginning of the fourteenth century. Even so, there is no mention of hotbeds in Britain until the late sixteenth century.

THE TUDOR HOTBED

The first directions in English, for making hotbeds, were given in 1577, by Thomas Hill. As we have already seen, much of his work was derived from the classical husbandries; to them we can now add de' Crescenzi. Like de' Crescenzi, Hill gave instructions for growing melons without the help of a hotbed, then offered it as an alternative. He gave no directions for making these dung beds (the term 'hotbed' had not yet been coined), but he did explain how to protect the young plants with light straw mattresses or wooden boards that could be lifted on and off.

Transplanted melons were given little shelters of dock leaves or wisps of straw, to protect them from excessive heat and cold. Hill also used hotbeds for growing exotic seeds such as oranges, lemons, pomecitrons (Gerard's *Citrus medica*), pomegranates, myrtles and dates, and noted that these plants 'ought to bee fenced by a succoure on the North side, that the colde ayre hinder or let not the comming up of them.'[14]

Within twenty years hotbeds were to be found in the gardens of all keen botanists and ambitious gardeners. By the end of the sixteenth century the flow of new and exotic plants from the Americas and the East had become a flood, and the hotbed was a necessary feature.

Many European universities now had botanical gardens (Pisa, Padua, Parma and Florence were among the first, in the 1540s), in which new plants such as oranges, lemons, potatoes, aubergines and tomatoes were tested for their economic or medicinal value, as well as being grown for their curiosity or beauty. Plants like these eventually reached the grander gardens (though not necessarily the dining rooms) of late Elizabethan England, making the springtime sowing of exotics on dung beds in the kitchen garden part of every serious gardener's routine.

In his *Herball* of 1597, John Gerard listed the times to sow a wide variety of vegetables.

He gave directions for the sowing on hotbeds of floramors (tri-coloured amaranths), Ginny peppers (capsicums), madde apples (aubergines), apples of love (tomatoes), apples of Æthiopia (Lobel's *Solanum pomiferum*), thornie-apples (datura, or Peruvian henbane) and balsam apples (*Momordica balsamina*, a kind of bitter melon or balsam pear) as well as Savoy cabbages and the hitherto unknown 'colie-flore'. They were covered with mats or canopies of sailcloth or canvas draped over hoops and poles until the seeds germinated. He also placed pot-grown plants, in their pots, in the dung, to hasten them along.

Neither Hill nor Gerard used the terms 'hotbed' or 'forcing': Parkinson appears to be the first to have done so, in 1629. By then kitchen gardeners had begun to sow their dung beds in January, in order to have lettuce and radish 'as early as the time of the year will permit them',[15] but the beds were still used chiefly to advance or 'force forward' cucumber and melon seedlings. Melons were 'of much esteeme . . . with all the better sort of persons', but, according to Parkinson, had only lately begun to be grown with any skill in England. Part of this skill lay in protecting tender exotics from the chilly climate of Britain, and managing dung beds so that the heat stayed regular and lasted as long as possible.

FENCES FOR THE MELONRY

'A sloping or shelving banke, lying open and opposite to the South Sunne',[16] was the best site for these beds. Hill had also recommended that the north sides be fenced. In the early seventeenth century, hedges, hurdles and walls were used to protect the beds on the east side as well; the cheapest fences for this purpose were made of reed matting.[17] As a defence against frosts and cold bitter winds these fences – often as high as six or seven feet – were apparently as good as a wall, if not better, for they deadened the wind rather than causing it to bounce off again.

The fences also enabled the enclosure to be provided with a door which could be securely fastened, not only against thieves but also against menstruating women, who, since gardening began, were supposed to have a disastrous effect on certain crops. Samuel Collins, John Laurence's protagonist (see Chapter 4), forbade ladies to go into his melonry altogether, 'Lest Nature should at that time prove in its Venereal discharge, which has not only an Imaginary, but so real an Influence on Mellons newly set, that they will most of them drop off'.[18]

Philip Miller, the head gardener at the Apothecaries' Garden in Chelsea, divided his mid eighteenth-century melon ground into four, using a different section each year and moving his reed fences annually, leap-frog fashion, as he built his dung beds in trenches and believed that melons did not do well for more than two years in the same bed. He warned against letting non-gardeners into the melon ground in case they did any damage to the fruit, and suggested siting it as close to the dung heap as possible for logistical reasons.[19]

GLASSES, BELLS AND FRAMES

Hill quoted the Romans on the protection of their cucumbers from 'boisterous windes, yea, frosts, the cold ayrs, and hote Sunne' with 'Glasses . . . made for the only purpose',[20] but neither he nor Gerard mentioned the use of protective glass on their own beds; they made do with canopies of canvas, straw mats and leaves.

The giant glass bell jar, bell glass or cloche was not introduced to Britain until early in the seventeenth century, with the French name of cloche. It seems likely that bell glasses, a product of the crown process, by which great discs of glass were blown through a rotating pipe, were first made in Italy late in the sixteenth century. They soon reached the south of France; the French horticulturalist Olivier de Serres (whose name, translated literally, means Olivier of the Greenhouses), described the culture of melons there in 1600 and appears to be the first to mention the big glass 'hats', one foot across at the base, made especially to cover the *fossette* of the plant. He says that earthenware pots were also used, if the sun was too hot, or if frost threatened.[21]

According to John Parkinson, 'Greate hollow glasses like unto bell heads' had reached the melon beds of England by 1629,[22] to be followed a little later by smaller, gourd-shaped bell glasses known as 'cucurbits'.[23] These glasses were originally made as

octagonal hand-light

cupping glasses, but John Evelyn had yet another use for them; he set them upside down as wasp traps (see Chapter 14).[24] Gardeners who could not afford such luxuries could make small glasses for young plants or seedlings from 'Large drinking glasses'.[25]

By 1677 square cases or hand glasses of leaded-glass panes were being made to order

Chase's barn-cloche

by English glaziers.[26] These had three advantages over the cloche. Firstly, one of their top panes could be hinged to act as a ventilator. (French cloches were sometimes made with a vent in the top but more usually they were propped up at one side or laid on a woollen cloth, so the condensation could be absorbed.) Secondly, square glasses could be made from old window panes. Thirdly, broken panes in a square case could be replaced; there was no way of mending a broken bell. Special covers of straw were made to protect bell glasses; if a hailstorm threatened, the gardener had to put them in place quickly.

LIGHTS AND SASHES

The glass 'lights' used on garden frames to this day also originated in seventeenth-century France. There gardeners used glass casements or window lights to cover their hotbeds as an alternative to bell jars. By the end of the century the toolshed of John Evelyn's Deptford garden contained 'wooden squares and one well glaz'd for the Hott-beds' as well as 50 melon glasses and '12 Mattrasses to cover Beds with'.[27]

The wooden frames supporting the lights sat on top of the beds and were made in varying heights, depending on the size of the plants below. The dimensions of the lights were less variable; they had to be long enough to reach from front to back of the bed (up to six feet), but no wider than would be convenient for two men to lift (say four feet). These qualifications regulated the size of the garden frame for as long as it continued to be made of wood and glass; the length of a framed bed would be measured by the number of lights needed to cover it, so that a gardener might refer to a 'one-light', 'two-light' or even a 'ten-light' frame.

PROLONGING THE HEAT

Although their heat could be conserved with various coverings, when hotbeds were first invented there was no way of prolonging the heat: dung heat lasted long enough to germinate seed and produce seedlings but it cooled off in about four or five weeks. If the seedlings were to be transplanted to the open ground at this point, the loss of heat did not matter, but if artificial warmth were still needed, they had to be transferred to a new and preferably gentler hotbed. If only the heat of the first bed could be kept going in some way, this inconvenience and disturbance to the plants could be avoided, and time and trouble would be saved.

Bassâl recommended the addition of pigeon dung to the original horse dung if it had cooled too much before the bed was made up. Six centuries later English gardeners were adding sea-coal ashes to the dung before making up the bed in order to make the dung hotter and help it to hold its heat for longer.[28] It was not until the early seventeenth century that another way was found of achieving this, without uprooting the plants. Once again it was Olivier de Serres, in 1600, who was the first to mention a new and very effective technique; he refreshed the heat of his beds by heaping them all round with 'linings' of fresh dung, about two feet thick and the same height as the bed. The idea was brought to England seventy years later in a translation by Evelyn, who described the addition of fresh dung to the outside of the bed as a way of keeping it 'in perfect temper'.[29]

RESTORATION HOTBEDS

A Royalist, Evelyn left England after the start of the Civil War for the Continent, where the art of horticulture was far more advanced. He returned in 1652 to live quietly in the English Commonwealth, designing gardens and translating the works of French horticulturists. In 1662, two years after the restoration of Charles II, the Royal Society was founded; its aims were to promote the welfare of the arts and sciences, and Evelyn was a founder member. Plant introductions from the New World and the East were increasing in number and it was a lively time for scientific activity. The Society's earliest transactions reflect the enthusiasm with which its Fellows cultivated their gardens. Proud and competitive gardeners vied with one another to raise the rarest fruits, the earliest vegetables and salads, the finest shrubs and the most exotic bulbs and flowers. They were considerably aided by the 'artificiall helpes' of their hotbeds and, increasingly, of hothouses and conservatories.

John Evelyn used his hotbeds for all the plants on Gerard's hotbed list, as well as canna lilies, geraniums, tuberoses, 'Hedysarum Clipeatum' (French honeysuckle, now known as *H. coronarium*),

purslane

'Humble, and Sensitive plants', marvel of Peru, oranges, lemons and myrtles;[30] while further north, in Scotland, hotbeds were used for forced asparagus, purslane and cauliflowers, as well as for melons.[31]

In 1675 Evelyn read 'A Philosophical Discourse of Earth' to the Royal Society. It contained another new idea, possibly his own. The dung was placed in a pit four feet deep which was lined with brick. This is one of the earliest examples of the use of a pit in gardening. The bed was made with hot dung as usual, but instead of covering it with a layer of earth, Evelyn filled long, open, wooden boxes with soil and sowed his seeds in them. The boxes were about twelve inches deep with holes bored in the bottom. They were nestled into the dung and could either be covered with individual glasses or by a mat sheltering the whole bed. The use of heated pits and earth-filled cases could continue indefinitely, for as the heat diminished the boxes could be removed and the pit refilled with fresh dung.[32] The other great advantage of a pit was that it helped to protect the plants inside it from frost.

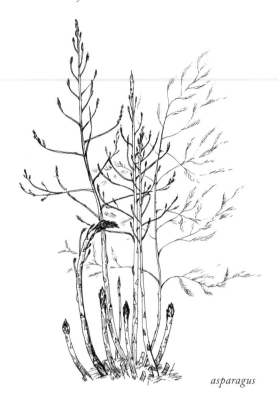

asparagus

PROBLEMS IN THE EIGHTEENTH-CENTURY FRAMEYARD

Hotbeds were still used mainly for raising melons and cucumbers, but by the eighteenth century the list of subjects for forcing or 'hastening forwards' had increased to include all sorts of salads and seedlings. Carrots, cauliflowers, potatoes and turnips, kidney beans, peas, asparagus, capsicums, aubergines, seakale, mushrooms and culinary herbs such as tarragon, mint and parsley were all raised on hotbeds, though not always without trouble.

If the conservation and prolongation of the hotbed's heat were the preoccupation of the sixteenth and seventeenth-century gardener, excessive heat, especially when the bed was newly made, was a major problem for his eighteenth-century successor. Dung heat itself could reach temperatures high enough to burn manure, mould and rootlets to a cinder, while steam from the bed, trapped within the frame, was capable of destroying precious seedlings or plants overnight. There was also the problem of the 'exhalations' and fumes which were carried into the frame with the steam. It was firmly believed that flavours were ruined and that plants could be poisoned by ammoniac gases and noxious vapours, if they had not already been stewed by steam or burnt to ashes by the rise in temperature. Eighteenth-century gardening manuals, journals and papers were full of suggestions and ideas for solving these and other problems connected with hotbeds. Sliding and hinged lights are nineteenth-century refinements, but the problems were still the same. The heat inside a hotbed could rise to as much as 49C/120°F – hot enough to cook a chicken and blister the paint on the frames, even when the temperature outside was low enough to turn drips of condensation from a melon frame into icicles.

In a gardening diary kept between 1751 and 1773, the naturalist Gilbert White recorded in detail the many problems that a gardener had to deal with, especially where melon and cucumber beds were concerned. White usually made a nine-light melon bed, some thirty-six feet long. One year it heated up so fiercely that it had to be remade, and the following year it failed to heat enough, so also had to be remade. As well as controlling the heat, one of White's chief concerns was the emission of 'foul vapours' from the steaming dung. In February of 1758 he began an experiment: to carry steam out of a cucumber frame, he inserted a tin chimney into his hotbed and then, 'in order to convey a succession of fresh air a-nights', he laid a leaden tube into the same frame, through the back. A fortnight later, he harnessed the heat from the frame by coiling up the end of the same pipe and laying it in a large seed box filled with two and a half barrows of hot dung. The nose of the coiled pipe projected about three inches from the box. He said the experiment worked.[33] A similar, but simpler device was designed for a hotbed some forty years later, in 1797. In this arrangement, made 'to remedy the injurious introduction of cold air into the glass frame of a hot bed by lifting the frame' the space above the bed was 'ventilated and heated' by air passing through a lead pipe laid in the dung. (The author adds that 'the air which has been rendered unfit for vegetation, will escape through the overlapping panes of glass'.)[34]

To maintain what White described as 'a fine, gentle, genial heat', the glasses of his frames were covered as usual in cold spells and at night with mats, layers of straw and more mats. Glass was another problem; taxed from 1745, it was expensive. It also increased the danger of scorching by the sun. Paper or calico, stretched over a ridge-shaped wooden frame, then brushed with boiled linseed oil, was found to be a cheaper and kinder alternative. But there was a drawback to paper lights as well. In 1754 White recorded: 'The paper lights torn by a storm, and the melon plants damaged'. Undeterred, he used paper again three years later, making on St Valentine's Day, 1757, 'a melon paper-house eight feet long and five feet wide: to be covered with the best writing paper'.[35]

The deliberate introduction of pure steam from boiling water, as opposed to the impure steam generated by dung, was first suggested in 1755 in *The London Magazine*. Pipes under the frame were fed with hot water from a boiler. The inventor, a Swedish brewer, assured his readers that perforations in the pipes would provide 'a warm and moist air like that which prevails in the Caribee islands' and they could grow cocoa trees with its help, if they wished. Excess water was drained off by a tap and the earth from the bed was prevented from falling into the pipes by a layer of coarse tanner's bark. However, at this date the management of boilers was primitive and the idea, though sound, was not to be taken up by the gardening fraternity until the end of the century.

In short, of all departments in the kitchen garden, the frameyard was one of the most demanding. First of all there was the constant carting or wheeling of manure, and then its preparation by piling it into heaps. Then there was the work of adding linings and the constant throwing on or off of mats, and the opening or closing of glasses. The dung sank, and with it the soil, so that the plants were too far from the glass; the heat was uneven; the ventilation was too much or too little . . .

SITING THE FRAMEYARD

Because a constant supply of fresh stable manure was required for a frameyard, it reeked of dung. The place was full of it, either waiting in heaps or made up into beds. Then there was the aesthetic problem of the frameyard's appearance. Compared to the rest of the kitchen garden, this department looked most disorderly; the beds were hard to keep neat, and even the best of frameyards was a squalid mess. The nineteenth-century gardener had strict instructions to keep his domain as clean and presentable as it could be; this edict extended to the frameyard, but here it was so difficult to carry out that in gardens with any pretensions to elegance it was essential to keep the place hidden from the gaze of the gentry. At the same time it had to be sited conveniently within the kitchen-garden complex.

A melon ground took up a considerable amount of room. Its size depended first of all on the number of beds. Each bed, when lined both front and back, could eventually measure eleven to thirteen feet across, so that sometimes the back of one row joined to the front of another; and each melon, even when planted five feet from its neighbour, would have roots and tendrils extending the full width of a lined bed. From the seventeenth century onwards, the simplest solution was to give the melonry a compartment to itself as close as possible to the farmyard or stables, either outside in the slips or inside, in one of the culinary quarters.

There was a practical element in having the melon ground in the slips: the carrying of litter would avoid dirtying the main walks; the hedges, hurdles, walls or fences that protected the beds from chilling winds and stopped bits of straw blowing about hid it from view as well; and time was saved in carrying and wheeling. The walks between the frames could be wide enough for a dung cart, sloping at each end but raised between the beds 'so that after your linings are made up, it may be kept as neat as if it were a pleasure ground'.[36]

frameyard, Heligan

TREATMENTS FOR MELON AND CUCUMBER SEEDS

Melon and cucumber seeds were thought to produce better plants – plants with less abundant, closely jointed foliage and more fruit – if they were kept for at least three to four years before sowing. Melon seed in particular was habitually carried about in the gardener's pocket for several weeks to harden and dry before sowing.

The dominant genes in cucumbers give the fruit a tendency to spininess, bitterness and tough skin. To combat these disadvantages, the classical writers advised soaking the seed in various liquids, among them ewes' milk, mead and honey, before sowing. A similar treatment, using wine and sugar, was given to melon seed.

THE MYSTERIES OF POLLINATION

The eighteenth-century landscape designer and architect Batty Langley, in common with 'many good gardeners at Twickenham' (where he lived), was in the habit of removing the male flowers from his cucumber plants. He had two reasons for doing this. As he said, firstly the male flowers 'never produce any Thing' and secondly they take nourishment from the vines and 'predjudice the Fruit belonging thereunto'. In other words, the fertilized fruit was unpleasantly bitter. Langley knew from experience that female cucumber flowers were able to form fruit without being pollinated, and that these fruits were always sweet.[37]

Langley's contemporary, Richard Bradley, disagreed. Bradley insisted that the custom of removing all the male melon and cucumber flowers, which he described as 'them that are ordained by Nature to set the Fruit', was not only needless but best avoided. He also thought that it was dangerous for cucumbers to be planted too close to melons in case their 'Male dust' gave the melons 'the Relish of the Cucumber in proportion as the Farina happens to fall in greater or lesser Quantity'.[38]

The cucumber (like the grape) has self-sterile, parthenocarpic, female flowers (i.e. flowers that will form fruit without fertilization), but this phenomenon was not to be understood for another half century. And the discovery of cucurbitacins, the elements responsible for bitterness in leaves and fruits, dates only from 1956.[39] Long before this, however, gardeners knew that if they allowed the female flowers to be fertilized they produced large, but bitter, seed-filled fruit, and if they were left unfertilized they produced smaller, but sweeter fruit. Moreover, they knew that while it was inadvisable, for these reasons, to fertilize cucumber flowers unless the fruit were needed for seed, it was essential to fertilize melon flowers, or the fruit would be small and tough. (Bradley was right on that point.) Modern cucumbers are now bred to produce plants specifically with only female or at least only hermaphrodite flowers, in order to have relatively seedless, sweet cucumbers; the only disadvantages of a fruit

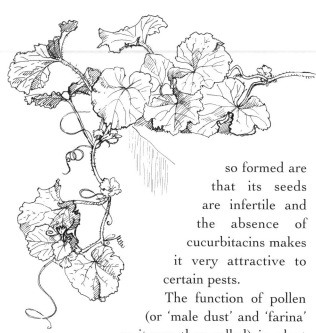

so formed are that its seeds are infertile and the absence of cucurbitacins makes it very attractive to certain pests.

The function of pollen (or 'male dust' and 'farina' as it was then called) in plant reproduction had been experimentally known for centuries, in the case of the date palm at least; the mechanics of its journey from stigma to ovary were yet to be discovered. All that was known in the 1720s was that pollen acted as a fertilizing agent by falling on the stigma of the female flower. Bradley shared with his contemporaries a fascination with hybridization in plants but he had a curious conception of the nature and transmission of pollen. He explained rightly that 'the Male Dust of plants may be convey'd by the Air from one to another, by which the generation and production of new plants [by which he meant hybrids] is brought about', but he also said that the 'Farina fecundens, or Male dust has a Magnetick Virtue . . . for it is that only which Bees gather and lodge in the Cavities of their hind legs to make their Wax with; and it is

well known that Wax, when it is warm, will attract to it any light Body'. It therefore seemed obvious that it was the magnetic virtue of pollen that caused fruit to form; it 'draws the Nourishment with great Force from the other Parts of the Plant into the Embrios of the Fruit, and make[s] them swell'.[40]

THE IMPORTANCE OF BEES

The contribution made by the bees themselves, as carriers of pollen, was virtually ignored by Bradley. However, in a letter to Bradley dated 6 October 1721, Philip Miller described the experiments made with tulips and spinach plants in his own garden that proved it was the 'farina' carried by bees, rather than the wind, that had impregnated the flowers.[41] Yet gardeners still tended to believe that pollen was transferred chiefly by the wind from the male flower to the female and that this was why plants confined in frames on hotbeds (such as melons) sometimes failed to set fruit. Further investigations into the mechanics of cross-fertilization were carried out in the 1760s by the German naturalist Joseph Gottlieb Koelreuter. It was he who discovered that the purpose of nectar was to attract insects, and that the co-operation of insects was, in certain cases, essential for pollination to take place. That is why, in fruit houses closed against chill winds, where forced fruit is flowering before bees are about, the gardener is obliged to pollinate the blossom with a rabbit's tail fastened to the end of a stick.

medieval mud bee-skep

(This was one of the first jobs a garden boy would be given. Good gardeners also took the trouble to move their beehives into the orchard in spring to ensure a bountiful crop of fruit.)

Although the keeping of bees had been closely connected with gardening for centuries, it was their wax and honey rather than their usefulness as pollinators that made bees valuable. The Romans sowed thyme, rosemary, savory and marjoram for their bees, or set their hives near flowers such as asphodel, narcissi, lilies, gillyflowers, roses, violets, larkspur and saffron, which the bees loved and made into the best honey [42]

The Celts had conical wickerwork hives daubed with dung or clay; similar hives, and hives made of straw, were placed in medieval gardens, either housed in 'bee boles' made in the walls or set out on little tables. 'Beehives of glass, very curious' were seen in the large kitchen gardens at Cannons, near London, by an early eighteenth-century traveller.[43] The decorative aspect of beekeeping appealed to the Victorians; wooden hives and decorative 'bee houses' or apiaries as well as ornamental bee-walls were common features of the nineteenth-century kitchen garden (see page 55).

The thirteenth-century Beaulieu Abbey accounts show that beeswax and honey were two of the most profitable garden products, for wax was sold to make church candles and tapers while honey was used as a sweetener, a preservative, a syrup and, when fermented, as mead. Until the middle of the eighteenth century, honey was the cheapest food and drink sweetener available to the poor. Thereafter the Germans began to develop the manufacture of cheap sugar from beets. Cane sugar had been imported since medieval times, but it was expensive and from the seventeenth century onwards it attracted increasingly heavy import duty. The removal of the Sugar Tax in 1874 made tart fruits such as rhubarb and gooseberries much more worth cultivating, and may account for the increased popularity of these fruits from then onwards.

M'PHAIL'S FRAME

Towards the end of the eighteenth century Evelyn's idea of using dung-filled pits for forcing, and especially for raising melons, began to take precedence over the straightforward, free-standing hotbed. James M'Phail described his pit, or 'brick-bed', in 1794, in *A Treatise on the Culture of the*

Cucumber. The cucumber was then grown under virtually the same conditions as the melon. The plants grew in pigeon-holed brick pits three feet deep and three feet square, containing well rotted and sieved leaf mould on top of a layer of rubble, the top of the mould being at ground level. Between the containers and the pigeon-holed walls, which supported the frames covering the beds, were spaces described by M'Phail as 'perfectly close flues'. The beds were flanked by wide trenches, front and back. Dung, fresh from the stable, was thrown into these trenches, transmitting its heat to the beds, and more importantly, to the air above them, by means of the pigeon holes and 'flues' (see page 118).

Finding that plants such as melons and cucumbers thrived on warm air, rather than warm soil, M'Phail had designed a frame that could be heated from the sides, rather than the bottom. He claimed that his frame possessed several advantages. The dung needed no preparation, as the heat passed only indirectly to the plants; the heat never rose above 35-36C/96-97°F on the extremities of the beds, or over 26–29C/80–85°F in the centre of the beds and, being within a pit, remained steady no matter what the weather. The dung, being also below ground in a pit, retained its heat better than outdoor linings and was easy to replenish; the earth in the beds would not sink as much as beds based on dung, and no 'pernicious vapours' from the dung could reach the fruit to taint it.[44]

Previously, cucumbers could be picked from February until October and melons from May until October, by forcing them on hotbeds of fermenting dung. M'Phail's pit not only enabled gardeners to grow both all the year round but also removed the mess from the frameyard and took away much of the worry of managing hotbeds as well.

THE NINETEENTH-CENTURY FRAMEYARD

This type of frame (now more usually called the forcing pit), could be described as an intermediate between a garden frame on top of a hotbed and an artificially heated glazed structure. It soon became the preferred method of producing early salads, melons and cucumbers, and also of raising young pineapples. Pits for raising pineapples were heated by smoke-filled hot-air flues in the eighteenth century (see Chapter 11), but the invention, early in the nineteenth century, of the hot-water boiler and the introduction, first of steam heating and then of hot-water heating (see Chapter 13), was seen as the greatest improvement for a gardener harassed by the exigencies of the hotbed. He could augment his dung heat with pipes containing either steam or hot water.

In the 1840s W. A. Rendle, a Devonian nurseryman, invented a tank system to heat melon, cucumber and pineapple pits. An appendix to M'Intosh's *Practical Gardener* of 1847 describes Rendle's method of 'producing uniform bottom heat from hot water tanks . . . with explanatory diagrams . . . exploding the expensive and unpleasant mode of smoke flues, iron pipes, the use of tan, stable manure, etc.' The tanks (divided along the centre, thus creating one channel for the flow and another for the return) could be made of well-jointed brick, stone, slate or wood, the water being heated by a small boiler situated at one end of the range. The tanks were covered with slates and the beds sat above. Steam could enter the beds through gaps between the slates (or later, via vertical pipes).

Finally, the gardener was able to do away with dung altogether and position his clean and tidy frameyard wherever he liked. By the end of the nineteenth century there was virtually nothing that could not be forced for the table either before or after its normal season. In 'some lordly places' even gooseberries were forced, as well as plums, currants, cherries, each in its own frame, pit or house, while the forcing of strawberries, rhubarb, carnations, lilies-of-the-valley and Christmas roses was widespread both privately and commercially.[45]

forced french beans

CHAPTER NINE

THE COMPOST YARD

To assist in the running of a kitchen garden, one part of the slips, or even a part of the frameyard, was usually set aside for the storage of unsightly but essential material. This included bundles of pea sticks and bean poles, firewood or other fuel for the hot walls and furnaces, and individual heaps of the ingredients for potting compost – broken crocks, rotted horse and cow dung, turf cut from pastures, decaying leaves, old ashes, sand, grit and peat. The place was known as the compost yard. Gilbert White used his melon ground for a similar purpose, building there a circular earth house (for storing turf).

The Pylewell Sale Catalogue of 1850 lists 'A Turf House and Fuel Store' among the buildings in the kitchen garden, which were presumably part of the compost yard, and in or near the melon ground or frameyard,

It was in the compost yard too that the gardeners had their plunge beds or pits full of old ashes from the boiler (there would have been similar pits at Pylewell, just in front of the old boiler sheds). It was also in this area that the fresh dung for forcing was heaped and turned, and suitable garden rubbish was transformed into that other kind of compost, a dark, crumbly, nutritious humus that enriched the soil.

Before the invention of artificial manures, even the humblest establishments had some sort of provision for the storage and preparation of fertilizing materials, for without them the kitchen garden would cease to be productive. In smaller gardens, compost would have to be made in any corner accessible to barrows and carts.

At Pylewell, the compost would have been made in a sheltered portion of the frameyard. The process required three separate compartments or booths: one for fresh garden rubbish, one for the previous batch that was in the process of rotting and one for the compost that was ready to use. This was dug into the beds in the autumn or forked in at planting time, in the spring.

THE COMPOST HEAP

'Compost', according to a 1921 textbook, 'is a heap of mixed vegetable and animal matter put up so that it can decompose and form useful organic manure'.[1] Evelyn puts it more succinctly: he says, 'Compost is all sort of Dung'.[2] Gardeners have always had much to say about compost. Each authority describes several methods of making it, with a variety of ingredients according to the soil or crop for which it was intended. They also have much to say about the virtues of different kinds of dung, other materials which may be added to it, composts that are suitable for potting and matter that is suitable for mulching.

There is a certain self-righteousness in making a compost heap, for something of value is being converted from garbage, rubbish or trash. More significantly, by using compost, the cycle of fertility is maintained; the soil is enriched by returning the nutrients that have been taken out, and its structure is improved by the addition of humus, which forms the bulk of both composts and farmyard manures.

A good compost heap works in a similar manner to a hotbed. Any waste that decomposes quickly by bacterial action is suitable for it. It can be made in a heap, in a pit, or in a bin. As in a hotbed, this waste will at first heat up, usefully killing all weed seeds, viruses and insect larvae. It should be left to rot down for at least six months, by which time the heap will have become a dark, sweet-smelling mass of rich, wholesome, friable

mould or humus. It may be necessary to turn the sides into the middle to ensure that everything rots equally well. The compost should also be kept damp (but not sodden), aerated and covered (to keep the rain off and the nutrients in). The decomposing process can be spurred on from time to time with nitrogenous activators.

Composts and manures have had their detractors, however. In the fourth century BC Theophrastus declared that pig manure and river water caused pomegranates 'to change character'.[3] As late as 1629, John Parkinson thought that manured ground 'alters and abates' the plants grown on it, so that they lose 'their natural Vigour and quicknesse of Taste'. He preferred things grown in 'a naturall fat or sandy Soile that is not so holpen'.[3]

Ninety years later, the Reverend John Laurence wrote in a similar vein, of 'untry'd Earth', meaning uncultivated topsoil from pasturelands. He thought it was preferable by far to 'rotten Dung or the common artificial Composts', at least in the fruit and kitchen garden. He gave three reasons: firstly, he claimed that dung when used in any quantity

'mightily fills the Place with many noxious Weeds'; secondly, dung contained many 'noxious . . . Juices' which spoilt the flavour of whatever grew in it; and thirdly, the 'untry'd Earth' was cheaper and easier to come by.[5]

Two hundred years later, gardeners were being told by chemists that non-organic, artificial manures were preferable at any cost to ordinary, home-made composts and farmyard manures. Admittedly, insufficiently rotted dung or compost is less beneficial than properly prepared manures, although a certain amount of uncomposted material or humus is helpful in keeping the soil open and well aerated. It also improves water retention. The addition of disease or weed-filled materials to dungs and composts is, of course, asking for trouble.

In the ideal kitchen garden, provision is made for both liquid and solid manures. An early eighteenth-century manual describes a large tank of water in which rotted horse or pigeon dung could be left to soak, 'which, after it has been heated by the Sun for some time, may serve the Occasions of the

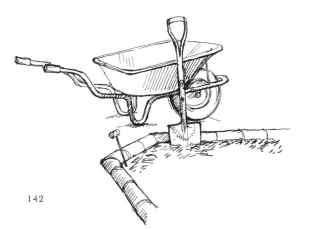

Garden'; there was also space set aside for the storage of rotted dung mixed with lime, ashes, dust and wood shavings, and left to rot for at least a year. This was used for seed plots and pot plants, and was guaranteed weed-free, 'especially if the Pots . . . be powder'd with the Earth in the hollow of an old Tree finely sifted'.[6]

MATERIALS FOR COMPOST

The solid part of dung, as modern gardeners know well, is rich in phosphates, while urine contains nitrogen and potash, both of which are vital ingredients for plant growth. (These two elements are also responsible for the frequently ammoniacal smell of the stable.) The most nutritious farmyard manure contains therefore a useful percentage of absorbent litter such as straw, sawdust, peat moss or bracken. Animals fed on a highly nitrogenous diet provide richer manure, as long as the urine is not washed away. For making hotbeds the dung of corn-fed horses (racehorses, coach horses, stallions and the like) was always recommended above that of poorer-fed pack horses or other beasts of burden; its greater nitrogen content made it heat quickly, to a high temperature. It was far more efficient than pack-horse dung and certainly better than cow or pig manure which is comparatively poor and wet.

Bird manure or guano (in which solid and liquid elements are combined) has been considered since classical times the most effective of all manures, especially when combined with litter. Neat, or diluted with

water, it makes an excellent compost activator. Poultry and aviary manure is six times richer in nitrogen and four times richer in phosphorus and potassium than the average manure of an old-fashioned farmyard. It is similar in value to top-grade guano.

The addition to the compost pit of human urine has a long history. Ibn al-'Awwam, writing in the twelfth century, gives the same advice to Moorish landowners as Florentinus had to Roman landowners in the third century: they should encourage their labourers to pee in the compost pits for a succulent compost.[7] The *hortus* or kitchen garden in the ninth-century plan found at the abbey of St Gall (see page 96) is sited between the poultry houses and the latrines, an arrangement that makes optimum use of both human and bird waste. Today, chemists and soil experts tell us that urine is still the best nitrogenous activator. The Moors also knew that the ashes of a burnt plant made a fine compost for any plants of a similar kind.[8] Centuries later, as we shall see, chemists found that plant ashes consisted of the same minerals as plant foods.

The waste products of any local forms of husbandry, housekeeping or industry made the most economical materials for composts. The authors of the classical books of husbandry had no scientific knowledge of the nutritional values of these materials, but the writers of more up-to-date manuals (who have access to a complete chemical analysis of every ingredient) list an astonishingly similar variety of compostable matter, beginning with all kinds of excrement, including nightsoil, sewage sludge and the emptyings of cess pits and privies, then going on to ashes, soot, dust; the debris from making vegetable oils, wine, beer, cider, tea and coffee; tanner's bark, leather trimmings, woodshavings, old mattresses and upholstery, cotton waste and wool shoddy; dead leaves, hay, straw, bracken and seaweed; hairdressers' clippings, feathers, dried blood, offal, carrion, bones, horns and the blacksmith's parings of hooves; shredded paper and cardboard; roadsweepings, ditch and pond cleanings; hedge, orchard and vine trimmings; lawnmowings, garden weeds and kitchen refuse.

ROMAN HUSBANDRY

By the first century AD, Roman agriculturists and gardeners were well aware of the effect of different soils, localities and climate on plant growth. They used marls to improve the land, differentiated between the value of one kind of manure and another and, where farmyard manure was in short supply, made compost and dug in green manures. Their practical, down-to-earth advice was taken to every corner of the Roman Empire, as well as to that of Islam, for the Roman husbandries were read and elaborated upon by Moorish gardeners in Spain throughout the tenth, eleventh and twelfth centuries.

Classical books of husbandry made a point of listing the manures of domestic birds and animals in order of merit, for the custom of fattening birds and animals indoors, in aviaries, dovecots, stalls and stables, meant that specific manures were always available. The Greeks, Romans and Arabs could choose from the dung of poultry, cattle, sheep, goats, pigs, horses, donkeys and mules as well as humans.

The Roman horticulturist Varro claimed that the best dung, not only for the land but also as fodder for cattle and pigs, was the droppings of thrushes and blackbirds, both of which were bred in aviaries to provide delicacies at banquets.[9] Pliny recommended: '. . . the residue of human banquets [i.e. human dung] as one of the best manures, and some of them place even higher the residue of men's drink [i.e. urine], with hair found in curriers' shops soaked in it, while others recommend this liquor by itself, after water has been again mixed with it and even in larger quantity than when the wine is being drunk'.[10]

Columella, writing in the first century AD, recommended human urine, kept for six months, as an excellent fertilizer for vines and fruit trees. The addition to it of old oil-lees was especially good for the cultivation of olives. He warned his readers of the danger of 'burning' the ground by using human and pigeon dung neat; he advised mixing them with other farmyard refuse. He also mentions the benefits of green manuring, the importance of ploughing-in the roots of leguminous crops, the fact that well-rotted manure helps to warm the soil (owing to its heat-retentive blackness), that gravelly land can be improved by the addition of clay and *vice versa*.[11]

THE IDENTIFICATION OF PLANT NUTRIENTS

In the mid fifteenth century the scholar-theologian, Cardinal Nicolas of Cusa, curious to discover the role of water and soil in plant growth, conducted an experiment which consisted of weighing separately a crop and the soil in which it had been grown, both before and after the crop reached maturity. It would be seen that the weight of the soil was scarcely reduced by the plants which grew in it, even though the plants increased in weight to equal that of the soil. The inference was that they must therefore take their weight from water, which contained some sort of earthy nourishment that was transformed into plant material by the sun.

Nicolas of Cusa's experiment was an isolated case. More typical of the state of botanic

science, even as late as 1608, were instructions given by Sir Hugh Platt for a preparation for a 'Philosophicall Garden' which was 'so enriched from the heavens, without the help of any manner of soyle, marle, or compost' that any plant you please would 'florish and fructifie in a strange and admirable manner'.[12] It owed a little to ideas about vegetative salts but more to astral influences and alchemy, which were the popular ideology of the time. By the mid seventeenth century the desire to rationalize this mumbo-jumbo and to discover the true chemical nature of such 'elixirs' and 'the humours' was irresistible. The celebrated scientist Robert Boyle grew plants in water only, and by analysing the ashes and distilling the plants grown as part of this experiment saw that they were reduced to a substance resembling 'salt and earth'. He concluded that water alone could produce not only salt and earth but also 'spirit . . . and even oyl'.[13]

No minerals other than 'nitre' and 'sulphur' were deemed to be present in plant ashes until the end of the eighteenth century, when experiments involving the repeated boiling and filtering of soil samples showed that the differences in the fertility of soils were not only due to sun, rain and air, but to 'neutral salt' and to what later became known as humus.[14] However, it was not until the nineteenth century that the essential constituents of plant food were identified. It was then seen that some plant disorders, previously labelled 'diseases', were caused by a deficiency of trace elements in the soil.

The understanding of plant nutrition was considerably advanced by the work of the Swiss chemist and naturalist, Nicolas-Théodore de Saussure. Early in the nineteenth century he discovered that plants absorbed nutrients selectively, through their roots; and by analysing plant ashes he discovered what the Arabs had known since the thirteenth century – that a plant's mineral constituents were similar to those found in the soil in which they grew. Finally, de Saussure listed the main nutrients of plants as water, carbon (mainly from carbon dioxide in the atmosphere), nitrogen (from ammonia in the air and compounds in the soil), plus other 'salts' and 'earths'.[15]

The next significant advances were to be made later in the nineteenth century by a German chemist, the renowned Justus von Liebig. He was the first to discover the full cycle of nutrition, first in plants and then in animals. By 1840 he had identified the nutrients essential to plant growth (carbonic acid, water, ammonia, potassium, calcium, magnesium, phosphate and sulphate) and had shown that plants could convert these nutrients into substances such as starch, sugar, fat and proteins. Moreover, when taken

in by animals as food, then excreted, these substances were reconverted to their original, simple components.[16]

THE BIRTH OF THE AGRO-CHEMICAL INDUSTRY

Liebig further stimulated modern agricultural and horticultural science by marketing an artificial fertilizer based on the same chemical components as guano, which had by that time become an article of commerce in Europe. Liebig's substitute was expensive and ineffective; he had underestimated the need for nitrogenous matter, believing that plants could derive all the nitrogen they needed from ammonia in the soil. Nevertheless, he proved that inorganic mineral salts could provide the soil with all the minerals needed for fertility, thereby laying the foundations for the artificial fertilizer industries of the late nineteenth and twentieth centuries.

Extracts from Liebig's books and papers were published in due course in various agricultural and horticultural journals. His work was encouraged in Germany because

there was, at that time, an urgent need to increase the agricultural output of that country. His researches into plant nutrition were continued in the second half of the nineteenth century by one of the first professional plant physiologists, another German, the botanist Julius Sachs. In 1860 Sachs astounded his fellow botanists by publishing a paper in which he described raising plants from seed to flowering in water to which only the essential mineral elements were added. By this experiment he clarified the different roles of nitrogen, nitrates and ammonium salts in plant nutrition.

It had taken almost a century to sort out these fundamentals, owing to the lack, at first, of any suitably delicate analytical apparatus. But in 1886 Hellriegel and Wohlfahrt (two more German chemists, engaged at the time in researches into the sugar-beet industry) were able to establish how it is that plants take in nitrogen from the soil. Their discovery was confirmed by experiments carried out at Rothamsted Manor in Hertfordshire by John Bennet Lawes and Joseph Henry Gilbert, pioneers of the artificial fertilizer industry and agricultural improvement in Britain.

ARTIFICIAL MANURES

Within fifty years, artificial manures were being applied to gardens as regular supplements to the minerals contained in composts, farmyard and stable manures. Gardeners could buy (at a price) nitrogenous manures in the form of nitrate of soda, nitrate of potash or sulphate of ammonia, using them either as a top dressing or digging them in. To these they could add potash manures such as kainit and sulphate of potash which, when dug well in, acted quickly and produced the same effects as wood ash. Slower-working superphosphate of lime, dissolved bones and basic slag were applied in autumn to boost the phosphates.

Today's gardeners now know that nitrogenous manures are fast working and make plants noticeably greener and more vigorous; that potash helps to develop the sugars and starches in seeds, tubers and fruit, being especially good for crops like potatoes and tomatoes; that phosphates are good for leguminous plants, turnips and fruit trees, assisting in the formation of fibrous roots and the early development of the plant.

But an even more conscientious effort has to be made to put back into the soil only that which will do good. As an ever-increasing network of roads connects a spreading mass of conurbations, the modern gardener's search for organic manures based on horse traffic and old-fashioned farming methods becomes more and more difficult. And he has learned to be chary of composting any old garbage; concentrates in poultry and animal feedstuffs make factory-farm manures dangerously rich in nitrogen (they are far richer than old-fashioned manures). They may even contain poisonous elements, such as copper, as well as antibiotics. Stable litter based on woodshavings needs to be well rotted-down before it is dug into the soil, as the woodshavings will otherwise cause an imbalance of carbon and nitrogen. Grass-cuttings, especially from municipal parks, might have been treated with pesticides and herbicides; spent mushroom compost may contain large lumps of chalk; paper printed with coloured inks may contain cadmium and lead; vacuum-cleaner emptyings may contain nothing but uncompostable man-made fibres. 'Fertilizers', as a John Evelyn of today might remark, 'is all sort of Chemicals.' Small wonder, then, that, on the one hand garden centres and potting sheds now look more like chemists' shops, and on the other that the organic movement is gaining momentum.

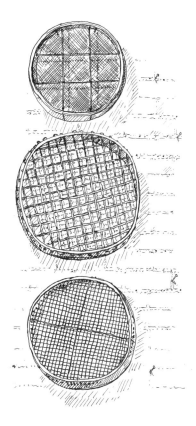

GREEN-HOUSES, ORANGERIES & CONSERVATORIES

A Dutch Orangery, c.1570
The windows are shuttered in cold weather. Heat is supplied by two STOVES.

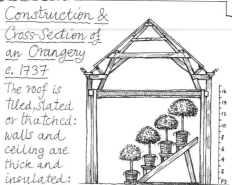

Construction & Cross-Section of an Orangery c.1737
The roof is tiled, slated or thatched: walls and ceiling are thick and insulated: tall small-paned windows admit light from the front only: stepped scaffolding allows more light to fall on each tree.

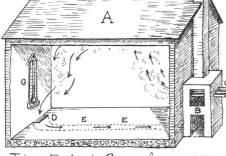

John Evelyn's Green-house, 1691
Fire-proof pipes (C) conduct warm, fresh air from an exterior furnace (B) to the house (A). As the air cools it falls into a duct (D) in the floor. It returns via an underground pipe (E, E) to the chimney (F). Note the thermometer (G) on the wall. The windows are on the south wall.

Various Designs, 1697 to 1804

Castle Bromwich, 1729

Norton Conyers, 1774

West Dean, 1804

Kensington Palace, 1705

Chatsworth, 1697 (later altered by Paxton)

CHAPTER TEN

GLASS AND HEAT

A SUCCESSION OF DELICACIES

A frameyard and a range of heated glass enabled a kitchen garden to supply luxuries – delicacies that are produced in an artificial climate at unnatural times – as well as a year-round succession of fruits, flowers and vegetables. In kitchen gardens without glass, and in kitchen gardens before glasshouses were invented, crops were grown on the open ground and in orchards in amounts that ensured a surplus big enough to last through the winter. The average family's winter fare was limited to fruit and vegetables that grew out of doors and kept well. The gardens of what used to be known as 'families of quality' were, however, expected to transcend these limitations.

In Mr Hamilton's time as head gardener at Pylewell, there were two kinds of kitchen gardener: those working in the frameyard and glasshouse department were called 'the inside men'. The others were called 'the outside men' because they worked in the open quarters, the orchard and the twelve acre field that supplied the kitchen with the more common vegetables such as potatoes, carrots and cabbages.

The under gardeners hardly ever saw Mr Hamilton with a spade in his hand. Like most head gardeners, when he was in the kitchen garden he worked largely in the glasshouses with the inside foreman Eric, who was in charge of the two other inside men, Les and Vincent. The division between the ranks of those who worked outside and those who worked inside was quite distinct; the outside gardeners scarcely ever entered the glasshouses.

The inside men gave food, water, heat, light and ventilation to the plants in their care so that they might thrive as naturally under glass as they would in their native habitats or, by the technique known as forcing, in seasons outside the norm. They provided Mrs Holmes, the cook, with new potatoes and salads at Christmas; strawberries and kidney beans in April; nectarines, muscats and figs all summer long; seakale, asparagus and rhubarb in November. Their duties were not, however, confined to the glasshouses. They also made up the floral arrangements for the table vases, *jardinières* and planters up at the house, filling them at all seasons with decorative arrangements of outdoor and greenhouse flowers and foliage, flowering bulbs and ornamental pot plants which they had raised themselves in the hothouses. They kept an eye on the plants in the conservatory. They made nosegays and buttonholes for special occasions and made sure that Mrs

'Ingham' Whitaker's 'signature' – a bunch of violets – was renewed whenever necessary. With heated glass and skilful management, it was possible for the kitchen garden to provide anything that could not be had from the open ground, whenever it was required.

THE GLASS AT PYLEWELL

Glasshouses are usually ranged along the southern side of the northernmost wall of a kitchen garden, so that they face inwards to the open quarters, but at Pylewell, where the ground to the north of the kitchen garden was once a gravel pit, it slopes steeply down to the farmyard. The hothouses and vineries are therefore ranged on either side of the main entrance, on the southern side of the southern wall, where the ground is level (see page 10).

Pylewell's range of glass was never flamboyant – it was modest but adequate. When Williams-Freeman bought the estate in 1850, there were, according to the Sale Catalogue, two forty-foot Vineries, a plant house of similar length (described as 'a Green House') and an Orangery with a twelve-light

(i.e fifty-foot-long) Pine Pit, as well as the 18-light pine pit in the Melon Ground (see Chapter 8). By the 1930s the number of glasshouses at Pylewell had increased. There were lengthy peach cases on the inner, south-facing wall, with another two lean-to houses, possibly for plums, on the inner south-west and west-facing walls and a fig house facing the frameyard on the outer, south-east facing wall. On the outer, south-facing wall the orangery had been pulled down to make way for an orchid house. The two 40-foot lean-to vineries doubled as forcing houses for French beans, strawberries and potatoes. There were also Hamilton's four new span-roofed greenhouses, consisting of a melon and tomato house, a carnation house and a new plant house, as well as the assortment of pits and frames described in Chapter 8.

Today, the fig house has gone, although the fig tree remains, a robust and unruly giant whose limbs, as soon as they were left

call went out for scrap metal; it was needed by the munitions factories. No one knew how long the war would go on; fuel was rationed and it was unpatriotic, if not pointless, to hold on to huge lumps of wrought and cast-iron machinery that might never be used again. Mr Hamilton, like countless other head gardeners of the time, watched dismally as the salvage men ripped out the bigger of the two boilers, leaving only the smaller one in place.

unpruned and unchecked, burst through the gaps left by missing panes and pushed apart the rotten timbers that supported them. The rest of the glasshouses are a sad sight; once-white timbers now show the dingy grey of old, bare wood. In the old days they were painted annually by Willy Woodford, the gardeners' handyman. He also kept the ventilating gear greased and painted, and the glass clean and intact, mending and replacing panes whenever one had slipped, cracked or broken. Now the old ratchets, rods, cogs and levers are immobile, red with rust; where glass remains, it is dirty and underlaid with plastic sheeting to act as insulation. The cast-iron guttering has fallen off and has not been replaced. There is no glass at all in one of the old vinery roofs, just wire netting between the rafters to keep the birds from any fruit which can be coaxed from the few remaining vine rods and peach trees below.

The greenhouses are never heated now. There used to be two boilers at Pylewell; a small one at the end of the early vinery and an older, larger one behind the late vinery. Sometime during the Second World War, the

THE EARLIEST GLASSHOUSES: THE HEYDAY OF THE ORANGE

Three fruits may be said to have influenced the evolution of the kitchen-garden glasshouse more than any others: the orange, the pineapple and the grape. The peach and the fig have done so to a lesser extent; the cultivation of melons and cucumbers (see Chapter 8) had more influence in the development of pits and frames. The orange had its heyday in the seventeenth century; the pineapple dominated the eighteenth; the grape, the melon, the fig and the peach shared the limelight in the nineteenth.

Of all the sought-after and pampered exotics in the fifteenth and sixteenth-century garden, the favourite was indubitably the orange tree. As natives of China and south-east Asia, oranges were unknown in the classical world; the only member of the citrus family mentioned by Theophrastus or Pliny is the citron *(Citrus medica)*. Oranges were probably introduced to the eastern Mediterranean by the Arabs. By AD 976

they were being grown in the open by Caliph al-Mansur in Cordoba, in southern Spain. The first Englishmen to encounter any sort of citrus fruits were the Crusaders at Jaffa in 1191. Thereafter, from the thirteenth century onwards, oranges, lemons, pomegranates and dried fruits were imported to England from Spain and Portugal. In 1411 Queen Leonora of Castile grew five orange trees from pips. In 1499 one of these trees was sent to Louis XII of France as a wedding present; it became known as *'Le Grand Connétable'* ('The Great Constable') of Versailles.

Oranges and lemons were grown in Italy from the fifteenth century onwards. They were not the first tender plants to receive protection from the Italian winters. Tiberius's cucumbers had had protective frames (see Chapter 8); and according to the Latin epigrammatist Martial, the Sicilian hero Entellus had his vineyard enclosed in transparent glass to protect his grapes from frost damage.[1]

Although the Imperial vines had glasshouses in the first century AD, fifteenth-century orange and lemon trees were protected from frost in open gardens only by straw coverings, wattle fences and fires. They were also grown as trees in tubs so they could be taken into sheds or caves for shelter in winter. These shelters gradually evolved into large wooden sheds with removable shutters.

Sub-tropical, half-hardy, evergreen exotics and their necessary shelters began to appear in the northern gardens of France, Germany, the Netherlands and England in the sixteenth century. Lord Burghley was one of the first to build a shelter for orange trees in England, at Burghley Court (now Burghley House) in Northamptonshire, in 1561, although it is doubtful if the trees bore fruit. Temporary sheds were replaced later by more elaborate houses of brick or stone, with large windows and glazed doors. They were heated with little stoves or pans of burning charcoal in very cold weather. One of the earliest glazed 'wintering galleries' was built at the botanic garden in Leiden in Holland in 1600.

It was the sour orange, not the sweet 'China orange' that was first grown in northern gardens. If the trees bore fruit it was used as a sauce for meats. The dried rind was made into sweet powders; fresh rinds were candied. The flowers made a perfumed water 'for gloves, to wash them', and a medicinal ointment. Seedling oranges, grown on hotbeds, were picked when only a few inches high, and put into salads, giving them 'a marvellous fine aromaticke or spicy taste, very acceptable'.[2]

THE ORANGES OF BEDDINGTON PARK

Part of the orange tree's popularity in England was due to its decorative appearance and the comparative ease with which it could be cultivated. The orange trees grown by one of Queen Elizabeth I's courtiers, Sir Francis Carew, at Beddington Park near Croydon in Surrey, in 1580 (possibly from pips given to him by Sir Walter Raleigh in 1560) were still alive, though much decayed, in 1700. In 1691 they were seen as standard trees, thirteen feet high and full of fruit; the previous year the gardener had gathered at least 10,000 oranges.[3] The number of trees is not specified, but they had portable wooden shelters in the form of a house some 200 feet long. The same trees continued to grow at Beddington in a brick and stone orangery until destroyed by the hard frosts of the terrible winter of 1739-40.

COLLECTIONS OF GREENS

Orange tree houses came to be known as 'orangeries' in the 1680s and in the most fashionable gardens were used mainly for these evergreen plants. Collections of 'greens' also included rarities such as bay trees and oleanders, cypresses, pomegranates and myrtles. The stove-heated shelters in which these 'greens' were 'conserved' were therefore known as 'stoves', 'green houses' or 'conservatories'. The plants were grown in large tubs or pots so that they could be carried outdoors in summer; John Evelyn said the crucial time for this was when mulberry trees started to put out their leaves.[4] When it was empty, the conservatory or greenhouse could be used for entertainments, in much the same way as

banqueting houses were before them.

As the seventeenth century progressed the craze for acquiring and cultivating half-hardy plants increased. By the end of the century all the best gardens in England had some form of conservatory, stove, orangery or green-house for exotics from the furthest colonies.

HEAT VERSUS FUMES

The priority was warmth, yet such heat as there was tended to be erratic as well as fume-laden. The windows usually, though by no means always, formed the south front of these early greenhouses, but light and air were seen as being of less importance in a house which was only to be used as protection from cold.

John Evelyn describes a conservatory built to a Dutch design. Shutters, mats or canvas blinds covered the insides of the windows and glazed doors on cold nights. The back and side walls and the ceiling were made of timber; the foot-wide space between the inner and outer boards was insulated with a filling of dry sawdust, well rammed in. The roof was tiled or thatched, and sloped backwards from the front. The conservatory was shut up and heated only in the most severe weather; if a damp cloth froze solid in the house it was time to close both windows and shutters. Continued frost meant that fires must be lit, otherwise the trees would 'grow musty'.[5]

Simple indoor stoves provided a safer alternative to the cheapest method of heating, which was to place pans of burning charcoal in the house, either on the floor, or hanging up by the windows. Burning charcoal in a confined space was not altogether advisable; its fumes could kill plants and, worse: the hapless gardener risked suffocation. The need to eliminate the noxious vapours emitted by charcoal-burning stoves led to the notion of heating a greenhouse by means of underground flues. In Liège in 1635 an over-wintering gallery 100 feet long was heated by coal-fired hypocausts.[6] By 1685, according to John Evelyn's *Diary*, the 'innumerable rarieties' [sic] in the greenhouse of the Apothecaries' Garden at Chelsea (the design of which was based on the contemporary greenhouse at Leiden) were kept warm in winter by 'sub-terranean heate, conveyed by a stove under the Conservatory, which was all vaulted with brick: so as he [Mr Watts, the gardener] leaves the doores and win-dowes open in the hardest frost, secluding onely the snow &c'.

This is the first mention of an English greenhouse with indirect heating, but that arrangement had its own drawbacks, for if the vault were badly mortared the fumes seeped into the house, and as ventilation was still only to be had by opening the windows, the plants were still at risk from icy draughts. (Mr Watts was removed from the post in 1693.)

EVELYN'S GREENHOUSE DESIGN

John Evelyn, however, was disapproving of 'ordinary iron stoves' and 'subterranean caliducts'. They wasted what he called 'the pent-in air', and he was concerned about their injurious effects on greenhouse plants. In 1691 he published his own design for a greenhouse ventilated with air that was heated, but also 'pure and genuine'. Fresh air was drawn in and heated by pipes placed in an external stove, then conducted by the same pipes into the greenhouse. The heated air rose to the top of the house, then fell as it cooled into an extract duct in the floor. This subterranean duct led back to the ash pit of the furnace so that the stale air finally exited through the chimney. The ends of the house were solid and the roof was tiled, but one side – the south side – was made entirely of glass, for Evelyn now recognized that 'the light itself, next to air, is of wonderful im-portance'.[7] (See page 148.)

As well as this novel arrangement for the circulation of heated air, the design was notable for two other innovations: a porch, so that when the door was opened the plants inside were protected from an inrush of cold air; and a thermometer, shown on the plan to be hanging on the wall facing the inflowing hot-air pipes. The thermometer was a comparatively recent invention; it was to become indispensable in heated glasshouses, and particularly so in pineapple houses.

Orangeries and greenhouses continued to be built to the old designs, with and without underfloor flues, well into the following century. Some were ornate, others were little more than insulated barns, but even in a garden as advanced as the Apothecaries' Garden in Chelsea, the greenhouse was still lit and ventilated as late as 1731 solely by tall front windows; gardeners' rooms occupied the floor above.

THE CHALLENGE OF TROPICAL EXOTICS

Once the art of keeping subtropical citruses, dates, myrtles, jasmines, oleanders and pomegranates had been mastered, the next horticultural challenge was to grow tropical plants – cocoa, banana and coffee trees, pineapples, and succulents such as prickly pears, torch-thistles, aloes, sedums and spiny euphorbias – with the same success. Most of these new introductions came from the East and West Indies; some had their origins in Central America or Africa, and a few had been sent from India or China.

Either as objects of curiosity or as plants with possible economic value, these were taken to Britain in their hundreds from their places of origin by Portuguese, Spanish, Dutch and British colonists, pirates and traders. But the over-wintering structures that were now to be found in the grandest gardens, while suitable for half-hardy

evergreens, offered inadequate protection to the more tender types of plant, which might at best flourish for one season, then perish. Few, if any of them, could be propagated, produce flowers or fruit, or stay alive through winter and summer in the old-style greenhouse. It was not only dark and fume-filled, it was also draughty and damp. 'Indian plants', as tropical exotics came to be known, needed constant heat, light and proper ventilation.

The pineapple or ananas, in particular, was the plant that was at the same time the most desirable and the most difficult of all the new introductions to grow in Europe. Indeed, it was the passion for pineapples in the eighteenth century that was responsible for the development of the hothouse, with well-regulated conditions for the cultivation of tropical exotics.

South American agave

155

STOVES FOR EXOTICS & PINES

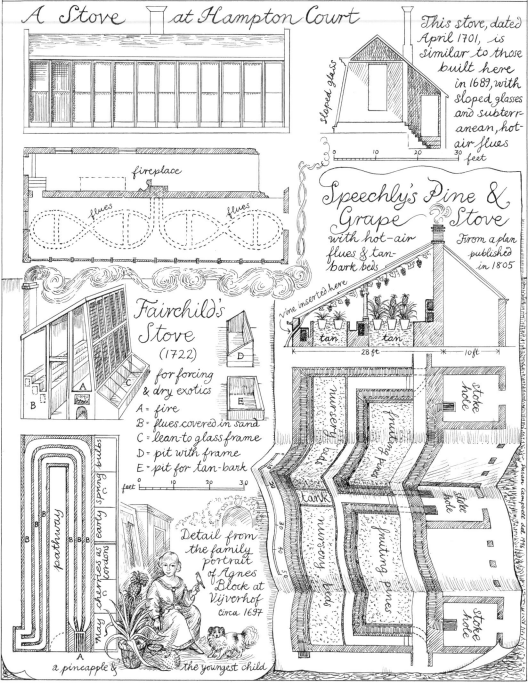

A Stove at Hampton Court

This stove, dated April 1701, is similar to those built here in 1689, with sloped glasses and subterranean, hot-air flues

sloped glass

0   10   20   30 feet

fireplace

flues   flues

Speechly's Pine & Grape Stove

with hot-air flues & tan-bark beds

From a plan published in 1805

vine inserted here

tan   tan

28 ft   10 ft

stoke hole

pea hrosum

fruiting pines

tank

pea hrosum

fruiting pines

stoke hole

stoke hole

Susan Campbell del. 1996

Fairchild's Stove

(1722)

for forcing & dry exotics

A = fire
B = flues covered in sand
C = lean-to glass frame
D = pit with frame
E = pit for tan-bark

A   B   C   D   E

feet   0   10   20   30

pathway

May cherries as early spring bulbs

cherries as cordons

B   B   B B B   C   C   C

A

a pineapple &

Detail from the family portrait of Agnes Block at Vijverhof circa 1697

the youngest child

CHAPTER ELEVEN

THE PINERY

The pineapple – described by Philip Miller, one of the first gardeners to produce it in England, as the fruit that 'surpasses all the known Fruits of the World' – is now so easy to buy in the shops that it is difficult to imagine the excitement that even the sight of one once engendered. Three hundred years ago it was a rarity in Europe; yet Christopher Columbus first tasted it two hundred years before that, on or a little after Monday 4 November 1493, when he and his sailors made their first landing in the New World, on the island now known as Guadeloupe. One of their first meals included pineapples, the flavour and fragrance of which astonished and delighted them.

When pineapples were at last grown in Europe, the production of a good, large fruit was regarded as a tremendous event, worthy of a commemorative painting, or even the striking of a medal. By the mid eighteenth century possession of one of these fruits was so prestigious that pineapples were hired out as decorations for dinner parties. If one of them happened to get eaten, the 'crown' or tuft of leaves at the top of the plant was sent back to the gardener for replanting. The diarist Parson Woodforde recorded his first sight and taste of the fruit, at the age of twenty-six, on 29 September 1766. As late as

the 1920s it was accounted a really grand dinner party only if there were present both 'a pineapple and Lady Curzon'.[1]

THE PINEAPPLE'S ORIGINS
The plant (*Ananas comosus*, of the *Bromeliaceae* family) is indigenous to tropical South America. *Ananas* is derived from its Indian name, *nana*; 'pineapple' came about because of the fruit's similarity to a pine cone. With maize, bananas, sweet potatoes and coconuts, the fruit was one of the South American Indians' commonest food plants.

The first published description of the pineapple (by Gonzalo Fernandez de Oviedo y Valdes) appeared in Spain in 1535. He enthused about its scent, beauty and flavour – a mixture of quinces, peaches and melons – 'but surpassing in excellence all those fruits together and singly'. As an emissary of King Ferdinand of Spain he sent some home from Haiti 'cut green to ripen at sea', but like most fruits when picked completely unripe 'in this way they lose their merit'. He also sent ripe fruit and shoots by which the plant could be propagated, but alas, the voyage was delayed and his shipment went rotten.[2]

However, as the pineapple was an excellent anti-scorbutic, it was carried by ships plying sixteenth-century trade routes as far afield as

South Africa, Madagascar, India, Singapore, Java, China, Japan, the Philippines, Peru, Ecuador and the Solomon Islands, and planted in all those places. By the end of the seventeenth century the pineapple was growing abundantly throughout the tropics.

THE PINEAPPLE'S HORTICULTURAL REQUIREMENTS

Unfortunately the pineapple was not so easy to raise in cooler climates, under artificial conditions. Its requirements were quite different from those of myrtles, pomegranates, oranges or lemons. These Mediterranean 'greens' could be overwintered in northern Europe with any sort of shelter that would protect them from temperatures lower than 8C/45°F, but the pineapple, which does not bear fruit until its second or third year, cannot thrive in temperatures below 16C/60°F and needs moisture as well as heat in order to prosper.

The pineapple's natural habitat is one of high humidity, although it also grows in arid regions with heavy dews; the trough on its tough, spiky leaves channels condensed water to its base, and storage cells in the leaves give the plant a high degree of drought tolerance. It also thrives in areas where the rainfall is confined to one season of the year. Under hot-house conditions the pineapple must have heat from the soil as well as the air; ideally it is grown at temperatures ranging between 16–30C/60–90°F. The fruit ripens during the mid-summer months at 24–32C/75–90°F/; it also needs a high percentage of sun and light if it is to ripen.

The Dutch botanist Paludanus tried, but failed, to keep a pineapple plant alive at Enkhuisen in Holland, in 1592;[3] no frame or greenhouse had yet been built that was capable of providing the necessary heat, light and moisture for such a plant. Further attempts to cultivate the pineapple in Holland produced only tiny, inedible fruit, on plants that had been brought by the Dutch West India Company (founded in 1621). The shipment of live plants was not easy: those which required light and air had to be kept on deck and protected from the salt spray, and the voyages were long.

Without a suitable pit or glasshouse, attempts to grow the pineapple in temperate or sub-tropical climates were bound to fail. Under glass the whole process, from rooting the suckers or crowns to ripening the fruit, was expensive, laborious, tricky and lengthy. The challenge brought all the horticultural technology and ingenuity of the late seventeenth and early eighteenth centuries into play, at a time when the Dutch had the horticultural lead over the rest of Europe. They imported live plants, herbaria, seeds and bulbs from their colonies, testing them for commercial exploitation and for pharmaceutical use, and enjoying them as rarities and status symbols in their own private gardens. Even so, they did not manage to grow pineapples at home until the 1680s, some thirty years after the first consignment of fruit came to Holland from the West Indies.

THE PINEAPPLE IN EUROPE

As there was a long-standing tradition of botanical and horticultural exchanges between Britain and Holland, it is possible that some of the same consignment was sent to England; although King James is said to have been presented with a pineapple in 1625,[4] an entry in John Evelyn's *Diary* noted that the first pineapples ever seen in the country were those sent to Oliver Cromwell in 1657. Evelyn later recorded the gifts of two pineapples to Charles II; the first ('ye famous Queene Pine brought from Barbadoes') was presented on 9 August 1661; this was also the first pineapple that Evelyn saw himself. A second pine was presented to the king in 1668.

A picture of Charles II being given a pineapple by a kneeling figure (said to be John Rose, the royal gardener) was painted not long afterwards, probably between 1668 and 1677, by the Dutch artist Hendrick Danckerts. This painting gave rise to the legend that the proffered pineapple was grown by Rose, but as the fruit was hardly known at that date in England, and had not yet been grown successfully even in Holland, it is far more likely that the painting is of the presentation of a pineapple that had just arrived. Moreover, Evelyn, a meticulous diarist as well as an ardent gardener, made no mention of pineapple growing in England.

The Dutch politician Pieter de la Court, a wealthy Huguenot immigrant from Liège, is said to have cultivated pineapples in his garden near Leiden in 1675. Further

attempts to grow pineapples with artificial heat were made at the botanical gardens (the *Hortus Publicus*) of the University of Leiden and at the *Hortus Medicus* in the City of Amsterdam; pineapple plants were sent from Surinam to both gardens in 1680. In 1687 a Dutch lady named Agnes Block became the first person to succeed in growing a pineapple to perfection – a feat notable enough for her to have a picture painted of the plant and a medal struck. A pineapple in a pot was also included in the Block family portrait of 1697. At the same time Jan Commelin, the Dutch botanist, had plants sent from Curaçao; they are said to have fruited in the *Hortus Medicus* in 1688 and 1689.[5]

Unfortunately, the means by which all these specimens were cultivated is nowhere described in contemporary Dutch gardening literature. What we do know, from a book on

gardening published by de la Court's son in 1737, is that the Dutch grew their pineapples in the early years of the eighteenth century in a new kind of hothouse or stove, first seen in a plan of 1682. This shows two small, sloping-fronted glass cases for tropical exotics at the *Hortus Medicus* in Amsterdam. They were heated (like the greenhouses at Leiden and Chelsea) by underfloor ovens, and faced south.

THE HAMPTON COURT STOVES

Three new stoves based on the Amsterdam design were erected at Hampton Court in 1689, when the Dutch Prince of Orange acceded to the English throne as King William III. His wife, Queen Mary, needed them for the royal couple's collection of rarities. Neither stoves nor plants like these had ever been seen in England before.

In 1690, the horticultural enthusiast Charles Hatton wrote to his elder brother Christopher: 'I heartily wish yr Loppe [Lordship] had been ther, for there is about 400 rare Indian plants wch were never seen in England. . . The stoves in wh. they are kept are much better contrived and built than any other in England.'[6] (See page 156.)

The Duchess of Beaufort, an ardent collector of rare plants, sent her steward, Mr Bale, to measure the stoves so that she might copy them herself. From his report we learn that each house was fifty-five feet long; each had two chimneys leading from two pairs of fireplaces in underfloor vaults. The fireplaces held little wheeled furnaces which could be drawn in and out at will, and the vaults were roofed with iron plates covered in sand one inch thick. Above the sand the floors were paved with closely mortared 'brick tiles', seven inches square and one and a half inches thick. Mr Bale explained that the fronts of the houses were sloping and south-facing to receive maximum sunlight. Ventilation could be adjusted by opening or closing the windows; there were fourteen of these, each one seven feet high and three feet four inches wide. They opened back to back. There was also 'an ayre hole' at either end of each house, with a glass pane 'to open and shutt on occasions'. The interior back and side walls were lined with inch-board painted white, to show up any smoking chimney flues.[7]

Another feature of the stoves at Hampton Court was their narrowness; although they had hipped roofs they measured only eight feet from front to back. The old-fashioned, opaquely roofed greenhouse or orangery was usually wider – the average was about twelve feet – but it was now realized that if the distance from front to back of the house exceeded the height of the windows the plants furthest from the windows did not receive enough light. One answer to this problem was to place plants on stepped shelves (see page 148).

The nucleus of the collection for which the Hampton Court stoves were built was a gift from Hans Willem Bentinck, Superintendent of the Royal Gardens in England from 1689 to 1700. Like Commelin, Frau Block, Pieter de la Court and the King of Holland, Bentinck had a major collection of exotic plants at his own estate, at Zorgvliet in Holland. However, although several pineapples were included in the Hampton Court collection, there is only one account of a pineapple ripening its fruit there, in October 1693.[8]

This occurred a year after Bentinck's collection arrived in England, but it is unlikely that the plant was raised entirely at Hampton Court. It is more probable that it was grown in Holland or shipped direct from the Indies with the fruit still unripe. According to Bradley, the Dutch still imported growing pineapples from the tropics to ripen at home,[9] and later in the eighteenth century British gardeners did the same.[10] A pineapple grown and ripened from scratch in Britain would have caused immense excitement in the botanical world of

1693, especially in England; it is inconceivable that such an event would have gone unrecorded in the diaries or letters of enthusiasts such as Evelyn or Hatton.

EARLY EIGHTEENTH-CENTURY HEATING IN THE PINERY

By the time of Queen Anne's accession in 1702, ornamental orangeries and conservatories were to be seen in every English garden of importance, as were greenhouses with underfloor heating, or heated houses built to Evelyn's 1691 design. Underfloor heating was supplied by stoves housed in sheds at the backs of the buildings. Room heating was supplied either by Evelyn's type of exterior stove or, in the old-fashioned way, by pans of burning charcoal, or by stoves inside the building.

Conservatory and greenhouse roofs were still tiled, thatched or leaded. Stoves with sloping glass fronts do not appear to have been built, as yet, anywhere other than at Hampton Court. However, by the beginning of the eighteenth century those who wished to have an ideal greenhouse were advised to 'let the length be from East to West, and have South Windows of Sashes, with close shutters, that when the South Sun is warm, even in Winter, you may open them a little to let in the comfortable Beams and fresh Air, which greatly cherish all vegetables'. The advantage of a south-facing house was at last beginning to be appreciated; greenhouses no longer faced the most convenient direction for their owners, which was often northwards.[11]

There had been progress too, in the provision of heat in the melon ground and warmth in the fruit garden. By the early eighteenth century, the hotbed (see Chapter 8) had become an established adjunct to British kitchen gardens, while in the fruit garden various experiments with fruit walls had been made (see Chapters 3, 4 and 5).

By 1714, when George I came to the throne, the enthusiastic gardener had a variety of heat-engendering and plant-protecting devices at his disposal. There were greenhouses with stoves or underfloor hot-air flues; heated glazed walls (either sloping or upright); and hotbeds covered with glazed frames. Evelyn's brick-lined pit or 'subterranean conservatory' was one of the most useful of these devices. It was originally designed to be heated by dung for the protection and forwarding of tender plants and seedlings; it could also be used unheated, simply covered with 'Fetheridge Boards' (feather-edge boards) like an old wooden greenhouse, for the sheltering of greens; but

it was in pineapple culture that its real worth was to emerge.

Evelyn's pit was ten feet wide and twenty feet long. Large pits like these could be heated by hot-air flues as well as dung. However, the best heat of all for pineapple growing was provided by pits filled with yet another horticultural innovation from Holland, tanners' bark.

TANNERS' BARK

Tanners' bark or tan bark is crushed oak tree bark. It is soaked in water to make a strong infusion or 'ooze', which is full of tannin, and used by tanners to convert animal hides into leather. The hides are steeped in the ooze for several months, with crushed bark laid between each hide. Eventually the ooze loses its strength and the moist (and by now fermenting) bark is thrown out.

Waste bark ferments and heats violently at first. Before it could become cool enough for use in a gardener's hotbed the bark was left for eight to ten days to drain and sweat a

little. It was then laid in a brick-lined pit on a bed of rubble where, after about five weeks, the heat became milder. It remained at a suitable temperature for plants such as pineapples without needing any attention for three to six months – considerably longer than a hotbed of horse dung. It also created less steam, which is injurious to plants under glass. Moreover, unlike horse dung, the fermentation could be reactivated by stirring the tan, or even by removing some of it when it had completely lost its heat and sifting the remainder with a proportion of fresh tan. In this way a tan bed could be kept going for as long as a year. A bed that retained a bottom heat of 75-85°F/24-30C and heated evenly without needing constant renewal was especially advantageous for pineapples. They could be left in a tan bed with the protection of glasses and frames, but with no other source of heat, from March to October, then moved into a heated conservatory for the next six months.

Although Evelyn was well aware in the 1680s of the fact that Dutch gardeners used tanners' bark both in pits for forcing, and as compost thereafter,[12] it seems odd that he never recommended it himself for hotbeds, nor is there any mention of a *rund-bak* (tan bed) in seventeenth-century Dutch gardening literature. Possibly the technique was so ordinary it merited no special comment. Its early use in Holland certainly suggests that this was the secret of their initial success with the pineapple. Philip Miller said that tan was invariably employed in hotbeds by Dutch and Flemish gardeners in the 1690s, but apart from 'two or three persons' at Blackheath in Kent, who were at that time using tan beds for raising orange trees, the practice does not seem to have reached England until 1716 or 1717.[13]

THE FIRST PUBLISHED ACCOUNT

The first instructions for growing pineapples were published by Richard Bradley in *A General Treatise of Husbandry and Gardening* (1721). Bradley had spent six months in Amsterdam, from May to December 1714. Here he met all the most prominent Dutch botanists and horticulturists of the day. Of the pineapples growing then in Amsterdam he says he saw about twenty different sorts, but only one had a fruit on it, which 'was not larger than a common Newington Peach, and even that was esteem'd a great Rarity'. Some plants had come from the Dutch East Indies and some from Surinam and Curaçao. Bradley also met the gardener of 'Mr Le Cour of Leyden' (Pieter de la Court van de Voort, son of the Pieter de la Court who had first tried to grow pineapples in 1675), and saw some of his fruit, which far surpassed the single pineapple Bradley had seen in Amsterdam. In fact, so many plants were raised each year that many were thrown away.

Some of those redundant plants were given to friends, with instructions for their cultivation. One of the recipients may have been a gardener in Germany, for in 1716 pineapples were served at the Hanoverian palace of Herrenhausen, the home of the future George II of England. As the necessary techniques were still known only to the Dutch, in all probability the grower of the Hanoverian pineapples was either a Dutchman, or a man with Dutch connections; he may have even been a friend of Sir Matthew Decker, a wealthy Dutchman living in Richmond in Surrey, whose gardener Henry Telende was on the point of producing the first pineapple to be grown and ripened in England – over thirty years after Agnes Block in Holland.

Bradley visited Decker's garden in the summer of 1721, two or three years after the establishment there of Decker's pine-stove. He was even more impressed with Decker's pines than he was with de la Court's. Henry Telende gave Bradley a precise account of their cultivation. The suckers or crowns were planted singly in small, six-inch pots in July and August. The pots were then plunged in a warm tan-bed pit, brick-lined and filled first with a layer of rubble, then with a layer of hot dung, one foot deep. The rest of the pit was filled wholly by fermenting tanners' bark pressed down lightly to soil level. It was surmounted by a sloping wooden frame divided equally into four lights.

The chief objectives in summer were to encourage the growth of roots and leaves on the first-year suckers and large, ripe fruits on the second-year plants. Ventilation was supplied by opening or closing the glass lights (glazed coverings); shade, when necessary, was provided by mats or canvases. At the end of October Telende would move his plants from the pit to the stove or conservatory. When winter was over the plants were returned to the outdoor tan bed, to be joined by more newly-potted suckers. In October the plants were returned once again to the stove. By February some of the older plants (now eighteen months old), would show infant fruits the size of tennis balls, covered in blue blossom. Now the tan bed was made up again, and in March, by which time the temperature was judged right, both first and second-year plants were brought out of the stove and put back in the pit. The fruit on the second-year plants ripened in July and August; the cycle which had started with the planting of suckers (and crowns) continued.[14]

The plants were grown in pots for the convenience of moving them from tan bed to stove and back again. There was also an idea that the roots should not come into direct contact with the bark, as the tannin might be harmful. Pine-pots were originally deeper in proportion to their width than the modern flowerpot, so that the plants could be packed more closely in the beds. In later accounts of pineapple growing, the gardeners wore leather gloves and hessian arm-bands while moving their pines, to protect themselves from the razor-sharp spikes on the edges of the leaves.

Skill was needed to ensure that the plants were given the correct amounts of water, warmth, air and light at all times under these relatively primitive conditions. Bradley was at pains to point out that tan was capable of warming only the soil and not the air above it. The heat in a stove-heated greenhouse was dry and still liable to be erratic – a thermometer was essential. Apparently Telende's success was largely due to his ingenuity in calculating, for the first time, the optimum temperatures for pines.[15] Thereafter, standardized spirit thermometers were made specially for gardeners by a Mr Fowler in the City of London. They were marked in inches as 'cold', 'temperate', 'warm' or 'pine apple heat', 'hot' and 'sultry'.

NEW STOVES AND FRAMES

Bradley was fascinated by the newly discovered art of making hotbeds with tan bark. By the summer of 1723 he had visited several gardens where bark pits were now used to raise not only pineapples but guavas and other exotics as well. The most notable place of cultivation was the Apothecaries' Garden at Chelsea, where Philip Miller was now in charge. He had brought tropical plants 'of the Latitude of 18 or 20 Degrees to the utmost perfection' in a new, bark-filled frame.

At the same time, at Hoxton (then a village on the outskirts of the City of London, well known for its nursery gardens), Thomas Fairchild, a renowned fruit grower, hybridist, cultivator and supplier of exotics as well as of Fowler's thermometers, was building stoves which incorporated several new features. The frontispiece of his *City Gardener* of 1722

shows a symmetrical range of lean-tos with long, low, sloping glass roofs. One of Fairchild's stoves featured a lean-to forcing frame on the front wall containing cordoned apples and cherries, spring flowers, roses and spring bulbs. Three-inch earthenware pipes fixed above the underfloor fire conducted warm air, as in Evelyn's stove, into the conservatory. Another pipe conveyed hot air 'at discretion' to the forcing frame. A further innovation was the use of glass partitions within the house. They created separate environments without casting shade and prevented the sudden loss of heat that could be caused by opening an outer door or a window. Access through an entrance lobby, or via the furnace shed behind the house, was also recommended.

No mention is made, though, of pineapple growing in this stove. For that purpose Fairchild made another stove in 1723. It was commended mainly for the improved dryness of its floors, achieved by having flues built (for the first time) above the floor. Although Fairchild's improvement was helpful to plants relishing dry conditions, it was not so good for pineapples, which need moist heat. This was ideally provided in summer by tan beds. But when the pots were removed for the winter to a stove or conservatory with fire heat alone, they were placed either in hot sand or on scaffolds and shelves. Skilful management by a gardener like Telende was needed to avoid the pitfalls of dry heat, where the extremities of the roots were liable to dry and harden. If they were watered too much, they rotted; if the fires went out the plants might die from cold. Continued growth was crucial – if large fruits were to be had the following summer the plants should be flowering and showing infant fruits by February.

The answer was to make tan beds inside the stove as well as outside; pines could now grow without check through the winter, with the combined help of moist bottom-heat and warm-air flues. In 1723 a stove was built at Croydon for one William Parker, combining tan-bed heat and stove heat within the same house. This was the first English stove, greenhouse or conservatory to contain a bark bed; it was not only ideal for pineapples, it also widened the range of plants that could be grown, and ushered in the great era of glasshouse horticulture in England.

By 1730 'the Nobility and Gentry' of England were in the grip of what can only be described as Pineapple Fever; the demand for pineapples at 'entertainments' meant that 'Stoves and Glasscases for the culture of the Pine . . . are now found in almost every curious Garden'.[16] The raising of pineapples for sale became a lucrative branch of gardening. At Shaw Hall, the Duke of Chandos's house near Newbury, pineapples were grown for sale at half a guinea each – half the price of a new wig.

The next development was the year-round use of outdoor tan beds or bark pits, which acquired heated flues. Young plants could remain in them all winter, leaving the larger stoves, now regularly equipped with bark pits, free for the fruiting plants. In both cases, the pits were sunk below ground level. James Justice, a Scottish horticulturist and author who introduced pineapples to Scotland, had the idea of putting both the fruiting and succession, or nursery, pits under one roof, and making access to the pits easier by raising them a few feet above ground level. He incorporated these improvements in his stove at Crighton, in 1732.

Meanwhile, the improvement of the glasshouse itself continued apace. Early in the eighteenth century Hermann Boerhaave, physiologist, botanist, and director of the Botanic Garden at Leiden, determined the best angle for the slope of glass on a greenhouse in winter. He calculated the slopes, at different latitudes, that provided the maximum heat and sunlight on the shortest day so that the sun's rays were at right angles to the glass when they were most required. His findings were elaborated upon by glasshouse designers until well into the next century.[17] However, low, sloping roofs were used increasingly where pineapples were grown, partly for economy and partly because the plants themselves were not that tall.

By 1851, Miller's bark stove in the Apothecaries' Garden (now also known as the Chelsea Physick Garden) had growing in it cashews, allspice, avocado pears, custard apples, cocoa, calabash, coconut, ginger, paw-paw, mimosa, tamarind and bananas, as well as pineapples. More significantly, this

Acacia baileyana

new stove incorporated all Boerhaave's findings. It had an upright glass front rising seven feet from a three foot wall of brickwork, with a sloping glass roof twelve feet wide, rising to the apex, sixteen feet high. The sloping glasses were made as sashes to slide open. At each end there were low sheds; one for the fire, one for tools. The stove house itself was thirty-two feet long and about twelve feet wide, with a path all round the bark bed. The back wall was heated by six upright flues in a criss-cross formation.

Ranges of glazed stoves became ornaments to botanic and kitchen gardens alike. The old-fashioned, south-facing orangery or greenhouse at Chelsea kept its classical, upright facade of tall windows, subterranean flues, opaque roof and rooms above, but by 1752 the two stoves flanking it on either side had been given glazed fronts, hinged to open for ventilation, and glass roofs sloping at an angle of 45 degrees, with sliding sashes. The back walls had serpentine smoke flues; the extra length provided by each return meant that more heat was used from each furnace.

The back walls and the greenhouse ceiling were whitewashed to reflect light. In bad weather, to protect the plants from cold and frost, to conserve heat, to keep out the rain and save the glass from being broken by storms and hail, the windows and sashes were covered with shutters or tarpaulins fixed in frames. Miller saw no reason why plants from all over the world should not be kept in one range, as at Chelsea, with different temperatures provided by 'the greenhouse in the middle and one stove and a glass case at each end'. Houses more than forty feet in length could have glass partitions with glass doors, and a fire to each section, thus providing more variations of temperature.[18]

As the popularity of the pineapple grew, stoves became longer, and, as we have already seen, the height of the roof was lowered. Miller saw this as a considerable inconvenience because of the resulting difficulty of watering the pines. By 1754 pineapple stoves fifty feet long, containing upwards of 120 plants, were not unusual.

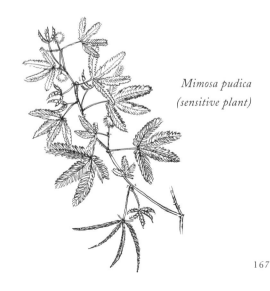

Mimosa pudica
(sensitive plant)

Beds eight feet wide were the rule, with a target of about ninety fruits a year. The houses could be ranged ornamentally (as in the kitchen garden at Wardour Castle in Wiltshire) on either side of an orangery or greenhouse. Heat was supplied by furnaces housed in sheds behind the back wall. By the end of the century, at grand, ducal gardens like Welbeck in Nottinghamshire, the fruit would be counted in hundreds rather than tens.

English gardeners could no longer meet the demand for suckers and crowns; these now had to be imported from the West Indies. With them came the thrips and mealy bugs that were causing such havoc in the sugar-cane industry. The best way to deal with afflicted pineapples was to take the plants out of their pots and immerse them in a tub of tobacco water for twenty-four hours.[19] Later remedies included a concoction of water, soft soap and quicksilver.[20]

By the mid eighteenth century stoves were still constructed as lean-tos, and used mainly for pines. Lean-to glasshouses were also built for collections of exotics, but they were rarely more than sixteen feet high; several specimens (avocado and banyan trees, for example) grew too large for a house to contain them. Heated houses were not yet built exclusively for other types of fruit such as peaches, figs or vines. As late as 1768, Miller's *Dictionary* stated that 'Far the greatest number of stoves which have been erected in England, are designed for the culture of the Ananas only.'[21]

GLAZING

In 1767 the first monograph on the cultivation of the pineapple appeared. John Giles, the author of *Ananas: or, a Treatise on the Pineapple*, suggested ways in which the glazing of stoves could be improved. He disliked old-fashioned leaded panes; 'imbricated' or overlapping panes set in putty would, he said, let in more light.

At this date frames, sashes and beams were still made of wood, and painted white. Iron was not to be used in greenhouse construction for another forty or fifty years, and it was not until 1789 that the ends as well as the front of a lean-to greenhouse were glazed.[22] Sashes were usually three or three and a half feet wide, with glazing bars six to nine inches apart; each pane of glass measured no more than six by eight inches – tiny by modern standards, but cheaper to replace, and stronger than large panes in an age when glass was the most expensive part of a hothouse. The Excise Act of 1745 included a tax on glass by weight of materials used; it was increased in 1777 and again in the 1780s, and not repealed until 1845, thus restricting the use of glass, especially in hothouses, for an entire century.

FUEL AND FURNACES

The expense of building a stove was one consideration; heating it was another. In coal-rich counties, for example, coal was cheap, but where carriage had to be paid for as well, it became dear; where economy mattered, wood, turf or peat was used instead. Small brick furnaces, some twenty inches deep and sixteen inches square inside, were the norm. They were built well below floor level so that the house received the maximum benefit from the lowest flues. Care had to be taken with the positioning of furnaces and flues – nearby timbers and tan beds could easily catch fire, and accidents like this had caused several stoves and orangeries to burn down.[23]

Furnaces had three iron doors; one in front of the fire for the fuel, one just above the grate to adjust the draught when lighting the fire, and one to cover the ash hole at the bottom. Houses longer than forty feet needed two small furnaces. Fairchild's fifty-foot-long forcing stove was heated by a massive brick oven ten feet long and five feet wide, covered in cast-iron plates, a layer of sand and square paving tiles.

Each type of fuel had its different qualities. First in order of preference came coal, which gave a more lasting, moderate heat, then turf, peat or wood. Pit coal, which burned to a white heat, was preferred to 'Newcastle coal', which ran into clinker and deposited heavy soot. Turf and peat were preferred in Holland; these gave constant, equal and relatively smokeless heat, though the smell of peat was not liked in an orangery. Wood came last, as it required 'much greater Attendance' and its heat was 'sudden and unconstant'. On the other hand, it made the hottest smoke and was therefore the best for heated walls.[24]

The heating of pits was also expensive. Tan had to be paid for, and brought from the tanner's yard. Horse dung also had to be bought and carted if supplies at home were insufficient. Various fermenting materials such as grass, weeds, bran and water, and straw mixed with sea-coal ash, were used to economize on tan.[25]

LATE EIGHTEENTH-CENTURY STOVE IMPROVEMENTS

In spite of the quantity of pineapple lore that was set down in every gardening book of the mid to late eighteenth century, Philip Miller's horticultural advice could not be bettered. The 'stoves', however, were still in need of improvement. Small advances occurred here and there, such as the insertion of iron 'regulators' or dampers in the flues to control heat, and the provision of doors in the flues to make cleaning easier. In 1767, to avoid the lengthy business of putting up large, unwieldy shutters, tarpaulins or mats on frosty nights, the horticulturalist John Abercrombie suggested covering the top glasses of the hothouse with roller blinds made of canvas or sailcloth.[26]

William Speechly, gardener to the Third Duke of Portland at Welbeck Abbey from 1767 to 1804, had several new devices in his hothouses, some of which may have been gleaned from a trip to Holland. He was sent there in 1771 by his employer (grandson of Hans Willem Bentinck) to learn what he could of Dutch gardening. He liked the double-pitted stove, but improved on Justice's design by adding a third line of flues under the windows along the front. He also

placed a large tank in the centre of the house to collect rainwater from the roof; apparently he was the first to do so, for he found it 'strange that an object of so much importance should hitherto have been so little attended to'.[27]

THE NINETEENTH-CENTURY PINERY

In 1820, four hundred Bermudan pineapples, the first consignment of that fruit 'as an article of commerce', were bought by a London fruiterer, a Mr Mart of Oxford Street. Two-thirds of them arrived in good condition; 'those pines which were packed with the roots arrived in a better state than others that were cut off in the usual manner'.[28] If it is picked just before it ripens, a pineapple can be kept in good condition from three to six weeks, depending on the

variety. Even though the steamship voyage from the Bermudas took only six weeks, this doubtless meant that the hothouse product was still better than the imported variety. Moreover, as the century progressed, several new cultivars were introduced, thereby lengthening the season, so that home-grown, hothouse pineapples were soon available all the year round.

The 'Black Jamaica' pine was an early nineteenth-century introduction. It was smaller than the spiny old 'Queen' pine (a summer-fruiting variety), but, by growing the 'Jamaica' in small pots at a higher temperature than usual, it could be encouraged to ripen its fruit in winter. Another new cultivar, the very large, winter-fruiting 'Cayenne' (now the most widely cultivated variety in the major pineapple-producing areas of the world) was introduced to France and thence to England from French Guiana in the 1830s.

Pineapples therefore continued to be cultivated in all the best British gardens, but as they thrived best in houses devoted exclusively to their needs, and as they required no more than four feet of headroom, nineteenth-century gardeners took to raising them throughout the whole cycle – from suckers to fruiting plants – in pits, rather than houses.

The twelve and eighteen-light pine-pits described in the Pylewell sale particulars of 1850 are typical of the span-roofed pineapple pits used from the early nineteenth century through to the early twentieth century. Heat

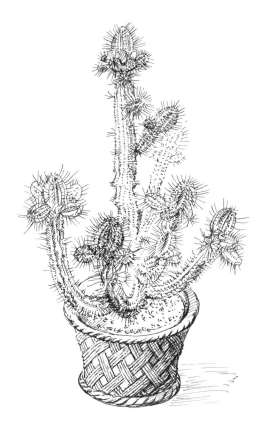

growing pineapples (mostly smooth-leaved 'Cayennes') in the Azores and sending them home by steamship. The journey was not only shorter than the trip from the West Indies, it was more rapid by steam than by sail, thus ensuring that the fruit arrived in better condition and making the British hothouse pineapple a redundant luxury.

was provided both by hot-water pipes beneath the staging and by tan-bark or fermenting oak leaves in the plunge beds above it. The young plants (rooted suckers and crowns) occupied the perimeter beds along the sides of the pit, where the eaves met the outer walls. The fruiting pines, being taller, occupied a central bed beneath the ridge of the roof. Divisions within the pit enabled different temperatures and densities of moisture to be maintained.

Pits like these continued to be used for pineapples until the First World War, but very few country-house gardeners were asked to raise pineapples after that date. Since the 1880s British gardeners had been

opuntia, or 'Indian fig'

VINERY

Forcing Vinery.

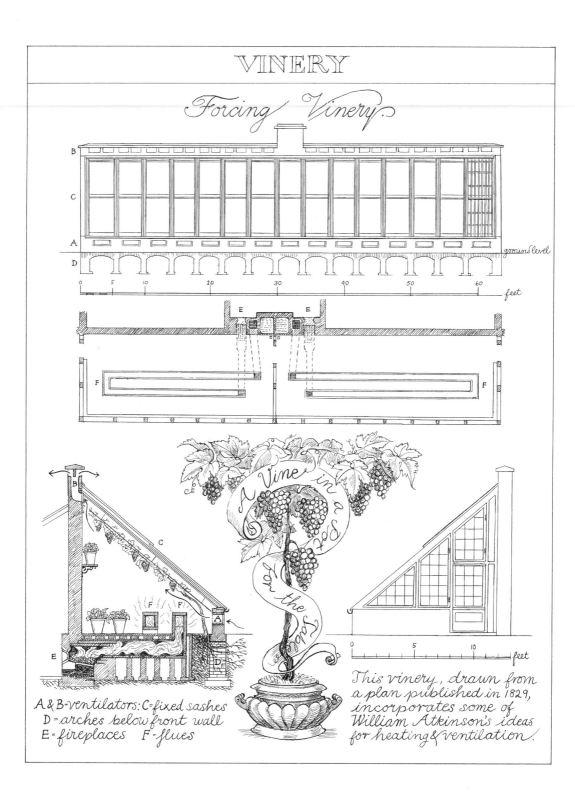

ground level

0	5	10		20		30		40		50		60	

feet

A Vine in a Pot for the Tropics

0   5   10   feet

A & B = ventilators: C = fixed sashes
D = arches below front wall
E = fireplaces   F = flues

This vinery, drawn from a plan published in 1829, incorporates some of William Atkinson's ideas for heating & ventilation.

CHAPTER TWELVE

THE VINERY

STOVES FOR EXOTICS

One of the earliest uses of the word 'hothouse' appears in 1749, in the title of a catalogue from James Dickson and Co., nurserymen and seedsmen of Edinburgh. It is a list of *'Hot-house, Green-house, Hardy and Herbaceous Plants . . . '*. The gardener hereby acquires a new term to add to the repertoire of 'stove', 'greenhouse' and 'conservatory'. The latter two words meant, at that date, exactly the same thing; a greenhouse or conservatory was usually heated, but it was cooler than a hothouse or stove. It would contain plants such as sedums, citruses, jasmines, myrtles, oleanders and geraniums, that could stand out in the open in summer.[1]

'Hothouse' quickly became a generic term for any stove containing tropical plants. The optimum temperature was 21C/70°F. Stoves and hothouses were kept 'wet' or 'dry' according to the needs of the plants housed within them. They were used for pineapples as well as certain forced vegetables, fruits and flowers, 'succulents' such as cereuses (members of the cactus family), 'African' aloes and euphorbiums, and 'woody' plants such as coffee trees, acacias and mimosas.

Eighteenth-century hothouses contained as many exotics as their owners fancied or, to be more precise, as their gardeners could manage. Richard Bradley, as early as the 1720s, listed some forty exotics for stoves that would need to be heated to between 50 and 75°F (10–24C);[2] six decades later Abercrombie named 105 tropical plants suitable for the pine house. Abercrombie also coined the word 'glassary', but this did not survive. In 1789 he came up with 'pinery', or 'pinery stove and pinery hothouse' as well as 'vinery'.[3] 'Pinery', and 'vinery', like 'hothouse', were here to stay. Before the advent of the vinery, however, there was the pinery-vinery, in which grapevines were planted in a bed outside a stove designed for pineapples or exotics, drawn inside through small holes in the wall, and trained up to the rafters. The idea was that the vines would benefit from the heat within the house, while the pines below enjoyed the shade of their leaves. The shared house meant economy in fuel, but Philip Miller, who first observed this technique in 1752, thought it impractical; 'because where the Stove is design'd for the Anana's, the Air must be kept warmer for them,

Aloe mitriformis

building. He argued that the roots of the vines, being outside, had a colder bed than the pines; that the pines benefited from the vines' 'kindly shade' and that no one's objections could be proved as long as the house was well managed.[6] Vines continued to be forced in the pine-house well into the nineteenth century. As late as 1847 Charles M'Intosh wrote that 'we ourselves have had, and have also observed in the case of many others, as good pines grown under the partial shade of vines, as we have ever seen in houses dedicated entirely to the former'.[7] Pots of strawberries, cucumbers and French beans were also accommodated for forcing in the pinery.

than is requir'd for any of the other fruits; so that they can never succeed well together'.[4]

Another Scottish gardener Walter Nicol, argued that it was 'unnatural that one part of a plant should be, as it were, in Greenland, and the other in the West Indies', and that pines would not thrive in the shade of other plants.[5] Some thought the pinery-vinery was too hot for grapes and too shady for pines; the vine leaves dripped on the pines, and the forced grapes, while gratifyingly early, were not as well-flavoured as those grown under more natural conditions. On a more practical level, the low, shallow-angled roof of a pinery made the tending of the vines extremely difficult. Nevertheless the system had its champions, among them William Speechly, gardener to the Duke of Portland at Welbeck, who appears to have coined 'pinery-vinery' as the name for such a

GROWING THE VINE

The horticultural requirements of the grapevine (*Vitis vinifera*) are very different from those of the pineapple. A vine will survive winter cold, frost and damp and in good summers will ripen its fruit out of doors during August and September, but the crucial time begins between mid April and mid May, when growth starts. If the temperature governing what is known as the 'growing threshold' falls below 50°F/10C at this time, delays and failures with fruit are inevitable.

Outdoor vines are therefore a risky proposition, Sweetwaters being the best varieties for this type of cultivation. Hamburghs thrive better under glass and will do well in relatively gentle heat, while Muscats, Alicantes and Colmars need greater heat, either to force them to ripen early, or to ripen them at all, although they will need relatively high temperatures for only a few weeks in the year.

The production of grapes in Britain without the assistance of heat or glass is, as the proliferation of English vineyards in recent years testifies, not without its rewards. Given good summers, suitable varieties and favourable localities, British grapevines will ripen their fruit in the open, either on sunny slopes or against warm walls, as far north as a line drawn from South Wales to The Wash. (This line is arbitrary; there is a very fine vineyard sixty miles to the north of it, at Renishaw Hall in Derbyshire.) Moreover, although vulnerable at times to variations in the climate, grapes have been grown in gardens and vineyards as far north as a latitude of 51 degrees in southern England, and in northern France and Germany, since Roman times.

As wine played an essential part in the Christian faith, viticulture was practised by monks as well as by royalty and nobles in medieval Britain. The Domesday Survey records thirty-eight taxable vineyards in 1086. Wine making decreased somewhat in the fourteenth century, possibly due to climatic changes (see Chapter 2) or competition from France, but dessert grapes were grown on a large scale in London as long ago as the early fifteenth century,[8] and when Henry VIII came to the throne in 1509 there were nearly 140 major vineyards in England and Wales, two thirds of which

belonged to the Crown and the aristocracy and one third to the Church. After the Reformation many old monastic sites were still associated with vineyards, but wine making went into decline.

In late medieval and Tudor gardens, vines were grown mostly for decoration. With their shady leaves and trailing, clambering habit, they were liked as coverings for arbours and alleys but were not expected to provide an infallible supply of edible fruit. Their grapes might be abundant and juicy, but they might also be small, seedy and fairly sharp, more suited for wine making or verjuice than for dessert.

THE FIRST DESSERT GRAPES

Serious attempts to grow table grapes in English kitchen gardens were made in the early seventeenth century, with vines trained over low, sunny walls and against house walls backed by kitchen chimneys (see Chapter 3). From the mid seventeenth century onwards, kitchen garden vines were trained against the newly introduced French espaliers or 'pole-hedges', kept fairly low and placed either in front of, or against, fruit-garden walls. Vines were still grown on arbours; they were also trained as standards, sometimes supported by stakes up to five feet high and three or four feet apart, as if in a vineyard.[9]

Early Stuart gardeners appear to have had much the same results as their Tudor forebears, with grapes ripening only 'when a hot yeare happeneth'. If wine were made, it met with little success.[10]

SEVENTEENTH-CENTURY GRAPE VARIETIES

By the seventeenth century, numerous varieties of grapevine were available. John Parkinson said that his friend John Tradescant the Elder had twenty different sorts of vine in his garden, but 'hee never knew how or by what name to call them'. Parkinson himself mentioned some two dozen, including the ancestors of many that are still grown today. He listed the 'Frontignack' (Frontignan or Muscat), 'Damasco' (Damascus), white and red Muscadines (kinds of Sweetwater or Chasselas which are confusingly known as 'not muscats'), 'Alligant' (Alicante, later known as St Peter's), 'Bursarobe' (Bar-sur-Aube, later known as the early Chasselas), 'Orleans', 'Burlet' (Bordelais, difficult to ripen and mostly used to make verjuice), 'Raison of the Sun' (better known in England as a dried raisin) and the small 'Corinth or currant grape'.[11]

More suitable varieties for English gardens were introduced later in the seventeenth century, in particular by Sir William Temple, for many years English Ambassador to Holland and later the owner of a celebrated walled fruit garden. In about 1660 he introduced and distributed among local gardeners and 'Persons of Quality' several varieties of peaches, nectarines, apricots, figs, pears and plums, as well as grapes. These, which he grew on walls between his wall-fruit trees, included the Canadian Parsley vine, the Arboyle (small, white and the 'most delicious of all Grapes that are not Muscat'), the Grizelin or Pale Red Burgundy (for an east wall), the Dowager (a black Muscat, 'ripens well') and the Grizelin Frontignac - 'the noblest of all Grapes I ever eat in England' ('needs the hottest wall and sharpest gravel').[12]

Forty years later, as Stephen Switzer observed, some of these varieties had disappeared. The names of others had changed beyond recognition. Nevertheless, some good kinds remained; Switzer recommended, for the open, in English gardens, the early varieties of blue Frontignan and Muscadine (also known as Sweetwater and Chasselas); Cluster

Currants; Zantoignes, Corinthian Currants or July Grapes; Parsley Grapes and Muscats of Jerusalem (Muscats of Alexandria).[13] He also mentioned the suitability of gravelly soils such as are found around London, the possibility of keeping ripe bunches on the vine in special glasses or bags, and the forcing of grapes on flued walls, which he himself first saw sometime before 1717, at Belvoir Castle.[14] The Second Duke of Rutland's vines – Frontignans, ripe by July – were grown at Belvoir on sloping fruit walls heated by smoke-filled flues. The walls were later covered with glass casements (see Chapter 3).

THE USE OF FLUED WALLS

The invention (see Chapter 3) of the hot wall or stove wall meant that grapes, like other tender outdoor fruits, could now be grown in all parts of England. Thomas Hitt, who had served his apprenticeship as a gardener at Belvoir under the second duke, was of the opinion that all large gardens in the north of England should have hot walls, if ripe grapes were to be obtained. He also supported the view that if early grapes were wanted the vines could share a stove house with other exotics, though 'the fruit is never so well flavoured as those which have the benefit of the dews'.[15]

Flued grape walls were now made upright (the sloping wall being 'attended with a great disadvantage, for the wet lodges upon and decays the fruit'), about ten or twelve feet high, with borders of a corresponding width

in front. The glasses sloped from the top of the wall to the front of the border, so that early crops of kitchen vegetables could also be forced beneath them. Hitt found, however, that his best-flavoured and largest grapes grew on a flued wall no more than four and a half feet high, with the vines protected by glasses on frosty nights.

THE FIRST PROPER VINERIES

From the 1770s separate hothouses – 'graperies' or vineries – began to be built for the benefit of the dessert grape. The vines were still planted outside, entering the house through holes in the low parapet walls which supported sloping glazed sashes above, where they were trained and bore their fruit as before. In the depths of winter, while the rods were leafless and forcing had just begun, pots, boxes and tubs of French beans, strawberries, spring bulbs and early summer flowers were also forced, making use of the floor space below the vine.

To admit more sunlight to the floor, the front walls of the forcing houses described by John Abercrombie in 1781 were given upright glasses to a height of six feet. These houses were forty to fifty feet long, twelve to fourteen feet wide, and provided with flued back walls ten to twelve feet high.[16] Besides grapes, Abercrombie forced peaches, nectarines, apricots, cherries, early figs, dwarf currants, gooseberries and raspberries. As well as the usual French beans, straw-berries, spring flowers and bulbs, he also forced peas, beans, carrots, cauliflowers, mint and celery.

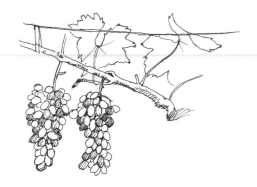

William Speechly's vinery of 1790 was similar. It was a lean-to running east to west, with a back wall ten to fourteen feet high and a border ten feet wide inside, but it had lower front glasses to allow for a slope on the roof of 43 degrees – the proper angle, he said, for vines forced after the vernal equinox.[17] Calculations of the angle of the sun's rays as they fell on a glass roof at different times of the year led to the creation of lean-tos with a 'sharp pitch' (45–50 degrees) for early forcing and a flatter roof (40 degrees) with longer rafters for main or late crops.[18]

THE DEVELOPMENT OF FORCING

Theoretically, any variety of vine could be forced as soon as its leaves had fallen, so fruit could be picked as early as March, but with the later varieties this was found to produce inferior fruit. Forcing was therefore restricted to early varieties.

If ripe grapes were wanted in May, forcing began early in the New Year. The parts of the stems projecting outdoors were wrapped with hay bandages, moss, bracken or hessian, and the outside bed was covered with dry litter. Inside, the heat was raised to a minimum of 50°F/10C and a maximum of 55°F/13C, slowly increasing as the buds swelled, then burst, sending out leaves, stems and flowers. By the time the fruit had set, the heat was up to a minimum of 75°F/24C and a maximum of 80°F/27C, though higher temperatures were not unknown. In the first stage of forcing, the right degree of humidity was provided either by means of evaporating pans laid along the heating flues or pipes, or by watering the paths within and syringing the leaves with water (warmed if necessary) at regular intervals throughout the day. Later, when vineries had beds inside as well as outside, humidity and nourishment were also provided by a bed of strawy, rotted dung laid on the borders inside the house. When the vines began flowering, syringing and watering ceased, so as not to impede pollination. These activities were resumed as soon as the fruit formed. As it ripened, the top and front ventilators were kept open, and 'a little warmth' was allowed to circulate – but in 1957, 'with the price of fuel at its present shocking high level' the gardener was advised to lay dry straw on all the borders, to retain heat, prevent the problem of split berries and create 'a warm, dry, buoyant atmosphere'.[19]

At the other end of the season, when late grapes were left on the vine to preserve them

through the winter and as far as possible into the early spring, the aim was to avoid damp, which would encourage mould on the fruit. The inside border was therefore covered in dry sand, ashes or gravel; leaves were removed from around the bunches, and gentle heat, combined with fresh air, was administered on damp, gloomy days. By letting the fires out in the afternoon and shutting the late vinery tight at night, varieties which had ripened in the late autumn, such as St Peter's, Black Raisin, the Syrian, the Black Damascus and the White Muscat of Alexandria, could be kept on the vine until February, if not longer. By this means, and by forcing the Frontignacs and Sweetwaters in his early house so that they ripened on 1 May, a record of some sort was achieved by Richard Arkwright, a gardener at Willersley in Derbyshire. He was able to provide his employer on that day in 1810 with freshly gathered table grapes of both the current and the previous year.[20]

The Victorian and Edwardian gardener was certainly expected to supply his employer with hothouse grapes all the year round. Early varieties would be ripe from the end of April and the best keepers, usually the last to ripen, could be stored on the vine itself or in the fruit room (see Chapter 18). Some varieties, most notably Lady Downe's Seedling, will keep for almost six months; ripening from August onwards, the grape can hang in the vinery until March, though it has been known to keep in the fruit room until the end of May or even into June.

At Pylewell, grapes like these were grown in the two vineries (one for early, one for mid to late-season fruit) until just before the Second World War. But vineries need subtle, watchful management. For old gardeners like Mr Hamilton, the forcing of grapes was akin to a form of religion; for his underlings it was more like a form of tyranny. Every part of the vine – its roots, main stems, shoots, leaves, flowers and fruit – received careful attention. The vine was fed, watered, syringed, warmed and shaded, ventilated, de-infested, pruned, disbudded, thinned and trained in a routine that demanded attention for three-quarters of the year. It was allowed to rest after forcing for three months, but in an establishment where vineries were kept in a constant state of successional production, the gardeners' vigilance lasted for 365 days a year.

THE GRAPE EARNS ITS ACCOLADE

By the 1780s the hothouse cultivation of the pineapple – the King of Fruits – had been mastered; but the horticultural secrets of producing superior table or dessert grapes, and forcing them so that they could be enjoyed all the year round, were still in the process of being discovered. It was another sixty years or so before it could be said that the produce of the vinery 'ranks next the pine, and is by some preferred to it'.

This accolade was eventually given to the grape by John Claudius Loudon in 1824.[21] By the end of the century hundreds of varieties were grown in British vineries and

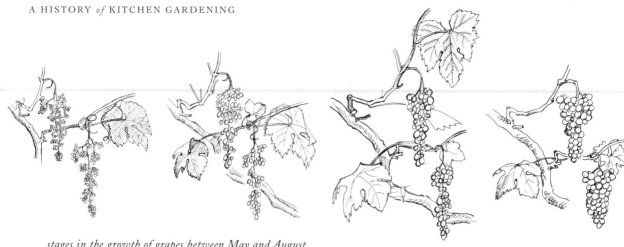

stages in the growth of grapes between May and August

the grapes that graced the fruit bowls of Victorian and Edwardian buffets and dining tables were the envy of the horticultural world. They came to be known as gourmet's grapes. They were presented either among elaborate arrangements of fruit or on separate dishes as perfectly symmetrical bunches; shouldered, long and tapering; small and cylindrical or compactly conical – always with their bloom intact and often with berries the size of small plums. They ranged in season, colour, shape and flavour from the early, tender-skinned Sweetwaters, such as the firm-fleshed, amber-coloured, oval-berried, honeyed Golden Chasselas, through the rich, mid-season, round-berried, musk-flavoured Frontignacs and Muscats like the red Catawbas and the purple-black Muscats of Alexandria, to the vinous Black Hamburghs, which yielded huge, late, large-berried bunches. (All these old varieties are still grown today.)

The reputation of English hothouse grapes in the first decades of the twentieth century was such that they were actually exported to America by commercial growers; Alicantes and Gros Colmars were the favourites. Early grapes were so highly prized in the 1870s and 1880s that they fetched what were then astonishing prices – from fifteen to twenty shillings per pound.

A CONTINUOUS SUPPLY OF GRAPES

Just as the fruiting season of the pineapple was extended by combining the art of forcing with a choice of early and late-fruiting varieties, so it was with the nineteenth-century dessert grape. Succession vineries were used to provide early, mid-season and late grapes. Grand establishments might even have a fourth vinery, for heat-loving Muscats. The use and timing of heat was different in each house. Once forcing had been started, a crop of ripe grapes could be expected five to six months later. If forcing began in the early vinery in November (the earliest practicable time), ripe fruit would be available in April. If it started at Christmas, fruit could be picked by May or June, in time for the London 'Season'. In the mid-season vinery, heat was only necessary to assist in the setting and ripening of fruit in cold summers. In the late vinery, heat would be needed partly for ripening and partly to keep damp and mould at bay, especially where grapes were left on the vine throughout the winter.

VINERY BORDERS

By the mid nineteenth century early vineries had beds inside the house for greater warmth. Mid-season vineries might have had the beds half in and half outside; late vineries had borders outside. As a general rule the border, wherever it was, should be as wide as the house is high.

When grapes were first grown in hothouses and trained above pineapples, the vines were raised annually in pots and trained to one stem or rod. When well-rooted, with sufficiently long stems, they were planted in an outside bed and the stems were poked through holes at the top of the front wall, just below the glass. (The advantage of a single stem, with short spurs, as Charles M'Intosh observed, was to reduce the amount of shade falling on the pines below).[22] The earliest vineries (circa 1770) had a similar arrangement of holes in the front wall, but in these vineries the borders, well provided with two feet of rich turfy loam lying over a one-foot layer of drainage provided by lime-rubbish, stones and gravel, were only five feet wide, for the vines were replaced every two years at least.

The provision of arches under the front wall of the vinery – similar to the arched foundations beneath fruit walls (see Chapter 5) appears to have begun in the early years of the nineteenth century. According to a description of the planting of the vinery at Shobden Court in Herefordshire, which had been built in 1805, both the front wall and its flue stood on wide arches, so that the roots of the vines 'had liberty to extend themselves either way without interruption.'[23]

William Atkinson, a London architect, was instrumental in promoting this, and other significant improvements to the form and heating of vineries. He did away with the upright glasses forming the front of the house, and reverted to the slope-roofed design of Justice's pinery of 1732. (This saved one-third of the gross cost of the glass, an important factor while glass was still taxed.) The front wall of the vinery was only two feet high, resting on arches below ground level. The glass roof, whose panes, for economy, measured only six by four inches, sloped from the top of the back wall to the top of the front wall. This alteration in design incorporated an improved form of ventilation (see Chapter 13).

Atkinson also made several improvements to the furnaces then used for heating hothouses, chief of which was a pair of 'dumb' or 'dead' plates which helped to carbonize the fuel and consume smoke. In another innovation (or rather re-invention, for this, too, is seen in Justice's pinery), his hot-air flues ran under the floor and along the front of the house, where they rose above floor level, leaving space for the vine

to be planted between the flue and the inside of the front wall. Atkinson later invented a hot-water boiler, which greatly simplified that form of hothouse heating (see Chapter 13).[24]

The border outside a vinery frequently sinks from disuse, so that the uppermost parts of the arches in the front wall are revealed. Previously, they would have been invisible; the soil would have just covered the tops of the arches. The borders would have sloped downwards towards the sun for good drainage and warmth. At Pylewell as elsewhere, any horse, cow, sheep, cat or dog that died on the farm was buried in this bed, which was in any case well manured. Fresh stable manure was heaped on it as well, in spring, to warm it up, the bulk of this being removed in mid-May to allow the heat of the sun to reach the soil.

New vine rods, when needed, were planted in the autumn or spring, but never in mid-winter, for the idea was that the roots should make rapid growth in warm soil. Good drainage also helped to warm the bed; if the roots entered cold, wet soil or subsoil, either split berries or 'shanking' (the drying-up of the berries and their stalks before the grapes are ripe) would be the result. While the berries were ripening, some gardeners would lay sheets of corrugated iron over the outside border, to carry away surplus rain and keep the roots warm and dry.

Warmth in the vinery border was so much sought-after that in the 1850s at Trentham, the Duke of Sutherland's seat in Staffordshire, the vinery borders (already provided with a ten-inch layer of stones and brickbats for drainage) were dug to the required depth of twenty inches, then permanently covered in a thin shell of concrete. 'As a deviation so great from formerly established rules, it created at the time no little speculation', but it was argued (by the landscape gardener Robert Marnock, whose description this is) that where the bed was in a low and damp situation, this unusual, impermeable covering did not deprive the vine of water, as its roots received moisture from below, by 'capillary attraction'. Manure, in liquid form, could be applied via drain tiles which would 'act as distributors'. An important virtue of the concrete shell was that it reduced evaporation; above all, it increased the heat of the soil beneath. In short, it maintained a uniformity of humidity and temperature in the border; moreover, it acted as 'a complete preventive' for what was then regarded as 'a common evil – . . . the all but irresistible temptation to dig up and crop vine borders'.[25] The famous Hampton Court vine was cited as a similar case; it flourished with no prepared border and it had a paved floor inside the house. The secret of its fruitfulness is likely, however, to be the fact that its roots were found to have travelled into a nearby sewer. Vines which had their roots under tan beds were equally fruitful. John Mearns, gardener to William Hanbury at Shobdon Court in Herefordshire, advocated 'chambering' the borders, by giving the roots of each vine its own compartment, the divisions to be made with brick or stone walls.[26]

PRUNING AND TRAINING

The vine fruits on shoots made the same year, and is usually pruned back in winter to within two or three eyes of the old wood. By tradition, pruning begins on the shortest day, just before Christmas or, in the case of early and late vines, as soon as the leaves had fallen. This is the time to wash the glass, walls, ironwork and timbers, to pull loose bark off the rods and to treat them with an insecticidal plaster (one old recipe was a mixture of tar oil or nicotine, Gishurst compound and sulphur, with cow dung and clay to make it stick).

The vine rods are taken off the roof trellis for pruning, then left in a horizontal position until growth or forcing begins, when they are tied up again. This allows the sap to reach the furthest extremities. Pruning and disbudding leaves the rods with just enough spurs and buds to supply the fruiting shoots for the next season. The new shoots are trained to fill all the available space on the trellis beneath the vinery roof while producing the optimum number of bunches at the optimum size – quality rather than quantity is the aim. The new shoots of established rods are trained laterally by tying them to the trellis under the vinery roof – about eighteen inches from the glass or the leaves and fruit will scorch – and stopped after the appearance of two or three clusters of flowers (the future bunches of fruit). Pruning and pinching-out continues throughout the summer, to allow sufficient light and heat to reach the fruit.

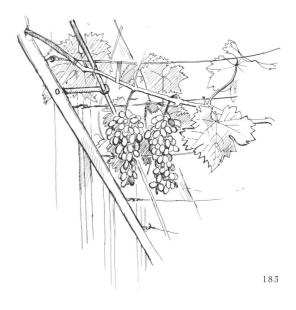

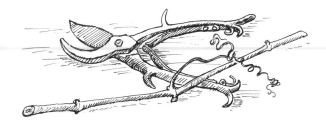

At first, when vines were trained on walls and espaliers in the open, they were given the same shapes as trained wall-fruit trees: that is, the main stem was allowed to send out branches which were then pruned and tied-in to take the forms of espaliers or fans. On bringing them into the vinery, the same form of training – fans or espaliers – was practised. By the end of the nineteenth century, however, the training of hothouse vines as single rods was favoured.

When the vine is in flower a wonderful scent fills the vinery. Mr Hamilton used to go through his vineries every day at noon, tapping the rods to shake the pollen free. He assisted the Muscats, which are known as 'shy bearers', by brushing their flowers with a rabbit's tail on a stick. Other aids to pollination were to stroke each cluster with the palm of the hand, or to shake the pollen on to a sheet of glass and blow. After the berries have set, the finest bunches are left and surplus bunches removed, so that each rod will only bear the number it can best support and nourish.

THINNING THE BERRIES

One of the earliest, if not *the* earliest descriptions of berry thinning appears in 1771.[27] It is a tedious but necessary procedure which is carried out more than once during the growing period. The aim is to have large, ripe, well-coloured berries and to prevent mould. When the berries are the size of small peas, the task of thinning begins. All the smallest interior and seedless berries are snipped out first, followed by enough to thin the bunches by as much as a quarter to a third of their fruit. Any berries that might give the bunch an unbalanced shape are also snipped off.

Thinning requires patience, skill and stamina. The job would usually be carried out by a young journeyman, who would spend long hours under the vine, with his arms stretched up to reach the overhead bunches and a soft silk handkerchief tied over his head, for at this stage the bloom on the grapes would be forming and any abrasion from rough hair or a cloth cap would remove it for good, ruining the final effect. To assist with the thinning, he would prise the fruit apart with a fine, pencil-length, pointed stick or, with the aid of a loop of raffia he would gently lift each cluster forming the bunch. The surplus berries were snipped out with special vinery scissors. The snipped-off grapes were kept and taken to the kitchen, either to make well-sugared 'spring tarts' and pies or to be pressed for verjuice.

Once the thinning had been done, if the grapes were of a variety whose bunches formed wide 'shoulders', the bunches were strung up to the wires or to lateral shoots to encourage the formation of a good shape.

SHADING AND VENTILATION

As summer approaches, heat and light from the sun increase and so shading becomes necessary. Gardeners of Mr Hamilton's generation painted a special wash called 'Summer Cloud' on the glass, or let down slatted blinds on rollers. Earlier gardeners relied on the vine's own leaves in conjunction with light blinds of bunting or tiffany. The pulleys for these blinds can still be seen on some old vinery walls, though the cords and rollers have long since vanished. Black grapes need more shade than white; Muscat houses were given no shading, as they needed all the sunlight they could get, but individual bunches of Muscats had sheets of tissue paper fixed over them to encourage a golden colour. Before the repeal of the Glass Tax in 1845, glazing had to be done with the cheapest glass, and irregularities in the smoothness or thickness of the panes, which might also be blistered, wrinkled or bowed, could cause accidental scorching to the leaves and fruit. Shading was therefore essential.

With thinning and shading completed, the routine of feeding, watering, damping-down and, above all, ventilating, continued. The rule in a vinery was, 'always ventilate at 70°F [21C]'. For gardeners like Mr Hamilton, the execution of this rule demanded constant vigilance. If a cloud hovered over the sun, the ventilators had to be closed instantly; as soon as it had passed, the ventilators were opened again.

Pulleys, winding wheels, counter-weights, connecting rods, levers and ratchets that opened and closed the sashes and ventilators are all still in place in the vinery at Pylewell, marked with the name of their maker, Foster Pearson. They were made to a design that was originally perfected for the royal kitchen gardens at Windsor in the 1850s. With just one handle, all the front glasses, or all the back ventilators, or all the roof lights can be opened or shut at the same time.

The crucial weeks were not only those when the grapes were ripening (when the air needed to be kept warm, mobile and not too muggy), but also, as always where fruit is concerned, during February, March and April, when the sun was hot but the air was cold. The temperature inside the vinery could shoot up to over 80°F/26C in a trice; if clouds hid the sun while the sashes or ventilators were open, the temperature could fall to near freezing, with devastating effect on bursting buds and young growth. While the fruit was ripening, all openings made by ventilating shutters and windows were covered with fine gauze or butter muslin to keep the birds and wasps out.

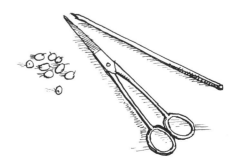

VICTORIAN HOTHOUSES

A Range of Glass (c.1870) *with a plant-house centre, three-quarter-span vineries either side & lean-to peach houses each end*

Paxton's Ridge & Furrow Roof (1835)

Paxton's Patent Portable Hothouse (1858) *with hinged roof and grooved wall-plates*

ground level

Ventilator mechanism (c.1880)

3 — ft
2 —
1 —
0 —

0 1 2 3 4 5   10 *feet*

Moore's ¾-Span Cucumber House with tanked bed (mid-19th c.)

warm, moist air
watering pipes
cucumber bed →
hot-water tank →
forcing bed →
hot-water pipes
cold air

0   5   10 *ft*

A Span-roofed Orchard House of brick, iron and glass (mid 19th c.)

0   5   10   20 *feet*

Susan Campbell 1996

CHAPTER THIRTEEN

THE NINETEENTH-CENTURY GLASSHOUSE RANGE

VENTILATION

As early as the 1690s John Evelyn had observed that plants would die (like animals or people) if they were confined in a space with 'pent-in air', and he duly suggested a means of solving that problem (see Chapter 10). But although the idea was sound, it was not taken up with any enthusiasm by the gardening fraternity as a whole.

The ventilation of hothouses was necessary for several reasons: to lower the temperature, to release stale air and replace it with fresh, to raise or lower the humidity of the house and to provide a beneficial current of air (a gentle movement, rather than a full-scale draught).

Air could of course be cooled and replaced simply by opening or closing the doors, windows and sashes, but the dangers of excessive heat or cold, of strong draughts or damage from rain, made this form of ventilation rather hazardous. In fact, the doors, shutters and glazing of the earliest glasshouses were often so ill-fitting that ventilation of a kind occurred willy-nilly.

Theories about the necessity of ventilation, and the bad effects of the lack of it in frames and greenhouses, proliferated during the eighteenth and nineteenth centuries. After making numerous experiments with the circulation of sap, the eighteenth-century scientist and botanist Stephen Hales decided that plants grew mouldy in 'a close, damp air' because the sap stagnated under those conditions.[1]

In 1846 the botanist and Secretary of the Horticultural Society of London, Dr John

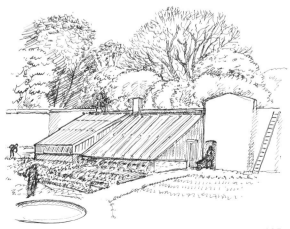

Lindley, described the situation of plants confined in stagnant air as 'like nothing so much as a criminal set fast in an everlasting pillory'. He claimed that moving air was essential because it increased the plant's capacity to absorb food (vital carbonic acid) through its leaves during the night, and assisted the removal of 'perspiration' during the day. It must therefore be constantly available, but once again: 'How to secure that is the great horticultural problem which now remains to be solved.'[2] The solution, which was not dissimilar to Evelyn's, had in fact been available for some time, but it was misunderstood and misused by the majority of gardeners, thus justifying Lindley's anxiety. The problem was solved by admitting air low down in the front of the house at a point where it would encounter some form of heat from a flue, steam pipe or hot-water pipe, and would therefore rise. By opening more ventilators high up at the back of the house, a current would be formed and the warmed air would exit, taking stale air with it. This form of ventilation is a great deal more satisfactory than the opening of sashes, doors or windows.

Walter Nicol used this method in a greenhouse at the beginning of the nineteenth century. He made ventilators in his hothouse at the top of the back wall, avoiding the shed behind it. They opened like windows. Where there was no shed, he built chimney-like apertures, with air tubes fixed inside and wooden sashes in front, to be raised or lowered as needed. At the same time he drilled one-inch holes in the front wall, six to eight feet apart. Into each of these holes he inserted a tin tube, with a funnel on the outside and a fine rose, similar to that of a watering can, on the inside.[3]

A few years later William Atkinson improved on this method by introducing hinged, horizontal, wooden ventilators low down in the front wall which corresponded with sliding, horizontal wooden ventilators just below the roof in the back wall. When the front vents were opened the air was drawn into the house over a heated front flue. It rose to the back of the house and exited through the top vents (opened by vertical slides operated by pulleys and weights) into a cavity in the wall which was open above the roof. The roofs did away with sashes and were made in one sealed piece.

Front and back ventilators worked in unison were so obviously the solution that it is hard to understand how their misuse occurred. However, their opening and shutting were apparently governed solely by the state of the thermometer and, with the roof sealed shut, they were opened only to reduce temperatures during the day; frequently only the top or only the bottom vents were opened, thus cheating the plants of their aeration, and the house was invariably shut tight at night. Eventually, sliding sashes, hinged front lights, ventilators front and back and ventilated floors were all to be found in the mid to late nineteenth-century glasshouse, and an understanding of their purpose was drummed into every apprentice, so that a perfect environment could be created for almost any plant.

IRON AND WOOD

Until early in the nineteenth century, glasshouses had been built only with masonry or bricks, glass and timber; now their builders began to use iron and copper as well as wood, and a debate immediately started as to the respective virtues and drawbacks of each material. The two main protagonists were John Claudius Loudon and Charles M'Intosh; both were the authors of numerous works on horticulture, but the former was more of a theorist while the latter relied on direct experience.

Loudon had 'no hesitation in giving the preference to metal over wood'.[4] With its flexibility, delicacy of appearance and 'greater latitude of form and dimension', iron was certainly more suitable than wood for curvilinear roofs. It was also an essential material for the large, domed conservatories that it was helping to make so fashionable. Malleable yet strong and durable, slender iron beams and rafters also allowed more light to enter the house than their counterparts in bulky wood. Iron, said Loudon, was cheaper to buy, and it transmitted heat more rapidly than wood.

Wood, for M'Intosh, was equally suitable: it was economical, durable and elegant. Iron, for him, had several disadvantages. The two main objections were that wrought iron was subject even more than cast iron to rust and both needed frequent repainting; also that its expansion and contraction in extremes of heat and cold caused glass to crack and sashes to stick. M'Intosh complained that

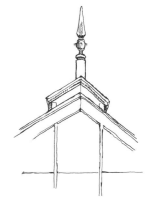

iron sashes expanded to such an extent that: 'The strength of two or even three men has not been enough to force down the sliding roofs for air'.[5]

M'Intosh compared the maintenance costs of two houses of the same dimensions, one made of iron, the other of wood; he found that the cost of repairing the iron house was nearly double that of the wood. Moreover, though wood was dearer, it was cheaper to build with because it was more easily taken to pieces and recycled. Twenty years later, with improved ventilation and heating, the general view was that iron was better for large houses but that small houses should be made of wood.

By 1870 a combination of wood and metal was used in the construction of greenhouses. Houses designed for the raising of plants in pots (other than pineapples) were provided with staging, rather than beds and borders.

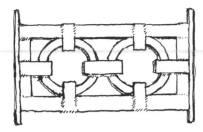

The staging was usually supported by an iron framework standing on iron legs, and made of slate, finely corrugated iron sheeting covered in small pebbles, or wooden battens. Iron was also used for the supports to staging, the interior paths or gratings that covered underground heating pipes, the mechanisms used for opening and closing ventilators, and the decorative grilles covering ventilator openings.

CURVILINEAR ROOFS

In 1815 the mineralogist and horticulturist Sir George Mackenzie suggested that horticultural glasshouses should have hemispherical roofs, in order to 'receive the greatest possible quantity of the sun's rays, at all times of the day and at all seasons of the year'.[6] Loudon discussed the idea and proposed improvements, inventing in 1816 a curved, wrought-iron sash bar. In the summer of 1820 the distinguished president of the Horticultural Society of London, Thomas Andrew Knight, built himself a new pinery at Downton Castle, his country seat in Herefordshire, with a curvilinear iron roof 'of the kind invented by Mr Loudon of Bayswater'. Knight's intention was to 'obtain the greatest possible influence of light, and command of solar heat' for his pineapples, in the hope that he could dispense with the use of bottom heat and tan beds, yet prolong their fruiting season from early spring to late autumn.

His new house had one fire, with a flue heating the floor in a triple turn. The iron rafters curved from a low parapet wall in front to the top of the back wall, which was eight and a half feet high and built, like the end walls, of brick. The glass panes were laid in a rock-hard composition of white lead, oil and flint sand, which also sealed the overlaps, so that with the ventilators shut the house was virtually airtight (it had ventilators similar to those invented by Atkinson). In effect, he had created an oven. Lack of attention to ventilation on a bright spring day caused all his closely shut-up plants (hitherto his best pines ever) to burn and spoil. Further attempts failed to produce the pineapples he desired. Eventually he gave up and grew vines through the pipe holes which he had added in the front wall as an additional form of ventilation.[7]

By 1872 curvilinear houses had fallen out of favour. They proved more expensive to build than the usual type of house and, since ventilation was insufficient unless they were provided with movable sashes, they were incapable of being made rain-proof. Moreover, the principle of letting in maximum sunshine also allowed them to admit maximum cold.

SPAN ROOFS

As early as 1805 Loudon illustrated a span-roofed glasshouse which, being made of glass on all sides would admit more light than a lean-to. The house should run north-south rather than east-west.[8] The extra heating necessary and the cost of glass inhibited the early development of this idea, although it was cheaper than a curvilinear house; but span-roofed houses were common by the mid-century. Ventilation at the top of such houses was by means of a hood above the central ridge.

Between the two World Wars the celebrated span-roofed late vinery at Longleat in Wiltshire, 180 feet long, was always used in the shooting season as a dining room for the guns' lunches. The guests could help themselves to grapes – black one end, white the other. In 1855 M'Intosh installed span-roofed vineries at Dalkeith (where he was gardener to the Duke of Buccleuch). These vineries were heated by 'air-drains' connected to a heated chamber below the central corridor. The air within was regulated by metallic traps; heated ventilation was thus provided above and below floor level, advantageously bringing the roots into growth before the buds.

In the three-quarter-span vinery at Windsor Castle vines could be grown at the back of the house as well as under the rafters; both the width of the roof and the height of the house were greater than they would be in a lean-to, and could be extended.

PAXTON'S RIDGE AND FURROW ROOF
Having invented the wrought-iron sash bar in 1816, Loudon is further credited with inventing, in the same year, the principles of the ridge and furrow roof, but it was the Duke of Devonshire's gardener, Joseph Paxton, who first put this system into practice.[9]

The ridge and furrow roof was designed to allow the sun's rays to enter the house both earlier and later in the day than it would in a plain lean-to; it also attracted less violent heat at midday. As the entire roof sloped gently downwards, the furrows or valleys between the ridges formed gutters for rainwater, which was directed into hollow, upright supports on the front of the house, to tanks within. Paxton first experimented with ideas for his 'angled roof' in 1828, and built the first of its kind in 1832 at Chatsworth in Derbyshire, symbolically bridging one and a half centuries by re-roofing the 1698 greenhouse in this manner. Visitors to Chatsworth will see another example of this type of roof on Paxton's peach case, or 'conservative wall' which was built in 1838. Paxton also used the system to build the magnificent three-quarter-acre Great Stove at Chatsworth between 1836 and 1840, and an even greater glasshouse in London, the two-acre Crystal Palace, built for the Great Exhibition in 1851.

PAXTON'S PORTABLE HOTHOUSES
In 1858 Paxton applied for a patent for his portable hothouses. These were designed not for great public spaces or the gardens of dukes, but for kitchen or market gardeners of 'short or uncertain tenure' who wanted to

take their hothouses with them if or when their agreements ended. The design was based on a folding hut frame that Paxton had devised for the Crimean campaign. The only masonry needed was for supporting walls and piers, to which a wall plate was fixed. This served a dual purpose as a gutter and a groove for the sashes.

The sashes were bolted together, top and bottom. Each one was four and a half feet wide and eight to sixteen feet high; they were separated by smaller sashes only nine inches wide, which opened outwards and acted as ventilators. There were no rafters; span houses had the tops hinged together, lean-tos used the wall as support. This form of construction, advertised in the gardening

press of the day as 'Hothouses for the Million', was used to make vineries, fruit houses, peach houses, and pits for bedding-out plants, pines, melons or cucumbers. By lowering the walkway inside to below ground level, plenty of headroom was created for the gardener (see page 186).[10]

THE ORCHARD HOUSE

An equally versatile form of glasshouse had been invented in 1848 by Thomas Rivers, the nurseryman and orchardist. This was the orchard house, a span-roofed or lean-to structure of any length from ten to one hundred feet, and as wide as possible. It was tall enough to accommodate a mixed collection of the dwarf fruit trees that were Rivers's speciality, either growing in pots or in borders within the house. The choicest varieties of apples, pears, peaches, nectarines, plums, apricots and cherries were grown in dwarf form, as well as grapes and figs (see page 186).

The expense of building a separate house for each kind of fruit, which was then the practice in the grandest gardens, was thereby avoided, and as fruit trees in pots are portable, the hardier varieties could be taken into the house for forcing or ripening and brought out again afterwards. Ventilation was simplified by sliding the roof sashes from one end to another and removing the end glasses altogether in warm weather, to provide as natural an environment as possible. Very cheap, unheated orchard houses could be made with weather-boarding for the sides and ordinary sashes for the roofs. These structures were advertised as being ideal for the amateur gardener, whose needs were increasingly catered for by greenhouse manufacturers and seedsmen as the nineteenth century progressed.

With extra heating, Rivers created a tropical environment in his orchard house. Here he grew oranges, mangosteens, cherimoyas *(Annona cherimola)*, pomegranates, lychees, guavas and mangoes. This house, he thought, with its warm dry air, would make a good sanatorium for invalids. He later had the idea of putting orchard houses on tramways, so they could be moved to an adjacent plot at the end of each season – a system that can still be seen today in market gardens.

THE GLASSHOUSE AFTER 1845
The repeal of the Glass Tax in Britain gave a tremendous boost to the building and design of glasshouses. The effect was seen almost at once. Amazing stoves and conservatories were constructed in the great gardens of the aristocracy, and there was a proliferation of more modest hothouses and conservatories in humbler gardens. The price of sheet glass fell to ten per cent of what it had been when the tax had been in force. (The cost of taxed glass was two shillings per foot; the same glass, untaxed, cost tuppence.)

With the repeal of the tax, panes became larger, the practice of sealing the one-inch overlaps of glass with lead or putty was gradually dropped, and a smaller, unsealed overlap of a quarter inch or less was favoured. Curvilinear overlaps, to carry rain away from the glazing bars, were invented at this time. With the cost of just one of the necessary materials reduced by almost ninety per cent, huge ranges of glass were soon to be found in all the best kitchen gardens. They were constructed primarily for forcing fruit, flowers and the choicer sorts of vegetables and salads, and could now be seen in a beautifully arranged variety of lean-tos, spans, pits and frames. These ranges would also include ornamental stove houses for orchids or palms, ferneries, heath houses and even aquatic houses. The greatest cost of a hothouse now was not its glass, but the fuel with which to heat it.

THE BOILER
Until the Second World War, the hothouses at Pylewell were heated by two boilers. The war effort spared the small one which heated the early vinery, but the big boiler, a Robin Hood made in Nottingham, was never replaced. The only evidence that it ever

existed is a cavity in the brickwork that once encased it in the cellar, the coal-chute door above and the chimney still standing behind the vinery.

A complicated system of four-inch-diameter pipes heated first the vinery, and then ran underground to the three span-roofed houses used for growing orchids, carnations, cucumbers and melons, heating several pits as it returned, via the vinery and the mushroom house behind it, to the boiler. The quantity, size and disposition of the pipes in each house ensured that the correct amounts of heat were directed to the appropriate places; round the front, back and ends of the vinery border, below the staging supporting the beds in the span houses, and under the beds in the forcing pits. The circulation of warm air was assisted by 'cold-air drains' set below the pipes in the span houses. The outgoing pipes were naturally hotter than the returning pipes; this too was taken into consideration.

As anyone who uses a boiler for their central heating or bath water will know, the circulatory system by which hot-water heating works depends on the expansion of hot water into the space occupied by colder water. It seems so simple that it comes as some surprise to learn that hothouses were not heated by hot water until the 1820s and that pressurized steam heat preceded it by several decades.

STEAM HEAT

Experiments began in the mid eighteenth century to see if dung or tan-heated pits could be assisted by steam heat. Steam pumps and engines had been invented in the early years of the century for use in the pumping stations of Cornish tin mines. The most enquiring minds of the day were fascinated by the novelty of steam and its potential in other industries.

The old smoke flues and vaults frequently proved ungovernable and liable to collapse, due to frequent dousings of water when they overheated, which destroyed the cement; and fermenting dung was thought by many to give hotbed melons, strawberries, forced vegetables and salads a disagreeable taste. In the event, however, the necessary steam pipes, stopcocks, alembics, cisterns and furnaces of the steam-heated bed were found to be cumbersome, and most gardeners were doubtful if the thing was worth the trouble for the sake of a few early cauliflowers, salads and lettuces.

The idea of steam heat was good, but ahead of its time. It reappeared at the end of the century, when steam heating for pineries became widespread. Two factors combined to bring this about. First, tanners themselves, finding the old methods of tanning both tedious and expensive, eventually chose vitriolic acid as a faster and cheaper tanning agent than oak bark. Secondly, advances had been made in the technology of steam heating. The first attempt to steam heat a hothouse was made by a Mr Wakefield of Liverpool in 1788 and was 'afterwards effectively employed in the vault of a cucumber house at Knowsley by Butler, gardener to the Earl of

Derby'.[11] In 1791 a Mr Hoyle of Halifax patented a steam-heated hothouse.

The Earl of Derby's steam-heated cucumber pit was followed by steam-heated pits for melons and pines. Here, perforated steam pipes of lead or copper ran under the pits, heating a gradated mass of stones and pebbles. Paving stones were laid above the rubble, with gaps to allow the steam to pass into a bed of ashes, sand or soil. Pots of pineapples were plunged into the bed, which could also be planted direct. Variations on this theme were developed over the years.

At the beginning of the nineteenth century all the most advanced houses were heated by steam, which was conveyed from the boiler by a complex network of stopcocks, valves, traps and pipes. This had many advantages over the old smoke and fume-filled flue-heating system (although that system survived in some gardens well into the twentieth century).

Steam circulated easily, and its temperature was reliable – it never exceeded 212°F/100C, whether in pipes close to the boiler or in pipes 2,000 feet distant from it. It also saved fuel and labour: where there were previously dozens of little stoke-holes, each with its attendant ash heap, pile of fuel and chimney belching smoke and smuts, now there was only one fire, neat and compact, and one chimney. Moreover, pipes conveying steam took up less space than the old flues and needed no cleaning. To conserve heat, the steam boiler could be situated within the hothouse itself, with the furnace in the shed behind. However, there were disadvantages:

the furnace needed almost constant attendance to keep the water boiling; moreover, steam heat required an exorbitant initial outlay and cost a good deal to maintain, as well as being very liable to 'derangements'.

HOT WATER REPLACES STEAM

The coal or coke-fired hot-water boiler was invented in France in 1777 by a Monsieur Bonnemain, to heat incubators for hens' eggs. It made its first appearance in an English kitchen garden in 1816, at Sundridge Park in Kent.[12] It was introduced to England by the Marquis de Chabannes, who published an illustrated pamphlet explaining the system in 1818, showing a boiler working on what was later known as the 'thermosiphon principle'.

William Atkinson was therefore not the first to bring hot-water heating to the glasshouse (see Chapter 12), nor did he employ the thermosiphon principle in his first boiler, although he did understand the theory of circulation. However, his hot-water boiler, planned for a garden in Wales in 1822, worked well enough for engineers to realize that this was the way ahead.

Atkinson's boiler was simply a large, square, cast-iron container fixed like a cauldron over a fire that heated the sides, which were flued, as well as the bottom. The boiler, set in a niche in the back wall of the house and covered with a wooden lid, was on the same level as its distribution pipes. The heated water flowed out through an upper pipe to the furthest extent of the space to be heated, where it entered a reservoir or bend exactly level with the boiler. The water, somewhat cooled, then returned to the boiler, entering it at the bottom.

Thereafter, there were improvements and designs for boilers of all shapes and sizes, though boilers were generally made to three basic designs: the conical or cylindrical (an upright boiler with the fire inside the water-jacket); the saddleback (a horizontal water-jacket with an interior fire burning from front to back); and the tubular (similar to the conical boiler, except that the water was contained in tubes).

The advantages of the hot-water system over steam heat and smoke flues were, at an early stage, summed up by Charles M'Intosh. The heat was almost equally distributed in every part of the house; it continued, once heated, to provide heat long after the fire had gone out; the person in charge could therefore 'safely go to bed at nine o'clock, and by seven next morning find his house nearly at the same temperature in which he left it'. Hot-water heat was free of noxious gases, and it consumed less fuel than either steam or flued furnaces. It was more expensive to set up than flues, but cheaper than steam. It lasted longer than either, needed no annual expense, no repairs and no cleaning (unlike flues).[13]

One of the disadvantages of a heated house is that the atmosphere tends to dryness. At first this was countered by syringing the plants and damping down paths and borders with water, or by opening the steam valves of a steam boiler. Evaporating pans fixed over the flues and pipes eliminated the need for these measures. By the 1850s, earthenware pans about fifteen inches long and five inches wide were being manufactured. Alternatively, water troughs were set into the tops of cast-iron heating pipes.

ORNAMENTAL BOILER CHIMNEYS

The boiler chimneys stood for all to see above the roofs of a modest glasshouse range like Pylewell's. They gave, it is true, a somewhat industrial air to the kitchen garden. As this was something that the designers of more superior gardens were anxious to avoid, their chimneys were sometimes given lengthy underground flues and were either removed to a distant part of the grounds where they might be hidden in a tall shrubbery (as was the chimney of the Great Stove at Chatsworth) or decorated with pleasing architectural features and placed in the centre of the kitchen garden (as at Castle Howard in Yorkshire). The boiler chimney might even be disguised as a tree trunk (as at Cliveden in Buckinghamshire). At Tyninghame in East Lothian the chimney pots of a small greenhouse boiler are shaped like Grecian vases, giving an elegant appearance to the top of the garden wall, and a row of chimneys on top of a heated wall at Tatton Park, in Cheshire, are also shaped like urns.

ALTERNATIVE METHODS OF HEATING

The amount of fuel needed by the boilers at Pylewell – some forty tons of coke each winter – was small by comparison with some of the neighbouring estates, one of which consumed three tons a day. Percy Gregory remembered one exceptionally cold winter at Pylewell when the boilers used fifty tons before Christmas. It was his job to fetch the coke with the pony-cart from the local railway station.

At a rough calculation, the annual fuel bill of a moderate-sized range of glass equalled the annual wages of three men. Those who found the heating of a hothouse relatively expensive might therefore have been interested in ways of economizing on fuel. For Joseph French, 'a farmer of eminence' living at East Horndon in Essex, the answer was close to hand. Since 1795 he had forced his vines and nectarines in March by piling fresh cow dung from one end to the other of his fifty-four-foot-long vinery and sixty-foot-long nectarine house. The heaps were six or seven feet wide, leaving a path five or six feet wide along the back. 'The vapours bathed the leafless branches and destroyed all insect eggs.' As the steam abated, the buds opened. Fresh dung was added and covered with the old dung to encourage new heat and lessen the vapours. Temperatures inside the house were kept up all summer, at around 65-70°F/18-21C. In the summer of 1816, French picked between 600 and 700 bunches of grapes, totalling eleven and twelve hundredweight, and 1,200 nectarines. His only expense was one man's wages to attend the two houses, at 2s.6d. (12.5p) a fortnight.[14]

An even cheaper method was discovered in Russia, where a cattle shed was situated behind the greenhouse and their steamy breath used as the only form of heating. The moisture from cow breath saved watering, and the expired carbonic gas quickened and promoted vegetation.[15] This idea was actually carried out in Wales, by a Mr Lawson who built a 'cow-house vinery' at Tirydail, near Llandeilo, in 1852, 'and very pretty they [the cows] look with a row of chrysanthemums on the wall in front of them . . . a scarlet geranium too, planted in the open ground, and trained on the same wall looks very well and luxuriant.'[16]

IN THE BACKSHEDS

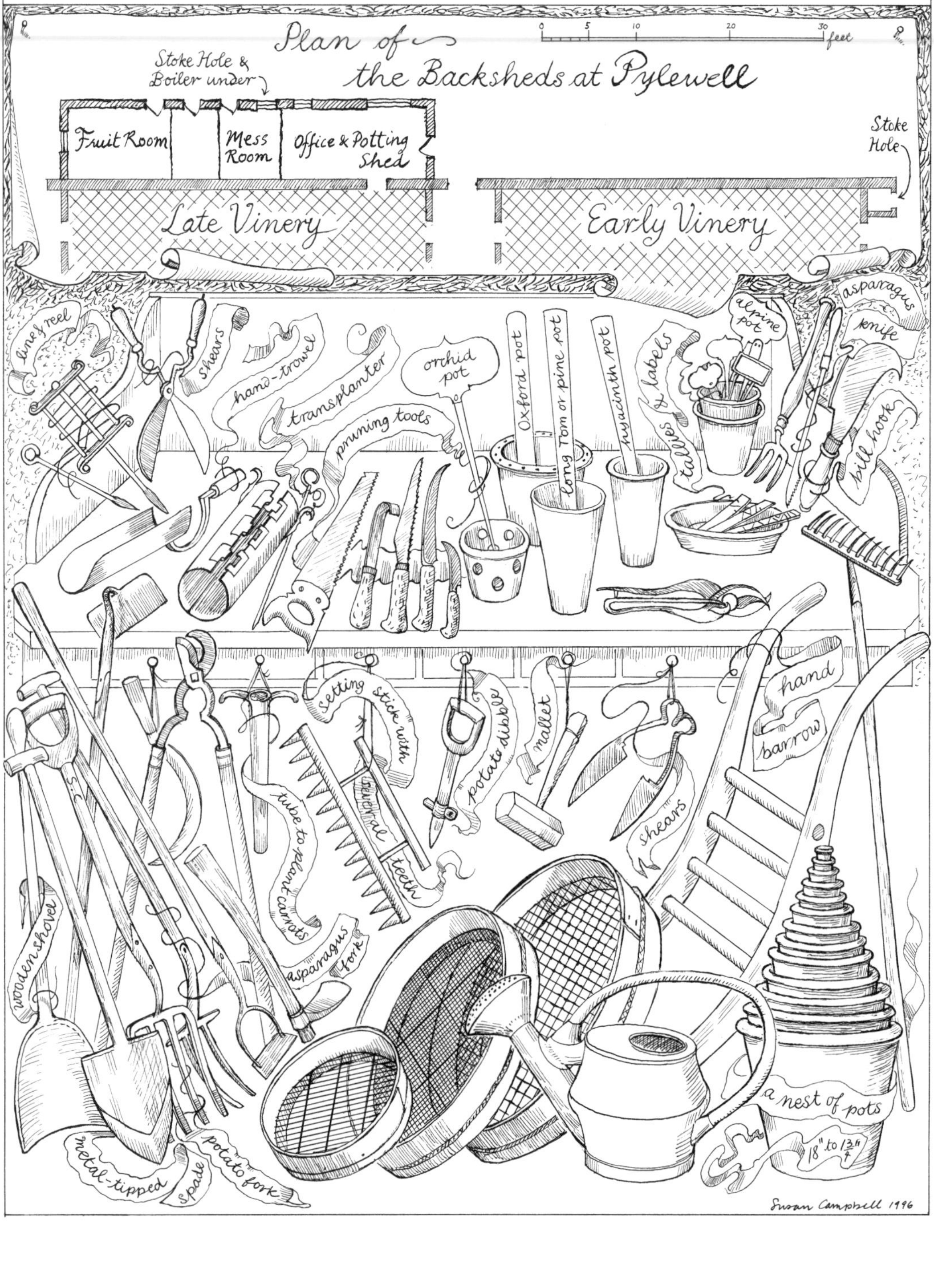

Plan of
the Backsheds at Pylewell

Stoke Hole &
Boiler under

| Fruit Room | | Mess Room | Office & Potting Shed |

Late Vinery

Early Vinery

Stoke Hole

0 5 10 20 30 feet

line & reel

shears

hand-trowel

transplanter

pruning tools

orchid pot

Oxford pot

Long Tom or pine pot

hyacinth pot

tallies & labels

alpine pot

asparagus knife

bill hook

setting stick with tube to plant carrots

crucial teeth

potato dibble

mallet

shears

hand barrow

wooden shovel

s.c.

asparagus fork

metal-tipped spade

potato fork

a nest of pots

18" to 12½"

Susan Campbell 1996

CHAPTER FOURTEEN

THE POTTING SHED

In many hothouse ranges, especially those with an ornamental plant house as the central feature, a door on the back wall would lead directly to the potting shed behind, so that the most tender plants were never subjected to an outside journey between potting bench and hothouse. Pot plants in transition stood on a small bench beside this door.

THE BACKSHEDS AT PYLEWELL

There is no such door at Pylewell, as the central gateway between the vineries gives easy access to the potting shed. It is the first shed one comes to in the range of slate-roofed, brick-built lean-tos that occupy the northern side of the late vinery wall. These backsheds are the direct opposite, both in situation and in appearance, of the warm, light-filled glasshouse on the southern, sunny side of the wall. They are well built but quite modest, and not as accommodating as the backsheds would be in a larger garden, which would include storage cellars and more storage, or even living space, in garrets above the rafters. By tradition backsheds were lined inside with dark brown, varnished matchboarding; storage rooms and mushroom houses would have insulated walls and ventilated ceilings. Here, the rooms are all plastered and whitewashed and the floors were made of plain deal. In a grander place they might be made of parquet or even (as at Windsor Castle) tessellated marble.

The size of the backsheds in most gardens was governed by the height of the wall behind them; obviously, the shallower the

boiler house and potting shed

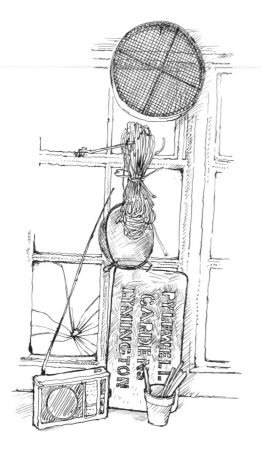

roof, the wider the sheds will be. Loudon, thought that an angle of 40 degrees was the minimum requirement if north-facing roofs were to dry off quickly in bad weather, and this would appear to be the angle of the roofs at Pylewell.

However, somewhat unusually, only one of the vineries, the late vinery at Pylewell, has backsheds built behind it (see page 198). There is no evidence, either on maps or on site, that they were ever built against the early vinery, which has only the smaller boiler room attached to it. (The old boiler is just visible in the cellar below, amongst a mass of ferns.) The existing sheds contain a

fruit room, a mess room, the large boiler room and a very long potting shed, which was also used as a packing room and Mr Hamilton's office. Mention is made in the 1850 Sale Catalogue of 'a range of Buildings for Tools, Stoke Holes, Mushroom Houses, Potting Houses . . . a Turf House and Fuel Store' which appear to be connected with Weld's Melon Ground and eighteen-light pineapple pit, and this was probably behind the early vinery (See Chapter 8). There is a small bothy or mess room with a cart shed on the outer, south-eastern corner of the wall and another tiny bothy faces it across the access drive in a little garden of its own.

With the possible exceptions of the fruit room and the head-gardener's office, the backsheds in grander gardens were the domain of the workforce. Because these were places in which the gardeners were given work to do whenever the weather outside was unsuitable, a good employer provided the workrooms with fireplaces, flues or heated pipes, and indeed someone has seen to it that Pylewell's mess room, potting shed and bothies all had little fireplaces. By convention and mutual agreement the worksheds were never visited by the gentry or their friends. Just as the boundary between the master's and servants' territory within the mansion – known there as 'above' and 'below' stairs – was marked by a physical barrier in the form of a green baize door, so in the kitchen garden the hothouse wall formed a boundary between master and servants.

THE POTTING SHED

No matter how old a kitchen garden may be, nor how long since it was abandoned, its potting shed tends to outlast all other garden edifices. This may be because it continues to be useful even if the rest of the garden and its staff have been made almost completely redundant. At Pylewell most of 'the offices', as the backsheds were called, were abandoned years ago and are in a state of ruin but, because the potting shed was still needed as a working shed, it is not as derelict as the rest. When I first saw it there was a transistor radio on the work bench and a good smell of tarred string, earth, machine oil and creosote. This room was not as cobwebbed or redolent of rot, rust and dust as the mess room, boiler room and fruit room. Although a broken window allowed a robin, a pair of swallows and a wren to make their nests in there, the roof was still intact and it was not overgrown or open to the skies like the rest of the sheds.

The potting shed even acted as a little museum. The initials of the last hired men from the old team were still painted on the wall beside pegs that once held their forks, spades and hoes, and here too was the set of stencils that was used to print those initials. They were made of thin sheet brass, each letter standing in its own slot in a little wooden box. Someone had propped up the stencilled template bearing the name of the estate on the window ledge, as if to remind themselves of the days when the garden produce was regularly packed up and sent

off to London. (Vegetable hampers and fruit-packing cases that have 'PYLEWELL GARDENS LYMINGTON' printed on them are still to be found in odd corners in the backsheds.)

Old-fashioned sulphurators, smoke diffusers, bellows and spray guns, red with rust, green with verdigris and blackened by smoke, stood neatly along the shelves above the door. Up in the rafters (supposedly out of the reach of a small garden boy), there was an assortment of battered tins, bottles, cartons, jars and canisters. Some of them still contained the listed poisons that Mr Hamilton used to buy from the chemist in order to deal with mildews, viruses, weeds, noxious bugs and various other horticultural nuisances (see Chapter 15). Another shelf was stacked with modern bottles, packets and plastic containers containing proprietary plant foods, slug pellets, insecticides, herbicides and fungicides.

There were separate hooks for bundles of cruel-looking traps for moles, rats and mice; and there was a box full of brass nozzles for watering cans, syringes and hoses, which are no use at all on today's plastic implements. Hanks of rope and cord, skeins of string and thread, coils of wire, wooden dibbers and cast-iron line-marking reels hung above the

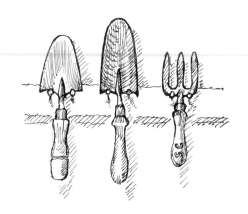

tools on the wall. A variety of antique wooden-rimmed sieves was hooked up along the window over the workbench; strung from a rafter there was a set of tiny leather boots that once protected the lawn from the sharp little hooves of the mowing pony. From another rafter hung an assortment of trugs and baskets, also a cluster of narrow-necked glass jars – patent wasp traps – and a large leather satchel, stiff with age, whose open top allowed the gardener the use of both hands when picking apples or pears. On the back of the door there were two hooks, one for a hank of raffia – blond, shaggy and brittle, unwanted for years – and one for an ancient blue apron, symbol of the gardener's trade, now almost fossilized into permanent folds.

POTTING SHED WORK

This is where everything to do with indoor sowing, potting-up, potting-on, taking cuttings and making up small quantities of potting composts took place. The potting shed also had enough light and space for all the other gardening operations that were once carried out in here. There is a tiny fireplace in

the corner, a relic of the days before the backsheds were heated by pipes from the hot-water boilers; it is still useful for heating the odd can, kettle or bucketful of hot water. This is where the men were given indoor, winter tasks such as mending tools and nets, mending and making brooms, besoms, screens, baskets and straw mats, cutting fruit tree ties or painting tallies, when it became too dark, cold or wet to work outside. This is also the place where Mr Hamilton mixed his plant foods and poisons.

In moderately sized kitchen gardens like this one it was quite usual to keep tools in the potting shed, but where more than seven or eight men were employed, they had a separate shed for the purpose. In grand gardens the owner supplied all the tools, and each department had a separate toolshed. Tool handles were branded either with the owner's or the garden's initials. Here, for example, you would find either 'W.I.W.' (for William Ingham Whitaker) or 'P.P' (for Pylewell Park), followed by an 'I.' for 'Inside' (greenhouse tools) or an 'O.' for 'Outside' (open-garden tools). Extremely grand gardens might have three or four toolsheds, in which case there would be an 'F.' for the Flower Garden, or a 'P.' for the Pleasure Grounds, and the tools would also be stamped with the gardeners' own identifying numbers. There could then be no confusion as to which tool went where, and who was responsible for it.

Here, as elsewhere in the gardens, discipline was strict, but it was necessary if

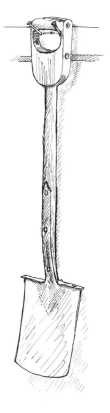

only to simplify the business of being able to lay one's hands on the right thing at the right minute. Mr Townsend Sharpless, of Philadelphia, is credited (in 1894) with the idea of making a silhouette of each tool on the space which it should occupy on the wall; 'The consciousness that there is such a tell-tale in the tool-room will stimulate any careless workman to return everything which he takes out'.[1] The idea is still in use and now known as a shadowboard.

GARDEN TOOLS

Gardening tools have, by tradition, ashwood handles; those of hoes and rakes are subtly waisted towards the top, to aid with the sliding action of the hands when hoeing and raking. A well-equipped gardener would have a range of spades, shovels and forks with a variety of handles, curved or straight, depending on whether tools are to be used for trenching, turfing or lifting.

Five hundred years ago the spade, arguably the one tool that no gardener can afford to be without, was made of wood, with an iron shoe acting as a blade. By the end of the eighteenth century this clumsy implement had been improved by making the entire blade of plate iron. It was forged with iron straps that were bolted to the handle. The top of a cast-iron blade could be almost as cutting as the edge, so gardeners protected their feet by strapping iron plates under their boots or clogs when digging; alternatively, the top of the blade would be flattened to form a tread. Towards the end of the nineteenth century, lighter, keen-edged, bright steel blades with treads, welded by a new technique to solid iron sockets and hollow shanks, were manufactured – a vast improvement on the heavy old iron spades, which were difficult to keep sharp and, being less smooth, became clogged with soil. A man's spade had, ideally, a blade measuring eleven by seven inches and a thirty-three inch handle; smaller, but equally good, spades were recommended for boys and lady gardeners.

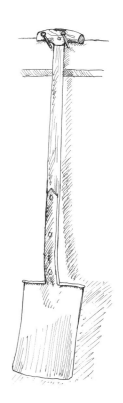

No mention is made of garden forks for digging before the seventeenth century. Lacking the strength given by steel, iron pitchforks and

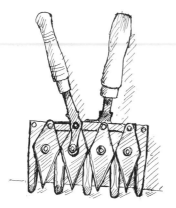

hedging shears

dungforks were used mainly for lifting or shifting litter, haulms and dung, loosening soil from roots or stirring the earth between plants. Short-handled hand forks were used for lifting small roots (such as asparagus) or making cavities in order to plunge pots into hotbeds. Lifting forks had two, three or four curved, long, slender and flexible prongs. Digging forks had four or five round, square, flat or diamond-shaped prongs; forks for potato digging had four firmer, shorter, flat prongs. The use of a steel-pronged fork as a digging tool came into general use only in the 1860s. Where the soil is heavy or wet, a digging fork is easier to work with than a spade. Forks are valuable too when trenching, for breaking the soil at the bottom of the trench, and for mixing the manure or fertilizer with the soil and breaking up surface clods.

Spade and fork handles were made in a variety of patterns; these depended as much on the locality as on the job for which the tools were designed. The handles of sickles, scythes, hooks, mattocks and axes were similarly shaped by tradition to provide balance and strength, becoming smoothed and lustrous with years of use. The metal parts - straps, bolts, blades and tines - were not allowed to show a hint of rust. None of Pylewell's tools would ever have been put away without being scraped or washed clean, then dried and oiled.

The gardeners at Cottesbrooke, in Northamptonshire, used a wedge-shaped piece of wood to scrape off the mud. Doug Brereton, the head gardener there, had a scraper made from a bit of old seed-box; it was about two by four inches in size, rounded at one end to fit into his hand and sharpened at the other end to do the scraping. The scraper lived in his jacket pocket, but in the days before Wellington boots, gardeners stored a similar tool in the leg bindings that kept their trousers tight below the knee. It is known in some localities as a 'man' and privately known as a 'minute-killer', for iron spades need to be scraped from time to time when digging, especially on heavy soils, and this provided a spare moment in which to straighten an aching back or light a pipe.

At the end of a day's work all gardeners would have to clean, then oil their tools by pushing blades and tines into a large box filled with a mixture of sand and sump-oil; this greased and polished them to a black shine. Any remaining specks of sand were brushed off with an old scrubbing brush. Gardeners had to pay equal attention to the sharpening of their tools, using an assortment of files and whetstones which would be kept in a box beside a grinding wheel on the work bench. When wear or damage eventually rendered tools useless, a head gardener would have to apply to his master or the estate manager for permission, and money, to replace them. A wise owner made sure that tools were renewed as often as need be: a short spade leads to what an old gardener might call 'titivating' of the soil, rather than deep digging.

JOHN EVELYN'S TOOLS

In the past, garden tools were made of wood and iron. Today they are made of stainless steel and plastic, but the tasks for which they are designed have changed so little that an eighteenth-century gardener would find most of the implements in today's potting sheds similar to his own. John Evelyn listed all the tools necessary for his garden at Sayes Court, Deptford, in 1686, illustrating them in his *Elysium Britannicum.* He had wheelbarrows and waterbarrows, rakes 'of several sizes and finenesse', hoes and spades; trowels, pails and watering pots 'of severall siz'd holes'; vermin traps, nets and bird clappers; shears, pruning and carpentry tools; tubs for making infusions, for water and for plants; plant cases, boxes and flowerpots; bags, trays and tin boxes for the sorting and keeping of seeds; measures for bushels, gallons and pints – even a set of stencils with letters and figures. As Evelyn was an enthusiastic designer of gardens, his list included quadrant levels for banks and alleys, an iron-shod tracing staff, a foot measure, a large wooden compass, measuring chains and levels, rulers, black-

lead pencils and paper. Also, in an age when clipped evergreens (especially phillyreas) were highly fashionable, Evelyn had trestles, ladders and boards for cutting hedges and, as befitted a garden on the banks of the Thames, 'sail cloths to dry seedes on and hang before blossoming wall fruit'. In the seventeenth century, wall fruit trees were tied with non-chafing shreds of woollen cloth, soft leather and felt (see Chapter 4).

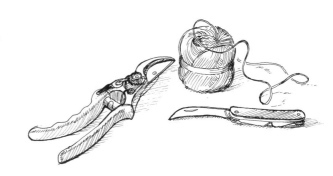

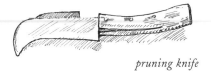

pruning knife

Old shoes and hats, or the parings and cuttings from shoe and hat-makers' workrooms came in useful here. (Gardeners today use strips of rubber cut from inner tubes for the same purpose.) Binding materials for other purposes included 'wyres, packthread and basse' plus 'finer thread to bind up nosegays with'.[2]

TRANSPLANTERS AND FORCERS

A curious instrument began to make its appearance in gardens in Evelyn's day. It was designed to remove trees and herbaceous plants from the nursery, taking the ball of earth surrounding the roots with as little disturbance as possible. This tool was called an extracting case or a transplanter, and looked like a tub or a tube sliced in half down the centre. The two halves were made of iron or tin, held together by hooks or hoops which could be tightened by screws. To extract the plant, a circular trench was dug round it, the extractor inserted and fastened, and the removal safely completed. The plant was transplanted to a hole matching in size, where the halves of the transplanter were removed one by one. Another, nineteenth-century design for a transplanter resembled two trowels attached to one another by a long handle, like a pair of sugar tongs. The advent of container-grown plants has made the transplanter obsolete; but the hand trowel, which is a far older tool, is still with us.

Tools connected with forcing have altered more than any others over the last fifty years or so. 'Precocious' crops used to be raised on hotbeds and protected from cold with wooden frames, sash lights, straw mattresses and bell jars (see Chapter 8). Evelyn used all these devices, but the modern gardener, with his plastic cloches, electric propagators, heated frames and glasshouses, has no need of them. Bell jars and hand glasses were put aside years ago in favour of Mr Chase's continuous tent and barn-shaped cloches (see page 129), and they, in their turn, have given way to plastic tunnels and garden fleece.

THE POTTING SHED BENCH

The Pylewell work bench stands below the windows looking out over the open quarters; its surface was once as smooth and well-burnished as the blades of the old gardeners' spades. It is made of sheet zinc nailed to a wooden top and was kept spotless by the ritual brushing-down that was performed after every session of pricking-out, potting-up or potting-on. These sessions formed part of the rhythmic cycle of seed sowing, taking cuttings and transplanting seedlings. Here, too, the inside gardeners 'twinked-up' their flowering pot plants before taking them up to the Big House; made buttonholes, nosegays and bouquets; trimmed, polished and arranged exhibits for horticultural shows and the harvest festival; mixed and prepared weedkillers, pesticides and fungicides.

At each end of the bench, to confine the potting compost as the work proceeded, is a wooden section, elegantly curved from back to front like the divisions between the loose boxes in the stables, and made by the same estate carpenter. The surface of a potting-shed bench was originally made of any close-grained hardwood that did not score or splinter easily, and in areas where stone or slate was common, these might be used instead.

Below the bench are drawers for smaller tools such as grape-thinning scissors, asparagus knives, grafting and pruning knives, wedges, secateurs, chisels, nails, hammers, files and pincers. Beneath the drawers are big, open wooden bins for potting composts. Gardeners buy ready-made proprietary composts now, in large plastic sacks, but in the past they mixed their own, either here on the workbench or, for larger amounts, in the open workshed next door. Mr Hamilton never allowed anyone else to mix the composts for, like all head gardeners, he was secretive about the ingredients and their proportions.

In the 1830s, according to the horticultural writer Charles M'Intosh, the basic ingredients of potting compost were peat (decayed heather, moss or wood, rather than bog peat), loam (light rather than clayey, from uncultivated downland) and sand (preferably fine and white), to which decayed leaves and dung, lime rubbish, pounded brickbats and gravel might be added. To a gardener of those days, 'sandy

loam' was shorthand for three parts of loam to one part of sand; 'rich sandy loam' meant, quite precisely, sandy loam to which one-third or one-quarter of well-rotted dung had been added.[3] There might have been as many as twenty different components in the bins under the bench at Pylewell, ranging from leaf mould to charcoal and bones, graded from large lumps to fine powder.

It was also at this bench that Hamilton potted up the indoor bulbs for forcing and sowed all the seed that was to be raised in the cold frames or hothouses. If he was wise he would allow no one else to do it, as he had to be sure that each batch was correctly labelled and dated, and that the job was actually done when it had to be done. After Hamilton's retirement, the gardeners still sowed seeds here for salads and bedding-out, sometimes

using the traditional pans and boxes, and sometimes old yoghurt pots and margarine tubs. This habit of recycling is nothing new. Long before the invention of plastic, propagating boxes were being made from the boxes in which tinned goods had been delivered to the grocer; the bottoms of butter and mustard tubs made ideal seed pans; half-tubs were used for blanching seakale, and whole tubs for blanching rhubarb.

A glance around any old potting shed will show that the tools for seed sowing are simple, and almost all these are recycled too. An old hand shovel will serve to fill pots, trays or boxes with compost, which can be shaken through an old kitchen sieve when it needs to be extra fine. The gardener lightly packs down each seedbox as it is sown with a home-made tamp that fits exactly. At Cottesbrooke, Doug Brereton used an old pricking-out stick for extracting and firming in all his seedlings; it was about ten inches long and was once the handle of a watercolour brush.

After labelling the pots, pans and boxes, the name, quantity and date of every sowing and pricking-out is recorded by a good head gardener in his garden diary, just as Evelyn's gardener was instructed. At the end of a stint of work Doug's bench would be completely cleared with a soft brush, leaving only two flowerpots in view; the biggest holding a selection of short canes, the smaller one containing labels and marking pens, the pricking-out stick and a miniature fork and trowel.

TALLIES AND LABELS

Durability – not only of the label itself but also of the writing on it – is of prime importance in a garden. For this reason, plant labels have been made in the past of horn, bone, ivory, earthenware and even leather, as well as wood and various metals. Modern tallies and plant labels are made of plastic, but Evelyn's gardener, like generations before and after him, had tallies or number sticks, name sticks and labels (in various sizes) made of lead, or of the narrow, wooden laths used by builders. Labels, of whatever material, were made more legible by whitening them, either by rubbing on white lead with a finger or by painting with a mixture of whitening and milk. Lead pencils were used to mark them, the writing becoming indelible if written on white lead. Favourite woods for making kitchen-garden labels were white woods such as hornbeam and laurel, which needed no painting. Alternatively, wooden labels could be branded with hot irons. Wooden labels intended for long-term marking had the pointed ends dipped in tar or a mixture of boiled oil and coal dust.

As a nineteenth-century precaution against theft, the name of the garden, or its proprietor, was imprinted on the back of lead, terracotta or cast-iron labels. By the end of the century, zinc labels had been introduced. These were sold already-stamped with the names of most of the varieties of orchids, fruits and roses grown at the time, at prices ranging from 1s.3d. to 3s.6d. per dozen, or unmarked at 1s.2d. to 3s.6d. per 100, with special indelible ink at 6d. a bottle. The thrifty gardener made his own metal labels, cutting the shapes of his choice from old tin cans or zinc rubbed bright with emery paper, and punching a hole for a copper-wire tie. He would either stamp numbers or letters with a little press, or use a quill pen to write with his own indelible ink made from nitro-muriate of platinum or a mixture of verdigris, sal ammoniac powder, lamp black and water.

FLOWERPOTS

The back wall of the potting shed at Pylewell was completely taken up by slatted shelves for the pots, trays and boxes needed for plants and seedlings. The boxes were stacked one above the other, according to size. The pots lay open-mouthed on their sides, each within the other, also according to size. Over the years, terracotta and wood were superseded by plastic, but broken flowerpots were never thrown away. Large pots with a bit missing might be used to shade newly bedded plants, large pieces were kept in a heap in the compost yard, and the smaller shards were put in a crock box in the potting shed. They could still be useful, acting as drainage in the bottoms of plant pots.

A large galvanized tank stands outside the potting shed, filled with water from a drainpipe off the guttering. This is where Percy, when he was the youngest gardener or 'pot boy', spent long hours scrubbing flowerpots, closely watched by Mr Hamilton. On his first day at work he learned that a dirty pot was liable to transmit fungus or disease from its previous occupant; it was also less porous than a clean one, porosity being a virtue in earthenware pots as it allows air to permeate the soil. He was taught to soak new pots before using them, as a dry pot would take moisture from the soil, but never to use pots soaking wet, as that would cause the soil, and eventually the roots, to stick. He had to stack wet pots in staggered rows so that they did not stick inside one another, taking care to leave them in a place where the frost could not crack them.

Earthenware flowerpots, and their design, are ancient. Before they were superseded in the mid twentieth century by plastic pots, they formed a high proportion of a potter's output, along with rhubarb, seakale and chimney-pots, roof tiles and drainpipes. Professional gardeners always referred to flowerpots by the number that were thrown from a single cast – a given quantity of clay from which two, four, six, eight, twelve, sixteen, twenty-four, thirty-two, forty-eight, sixty or eighty pots could be made. It follows that the 'eighties', which are also called 'thumbs', are very small – only 1¾ inches across and 2 inches deep, while the 'twos' are 18 inches across and 12 inches deep.[4]

Flowerpots were always unglazed but their saucers were usually glazed on the inside. Variations on the usual design of pot (fez-shaped, with a rim) included tall, rimless pots known as 'Long Toms', useful for growing bulbs such as hyacinths, as well as pineapples (see Chapter 11); 'Oxfords', which had broad rims pierced with holes for tying down the branches of blossoming plants; double-rimmed pots for cuttings, the rim being grooved to accommodate a bell glass; orchid pots, perforated all over with holes for the roots to escape; and double pots for alpines, only the inner pot having a drainage hole (the space between inner and outer being filled with water or moss to act as insulation). There were also flat earthenware pans for raising seeds and cuttings, and a wide variety of ornamental pots (see page 198).

TRAPS AND POISONS

The potting shed is the handiest place to make concoctions of any kind to do with the garden. It is also the logical place to keep traps and poisons but, although he had no legal obligation to do so, a responsible owner would insist that the head gardener kept the poisons in a locked cupboard in his office.

By the end of the nineteenth century, the potting shed was, both in fact and fiction, the first place in which the police, or a potential murderer, would look for poison. During this period, kitchen gardens, frames, hothouses and storerooms were kept free of woodlice, ants, cockroaches, rats and mice, by using bait such as lard, oatmeal, bread, potatoes, parsnips or honey, laced with arsenic, strychnine or mercury. At the same time, greenhouse pests such as aphids, red spider, thrips, mealy bugs and the like were destroyed by fumigants based on cyanide, tobacco or even pure nicotine, only one drop of which, it was said, 'will kill a dog'.[5]

Supplies of sulphur, paraffin, soda (both caustic and crystals), camphor, Paris green (aceto-arsenate of copper), copper sulphate, potassium permanganate, soft soap, soot, quassia chips, hellebore powder, pyrethrum and lime (both quick and slaked) were kept to hand for application as weedkillers, fungicides and insecticides in the form of powders, washes, pastes and sprays. All were prepared here, with the aid of barrels, buckets and boiling water. For the gardener, the potting shed was also a laboratory.

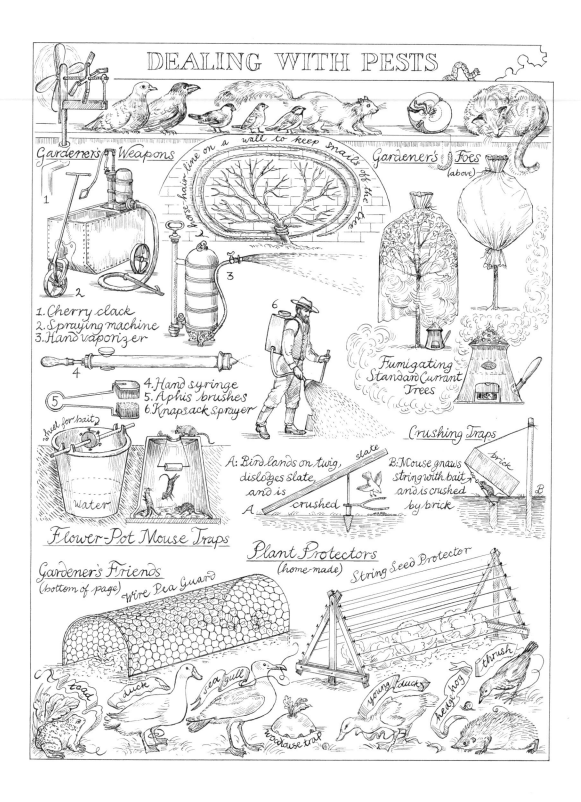

DEALING WITH PESTS

Gardener's Weapons

horse hair line on a wall to keep snails off the tree

Gardener's Foes (above)

1. Cherry clack
2. Spraying machine
3. Hand vaporizer

4. Hand syringe
5. Aphis brushes
6. Knapsack sprayer

wheel for bait

Water

Fumigating Standard Currant Trees

Crushing Traps

A: Bird lands on twig, dislodges slate, and is crushed

slate

B: Mouse gnaws string with bait and is crushed by brick

brick

A

crushed

B

Flower-Pot Mouse Traps

Plant Protectors (home-made)

String Seed Protector

Gardener's Friends (bottom of page)

Wire Pea Guard

toad

duck

sea gull

woodlouse trap

young duck

hedge hog

thrush

CHAPTER FIFTEEN

PESTS AND DISEASES

The contest between gardeners and their foes is ages-old. The fight against weeds and marauders is relatively straightforward, but to deal with insects, and viral and fungal diseases, a multitude of antidotes, both practical and superstitious, has been invented over the years by gardeners, with the help of chemists, mycologists, entomologists and not a few old wives. The necessary understanding of plant pathology, however, was slow to evolve and without it the success of some of these remedies was more a matter of luck than of design.

Only in the mid nineteenth century did it become accepted that a large number of plant diseases were caused by fungi. Until those fungi and their habits were identified, gardeners from Theophrastus onwards had supposed that knots, scabs, blisters, rot, rust, canker and mildew, as well as the complaints known as 'freezing and scorching', were due (if not to the wrath of God or the quarters of the moon), to insects or bad weather, or to a combination of the two.

Apart from a variety of spells, talismans and incantations for the superstitious, the gardener has always had a choice of several methods of dealing with his enemies.

EARLY PESTICIDES

Most of the classical pesticides were non-residual and non-poisonous to warm-blooded creatures. They consisted of sticky, bitter or smothering ingredients such as tar and bitumen, soap and soap ashes, dung, soot, ammonia (made from sal-ammoniac, urine or spirit of hartshorn), lime and salt. Sulphur (known as brimstone) and compounds brewed in copper pots were also used, but without a very clear understanding of the effects.

One of the most effective and dangerous Greek and Roman pesticides was amurca, a by-product of olive-oil making. Early European gardeners also used dangerous poisons like arsenic, mercury and strychnine *(nux vomica)*. Cyanide was not employed as an insecticide until 1886, by which time gardeners were also using hellebore and pure nicotine. These chemicals are poisonous to warm-blooded creatures as well as to insects. They were used mainly to kill ants, wasps, rats, mice, moles and rabbits, but some of them were also used as fumigants. These substances are dangerous, not only because they are as deadly to humans, fish, birds and domestic animals as they are to insects, fungi and viruses but because some of them remain toxic for weeks or months.

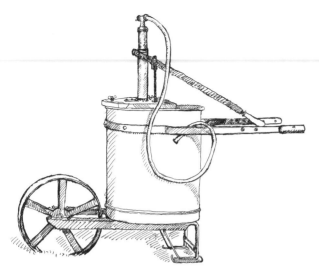

Far less alarming pesticides included the relatively harmless tobacco refuse (a seventeenth-century introduction from the Americas), as well as paraffin oil, introduced in the mid nineteenth century, West Indian quassia chips and Dalmatian pyrethrum powder, both used for centuries in their countries of origin but not imported to England for use as insecticides until the late nineteenth century. Tar oil and derris dust are two twentieth-century pesticides that are fairly harmless.

These ingredients, which could be combined with one another or used on their own, were applied as drenches, washes, pastes and powders with simple syringes, watering cans, sponges, brushes or bellows. Drenches made of brine, lime and copper were used in the preparation of seed corn and potatoes. Washes were made from infusions of bitter leaves, urine, alum root and vinegar. The addition of soft soap to these washes would smother aphids, mealy bugs and

unspecified 'blights'. Irritant powders were made from lime, soot, sulphur or tobacco dust to combat slugs and caterpillars; disinfectant plasters based on cow dung or mud, ashes and lime were painted on tree wounds and grafts. Most of these remedies worked, especially when based on soft soap (which spreads and smothers), lime combined with sulphur (the basis of lime-sulphur) and tobacco (which contains nicotine), though it was largely a matter of hit and miss until the causes of plant disorders such as mildew and leaf curl were accurately diagnosed.

MODERN PESTICIDES

Many of the most lethal pesticides date only from the end of the nineteenth century. They were made from 'synthetic' poisons – chlorinated hydrocarbons, which were based on organo-chemical compounds. They were invented primarily as agricultural fungicides and soil sterilizers (although some are offshoots of research into anti-personnel poisons for use in the two World Wars), but gardeners of Mr Hamilton's generation used them as enthusiastically as the farmers.

Some pesticides (or, to put it more correctly, 'plant protection products') have since proved so dangerous that they are now banned. Others, which may or may not be dangerous to the environment or to health, are currently withheld from use under directives from the European Union, until their suitability can be proved. The first organic compound was produced in 1885. It was formaldehyde (sold as formalin). An organic mercurial compound (chlorphenol-mercury) followed in 1913 and was sold under various trade names. Later discoveries – all to be found on potting-shed shelves in the 1950s and 1960s – include the now notorious insecticides aldrin and dieldrin (first used in 1948); calomel (another mercurial compound); the powerful organo-phosphorous insecticides parathion, benzine hexachloride (also known as BHC or Lindane) and dichlorodiphenyl-trichloro-ethane (DDT); the selective, synthetic organic weedkillers Simazine and Monuron (discovered in 1942) that remain effective for at least a year, and the fungicides Thiram and Captan (invented in 1937 and 1951 respectively).

It was during the 1950s that both economists and ecologists began to wonder if the manufacture and widespread application of these synthetic chemicals were altogether wise. The agricultural and horticultural benefits were undeniable but those miracle-working pesticides were extremely expensive. A fifty per cent increase in production went hand in hand with a four to five-fold increase in food prices. Added to this, the pests the new chemicals were intended to destroy gradually evolved into resistant strains, which could not be beaten without more expensive research and new, even more expensive and complex pesticides.

The environmental and health lobbies had stronger objections to their use. An Agricultural (Poisonous Substances) Act was passed in 1952 to protect employees from the risks of poisoning; synthetic pesticides had been found to cause cancers and hitherto unheard-of allergies in humans, while widespread spraying, which had become the easiest method of applying these pesticides, not only failed at times to eliminate the pest, it also allowed pesticides to enter the food chain. This caused harm, if not death, to other creatures, some of which (such as foxes, birds and ladybirds) are the pests' natural enemies.

The publication, in 1962, of Rachel Carson's *The Silent Spring* brought the more horrific aspects of this industry to the public's attention, and it is now accepted that it is in everyone's interest to minimise the use of pesticides.

However, the old head gardeners had an extremely militant attitude towards the army of beasts, birds, bugs and bacilli that threatened their crops. They were constantly on the look-out for evidence of destructive rodents, birds, insects or molluscs, and attacks by viruses, bacteria and funguses. At the first signs of blight, canker and

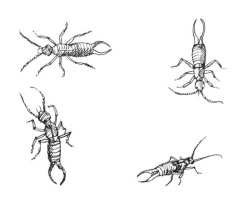

mildew; maggots, mice, mites and weevils; discoloration and wilt; of blotching, nibbling, tunnelling, spots, scabs and blisters, they took action. Like generations of gardeners before them, they studied the heavens and mixed their toxins. With only half an eye on the ecological mayhem they might be causing with their traps, shotguns, spray guns and puffers, they would fill them with the necessary bait, ammunition or poisons and apply them cheerfully wherever and whenever necessary. Conscious that their jobs were at stake if they failed to produce what was expected of them, their rationale was: 'It's them against us!'

Gardeners in the 1930s had a typically relaxed attitude to the dangers lurking on the potting-shed shelves. They would take a good sniff from a tin of Cheshunt Compound to clear their heads of a cold or a hangover. Percy Gregory told me with glee of the day when a pair of boots, put by a fellow gardener to dry by the potting-shed fire, burst into flames. The man had been spraying the paths with a weedkiller made from highly inflammable sodium chlorate and his boots had been soaked in it.

COMMERCIAL PESTICIDES AND THE LAW

Before the availability of commercial pesticides towards the mid nineteenth century, gardeners mixed their own brews, usually over a stove in the potting shed, according to tried and tested recipes inherited from their forebears.

The necessary ingredients could be obtained easily and cheaply enough. Some, such as soot, elder leaves, dung, urine and ashes, cost nothing; others – soft soap, lime, sulphur, tobacco and so on – could be bought at little cost from the gardeners' sundriesmen or tradesmen. It was not until 1851 that the Arsenic Act was passed, limiting the sale of that poison to persons of over twenty-one, known to the vendor, and ruling that all such transactions, with a note of the purpose for which they were intended, had to be recorded in a Poisons Book. In 1868 the law was extended (by the Pharmacy Act) to include the sales of other poisons, as well as the registration of all vendors and the manner in which those vendors kept, bottled, packeted and labelled their poisons. The Pharmacy Act of 1933 set up a Poisons Board and enabled local authorities to license the sale of poisons only by registered pharmacists from registered premises.

But as scientists discovered more about the causes of plant disease, so their cures and preventions increased in complexity. It began to be easier to buy pesticides, herbicides, insecticides and fungicides ready-made, rather than go through a series of laborious, smelly and dangerous chemical processes in the potting shed. By the beginning of the twentieth century, gardeners were able to buy all sorts of ready-made concoctions. But they had to be on their guard. Products varied in quality. Pyrethrum powder, for example, which is derived only from the dried flower buds, might well consist largely of ground stalks; and it was often adulterated with sawdust. And although a product might have a brand name and claim to cure every ailment, there was rarely any description of what went into it. Moreover, the customer often paid dearly for stuff made from the cheapest ingredients, merely to increase the maker's profits; anything 'new' went for an even higher price.

Gardeners also ran the risk of inhaling poisons accidentally or splashing corrosives on their clothes or skin. The manufacturers took pains to print warnings on the labels and good head gardeners took care to have antidotes to hand, as well as keeping their poisons locked in the poisons cupboard. Eventually, legislation, plus the increasing availability of preparations that needed only to be taken out of their packets and sprinkled on the soil, or puffed from bellows, or mixed with water, or set alight, meant that gardeners gradually ceased making their own potions. There are a few thrifty and ecologically conscious 'new age' gardeners who make their own nicotine smokes or sprays from cigarette ends; they also brew their own anti-aphid sprays by boiling up rhubarb, elder, wormwood or walnut leaves, but old-fashioned gardeners think they are rather eccentric to give themselves so much trouble.

FUMIGATION

The idea of using smoke as an insecticide is ancient; the fumigation of orchards was practised by the Romans. What is more, the smoke favoured by the Romans was mingled with the steam from copper cauldrons in which a sulphurous pesticide – surely the classical forerunner of Bordeaux mixture – was brewed. Roman books on husbandry suggested that gnats, cankerworms, mists, frosts and mildews could all be banished from gardens by the smoke and fumes of open-air bonfires. Suitable smoke was created by burning chaff or prunings and bundles of garlic leaves: smoke pellets were made of powdered ox dung, goats' hooves, hartshorn, nigella, pellitory and the resinous *gum galbanum* mixed with vinegar, formed into balls and dried. Other smokes were created by burning 'mushrooms from under a nut-tree' or lime and brimstone (sulphur). The fumes from sulphur and amurca would have been particularly toxic.

All these remedies (including amurca, which he called 'mother of olive oil') were

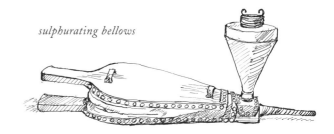

sulphurating bellows

quoted by Thomas Hill, though whether he actually made use of all of them is open to question.[1] Pipe tobacco, long known to the natives of South America as an insecticide, had been introduced to England in 1573, only three years before Hill's death. It is not mentioned by him as a pesticide, but in Britain it was well established as such, not as a fumigant, but as a decoction or powder, by the end of the next century.

Tobacco water, the liquid in which tobacco refuse (stalks and the parts too tough to smoke in pipes) had been boiled, was sprinkled on gravel walks in April as a weed and worm killer: the stalks were also powdered and scattered to a depth of half an inch under fruit trees to prevent 'Pismires [ants] and other crawling Insects, from invading the Fruit &c'.[2] At first tobacco was grown in England, but its cultivation at home avoided the obligation to pay import duties, and so the crop was banned in 1655.

Richards' patent fumigator

Tobacco smoke began to be used as an insecticide only at the end of the eighteenth century. An early mention of tobacco as a fumigant, in a peach house infested with aphids, appeared in 1794.[3] April was the month for destroying aphids by fumigating wall trees with tobacco smoke. Oilcloth, old blankets and carpets or doubled garden mats were securely fastened over wall trees, dwarf trees or fruit bushes, preferably on a dull evening, and the smoke applied either with fumigating bellows or by burning shreds of tobacco, mixed with a little damp hay or tansy, in a flowerpot. Next day the tree was powerfully syringed with the water engine and the ground beneath it lightly dug over, to bury any insects washed off but still half-alive. Fumigation was easier in hothouses, which needed only to be closely shut up during the process. 'Shut the house up close at night', wrote Walter Nicol, in his *Gardener's Kalendar* of 1810, 'and fill it so full of tobacco smoke that one person cannot see another.'

Like other pesticides based on poison, fumigants may be lethal to humans. None are now considered safe for gardeners to work with unless they wear masks and protective clothing. However, a set of instructions written in 1922 on activating cyanide as a greenhouse fumigant says the job is best done on a still evening, so that the fumigation can take place overnight. The gardener (advisedly an 'experienced and reliable person'), having previously sealed all windows, doors, ventilators, cracks and crevices, should take care to lock the door of the house and hang a card on it forbidding entry. The cyanide itself should be broken into small pieces, wrapped in a piece of wire gauze or muslin and 'by some arrangement lowered from the outside' into a jar containing diluted sulphuric acid: '. . .the gas will commence to be liberated at once'.[4] The risks of handling fumigants like these had been somewhat alleviated by the manufacture, towards the end of the nineteenth century, of nicotine-based fumigating liquids, shreds, and cones, which could be vaporized or burnt in so-called 'safety machines' by water, a spirit lamp or a night light.

Late eighteenth-century scientists developed a good understanding of plant pathology and other, related, aspects of biological science. While still not fully appreciating the role of fungi in plant disorders, they placed the blame for garden diseases and blights on poor hygiene and carelessness rather than on insects or such things as the east wind or hailstorms. Mildewed fruit trees were washed or sprayed with a mixture of urine and lime-water, or washed with a woollen cloth soaked in a mixture containing tobacco, sulphur, unslaked lime and elder buds.[5] This recipe, first given by the royal gardener William Forsyth in 1802, is the basis for lime-sulphur, which was still used as an insecticide by twentieth-century gardeners.

Remarkably, as late as the 1820s it appeared to John Claudius Loudon that '. . .very little could be done by art in curing [plant] diseases; but that much might be done to prevent them by regimen and culture'.[6] Hence the good head gardener's insistence on cleanliness and tidiness and Charles M'Intosh's observation that, 'Insects are probably, in all cases, the effects of bad management, and the effects of disease more than the cause of it. When plants are well-cultivated, and kept in a growing state, few insects appear to molest them; but whenever they become sickly, insects are sure to follow.'[7]

FUNGI AS A CAUSE OF DISEASE

It was discovered in 1846 that a parasitic fungus was the cause of the murrain, potato disease or potato blight – one of the worst diseases ever to strike the farm or garden. Until then it was believed that 'the moulds' on the damaged plant tissues were the *effects* of the disease; no one understood that 'the moulds' *were* the disease, and that healthy tissue could also become infected. The fungus was identified in 1876 as *Phytophthora infestans* by Anton de Bary. The following year another scourge – club root – which attacks the roots of brassicas and had hitherto been thought to be a form of hernia, vegetable syphilis or the ravages of an insect, was found by Michael Stepanovitch Woronin also to be caused by a fungus – *Plasmodiophora brassicæ*.

As soon as plant breeders and scientists realized that these two disorders, and many other mildews, rusts, moulds, cankers and blights, were all caused by fungi, the search

began for disease resistant plant varieties and the appropriate fungicides. The fungicides were mostly based on mercury, lime and sulphur. Club root could be controlled by burning the roots and treating the soil with lime, but apart from the discovery of a few disease resistant varieties, nothing seemed capable of dealing with potato blight.

BORDEAUX MIXTURE

The antidote to this scourge was discovered in France in the vineyards of the Médoc, where to discourage pilfering the wine makers sprayed the vines growing beside public roads and pathways with a mixture of copper sulphate and slaked lime. This turned the leaves and fruit a vitriolic blue and had the desired effect.

In 1882 a Professor of Botany at Bordeaux University, Pierre-Marie-Alexis Millardet, noticed while walking in the vineyards that the spray also seemed to protect the wayside vines from the effects of an epidemic of downy mildew *(Plasmopara viticola)* that was quite visibly wrecking the rest of the crop. It

occurred to him that a fungicide based on copper sulphate and lime might be the cure. Three years later the professor had perfected his *'bouillie bordelais'* and Bordeaux mixture was ready for use as a fungicide for the afflicted vines. In 1888 French horticulturalists tried treating blighted potato plants with Bordeaux mixture; the experiment worked.

'Bouillie bordelaise' became the first universal fungicide. It is still used in varying strengths against potato blight, apple and pear scab, peach leaf curl, tomato-leaf mould and blossom end rot, bean anthracnose, gooseberry botrytis et cetera; it also acts as a weedkiller. A monument to its inventor stands in Bordeaux.

MECHANICAL DETERRENTS

Mechanical pest controls, which are usually harmless to creatures other than the intended victims, deal mostly with sizeable insects, caterpillars, snails and slugs or small creatures such as mice and birds. They include syringing infested leaves with water, agitating affected branches, catching flying bugs in nets, protecting with fencing, netting and tar bands, hand picking, trapping, scaring devices and so on.

Charles M'Intosh removed pests by hand or by mechanical means. Diseased shoots and leaves were picked off or pruned away. Insects were physically 'annoyed to death' by the creation of what M'Intosh's contemporary, Loudon, described as 'artificial bad weather'.[8] This old-fashioned remedy was achieved by syringeing fruit trees vigorously with either plain water or a light brine, then shaking them to rid them of aphids, as well as of caterpillars and cobwebs. Boiling water was poured over ants' nests.

Children, weeding women and garden boys were employed in the destruction, by hand, of the eggs, caterpillars and larvae of cabbage butterflies and gooseberry, currant and codling moths. They were rewarded with money for finding wasps' nests. M'Intosh wanted every nest within a radius of one mile of his fruit garden to be destroyed by the end of July. He recommended stupefication with squibs of gunpowder or burning brimstone (sulphur). If wasps were still about when the fruit was ripening, bags of paper or crêpe were tied over the choicest specimens.

Garden boys, and generations of boys before them, when not exterminating wasps, were kept busy catching butterflies with large gauze nets. They were also responsible for catching snails by hand (they were found most easily at night with the help of a candle on walls and paths after a shower of rain). To kill slugs they sprinkled them with quicklime or barilla; to lure them they laid out cabbage leaves, warmed in the oven and spread with lard, or they might leave out piles of bran and collect the slugs from them in the morning. Their successors were to do the same in the 1950s, using metaldehyde as bait.

For centuries, slimy molluscs were kept off fruit trees and seedbeds by lines of soot,

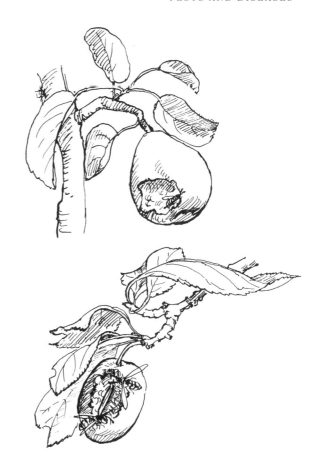

sawdust, prickly barley-awns or ashes. The Romans invented a sort of tar band, smearing tree trunks with that and a mixture of red earth, again to deter ants. 'The husbandmen of Flanders', according to Thomas Hill, twisted straw bands round their fruit trees to stop caterpillars climbing up them.[9] Ropes of horsehair were used in the same way in the eighteenth century. Ants were deterred from climbing fruit trees in early nineteenth-century gardens by pieces of cord, dipped in tar and tied round the trees – the precursors of our modern tar bands.

PREDATORS AGAINST PREDATORS

Percy Gregory claimed that pigeons and squirrels were kept away from Pylewell by the sheer number of gardeners there, plus the rattle of their water carts and the odd pot-shot from Fred Thomas's gun. The kitchen garden cat was looked on as an unpaid member of the garden staff. She was an excellent hunter of birds, rats and mice; but like most gardeners Mr Hamilton had an ambivalent attitude towards Tibbles's talents. He regarded birds as allies as well as enemies: moreover he thought Tibbles was less efficient than traps for rodent control and her toilet habits annoyed him. Nevertheless she was tolerated in the backsheds, as long as she earned her keep as a mouser. In some kitchen gardens cats were employed in the strawberry beds as temporary, but tethered, bird-scarers.

Tomtits, toads, hedgehogs and even guinea pigs were kept as guests in greenhouses and mushroom sheds, where they were welcome to eat all the slugs and woodlice they could find. Young ducks were allowed in the kitchen garden for a few days at a time, to deal with slugs and snails; an enterprising eighteenth-century gardener at Woodford, in Essex, was reported (by the Swedish traveller Peter Kalm) to have kept four tame seagulls for the same purpose. Birds that were more of a nuisance than a help were warned off the garden by the sight of corpses and strewn feathers of their own kind; Kalm describes cherry orchards in Kent, their branches hung with dead, stinking jackdaws, crows, rooks and magpies.[10] The use of feathers in the garden has a long history. Birds are territorial creatures; they are thought to be put off by the sight of another bird's feathers stuck in the ground or twirling in the wind.

TRAPS

Woodlice were particularly troublesome in nineteenth-century mushroom beds, but they could be kept at bay by standing the feet of the posts supporting the beds in troughs of water. They were also a nuisance in melon and cucumber frames; a trap made from a boiled potato, wrapped in hay and placed in a flowerpot was guaranteed to attract them 'in great numbers'.[11] Raw, hollowed-out potatoes or turnips were also left as traps for millipedes; glazed pots were sunk in the beds with decoys in them, to trap mice and moles, or filled with beer to drown slugs. Jars of sugary liquid are still hung in fruit trees to catch wasps. John Evelyn set small gourd-shaped bell jars, the 'new-invented Cucurbit Glasses', upside down, filled with a mixture of beer and honey, as wasp traps.[12]

Traps for earwigs were made of sheep's hooves (preferably with the skin still attached), placed upside down over canes stuck in the ground; earwigs climbed into the hooves and were collected each day by Evelyn's gardener, who kept a supply of 'canes and hoofes', for the purpose.[13] This kind of trap was still in use in 1858. Another popular trap, especially for earwigs in fruit trees and bushes, could be made of short bundles of hollow broad bean, Jerusalem artichoke or sunflower stalks, which have attractive sweet sap; the gardener was told to 'examine [them] daily and blow the earwigs out into scalding water'.[14] A variety of Heath Robinson-like mousetraps was fashioned in the potting shed. Most depended on the prey nibbling the string which was attached to the bait, thereby causing a brick or tile to fall on it, with lethal effect. Seeds soaked in paraffin or sown with holly leaves caused mice to give them a wide berth.

PROTECTIVE NETTING

One of the earliest references to protective netting for fruit trees comes from Columella. Rooks and crows were kept off pomegranate trees with 'nets made of broom'.[15] The use of hempen or flaxen nets to protect garden crops is presumably as ancient as the use of nets themselves to catch fish, although a reference by John Evelyn in 1686 to 'a Net to preserve seedes from Birds' appears to be one of the earliest references to its use in English gardens.[16]

Wire netting was used for a bejewelled aviary at Kenilworth in Warwickshire in the late sixteenth century,[17] but there are no references to a wire fruit cage as such until early in the nineteenth century when, according to M'Intosh, 'in some parts of England, cherry grounds are enclosed with high wire fences . . . and secured over the top by means of large nets'.[18] The cherry trees were dwarf standards, underplanted with strawberries, currants and gooseberries.

Wall brackets furnished with hooks from which to hang nets are a feature of nineteenth-century garden walls (see Chapter 4). Nets were also used in the spring to protect wall-fruit blossom from frosts and titmice. Large mats, hurdles, oiled bunting, canvas and pieces of evergreen were fixed

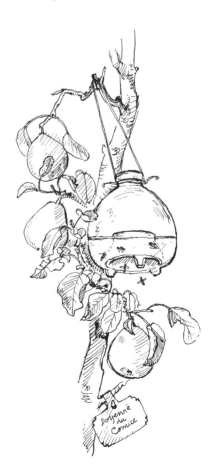

Doyenné du Comice

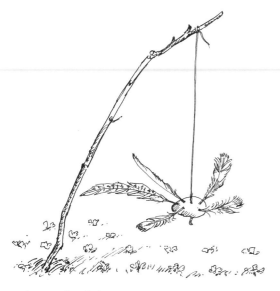

a 'potato-dangler'

over seventeenth and eighteenth-century dwarf and wall-fruit blossoms to protect them from frost, rain and hail: and coarse woollen nets were woven especially for fruit walls. The practical gardener has always built defences for his crops against the wind, frost and driving rain.

LONG-LIVED SUPERSTITIONS

Ignorance of the true causes of blight, disease and infestation, plus a feeling of helplessness in the face of tempests, droughts, frosts and floods that threatened lives as well as crops and thus the very sustenance of life, gave strength to a belief in a wealth of superstitions connected with ancient kitchen gardening. Some are still remembered even now, in gardening lore. I have read accounts written within the past sixty years of fruit growers who believe that if the sun is not shining at noon on 6 January (Old Christmas Day), it will be a

poor apple crop;[19] and of ladies who were not allowed to view the mushroom-growing caves of France when they were menstruating.[20] Many gardeners still deliberately sow parsley on Good Friday, and religiously plant and harvest shallots on the shortest and longest days, respectively. They also believe that stolen seed is better than seed more honestly obtained.

In fact, few of the old beliefs are as daft as they seem. Symbolism gives meaning to them, even if sense does not. Many of them are the direct descendants of the rituals, religions, myths, legends and folklore of our European ancestors - the Etruscans and Indo-Europeans.

The rational Greeks relied on rituals as alternative, or supportive lines of defence, and in particular of prevention, against garden troubles. The superstitious Romans relied more strongly on spells and talismans. And from the fifth century BC, both Greeks and Romans paid more and more attention to theories based on the doctrine of the four humours. To counter the threat or the actual occurrence of a horticultural disaster, creatures or objects possessing the appropriate humours were displayed or sacrificed. Aquatic and amphibious creatures represented water, reptiles represented earth, birds represented air, and mammals represented fire.

Thunderbolts, the weapons of Jove, would never strike bay trees (sacred to his son Apollo and therefore protective to garden crops) but they were attracted to thorn trees (emblems of witchcraft, useful as a hedge on the perimeter, but bad for grafting onto). When storm clouds threatened, the gardener held a large mirror to the skies because mirrors, according to classical folklore, absorb what they reflect. Vines could be protected from coal blight by burning three crabs alive among the trees (cold-and-wet destroyed by hot-and-dry). Caterpillars were banished by fixing the skull of a mated horse or she-ass on a stake in the centre of the garden (which also acted as a fertility symbol). A girl menstruating for the first time, if led three times round the garden, hair uncombed, bare-bosomed and unbelted, had a devastating effect on caterpillars; after this rite had been performed they would literally fall off the trees.

The classical kitchen gardener kept effigies of the gods and goddesses of fertility in his garden, primarily to make sure of bounteous crops, but statues of Priapus, who was symbolized by his maleness, were intended to scare intruders too. He would be fashioned if possible from a fig tree, and given an apron to conceal his rampant private parts, then placed either in the centre of the garden, or by the beehives, holding a reaping hook. Wives with 'sluggish husbands' were advised to feed them with rocket grown beside this effigy; his role as a garden god was always combined, however, with that of a scarecrow, which is perhaps why gardeners still make scarecrows man-shaped rather than woman-shaped.

Companion or companionate planting, whereby certain plants appear to release toxins which control pests on neighbouring plants or in the soil, is still one of the least well understood forms of pest control. The best-known example, that of planting French marigolds *(Tagetes patula)* between rows of any crop susceptible to eelworms or whitefly, was always practised in the kitchen garden at Pylewell, and as long ago as 1660, the Turkish garden book of Ibrahim ibnülhaç Mehmet recommended mustard sown round garden beds to keep bugs at bay.[21] An eighteenth-century explanation for the effects of companion planting is that 'Where different plants draw different juices from the earth for their nourishment: they must thrive best when planted near each other; for example, rue will thrive best near a fig-tree, and the figs will be sweeter; so a rose near garlick will be sweeter than common. . . . the bitter pungent juices being drawn by the rue and garlick from the fig and rose, . . .'[22]

CULTIVATING MUSHROOMS

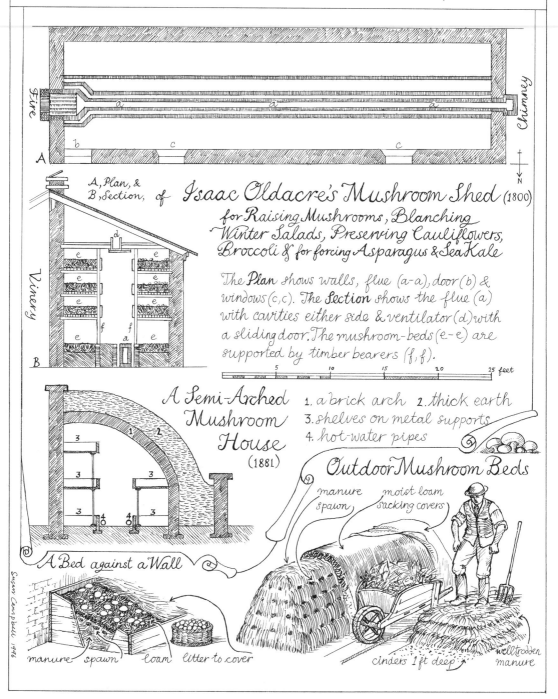

A, Plan, &
B, Section, of **Isaac Oldacre's Mushroom Shed** (1800)

for Raising Mushrooms, Blanching Winter Salads, Preserving Cauliflowers, Broccoli & for forcing Asparagus & Sea Kale

The **Plan** *shows walls, flue (a-a), door (b) & windows (c,c). The* **Section** *shows the flue (a) with cavities either side & ventilator (d) with a sliding door. The mushroom-beds (e-e) are supported by timber bearers (f, f).*

5   10   15   20   25 feet

A Semi-Arched Mushroom House (1881)

1. a brick arch   2. thick earth
3. shelves on metal supports
4. hot-water pipes

Outdoor Mushroom Beds

manure   moist loam
spawn   sacking covers

cinders 1 ft deep   well trodden manure

A Bed against a Wall

manure   spawn   loam   litter to cover

Susan Campbell 1996

Fire   Chimney

Vinery

CHAPTER SIXTEEN

THE MUSHROOM HOUSE

A backshed that has windows fitted with shutters, or one that has no windows at all, is invariably a mushroom house or a fruit store. Fruit stores, also known as fruit rooms, are furnished with slatted wooden shelves, and the one at Pylewell was used until very recently for storing apples, pears and grapes (see Chapter 18). Mushroom houses have a layout similar to that of a fruit room, with a central path and shelves on either side, but they may also have a double row of pipes running underneath the grating that forms a central walkway, to supply heat. Both types of building would have ventilators in the roof, or high up in the walls.

Although a mushroom house is listed in Pylewell's Sale Catalogue of 1850, and mushrooms were apparently on hand for the cook in the 1930s, its whereabouts is a mystery. If it was a typical mushroom house it might have had three rows of shelves, built of brick and supported by hefty cast-iron frames, running along either side of a central passage. Each row would be divided into bays, giving the place the appearance of a giant's linen cupboard, for each bay would be about two feet high, three feet deep and four and a half feet wide. The top shelf would be about six feet from the ground. Thick wooden boards, or sheets of iron, stone or slate would keep the contents of each compartment from spilling out at the front. Strong wooden planks or sheets of slate would have formed the base of each shelf. Where mushroom houses still exist, but are no longer used for their original purpose, which included the forcing of endive, rhubarb or seakale, their shelves make useful storage space for spare seed trays and plastic flowerpots, chemical sprays, powders and pastes.

MUSHROOM GROWING IN THE OPEN

It was in about the middle of the seventeenth century that French gardeners began to experiment with the cultivation of mushrooms in their gardens. In Paris, in1650, Nicolas de Bonnefons published *Le Jardinier François*, which described a method of growing mushrooms in a garden. Here, the kitchen parings and the water in which mushrooms had been washed were poured on to a hot bed consisting of mules' or asses' dung. This book was translated into English in 1658 by John Evelyn under the pseudonym 'Philocepos' with the title of *The French Gardiner*, but by the beginning of the eighteenth century a more certain way of

producing 'Bed-mushrooms' had been discovered. This involved inserting the spawn or mycelium of the edible field mushroom from old, infected horse manure into a hot bed of fresh, fermenting horse manure. Mushroom spawn was first described in detail by the French botanist Joseph Pitton de Tournefort in 1707.[1] There is a very brief account of a similar process in François Gentil's *Le Jardinier Solitaire*, first published anonymously, in Paris in 1704, but it is more hit-and-miss and omits the insertion of spawn.

London and Wise's translation of *Le Jardinier Solitaire*, published in 1706, advises the gentleman owner to dig a trench six inches deep and three feet wide in his garden in November, filling it with a well-rotted mixture of wheat straw and fresh horse dung to form a long, ridged bed two feet high, covered with two inches of earth.

The following April, to protect it from the summer heat, he was to cover it with unrotted litter, watering it whenever it appeared to dry out. 'This, Sir, is the cheapest way of raising Mushrooms.'[2]

Philip Miller elaborated on de Tournefort's instructions in his *Dictionary* of 1731, so that by skilful management of the spawn, the beds' coverings, the heat generated by the manure, and the moisture within the bed, mushrooms could be grown more or less all year round.

The beds were usually sited in the melon ground or frameyard beside the melons or cucumbers. Thick straw and coverings of canvas or matting were placed over them during times of heavy rain, frost or snow. The covers had to be lifted with care in order to pick the mushrooms.

THE ORIGINS OF THE MUSHROOM HOUSE

The mushroom house, or shed, evolved from the forcing house and could, if necessary, be used for that purpose as well. Mushroom houses were first built in Germany early in the nineteenth century, at a time when French gardeners had begun to grow mushrooms with great success in the darkness of underground caverns. Forcing houses, both glazed and darkened, were already popular in northern Europe, where the long, cold winters made outdoor cultivation of winter vegetables such as cabbages, cauliflowers, turnips and carrots difficult, if not impossible. German gardeners therefore hit upon the idea of growing mushrooms in their unlit forcing houses, using beds or boxes not already occupied by seakale, rhubarb or chicory (all of which were forced in warm, dark conditions).

In 1810 a Frenchman, Monsieur Chambry, began to grow mushrooms in the abandoned quarries and catacombs around Paris. As it turned out, he was the instigator of a massive, government-controlled, mushroom-growing industry. The industry flourished, taking advantage of the huge new underground quarries created by the Napoleonic and post-Napoleonic building of the city, and also of the amounts of horse dung generated by the city traffic. By 1860 there were thousands of caves containing literally miles of mushroom beds in the region. In 1867 William Robinson, the English gardening writer, visited Méry-sur-Oise (a village some eighteen miles from the centre of Paris) and there saw a cave with beds measuring a total of twenty-one miles that produced 3,000 pounds of mushrooms a day.[3] As with the German mushroom shed, underground mushroom culture avoided all the bother of covering the open beds in winter and, like the caves in the wine-growing areas of France, ensured both steady temperatures and humidity.

'The German mushroom-house' soon reached Russia, where it was seen by Isaac Oldacre, an English gardener working in the Czar's gardens at St Petersburg. In 1814 Oldacre built a similar house at Hounslow in Middlesex for Sir Joseph Banks, his new employer and a founder member of the Horticultural Society (later the Royal Horticultural Society). The mushroom house was visited by a committee from the Society. In due course

beds in a mushroom house

Oldacre published the plan, complete with hints on the cultivation of the mushroom (see page 226).

Oldacre's pamphlet, which was doubtless supported by Banks's patronage, included among its subscribers royalty, the nobility and the gentry as well as nurserymen, seedsmen, fruiterers and gardeners. By the 1820s cultivated mushrooms were so much in demand in Britain that no kitchen or market garden of any repute was without a mushroom house of some kind. It was usually built behind the vinery, but any dark, out-of-the-way place would do. Pits, darkened frames and cellars were also pressed into use. When all went well their produce was immense. An area of spawned compost measuring nine by two feet, for example, could yield eight pounds of mushrooms a week.

Mushrooms, picked daily at all seasons, were served at Victorian and Edwardian breakfasts, luncheons, high teas, dinners and suppers. Large, flat, open mushrooms (called 'flaps') were baked, broiled and stewed, or were made into soups and sauces, *gratins* and *ragoûts*. Young, unopened 'buttons' were sliced, fluted or finely chopped for garnishes and stuffings. If there was a glut they were potted in butter, pickled in vinegar, made into ketchups or dried and kept either whole or powdered for flavouring.

If Mr Hamilton had failed with the mushrooms at Pylewell he would have been considered worse than useless. Up at the house the demand for them in the 1920s and 1930s was constant and, as it seemed to the gardeners, always urgent, for Mrs Holmes, the cook, whom I interviewed in the 1980s, told me she would never resort to buying them. At that time shop mushrooms, if available, were extremely expensive (4s.6d per pound – the equivalent of £4 per pound today – wholesale, in winter) and rarely fresh.

Mushrooms continued to be grown in private gardens in the 1940s, but eventually their erratic growth and vulnerability to disease, plus the difficulty of obtaining suitable manure, the need for heat and the expense of keeping skilled gardeners led to the decline of the private mushroom house and the rise of the commercial grower. Mushroom houses were still useful though, as forcing houses.

The earliest mushroom houses, built according to Oldacre's design, had wooden shelves and hot-air flues beneath the walkway. But the fermenting compost on which the mushrooms were grown inevitably caused the wood to rot, endangering both the mushrooms and the gardener on his ladder. Supports of brick and cast iron, with slate or stone shelving, soon replaced the timber. At the same time, furnaces and hot-air flues gave way to boilers and hot-water pipes. Unglazed but shuttered windows were installed in some houses, to provide enough daylight to work by.

However, Oldacre's instructions for growing mushrooms remained the same, even a century later, and this would have been how mushrooms were grown at Pylewell before the last war. The instructions were as follows: the compost for the beds was made by mixing three parts of horse dung, fresh from the stable, with one part of litter. This was mixed with a fifth part of dried cow, sheep or deer dung. The compost was laid three inches thick on the shelves and beaten flat with a mallet. Another layer was added and again beaten flat until finally each shelf contained a compact mass of compost six inches thick. It started to heat up immediately, thanks to the fermentation of the fresh dung. When it reached 80-90°F/26-32C, holes were made in it with a dibble, two inches across and nine inches apart. These holes were planted with small pieces of mushroom spawn, but only when any excess of heat had cooled off, and the beds had settled down to a steadily declining warmth. If the temperature rose too much, slides in the ceiling were opened to let the heat escape through chimney-like ventilators.

After two weeks one or two beds were covered with one and a half inches of good loam which was again well beaten down. Five or six weeks later mushrooms would start to appear. The temperature of the house had to be kept between 50 and 55°F/10 and 13C and the pond or river water with which the beds were now cautiously sprinkled or syringed had to be as warm as milk fresh from the cow. According to Oldacre, once spawned, the

mushroom spawn

beds would continue to bear mushrooms in succession for several years, activated only by mould being placed on top and watered, and halted by being left to dry out. When bearing ceased completely, the old compost was replaced and re-spawned.

COMMERCIAL VARIETIES

It is generally supposed that the richly flavoured field mushroom *Agaricus campestris* differs in taste from the tasteless, cultivated 'shop' variety only because the one grows 'naturally' while the other is forced indoors. But it was not until 1951 that the shop mushroom was recognized and named as a different variety – *A. bisporus*. This mushroom, which ranges in colour from snow white to dusky brown is, or was, every bit as wild as *A. campestris*, but it grows on dung heaps and roadsides, and not in grassland. It is the mushroom that early gardeners would have found growing spontaneously on old hotbeds and mill tracks (the pre-steam-age tracks created by mules, donkeys or horses turning mill

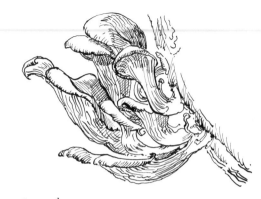

oyster mushrooms

wheels, threshing machines, pumping gear or engines). Indeed, 'Milltrack Mushroom Spawn', being virgin spawn of greater strength than manufactured spawn, was still being offered for sale in the late nineteenth century.

Both varieties of mushroom were cultivated by Oldacre and his predecessors, but they would have been unaware of the botanical differences. However, with the development of the nutritious, sterile, modern, commercial composts that have been developed to combat disease, *A. bisporus* has become the most commonly cultivated variety of Agaricus; unlike *A. campestris*, it thrives in such stuff.

Britain is almost the only country in Europe, if not in the world, where the eating of any kind of mushroom other than shop or field mushrooms is regarded as reckless, although it must be said that this attitude is changing. The gathering and eating of wild mushrooms is becoming quite popular, and at least two species of wild

mushroom are now being cultivated – the oyster mushroom *(Pleurotus ostreatus)* and the Japanese shiitake *(Lentinus edodes)*. These were first grown by the French and the Japanese respectively; they are now sold to the British supermarkets in some quantity by commercial growers.[4]

MUSHROOM PHYSIOLOGY

The cultivation of mushrooms is a process unlike any other in the kitchen garden, for here the gardener is dealing with plants that have no visible roots, slips or seeds. Lacking the chlorophyll found in every other fruit and vegetable, they have no need of sunlight – they can be grown in the dark. Their reproductive system too, is quite unlike that of any other product of the kitchen garden, for the true plant is the mushroom's spawn, or mycelium, while the mushroom itself is only the fruiting body. Above all, because the necessary conditions for the deliberate production of most varieties of edible fungi are so difficult to create artificially, their culture, even today, is limited to the few species that take kindly to domestication without being fussy about heat, dependent on another kind of vegetation or prone to disease.

Because their habits were so inexplicable, the earliest references to the cultivation of fungi amount to little more than a rough and ready re-creation of the conditions favoured by mushrooms in the wild, namely dung, humus or rotting wood, warmth and moisture. The manner in which mushrooms reproduced themselves was as mysterious as their apparently spontaneous growth. While on the one hand fire or (as some said) thunderbolts could cause them to grow, it was thought on the other hand that they could be produced by slime and damp. The word 'mycology' itself is derived from Greek *mukes*, which means 'fungus', but *mukes* also has associations with 'mucilage' and 'mucus'; the subconscious connection between slime and mushrooms persisted well into the Age of Enlightenment.

Richard Bradley, Professor of Botany at Cambridge from 1724 to 1732, knew well enough that field mushrooms could be grown from 'spawn'. Spawn had been discovered with the aid of de Tournefort's microscopes in 1707, when the French botanist published his observations of the way in which mushroom spores (the minute seeds shed by the gills in the mushroom's cap) became the little white threads which were later (in 1830) known as mycelial cords or mycelium. Moreover, in 1718 the Italian mycologist Pier' Antonio Micheli had succeeded in growing mushrooms from their own spores, on patches of dead leaves in the Boboli Gardens, Florence.[5]

Nevertheless, Bradley thought that the circles created by fairy-ring mushrooms *(Marasmius oreades)* were caused, not by the spittle of dancing elves, which was the popular view, but by the putrefying slime of copulating slugs which he had seen 'creep in a Circle for more than half an Hour, going over the same Ground at least twenty times before they could join, leaving on the Grass where they had crept, a viscous shiny Matter'.[6] He was unaware that the spawn itself inhibited further growth in pasture or on lawns where the mushrooms had already thrived. The spawn could only spread outwards, like ripples on a pond.

However, a scientific understanding of spores, mycelium and the sexual triggers that converted one into the other was of little concern to those who used mushroom spawn as an article of commerce. As we have seen, the best spawn for cultivated mushrooms came from mill tracks. Dry, compacted horse-droppings were collected from indoor exercise yards or the circuits of horse mills or threshing machines. Oldacre actually preferred fresh droppings. He mashed them with earth, formed this into bricks, dried them a little, then inserted bits of dry spawn. He stacked his bricks on a bed of dung, covered them with more fresh dung and allowed 'a gentle glow' to suffuse the stack so the spawn spread itself throughout each brick. They were then laid up in a dry place till needed; if necessary they could be kept for years. The market gardeners at Neat-House Gardens in Westminster sold spawn in the 1770s at eight to ten shillings a bushel. It was packed safely in hampers so that it could be sent far and wide to gardens all over England.

Alternatively, the gardener found his own mushroom spawn, either in the decayed manure of old hotbeds and dunghills or underneath the turf in pastures. He looked

Polyporus tuberaster

for 'that sort of earth that is found about their roots and is full of fine white threads, and sometimes white knots' and kept it carefully in a dry place until it was needed.[7] Every bit was precious, as a half-inch cube could cover two square feet with mushrooms.

THE MUSHROOM STONE

A certain sort of mushroom could also be obtained astonishingly quickly (literally overnight) by placing 'a kind of fossil, extremely curious'[8] in a pot of earth and watering it. This stone was known to the Greeks. Theophrastus described a kind of seaside mushroom that was spurred into growth by heavy rain and turned to stone by the sun.[9] The Romans called it *lapis fungifer*, *pietra fungeia*, or the mushroom stone. As it was already acknowledged that mushrooms had a kinship with fire, it was believed well into the eighteenth century that these stones

were pieces of volcanic lava, for one of the places in which they were most commonly found was the vicinity of Naples and, being otherwise unidentifiable, they were thought in that case to come from Vesuvius.

Giacomo Castelvetro, an Italian exile who took refuge in Jacobean England, had memories of mushrooms growing from a mushroom stone all summer, 'hard to believe unless one has actually experienced it'.[10] Stephen Switzer also knew of this phenomenon. In 1742 he wrote that one of these Vesuvian stones, when covered with nine inches of earth and sprinkled with warm water, blood or wine, would send out mushrooms in four days, thanks to the 'petrifaction of certain bodies' and their 'spontaneous productions'.[11] In 1758, the botanist and apothecary Sir John Hill described a large lump of *lapis fungifer* that produced excellent mushrooms. They were grown outdoors in a pot from early spring to late autumn, covered with a hand glass or cloche. The pot was moved to a warm, sheltered place between August and November and covered on cold nights with straw. From November to March it was kept in a cellar and continued to yield. One specimen from this stone increased in size by an inch a day between 19 and 24 June. Its head was six and a quarter inches across and it weighed one pound two ounces; the flesh was white and firm and the flavour both 'delicate and high'.[12]

This mushroom has been identified by modern mycologists as a bracket fungus –

Polyporus tuberastor. The 'stone' is an almost solid formation of this particular polypore's mycelium, which is scientifically referred to as a *pseudo-sclerotium* and is as hard as iron. When it becomes bound up with earth and pebbles it resembles porous rock or, as Mrs Beeton said, in her description of two kinds of Italian mushroom stone: 'The one found in the chalk hills near Naples ... has a white, porous, stalactical appearance; the other is hardened turf from some volcanic mountains near Florence'.[13] However, she did not tell her readers how to cook the polypore.

CHAPTER SEVENTEEN

THE SEED ROOM

In large establishments the supply of seeds, bulbs, tubers and corms was either given a room to itself, or it was kept in the head gardener's office in a cabinet provided with various-sized drawers; small ones at the top, large ones at the bottom. There would also be cupboards and drawers filled with sheaves of wrapping and tissue paper, bales of gauze and linen, cartons of neatly folded canvas and paper bags, balls of string, hanks of twine, pencils and pens, ink bottles, glue bottles, boxes of ungummed labels and various sizes of envelopes (some no larger than a visiting card). In the ceiling hooks were fixed, for hanging bags of threshed seed, seedheads and capsules out of the reach of mice; sieves were hung there too. Beneath the window there would be a worktable with weighing scales and a small winnowing machine attached to it, with more sieves, of various gauges, in a rack below. Mr Hamilton's seed supply was stored at Pylewell in a small cabinet in the potting shed and the gardening sundries connected with seed saving were kept in a cupboard.

In kitchen gardens large and small, gardeners spent long hours in the seed room, potting shed or office, drying, de-husking, cleaning and storing seeds. The seed room was not only the repository of the kitchen garden; it acted as a seed and bulb bank for the flower garden, pleasure grounds and shrubberies as well. Herbs for drying were bundled and stored here too. Most of this activity took place in August and September, when the herbs were full-grown and the majority of seeds were ripening, but the collections would have to be inspected every ten days or so, all through the year, to make sure nothing was going mouldy or being gnawed by vermin. Although most of his seeds were supplied by commercial seedsmen, Hamilton, like most gardeners of his generation and before, always grew some plants for seed, partly for economy and partly because not all of their favourite plants and vegetables were obtainable commercially; these might be their own hybrids, or local varieties that did well in that particular area and were unheard-of elsewhere.

Once they were clean and well dried, the seeds would be put into paper wrappings or envelopes and carefully labelled, named and dated; the smallest seeds were stored in the smallest, upper drawers. Larger seeds had larger, lower drawers; tubers, corms and bulbs went into the biggest, bottom drawers. Specimens from very valuable plants were individually wrapped in tissue paper. Most seed cabinets had brass label-holders on the fronts of the drawers holding neatly written cards to indicate what was inside, but the Earl of Derby's seed cabinet at Knowsley, near Liverpool, had the contents of each drawer written on the front in gold leaf. Large seeds such as acorns or nuts needed moisture to preserve their vitality; they were packed in mouse-proof wooden boxes, on a layer of damp sand or sphagnum moss.

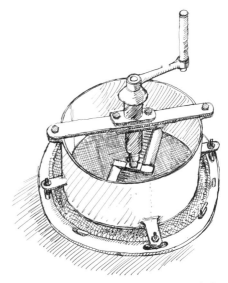

patent seed-sieve

SEED SAVING AND THE COMMERCIAL SEEDSMAN

There are a few disadvantages to home-grown seed. It is often variable; it may eventually produce inferior plants; it may also become infected with moulds. As long ago as 1285 Walter of Henley wrote of the benefit of obtaining 'foreign seed' [1] and in 1629 John Parkinson observed that it was a waste of time to conserve any seed other than that which came from the best plants; also that seed ripened abroad was superior to that ripened in Britain and that even the best of our gardeners 'hath not ground sufficient for all sorts, . . . and therefore the seede of some things are continually brought from beyond the Sea unto us'. Furthermore, plants grown for their seed needed more space than those grown solely for their leaves or roots. For example, to grow carrots for seed, 'You must . . . pull them up when they are too thicke, if you will have them

grow . . . for seed, that they may grow at the least three or foure foot in sunder.' [2]

For these reasons, whether their gardens were large or small, wise gardeners relied on commercial seedsmen for some of their seeds. The seedsman could concentrate exclusively on growing seed, on land ideally suited to a particular crop. He also offered a wider choice because he traded with other producers, including foreign seed growers. Modern seedsmen have these advantages, and more: they have assistance from government-sponsored research stations and laboratories, and access to seeds and seed trials in many different parts of the world. To benefit from these advantages, all the gardener has to do today is fill in an order form.

SEVENTEENTH-CENTURY SEEDSMEN AND NURSERYMEN

According to the centenary catalogue published by Sutton and Sons in 1906, the seed trade 'as a distinct industry did not exist, and illustrated and priced catalogues were unknown' before 1806, when Sutton's was founded.

As far as priced seeds are concerned, Sutton's claim may be true, but catalogues, or rather, lists 'of divers ordinary Herbs and Roots' to remind the gardener of the sorts he might need, began to appear in late seventeenth-century gardening books. The means by which the plants were increased was also briefly described: they were by seed, slips, tops or roots.[3]

Medieval garden accounts show that seed was sold by itinerant salesmen with packhorses. Their trade was not necessarily exclusively in that commodity, but the *Oxford English Dictionary* gives no reference to 'seedsman' before 1678, when the profession was just beginning to establish itself. One of the earliest seed shops in London was that of William Lucas in the Strand; a copy of his

seed list has been found in a notebook of *circa* 1677. At that time, according to the twentieth-century garden historian John Harvey, there were probably only three major seed businesses in London, but the horticultural trade was growing. By 1691, of the twenty-eight significant gardens in the London area, at least five were commercial nurseries. By 1700 the number had increased to fifteen.[4]

One of them was the enormous nursery at Brompton Park. It was founded in 1681 and occupied over 100 acres of land that is now the site of the South Kensington museums and the Albert Hall. In 1690 the nursery was managed by George London and Henry Wise; their foremen included Charles Bridgeman (who succeeded Wise as the royal gardener), Stephen Switzer and Leonard Meager. By 1700 London and Wise had a virtual monopoly of the seed and nursery trade in London.

Between them, London and Wise designed and supplied all the noblest gardens of the day – Kensington Palace, Longleat, Melbourne, Chatsworth and Blenheim among them – sending huge numbers of trees, shrubs and exotics, 'mural', standard, dwarf and other fruit trees, seeds, bulbs, roots and slips to all parts of the country. They designed and planted flower gardens, topiary gardens, walks, wildernesses, groves, canals, parterres and avenues, as well as 'that most useful (though less pompous part of Horticulture) the Potagere, Meloniere, Culinarie Garden'.[5]

seed-box and tamp

SEED GARDENS AND FARMS AROUND LONDON

As time went by, British nurseries and seed gardens were often combined with market gardens, and situated on the outskirts of towns; they were particularly numerous in the counties around London. Different localities favoured different seed crops. Essex was famous for brassicas, Bedfordshire for carrots, and so on. In the early part of the nineteenth century, Loudon wrote that 'Chervil, radish and cress seeds are grown chiefly in the neighbourhood of Saffron-Walden in Essex; cabbages at Battersea; onions at Deptford; peas in Kent; turnips in Norfolk; rape in Lincolnshire; mustard in the county of Durham, &c.'[6]

By the late eighteenth century it was acknowledged that the banks of the Thames above and below London 'has been as long, or perhaps longer, in the occupation of kitchen-gardeners, than any other land in Britain'. The market gardens and orchards around the city covered some 10,000 acres, with an annual income of £645,000 earned from vegetables and £400,000 from fruit.[7]

From the eighteenth century onwards, seedsmen and nurserymen made trials and grew sample crops, then had their seed grown for them on seed farms. It was ripened, harvested, cleaned and sent back to them by the hundredweight or bushel, to be sold in their shops and at seed markets in the metropolis. Samples of seed from successful vegetables and fruits grown in market gardens would also be taken by seed merchants and grown *en masse* on their farms. To keep the seeds true to type, growers were careful not to raise too many varieties of the same species or, if they did, they took care to have varieties that flowered at different times.

The most famous Thames-side kitchen gardens were the 200 acres at Neat-House Gardens, in Westminster (renowned for celery). There were more gardens at Chelsea and Battersea, specializing in cabbages and cauliflowers, and flower and fruit nurseries at Hammersmith, Bethnal Green, Hackney, Hoxton and Whitechapel. As London grew, the trade developed further away from the city, at Islington, Earls Court, Fulham, Mortlake (famous for asparagus), Charlton, Plumstead, Deptford (asparagus and onions) and Isleworth.

Some nurserymen and their gardens are still remembered by their products; John Wilmot and Michael Keens of Isleworth have given their names to the strawberries and plums they bred there; Joseph Myatt of Deptford is immortalized by his rhubarb; Battersea is remembered by its cabbage, Charlton by its peas. The roads from London to Heathrow Airport lie alongside some of these enormous gardens, which display remnants of walls and old orchards to this

day. One of them, in Colnbrook, is the birthplace of the seedling apple that became Cox's Orange Pippin.

THE FIRST
COMMERCIAL CATALOGUES

The first printed, commercial gardening catalogue to have survived contains alphabetical lists of seeds, bulbs, trees and shrubs in pamphlet form. It was issued by the nurseryman Robert Furber in 1727, to be followed in 1730 by his beautifully illustrated catalogue *The Twelve Months of Flowers*. By 1725, with a network of newspapers and weekly magazines covering most of the country, nurserymen and seedsmen were able to advertise their wares in the press, although not in the extravagant manner adopted by Furber with his flower catalogue. This development coincided with a pro-liferation of new, provincial nurseries.

Lists with prices were printed from the 1770s, but as costs and crops varied from year to year, most catalogues at this time gave no prices unless they were inked in, and they were rarely dated. Sutton's claim to be the

first seed company to print prices in its catalogues is therefore almost certainly justified. The company also takes credit for producing the first catalogues to contain advice, not only on when and how to grow its seeds but also on how to cook its more unusual vegetables.

TWENTIETH-CENTURY
SEEDSMEN

Packets of commercially grown seeds would be stored in the seed room as soon as they arrived. Like other head gardeners, Mr Hamilton sent off his main order in January, after consultation with his employers and the cook.

Piles of old catalogues are often to be found mouldering in the cupboards of head gardeners' offices, and they make interesting reading, but one of the most useful catalogues of the early twentieth century is in the form of a large book; it is a translation, published by William Robinson in 1904, of Messrs Vilmorin-Andrieux's *The Vegetable Garden*. (At that time the Vilmorin-Andrieux family included several prominent French horticulturalists and seedsmen.) This book is an illustrated, classified and descriptive compendium of all the 'garden vegetables of cold and temperate climates' then grown in France and England. The numerous varieties of every kind of vegetable listed – some 170 sorts of pea and as many lettuces and potatoes, 150 types of melon, 145 kinds of cabbage, 74 varieties of onion and 58 of beet, for example – might put our modern catalogues to shame, were it not that even then, according to Robinson, vegetables were being bred for size (possibly to suit the enormous families of those days) rather than quality.

The 1960s saw the introduction of the F1 hybrid – a plant raised from commercial seed, obtained by crossing two highly selected inbred lines. It will never produce true seed of its own but, being a first cross, it will have hybrid vigour. By selling F1s, the modern seedsman has, to a certain extent, made sure that the gardener must always return to him for his seed. A glance through any seed catalogue today will reveal that the majority of vegetable seed is F1; it also shows exactly how tastes in vegetables and marketing have changed in this century. Fewer varieties of vegetable are sold, and their earliness or lateness, productiveness and keeping qualities are still of importance, but the selling points – for the domestic gardener at least – are now on flavour, sweetness, crispness and texture.

KEEPING THE STRAIN TRUE

Some gardeners still try to keep the seeds of those vegetables, salads, fruits and flowers that best suit their soil, win them prizes at produce shows or most please the family, just in case they disappear from the catalogues. Gardeners have always experienced considerable difficulty however, in keeping their favourite strains true, especially with freely hybridizing vegetables such as brassicas and lettuces. The problem is ancient. The domestication of wild food plants – the ancestors of the cereals, vegetables and fruits we grow today began as long ago as the neolithic 'revolution' in agriculture, some 10,000 years before the birth of Christ. Some plants resisted and remained 'wild', others – grown by the earliest farmers and gardeners from seeds selected only from plants exhibiting the characteristics they wanted – became improved or 'ennobled'.

There is always the risk of a cross-mating that displays unasked-for characteristics, sometimes good, but all too often 'degenerative'. By selecting the best seeds from the finest plants, or from plants with the most desirable charac-  teristics; by removing 'rogues' from the crop; by taking advantage of the better kinds of sports and chance seedlings; by deliberately breeding hybrids; by rooting layers, taking cuttings and, in the case of trees and shrubs, by making grafts, generations of gardeners and nurserymen have propagated the best and enlarged the number of varieties available.

Plant breeding is now in the hands of biologists and laboratory technicians, well versed in genetics, hormonal and molecular behaviour. The first gardeners, nurserymen and seedsmen had none of this knowledge, but they gradually widened the choice and improved the quality of what could be grown in their kitchen and fruit gardens. They multiplied, within a species, the number of available varieties; they increased size and yield; they developed earlier, later and disease-resistant crops; they discovered, by trial and error, which varieties of fruit and vegetables suited specific soils, localities, seasons and climates. It is no accident that the kitchen garden has been the source of some of the most important botanical discoveries. The gardener is by nature closely observant and as keen to discover the reasons for any abnormal plant behaviour, or to improve his crops, as any scientist. Moreover, his workplace is the ideal situation for trials and experiments.

Much of what an intelligent gardener does is based on common sense, experience and observation. The most primitive of gardeners could see that plants benefited from feeding, protection and watering, and that the best plants produced the best crops, as well as the best seed. It had long been the practice to reject the smallest seed, and to choose the earliest seeds to form (these were usually the largest, and therefore the best). In spite of this, crops still tended to degenerate; the size of the sown seed was thought to be one of the main causes.

By the eighteenth century, the benefits of crop rotation and seed exchange had long been accepted, but the reasons for these benefits could not be explained. It was hardest of all to understand why seedlings sometimes failed to reproduce the good characteristics of their parents. The 'diverse nature of the soil' was held responsible for the 'many and prominent varieties of plants in use in the kitchen' until the mid eighteenth century, when this theory was shown to be flawed. Carl Linnæus unravelled the secrets of hybridization, discovering that it was the cross-fertilization of two different varieties of the same species that was responsible for these vagaries of plant behaviour.

TRANSPLANTING FOR SEED

The mechanism by which plants produce, first flowers and then seeds, was of little concern to primitive gardeners, but by the early seventeenth century it had been noted that the transplanting of certain plants as they approached maturity was a stimulus to flowering. The interruption in their growth and their removal to a larger space in a different plot caused them to flower far sooner than they would have done if left undisturbed; they also produced larger, better seeds.

When seed was required it was the custom, as with all seed plants, to save the best specimens in the crop. Seed plants to be transplanted were lifted when they reached the point at which they would normally be harvested. In the case of plants grown for their leaves or roots this would be before they flowered, usually as winter approached.

Roots such as carrots, parsnips and turnips had their leaves cut off and were stored as usual in clamps (see Chapter 18). They were then replanted in the spring, at very much wider spacings, because in their second, seed-forming year they could grow to as much as five feet high and three feet across, producing seed by midsummer.

This transplanting or replanting process was described by John Parkinson as 'the best way to have the fairest and most principall seede' from radishes, lettuces, turnips, parsnips, onions, leeks and carrots. As winter approached, cabbages were dug up, roots and all, to avoid the risk of frosts rotting their stems, then wrapped in cloths and hung in sheds until the danger of frost had passed. In March they were planted again, in trenches, with their heads almost buried in the ground and protected with straw, to flower and form seed pods in due course.[8] This technique for procuring seed was still recommended by Loudon in 1825.[9]

RIPENING THE SEED

Most types of seed, but especially those in pods or clusters, were picked before they were fully ripe, to make sure of securing them. They were then dried in the sun, or in a greenhouse or potting shed. After drying they were rubbed or 'thrashed'. Parkinson's radish plants were pulled up entirely when the seedpods became 'whitish', then hung on bushes or fences until they were completely dry. His lettuce seed had to be gathered before it fell, still attached to its stems, when

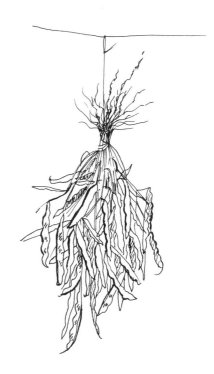

it was almost ripe; then the stalks were laid on mats to ripen in the sun. This procedure was also used for ripening borage, aniseed, carrot, balm, leek and onion seed.

CHOOSING THE BEST

As the first seed to form was always said to be the best, by allowing only this to ripen, especially in the case of cucumbers, peas or beans, the crop was naturally reduced; the plant had achieved its purpose and lacked the stimulus to produce more flowers or fruits. Besides taking the earliest seed from any plant, the part of the plant from which the seed came was also taken into account. The best seed of a melon was said by John Mortimer to come not only from the earliest fruits to ripen, but also from the sunniest side of the fruit.[10] And for parsnips, John

bolt-resistant varieties are now available. But neither these, nor any explanation for bolting, was available to gardeners in Parkinson's time. Bolting was usually caused by a cold spell in early spring. If the days, as well as the nights, are cold enough, a young plant will be triggered into flowering a few weeks later. It will stop making the large leaves or swollen roots that were hoped for, and send up a flower stem instead. The effect, referred to (since the 1930s) as vernalization, is the same as if the plant had spent the winter as a mature plant, to flower in the following year – which, under ideal conditions, it would have done.

VIABILITY

Theophrastus advised sowing all seed when it was fresh in order to obtain the best results, but he remarked that the keeping capacity varied from one species to another. He thought vegetables with a 'pungent taste' such as coriander, leek, mustard and rocket kept better than mild vegetables such as cucumbers, gourds, orach and basil. He also noted that the viability of all seeds was affected by the way in which they were stored. Seed corn, for example, remained viable for forty years, and 'food-seed' lasted sixty to seventy years, without being 'evaporated' or eaten by worms, when stored at Petra, in Jordan; the reason was that this region is 'elevated and exposed to fair winds'.[12]

The eighteenth-century gardener Philip Miller, on the other hand, ascribed viability

Parkinson recommended only saving seed from the main or central flowerheads,[11] while according to the *Gardeners' Chronicle* of 25 October 1890, in order to achieve plants with short stems, the Earl of Derby's gardener at Knowsley cut the heads off his Brussels sprouts and saved only the seed which came from the sprouts.

On the other hand, plants that 'bolted', or ran to seed before time, were not welcome and were weeded out. Bolting occurred both in root crops and leaf crops, especially if they were sown early; cabbages, onions, lettuces, carrots, turnips and beets were, and still are, particularly vulnerable, although modern to the oiliness, or otherwise, of certain seeds; and further suggested that it depended on the 'nature' of the oil (hot or cold), and the texture of the seed coat. Seeds possessing oil of a cold nature and 'thick horny Coverings' – cucumbers, gourds and melons – 'continue good eight or ten Years' (contrary to Theophrastus's view). Oilier seeds such as radishes, turnips and rape keep only three or four years; this is because their oil is of a warmer nature, and their coats are 'not so hard and close as the others'. Seeds from umbelliferous plants such as carrots, parsley and parsnips contain little oil and 'seldom remain good longer than two Years'.

From 1722 to 1770 Miller was head gardener to the Society of Apothecaries at their Botanic Garden in Chelsea. He was therefore constantly growing new seeds sent to him from all over the world, hence his preoccupation with viability. In the second volume of the third edition of his *Gardener's Dictionary* (1739) he set out the first table showing the length of time seeds would keep, provided they were 'well saved'. He wrote that seeds which keep for three years or more, including cucumber and melon seeds, 'are generally preferr'd for being three Years old, . . . because when the Seeds are new, the Plants grow too vigorous, and produce a small Quantity of Fruit.'[13]

Like many gardeners before him, Miller believed that if old seed was not to be had, new seed could be 'aged' by keeping it in his breeches pocket for a couple of months. This belief, and the preference for old, rather than fresh melon and cucumber seed, persisted late into the nineteenth century until another gardening writer, James Anderson, declared that the idea that the long keeping of certain seeds improved them should be treated 'with deserved ridicule'.[14]

PICKING AND PRESERVING

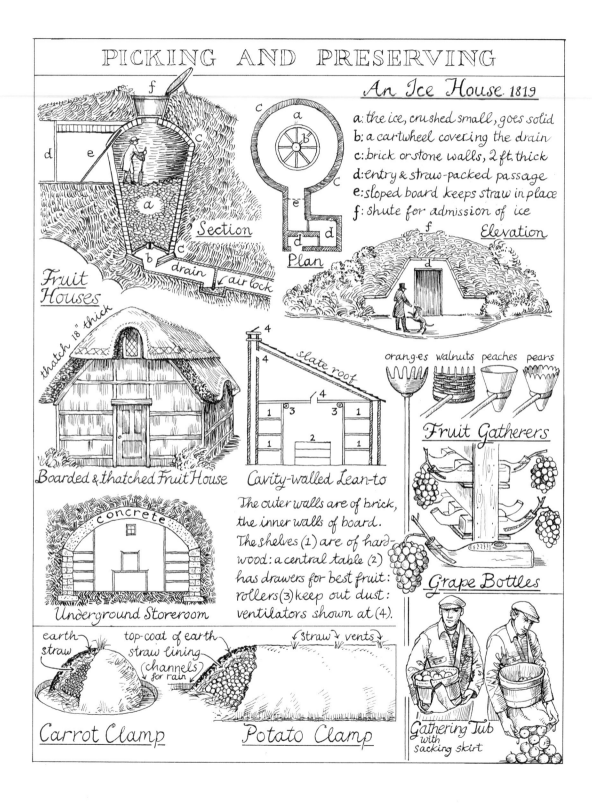

An Ice House. 1819

a: the ice, crushed small, goes solid
b: a cartwheel covering the drain
c: brick or stone walls, 2 ft. thick
d: entry & straw-packed passage
e: sloped board keeps straw in place
f: shute for admission of ice

Section

Plan

Elevation

drain   air lock

Fruit Houses

thatch 18" thick

Boarded & thatched Fruit House

Underground Storeroom

concrete

Cavity-walled Lean-to

The outer walls are of brick, the inner walls of board. The shelves (1) are of hardwood: a central table (2) has drawers for best fruit: rollers (3) keep out dust: ventilators shown at (4).

slate roof

oranges   walnuts   peaches   pears

Fruit Gatherers

Grape Bottles

Carrot Clamp

earth straw
top-coat of earth
straw lining
channels for rain

Potato Clamp

straw   vents

Gathering Tub
with sacking skirt

CHAPTER EIGHTEEN

PICKING, PACKING AND STORING

THE COOK

'Mrs' Holmes was the Whitakers' cook at Pylewell during the 1920s and early 1930s. She left to take up a position with royalty, and then married the old Pylewell coachman's brother, who lived in Winchester (the 'Mrs' was a courtesy title always given to unmarried cooks), but her husband suddenly died and she returned to Pylewell just before the war. She cooked for Billy's mother after the war, and then retired. She was, according to Jean and Penelope Whitaker, 'the best cook ever', but as terrifying to the gardeners as she was to her own staff. Her pre-war responsibilities were enormous; apart from laying on meals for special occasions and numerous guests, she had to oversee the cooking of five different breakfasts, luncheons, teas, suppers and dinners for the whole household. These meals were eaten more or less simultaneously in five different parts of the house; in the dining room, the school room, the nursery, the housekeeper's room and the servants' hall.

She claimed that 'Hamilton *always* had what was wanted', and that apart from citrus fruits she never had to buy fruit or vegetables from the shops. Nevertheless, she demanded undamaged garden produce in tip-top condition, and fruit at the correct stage of ripeness. She did not expect to find mud, strands of hay or straw, stray twigs, wispy roots, tough stems and surplus, dead or mouldy leaves in her daily consignments from the kitchen garden. Nor did she want to rummage through a jumble of produce piled hugger-mugger in their boxes, barrows or baskets. Before any fruit, roots or greenery were sent to her they had to be cleaned, neatly bundled and sorted. Then, to avoid jostling, everything was carried to the house by two gardeners on a stretcher-like hand-barrow.

Mrs Holmes had a book of menus, written in French, for Mrs Whitaker to choose from. She would take it to the boudoir, first thing every morning, to discuss what to have, and find out how many it was for. By 9.45 a.m. Mrs Holmes's head kitchenmaid had written a list to give to the gardener waiting at the kitchen door for any extra items to add to the main delivery, which would have come to the kitchen by nine o'clock.

The gardeners did the basic washing, trimming and boxing-up, first thing in the

morning, or last thing at night. This work took place in the washroom at the far end of the potting shed, behind the late vinery. Here the produce, fresh from the garden, would be prepared for the kitchen, for storage, or for sending to the family when it was away in London. When I first knew Pylewell, the packing bench, and a big stone sink with a single cold tap, were still there, with a well-worn trimming knife and an old scrubbing brush on the window sill above them. On the workbench was a set of scales, with some of the original weights. Piles of old newspapers, wooden and cardboard boxes, balls of string and reels of sticky tape lay abandoned on the shelves.

Vegetable washing was normally the work of the under gardeners, with the boys giving a hand when there was a big order. Even as late as the 1980s, at Cottesbrooke in Northamptonshire, the gardeners prepared vegetables meticulously before sending them up to the house. Potatoes were scrubbed, leeks and heads of celery were washed, topped and tailed; asparagus was cut into equal lengths and graded, then tied in bundles with raffia; sprouts, peas and beans were sent in baskets; trimmed cabbages and cauliflowers went loose. Tiny beets, carrots and turnips were carefully washed, but their leaves were left on so that the crop could be tied in neat bunches. Radishes, spring onions and fresh herbs were also bunched, and put with the other saladings, which were trimmed and lightly rinsed. Doug Brereton, the head gardener there, always sent his cucumbers with their withered flowers still attached, as if proof were needed that they were fresh and home-grown.

Tomatoes, cherries and soft fruits were tenderly laid in wood-chip punnets lined with white paper (all the packing materials were bought by the gross and the ream from the sundriesman). The choicest melons, peaches, apricots, nectarines, plums, figs and grapes were laid in flat baskets, on beds of fig or vine leaves. Doug picked these fruits himself, and would have preferred to have arranged them for the table himself as well, for his greatest fear was that the bloom might be damaged or the fruit bruised by less experienced hands. However, this job was always done at Cottesbrooke by the cook, and at Pylewell by Mr Manley, the butler.

Taking care of the best fruit was one of those jobs (like sowing the best seeds) that was the head gardener's sole responsibility; dessert fruits were virtually untouched by anyone other than him, the cook, or the butler until one of the family, or one of their guests, chose to eat it. Mr Hamilton also told Mrs Holmes when any fruit was ready to make into jams or preserves.

SENDING AWAY

Some green, tin, cone-shaped florists' vases were stacked on the open shelves at the back of the washroom, reminders of the days when cut flowers were trimmed and tied into bunches here too, ready for taking to the house or for sending, in specially made boxes, with the rest of the produce when the family was away. Gardening treatises from the early eighteenth century onwards contain detailed instructions on the packing of produce, especially fruit, for carriage. Everything would have to be trimmed neatly to reduce carriage weight, and fruit was packed in wood or paper shavings, tissue paper or newspaper, before being gently but firmly stowed in large, lockable boxes or hampers. Heavy things such as melons and cabbages went at the bottom, with bran or wood wool between the spaces; lighter, delicate soft fruits and flowers went in their own shallow boxes or baskets on top. An ingenious system of padding and false bottoms ensured that everything arrived safely.

Grapes had a box to themselves. It was lined with moss that had been gathered early in the summer, then well dried and beaten, to make it soft, elastic, and free from dust. Paper was laid between the moss and the bunches of grapes, which were tightly packed with bran or wadding and silver paper so that they could not be shaken. In order to minimize the risk of blemishing, they were packed in the vinery as they were picked. On arrival, if they were packed in bran it would be removed with bellows.

In great houses, it was customary each week to send from the family's country seat to their town house a supply of fruit, flowers, vegetables and salads from the gardens, as well as butter, meat, eggs and poultry from the dairy, farm and poultry yard, preserves from the kitchen and still-room and even fuel and clean laundry. Before the advent of the railways, carriage would be by water or road. A horse and cart was fine for 'hard baking pears and apples', but for tender fruits the best form of transport was 'Water Carriage, or the Back or Arms of a Porter, for fear of jogging'.[1]

The River Thames was a valuable thoroughfare and amenity in this respect, especially for those living close to its banks and in London. Watermen and barges took goods to and from the great houses and palaces at Syon, Richmond, Greenwich, Hampton Court and Kew, and their owners' equally palatial mansions in London.

The coming of the railways made it possible, by the early twentieth century, for goods to be sent all over the kingdom with their arrival ensured within one or two days. Twice a week, on Tuesdays and Fridays when the family was away, it was young Percy Gregory's job to harness the mowing pony to the garden cart at 8 a.m., load it with the garden boxes and hampers (securely padlocked and stamped 'PYLEWELL GARDENS LYMINGTON'), and accompany them to Lymington Town railway station, three miles away, to see them weighed. From here, when the family was in town, the hampers were sent by the 9.15 passenger train, in the goods van, to Waterloo, whence they were taken by carrier to the Whitakers' house at 41 Upper Brook Street, Mayfair. The pony-cart would return from the station with last week's empties and, if necessary, a load of coke for the boilers. (Percy remembers one particularly bad winter when the two boilers used 50 tons of coke before Christmas.) Percy would be back at the gardens by midday, in time for his dinner. The system also allowed the returning baskets to bring goods for the gardens from the metropolitan nurserymen. Before the advent of the telephone, the gardener would make his requests in the notebook that accompanied every transmission. His employers, the butler or the cook would use the same notebook for their requests and comments. Virtually all the house servants from Pylewell, including the chauffeur and a fleet of cars, would accompany the family to town. (Although the Whitakers' first car – a Rolls Royce – was bought in 1910, they referred to its driver, Mr Newstead, as 'the coachman' for years afterwards, as that is what he had been until then.) The family's town house was used not just for the Season, which lasted from Easter to the end of July, but for a month or so in early spring, for dresses to be made and fitted, and again for a 'little season' in the autumn. In 1925, when the family went to Scotland for six weeks of grouse shooting, the Pylewell children, servants, bicycles and dogs were sent ahead by train, occupying one whole coach and sleeping in it overnight in a London siding, before being hooked to the train for

Elgin. The senior Whitakers followed in the Rolls and hampers from Pylewell gardens duly appeared twice-weekly.

It may seem strange that families should have continued to have kitchen produce sent from the country-house kitchen garden to town well into the twentieth century, even though as town dwellers they, or rather their servants, could buy all they needed from the greengrocer or street market. The old custom owed something to economy, because apart from the certainty that one's own fruit and vegetables were better than shop-bought produce, the gardeners at home were working – and being paid – whether the family was in residence or not.

These long absences from the country house were usually controlled by regular fixtures in the calendar, caused by affairs of state, business, social occasions, or holidays connected with hunting, shooting and fishing. The gardener was therefore forewarned, and could plan ahead to some extent, but once crop production was underway the kitchen garden of a country house was more or less unstoppable. Like a liner in mid-ocean or a moving train, it was no simple matter to shut down the engines and expect all movement to cease at once. Cucumber seed was sown first in March and again in September to provide cucumbers for eating all the year round; broad beans were sown from November to April for eating from June to August; trees bore fruit within six months of forcing. With these procedures once begun, there was no turning back.

STORE ROOMS FOR WINTER

It took good management to supply the household with enough garden produce to last through the winter. To achieve this there had to be a surplus of the types of fruit and vegetables that could be made into preserves or would otherwise keep well – and keeping over winter meant having proper storage places. At Pylewell, there was a shed by the kitchens for the storage of potatoes or roots, and the old dairy, as well as the fruit room in the backsheds, was sometimes used to store fruit.

Rooms over stables, sheds in various parts of the gardens, gazebos in the garden walls, cellars, lofts and rooms in the mansion itself did well enough for storage until the latter part of the eighteenth century. Thereafter custom-built fruit rooms and root cellars were found to be more satisfactory and the sheds behind the hothouse range (the backsheds) were found to be the best place for them. For one thing, temperature, light and humidity could be monitored by the gardeners; also, with easier access the gardeners could look over their stores regularly, sending produce whenever it was ready and making sure nothing was shrivelling up or going mouldy. Harvesting methods were perfected to ensure success in the store rooms.

GATHERING APPLES
AND PEARS

For the successful storage of apples and pears there were several rules. The pomologist Robert Thompson was particularly anxious to avoid 'careless gathering'. 'When a large fruit-room has to be filled with produce to be reserved for use over a period of several months, the greatest care in every detail should be exercised. Avoid clasping and pinching the fruits in the hand; place them in padded shallow baskets, and remove them from these to their final quarters with the same care.' [2]

Before picking could begin, the day had to be dry, the fruit perfectly ripe – dropping into the hand when lightly pushed upwards – and the dew gone off it. On fruit-picking days, William Forsyth, gardener to George III, saw to it that the grass below the trees in the royal orchards was mowed, then strewn with previously dried mowings, perfectly dry pea-haulms, oat or barley straw. Special fruit-picking steps were brought out, with detachable ladders at the back and a broad

step with room for a basket on top; baskets, hampers and wheelbarrows were assembled. The baskets were lined with 'short-grass mowings, perfectly dry (which you ought to provide for the purpose in Summer, and keep in a shed . . . till wanted)'.[3]

If the fruit were in the least bruised, it would not keep. Windfalls were therefore kept separately from the hand-picked fruit, and used first. Once all the fruit had been gathered the dry mowings were raked up and put on the compost heap; if left, they would harbour slugs. In fine weather between September and late October, the latest apples and pears on the espaliers, walls and orchard trees would be carefully gathered from midday onwards and taken in baskets to the fruit room. There, the windows were left open and the fruit was laid in heaps, each of its own sort, to 'sweat' for a couple of weeks before being wiped dry, sorted and finally stored.

The sweating procedure was criticized in the early nineteenth century for, at best, serving no practical use and, at worst, giving the fruit a bad flavour or making it dry and mealy. Many gardeners abandoned the practice, but it still had its adherents, who argued that sweating had always been done before and that, as it removed a quantity of moisture (so much, according to William Forsyth 'that on putting your hand into the heap, it will come out as wet as if it had been dipped into a pail of water'),[4] and Loudon considered that 'it must, to a certain extent, be a beneficial practice.' [5] It was reinstated by twentieth-century fruit growers.

RETARDING RIPENESS

There were two schools of thought as to whether fruits (pears in particular) should be picked only when perfectly ripe, or whether they should be picked at intervals when unripe, nearly ripe and fully ripe. The advantage of the latter approach, as explained by the nineteenth-century nurseryman George Lindley, is that 'the last-gathering will be the first to be brought to table; the second gathering will be next; and the first gathering will continue the longest fit for use'.[6] On removing winter pears (pears stored from October to March or even longer) from storage, it was, according to Benjamin Whitmill, writing in the eighteenth century, the custom to warm them by the fire 'before they are eat, as they do a Bottle of Wine, which will heighten the Flavour of the Fruit'.[7]

Early in the nineteenth century, scientists began to experiment with other ways of retarding ripeness in fruit. In 1821 a prize was awarded to a French scientist for a paper in which he explained how he delayed the ripening of fruit by sealing it in a bottle which contained, in a separate compartment, a paste made of lime, sulphate of iron and water. The subsequent retention of carbon, he said, prevented the fruit from ripening, as that process needs carbonic acid, a combination of carbon and oxygen. He kept unripe peaches, plums and apricots like this for a month, then ripened them perfectly on exposing them to air.

FRUIT-GATHERING IMPLEMENTS

If there were any risk of damaging the tree and its fruit by using a ladder, gardeners used special gadgets for gathering the best fruits growing out of reach. These implements began to appear in early nineteenth-century gardening manuals, and later in their manufacturers' advertisement (see page 246).

For large fruits such as apples, peaches or pears, fruit gatherers took the form of a cup-shaped receptacle of tin or basketwork attached to the end of a long rod. For really delicate fruit, a tin cup might be lined with velvet. Another type of fruit gatherer had a pair of leather-covered forceps attached to a pole. Alternatively, the pole supported a combination of scissors and tweezers activated by wires, pulleys, springs and levers. These were designed to pick bunches of grapes and other berries, first cutting the branch, then holding on to it.

Grape and berry gatherers, while helpful for the picking of fruits such as gooseberries, strawberries, raspberries and, of course, grapes, were essential if the owner had the idea that 'such fruits . . . should be touched by

no other hand than that which conveys them to the mouth'. A dining table ornamented with fruit growing on miniature trees in pots was one way of doing this. Alternatively, entire branches of fruit were cut off the trees or bushes on which they grew, 'and brought to the table, as bouquets, in elegant china vases'.[8]

THE FRUIT ROOM

By tradition the fruit room has insulated walls and a ventilated ceiling lined with dark brown, varnished matchboarding; some fruit rooms had ventilators in the form of chimney-like shafts, inclined towards the back wall; they had top and bottom shutters that could be opened or closed by pulleys. In many cases there is a fruit cellar below. At Pylewell, there are no such refinements; the walls are merely painted white, but in one corner there is an arrangement of slanted shelves, for the accommodation of burgundy-shaped grape bottles.

The fruit room was used mainly for the best mid and late season dessert apples and pears; they would take up most of the space from the time of their harvesting in September and October until early to midsummer, when even the longest keepers would all have been eaten. This was the time when midsummer fruits such as pineapples, melons and peaches would be lodged there for a short while after picking: a few days' delay between picking and eating was supposed to improve the flavour. 'Kitchen' or cooking apples and pears were stored in heaps under the lowest shelves or kept in boxes, baskets and hampers in the cellar.

The requirements of a mid nineteenth-century fruit room, as set out by M'Intosh in 1853 are as follows: 'exclusion from air, a cool and uniform temperature, an atmosphere neither too dry nor too moist, and total darkness'.[9] Some fruit rooms were divided in two, with a door connecting them. Although invariably sited close to the boilers, fruit rooms were never heated – the best temperature for keeping fruit is now reckoned to be between 40 and 45°F/5 and 12C – and the insulation in the roof and walls was intended to keep the temperature stable. The room furthest from the boiler would be the coolest, so the longer-keeping varieties of fruit (especially pears) would be stored there, and brought into the first room as they were needed. The cellar was even cooler, and was sometimes used as a retarding room for the later varieties. If the fruit was picked when only just ripe, or even slightly underripe, the transfer into a slightly warmer room would bring it to perfection.

Both the back and front walls of the fruit room at Pylewell are furnished from floor to ceiling with slatted shelves. There is one foot between each tier and the shelves are about thirty inches deep and four feet wide. They are well made, of well-seasoned white deal (red deal was never used, as it gave a resinous taste to the fruit). In very grand fruit rooms these shelves would slide in and out on little brass rollers and be tilted very slightly downwards to enable the gardener to see if any fruit had started to spoil.

Each variety of apple and pear was given a shelf to itself; the apples, but not the pears, might be stored in two layers per shelf. At Pylewell the varieties were simply jotted on a card that was propped up among the fruit, but in grander gardens each shelf had a number stencilled on the front that tallied with a number painted on a blackboard by the door. The fruit variety was recorded against it in chalk; this system also served as a record of how much fruit had been taken out of storage.

Grand fruit rooms such as those at Tylney Hall in Hampshire (where the store room and office floors were of parquet), were fitted with canvas blinds in front of the shelves, to keep moisture in and dust and light out. In more modest places, the fruit would be covered with old canvas or sheeting. The shelves in George III's fruit room at Kensington Palace had coarse, canvas coverings under and over the fruit, which was never laid in more than a single layer, and was turned two or three times during the winter, to keep it sound. The laying-out on the shelves and the necessary inspections were a laborious business, jobs that were given to the men in wet weather, or on dark afternoons, when no work could be done outside.

The fruit room and the office were the only places in the backsheds which might be visited by an interested owner. For this reason the fruit room had to be, 'at all times kept neat and clean, furnished with chairs and writing materials, paper, &c for packing, and be in such a state that the owner may visit it with his friends'.[10] One such owner was the Earl of Derby. At Knowsley, his estate near Liverpool, he had a fruit room some 80 feet wide and 100 feet long, with a table on which to display the fruit running the length of the room. At Windsor Castle, when royal visitors were expected, the best fruit was taken from the cellar where it was normally kept, displayed in the magnificent fruit room above, then duly returned to the cellar when the visit was over. As backsheds were usually long and narrow, and very much the domain of the workforce, fruit rooms were sometimes built as ornamental houses or gazebos elsewhere in the garden, as at West Dean, in Sussex where there is a little circular, thatched house of flint by the owner's entrance to the kitchen garden. George Bunyard's fruit houses of the early twentieth century (one of which can be seen at Chilton Foliat, in Berkshire) were also thatched, as much for insulation as for decoration, and for the same reason were given double doors and reed walls insulated with furze (see page 246).

plums packed in nettle leaves

THE METHODS OF PRESERVING FRUIT

Authorities differed on the question of the best bedding material for fruit. Some said straw, others preferred hay, or fern, or moss, or nettle, vine and fig leaves; Varro, a Roman authority on husbandry, even suggested wool. All of these are capable, when old, musty or damp, of transmitting a dis- agreeable flavour, and so, from the early eighteenth century onwards, two or three layers of thick, soft paper were laid between the bedding or packing materials and the fruit. The finest fruits were laid only on the best writing paper. Later they were also wrapped in tissue paper and their stems tipped with sealing wax; inferior sorts were given newspaper. The latter were also stored in tubs, barrels and glazed earthenware jars or steens.

These techniques have remained unchanged since classical times. The jars used and described by the horticulturist Thomas Andrew Knight for preserving his pears and apples were of one gallon capacity, one foot high – like Roman preserving jars (see page 260) – perfectly cylindrical and designed to stack one above the other. As instructed in the classical husbandries, the gardener or orchardist arranged the contents in layers, with a filling material such as bran, chaff, sawdust or very dry sand, so that air was largely excluded. Nuts were kept in dry salt, and quinces were put into honey.

The jars were then closed with a lid, which was sealed with pitch, resin or plaster. Knight filled the space between the top of one jar and the base of another with a cement made of two parts milk curds and one part lime, keeping the jars in 'a cold and dry situation'. Alternatively, after sealing them up, barrels and jars were buried in the ground, upside down, or placed in the ice-house (see page 246). Being completely watertight, they could even be put at the bottom of a deep well. The fruit inside kept perfectly from October to March; some varieties of apple and pear could even be kept until June or July.

The exclusion of air from a container with food in it, in order to preserve it, is as ancient as smoking, brining or desiccation, but the use of heat to expel air was not discovered until 1807, when a Mr Saddington invented a way of heating vessels of fruit, filling them with boiling water and closing the vessels with hermetic seals – precursors of the Kilner jar.[11] In 1823, a method of preserving cherries, grapes, pears, apples and chestnuts in glass vessels filled with carbonic gas (made from carbonic lime and sulphuric acid) was found to keep the fruit for over two weeks, without any alteration of taste.[12]

In the 1880s ways of artificially excluding air from containers by using heat, carbonic acid, or salt and water, were regularly described in the gardening press. These methods of preserving may seem to us to belong to the kitchen rather than the garden, but the gardener's role until well into the twentieth century included, by tradition, the preserving of his crops by whatever means.

ROOT CELLARS AND TUNNELS

Coldness and the exclusion of air had long been recognized as conducive to the keeping of sound, plump fruit. This was also the case with vegetables. By wholly burying roots such as potatoes, scorzonera, salsify, turnips, parsnips, beets and carrots in sand or in earth-covered clamps, and by partially burying leafy vegetables such as cabbages, lettuces, endives and chicory (dug up for the purpose with their roots intact), the kitchen was supplied with those necessities throughout the winter and early spring.

Root cellars should be cool and dark but neither too damp nor too dry. They were often built under the fruit room, and divided into stalls or bins, a little like a wine cellar or a stable. Each compartment would be filled with roots stacked in layers of sand. Leafy vegetables could be kept here too. There was no root cellar in the Pylewell kitchen garden, but the large shed by the kitchen, capable of storing fifteen to twenty tons of potatoes, was also used for storing roots.

Root tunnels can still be seen in some old kitchen gardens: they stand high enough for a man to walk into, and are thickly covered in earth and ivy, and lined with closely jointed stone or brick. They look rather like long, narrow air-raid shelters (which, indeed, made excellent root stores too, after the Second World War).

A ROOT CLAMP

Some gardeners actually preferred to clamp their potatoes, finding that they kept better and were easier to get at this way than when kept in bins in a cellar. To make a clamp, a gardener must wait until the garden has had some autumn rain, then he marks out a rectangular patch on a fallow piece of ground, covers it with a thick bed of straw and heaps his potatoes on it in a long, wide ridge. Only big potatoes are suitable for clamping, the smaller ones would be sent (after washing) direct to the kitchen, or to the farm for the pigs.

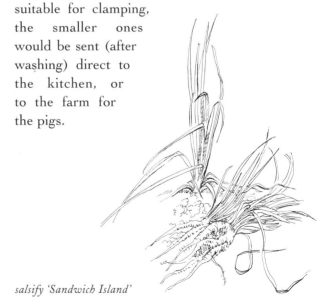

salsify 'Sandwich Island'

Potatoes and other roots are clamped a little while after they have been dug up because, like apples, they need to sweat for a few days before being stored. When each batch of potatoes had been stacked, it was covered with more straw, leaving a topknot at intervals along the ridge for ventilation because the potatoes would continue to sweat and might even heat up slightly. The final covering was a thick layer of earth, which was dug in such a way that a shallow trench was left all round, for rain to run into.

The longest-keeping varieties went at one end, and the early main crop at the other. To take them out, the earth and straw was carefully removed from the early end, the chosen potatoes were taken away in sacks and the coverings were as carefully replaced. The clamp had to be well made so that neither frost nor rain could penetrate it; the only enemy is the rat. If rats got in, the gamekeeper's terriers would be sent for and the whole clamp dismantled while the gardeners stood by with the dogs, spades and sticks. When the rats were safely dead, the clamp was built up again.

Carrot clamps were made in the same way, except that these were round instead of long, because carrots are stored with their leaf end outwards and their pointed ends inwards; their conical shape leads naturally to a circular clamp (see page 246).

THE GRAPE ROOM

One day a gardening friend gave me one of the strange-looking bottles that he had found in a box, when he was having a clear-out in the fruit room of a large house. It was made of pale green glass, square in section, with a hole in one side and a turned-up neck. It was stamped: 'Copped Hall Grape Storing Bottle Patent Applied for no. 25693 Wm Wood & Son Ltd Wood Green'. Later I met a man who had ended his gardening career in the Royal Kitchen Gardens at Windsor. He could remember seeing rows of these bottles when he was young, lined up along the edges of special shelves, each one full of water, with a bunch of grapes on its stem hanging from the bottle's mouth. It was his job to snip out any grapes that had begun to go mouldy and to top up the water through the hole in the side of the bottle, using a watering can with a long, thin spout (see page 246 and opposite).

Before the patent bottle was invented, ripe grapes were kept for months in bottles somewhat resembling a modern milk bottle, or in clear burgundy bottles (clear, to see if water needed renewing; burgundy because the sloping shoulder was more suitable than that of a claret bottle). Some fruit rooms had special stands made to hold the bottles, but in others notched wooden rails were fitted to the fronts of the top fruit shelves so that the bottles could be placed at an angle, by their necks. At Pylewell the shelves were simply built at an angle. Bunches of grapes were cut with one part of the stem long enough to reach the bottom of the bottle. This was filled with rainwater kept sweet by the addition of a lump of charcoal. A bung of wadding

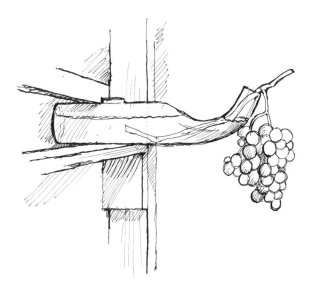

prevented evaporation and kept the stem in place. A sheet of white paper was tucked between the neck of the bottle and the shelf, to keep the bunch of grapes clean and to protect the bloom.

Dessert grapes have been kept over winter since ancient times, on the vine, as desiccated fruit, or in airtight containers. Pliny wrote of keeping grapes on the vine until they became 'glassy and transparent'; if they were to be picked it had to be done at the time of a waning moon, on a fine, dry day. Their stems were dipped instantly in molten pitch; a vat of it was kept at boiling point for this purpose on a fire by the vines. Alternatively, a squill bulb was stuck on either end of the 'hammer-shoot' of stalk that was obtained by cutting the stem so that some of the main branch was included, to form a 'T'. The bunches were hung by strings from the ceiling. A fire in the room gave them 'a smoky flavour'. Grapes were also dried by the fire or in the sun to become 'raisins of the sun'; the small black variety grown and dried near Corinth thus became known as 'corans' or currants.

PRESERVING ON THE BRANCH OR STEM

Fruits such as cherries, currants and gooseberries were occasionally preserved in the fruit room on their severed branches. The hanging fruit kept better like this than if it was stored in baskets or boxes; in the same way, plums were suspended by their stalks on twine. Late-ripening plums, such as Coe's Golden Drop, were said to improve in flavour with this treatment, especially if they were kept hanging for a few weeks inside a south-facing window. This, according to an early nineteenth-century *Kalendar of Work*, should be done in October. A slow process of desiccation then begins, and if the plums are next 'wrapped in thin, soft, white paper, and put in boxes in a dry room, they may be kept perfectly well for twelve months, when they become an excellent sweetmeat'.[13]

While many vegetables and most fruits need dark, not too dry, cool storage places, there are some that keep best in light, airy lofts and garrets; onions strung on ropes, bunches of shallots, plaits of garlic, marrows, gourds and pumpkins, cabbages and cauliflowers come into this category. The latter were hung up by their roots and stems, out of the reach of mice. The only other dangers to guard against were damp and prolonged frost.

PRESERVING IN CROCKS, CASKS AND JARS

Columella described a method of sealing his best grapes and pomegranates on the living branch inside specially shaped earthenware crocks. He also preserved his grapes in chaff, 'green, for as much as a year', in sealed earthenware pans stored in lofts and covered with more chaff. He had similarly shaped vessels submerged in spring water; alternatively, they were placed in airtight casks with various preservatives or 'pickles', such as oil and lye, honey, brine, vinegar, boiled-down must (unfermented grape juice, also known as *defrutum*) and grape skins from the wine press. These liquids made a preservative for grapes themselves, as well as for quinces, pears, olives, and the roots of herbs such as alexanders.

Roman jars for preserves in liquid were straight-sided and cylindrical, made of earthenware or glass. This shape meant that equal pressure was kept on the food at the bottom and it was always covered with pickle.[14] Early seventeenth-century English gardeners also made pickles and hung their bunches of grapes indoors, a piece of the branch with every cluster, and an apple at each end, to keep them until Easter.[15] The dipping of the ends of the branch into tar and the use of *defrutum* continued. John Parkinson said that the Turks kept grapes in jars all winter and into the following summer by strewing the bunches with mustard meal, pouring new wine over them 'before it hath boiled', then stopping up the vessels for as long as need be. The spicy liquor was washed off the grapes before they were eaten. This method has remarkable similarities to a Roman recipe, in which pounded mustard seed was steeped in new wine for a relish, and to the Italian mostarda (whole fruit pickled in mustard-flavoured syrup). Grapes stored in jars of sand were likewise 'washed clean in faire water' before eating.[16]

THE ICE-HOUSE

The ice-house at Pylewell is situated close to the Mill Pond, some distance below the kitchen gardens. It predates Joseph Weld's ownership and is not part of the kitchen-garden complex but, because its purpose was to supply ice to the kitchen, its care was always one of the kitchen gardeners' responsibilities. By the 1920s, when ice was more easily bought by the hundredweight from the fishmonger in Lymington, use of the ice-house had pretty well ceased, but before then, as the kitchen gardeners had access to it, they could use it in the summer months when it was half empty, for the cold storage of certain roots and vegetables, well insulated in straw.

Ice-houses began to be built for wealthy British landowners in the seventeenth century. The idea of storing winter ice and snow in deep brick-lined pits was probably taken from Italy where, since the time of Pliny, ice and snow had been used to make cool drinks and, later, icecreams. Charles II installed some of the first ice-houses (then called 'snow-wells') in England in the 1660s, in the gardens of his palaces at Greenwich, Windsor and St James's, setting a trend for 'iced creams' that appear increasingly often in records, recipes and reports thereafter.

Ice houses were usually sited close to water on a slight, north-facing rise so that, as the ice inside them melted gradually, a sloping drain at the bottom would carry the melted water back to the pond. Two-thirds of the structure would be below ground level and the top was covered in a natural-looking mound of soil. The Pylewell ice-house is in just such a situation about 100 yards from the pond. It stands at the edge of a spinney, opposite the old orchard, its domed top almost hidden by elders and hazels. It is reached by a cart track leading up from the pond. The entrance is boarded-up now, for safety; once inside, it is pitch-dark. At the end of a short passageway there is a sheer drop of some ten feet to the bottom of an egg-shaped void.

To fill this void with ice, the kitchen-garden workforce was summoned to break up ice on the mill pond as soon as a one-inch-thick layer had formed. They then carted it to the ice-house. The drainage hole at the bottom was covered with faggots of wood overlaid with reeds or straw. The men used mallets to pound the ice almost to a powder, and then rammed it down in the ice-house to form a solid mass. It was so densely packed that it took a crowbar to remove it. A lining of straw was put between the ice and the wall to encourage the run-off of thawed ice. To insulate the house still further, the entrance lobby was filled with straw.

During the summer, roots such as turnips, carrots, beets, celery and potatoes, as well as peas, beans and cauliflowers, were kept in the ice-house. The top of the mass of ice was covered with straw and the vegetables were packed into boxes and baskets above that. Sometimes ice-houses were constructed with double walls. The inner section contained the ice, and the outer had recesses in it for the storage of fruit or vegetables and the retardation of fruit trees in pots.

It comes as a surprise to learn that, as long ago as 1823, the ice-house was also used as a freezer. Cherries, strawberries, raspberries, plums, peaches, 'or any other succulent fruit whatever', were put into containers, rather like those once used for freezing ice-creams, with salt and ice round them. When the fruit was frozen, it was carried to the ice-house, and placed in a hole dug out of the centre of the ice. Over the top of the hole went 'a quantity of powdered charcoal . . . secured by a common blanket. When the winter season arrives, the containing vessel may be opened, and the fruit taken out in its frozen state; then place it in cold water to thaw, and it will be found as delicious as when first gathered.' [17]

DIGGING, BLANCHING and SOME EDGES

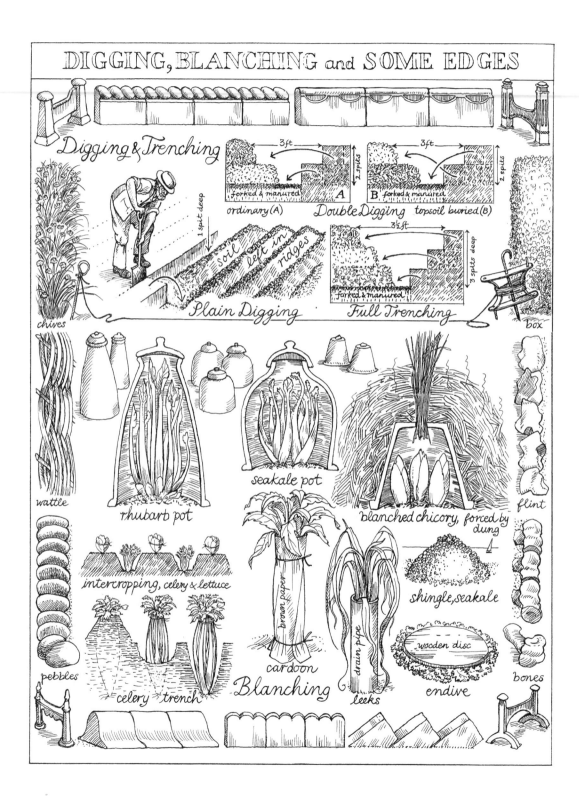

Digging & Trenching

ordinary (A)

Double Digging   topsoil buried (B)

3ft / 2 spits / forked & manured / A

3ft / 2 spits / forked & manured / B

Plain Digging

1 spit deep

soil left in ridges

Full Trenching

3½ft / 3 spits deep / forked & manured

chives

box

wattle

rhubarb pot

seakale pot

blanched chicory, forced by dung

flint

intercropping, celery & lettuce

cardoon

Blanching

leeks

drain pipe

bran paper

shingle, seakale

wooden disc

endive

pebbles

celery trench

bones

CHAPTER NINETEEN

THE GARDENERS

THE GARDENING HIERARCHY

Just as Mr Manley, the butler, was overall head of the household staff, with Mrs Holmes, the cook, as head of the kitchens, so Mr Hamilton, as head gardener, was chief of the park and garden staff. In Victorian times his rank would have equalled that of the butler and the cook, as well as that of the coachman, the land steward and the farm bailiff.

The head gardener of what was known as 'a first-rate residence' (a country house that Loudon would describe as a mansion, hall, court, abbey, priory, palace or castle, and a demesne of between 500 and 10,000 acres, if not more) would have under him: 'A forester, for the demesne-woods and park-trees; a pleasure-ground foreman for the lawns and shrubbery; a flower-garden foreman, a forcing-department foreman, and a kitchen-garden foreman'.[1]

The ranks were virtually the same one hundred years later, in 1930. Of the sixteen gardeners working at Pylewell, one (Mr Hamilton) was the head gardener, three were foremen, five were journeymen, five were variously described as labourers, 'improvers' or apprentices, and two were 'boys'. There was a distinct division between the men who worked in the park, pleasure grounds and flower garden under the pleasure gardens'

foreman, and the two groups who worked 'inside' and 'outside' in the kitchen gardens.

The kitchen gardens were directly under the head gardener's eye, with George Tarrant and Fred Thomas as the outside and inside foremen respectively. Vic, Ron and Frank were the outside journeymen and Percy was the labourer. These were the four gardeners who worked in the open quarters, the field and the orchard (see Chapter 6). When extra help was needed, the gardeners' wives, or women from the village might be called in as weeders or pickers. Les and Danny, the inside journeymen, worked with Fred and Mr Hamilton in the glasshouses (see Chapter 10).

THE HEAD GARDENER'S HOUSE AND OFFICE

As the productions of the kitchen garden were the most labour-intensive and most valuable, with those of the hothouses deserving top priority, it followed that the head gardener's house should be situated as near to them as possible; in this way, a close watch could be kept on them should a crisis arise. The head gardener's house was therefore often built against the north-east or north-west wall of the kitchen garden itself. In very large gardens, such as at Castle Howard in Yorkshire, it was sited in the

Mr. Hamilton's cottage

centre of the kitchen gardens; at Windsor, in the royal kitchen gardens, it was placed half-way along the immense glasshouse range. The head gardener's house was usually commensurate in grandeur with the rest of the gardens, the mansion and the estate.

At Pylewell Mr Hamilton's cottage was at the entrance to the drive leading to the kitchen gardens, and some distance away. However one of the bothies occupies a small plot to itself, just outside the garden wall, but right next to the glasshouses (see page 9). It was therefore the 'bothy boys' job to keep an eye on the boilers and glasshouse ventilators at night and at weekends. Hamilton's cottage was quite modest, thatched in the style of the rest of the mid nineteenth-century estate workers' cottages, with a thick hedge round its own small garden. A head gardener's cottage on an estate such as this rarely had more than the one main bedroom, spare bedroom, small parlour, kitchen and scullery that we find here. The exceptions occurred when an enlightened owner provided bedrooms for the journeymen in the head gardener's house, rather than in the bothy. If the situation of the head gardener were grand enough, he might also have rooms for a living-in servant. In a place such as Windsor Castle, Welbeck or Knowsley, where there might be twenty or thirty gardeners at least, a whole block of gardeners' bedrooms was built, with a communal dining room and reading room, the cooking being done for them in one kitchen.

Sometimes the head gardener's office was within, or adjoining, his house, but here at Pylewell the office is within the potting shed. A head gardener spent a fair amount of his time in his office; it would need to be furnished with a desk, bookshelves, a map of the entire estate and another of the gardens, and a lockable cupboard for ledgers, account and memo books, stationery, spare thermometers, budding knives and the most dangerous poisons. For decoration, the walls would be hung with certificates of awards won in the local horticultural shows.

Time sheets and accounts had to be kept for wages, machinery, tools, fuel, seeds, plants, fruit trees and sundries. Sales of surpluses were registered; the weather and hothouse temperatures were recorded; produce sent to the kitchen was listed; trenching, plantings and sowings were noted down. Every day's doings were written down in a garden journal, and a diary was kept of future events which might affect the gardens – weddings, fêtes, garden parties, holidays, banquets, important visits, open days and sporting weekends.

THE DUTIES OF
HEAD GARDENER

The head gardener might reach the pinnacle of his career at any age between twenty-five and fifty-five. Once there, if he were in charge of a large workforce, he never needed to touch a spade or barrow again in his life. His was a responsible job, depending on the management of and co-operation from three or four men in a small place (where his post would be described as that of working head gardener) to over fifty men (before the First World War) in a garden the size of Chatsworth. He was answerable for every single production from the kitchen gardens, for the beauty and management of the rest of the gardens, and for hiring and firing, wages and the sale of surplus produce. As a measure of his importance, the head gardener was often the only gardener allowed to smoke in the gardens; he was also entitled to the use of a stable and a cow shed, a messenger boy and a pony chaise or small van.

The head gardener's character was therefore scrutinized closely before he was appointed. It was assumed that he was already master of his profession, but did he have 'A Shape and Motion denoting a Sturdy, Vigorous, Nimble Man' and was he 'not affecting to be dress'd or adorn'd above the common Station of a Gard'ner'? If married, would 'his Wife and Children work in the Garden'? If his wife were able to act as a helpmeet so much the better (but before appointing her 'see whether she be Cleanly and has nothing Disgusting in her'). Could he

write and draw? Was he 'Always the first and last at his Work . . . delighting in his Gardens above all other things, especially upon Holy Days; so that instead of debauching and carousing at such times, as is most common for most Gard'ners to do, he may be seen walking in his Gardens with his Servants'? If so, would this paragon point out to his staff what wanted doing 'every work-day of the Week', pinching insects and squashing caterpillars as he walked through his domain, fixing a stray branch here, picking fruit that was about to fall there, and so on?[2]

The requirements for a perfect gardener remained virtually the same for two hundred years. A sample of the 'jobs vacant' and 'wanted' columns of *The Gardeners' Chronicle* of 1884 throws up the same desirable characteristics: the gardener must be hard-working, a master of his business, sober (even teetotal), active, intelligent; he must understand bees (and cows); his wife should be willing to do laundry (or look after the house); he should be thoroughly up in all classes of fruit, flowers and vegetables, vines, melons, orchids; bouquet-making and table decorations; forcing, propagating, et cetera.

SHOWS AND EXHIBITIONS

An ambitious gardener relied on prizes for recognition of his own prowess, especially if he had bred any new variety of fruit, flower or vegetable. In the 1860s the Royal Horticultural Society set the rules by which all shows of any significance were to be judged. The traditional time for these shows, which ranged from the international to the purely local, was the third week in August. Professional gardeners, who stood to gain most for their businesses or reputations, were allowed to show produce in their own names only if the garden belonged to them; when Mr Hamilton exhibited rhododendrons (at which he excelled) at the county show they were entered under Mr Whitaker's name. However, if any gardener had a private passion to enter plants from his own patch – giant gooseberries and leeks were, and still are, two particular favourites for showing in the north – he was at liberty to do so.

The village horticultural show and the local county show were two highpoints in the gardeners' year. A half-day off was given to the most deserving men, so they could visit it. Mr Hamilton judged the amateurs at the village show, and Mr or Mrs Whitaker gave the prizes. The greatest honour for any head gardener, though, was to exhibit and win at the Royal Horticultural Society's annual show at Chelsea. For this occasion, if the head gardener were to accompany his master he wore a top hat, white gloves and morning suit.

THE FOREMEN

The foremen were supposed to keep an eye on all the journeymen and apprentices beneath them, making sure that they began work punctually, that they looked clean and presentable (at the start of the day at least), that their tools were kept clean and tidy and returned to their proper places, that manners and decorum were observed, especially in dealings with the proprietor, his family and friends, that bills were paid when owing and that the no-smoking-at-work rule was strictly observed.

In some gardens the inside or glasshouse foreman was responsible, with the head gardener, for arranging all the fruit and flowers for the table. At a great house such as Holkham Hall in Norfolk in the 1930s, the table decoration was changed for breakfast, lunch and dinner, and there it was the inside foreman's job to pick the fruit himself and arrange it in baskets or dishes, placing on each variety a white card with its name written in his best copperplate hand. He would line the dishes with vine leaves or zonal pelargonium leaves from plants grown specially for that purpose. One of the traditions at Pylewell was to present at table a whole pot of growing, forced strawberries (suitably housed in a cache-pot) on 3 April, Mr Whitaker's birthday.

Mr Manley might arrange elegant silver or crystal fruit stands and dishes with apples, pears and nuts in winter, and with berries and currants in the summer, but it was always understood that Fred Thomas and Mr Hamilton would pick the best fruits themselves. They would also be responsible for the flower vases, epergnes, and trailing sprays of ivy or smilax that wound their way gracefully across the tablecloth, as well as for all the vases and displays in the rest of the house and the plants in the conservatory. They would fill the vases in the flower room by the front door of the mansion and, wearing galoshes over their gardening boots to protect the carpets that were already covered with druggets, they filled the planters and *jardinières*, working in deathly silence while the family still slept. Bedroom flowers were taken upstairs by the household staff and, as Percy remembered: 'There would be hell to pay if they didn't match the curtains!'

SCOTTISH GARDENERS

Many of us have already met the most famous Scottish gardener, in fiction at least; he is Mr Macgregor, the gardener in Beatrix Potter's *The Tale of Peter Rabbit*. The high proportion of Scots in the gardening profession has often been commented on, and is certainly noticeable in almost every branch of gardening. As George Eliot wrote in *Adam Bede*, 'a gardener is Scotch as a French teacher is Parisian'.

An explanation for the prominence of the Scots in horticulture is given by the twentieth-century garden historian John Harvey, who notes that after the Act of Union with Scotland of 1707, when Scotland became economically depressed, large numbers of Scots emigrated. Many came southwards from the Lowlands to England, sought and found places in the gardens of large estates and, thanks to their capacity for hard work, a better education system than the English and their habits of thrift, gained a reputation for excellence.[3]

WEEDING WOMEN

Although there was an ancient superstition about the danger of menstruating women being allowed into the kitchen garden (see Chapters 8 and 15), this was no bar to their employment as a cheap form of part-time labour. Women were paid little more than a child or garden boy, and never more than half as much as a man for the same hours of work, no matter how experienced they were. They were given the most finicky jobs, mainly weeding, but they might also search for insects and caterpillars, gather fruit, and drop potatoes into holes dug with a dibber by the gardener walking ahead along the rows.

THE APPRENTICE AND THE GARDEN BOY

Life as a garden boy and apprentice was characterized by strict discipline and long hours, some of which were spent on jobs of unrelieved monotony. Mr Hopkins, head gardener at Chatsworth in the 1980s, started there as a garden boy aged fifteen in 1939. His first three days were spent entirely in the compost yard, teasing rotted turf fibres apart for the potting compost.

Other jobs were less arduous, although if they were badly done there would certainly be reprimands. Mr Hopkins's predecessor in the 1920s spent his midsummer days as a boy watching the peaches, which were protected by tiffany blinds on rollers; he had to be always at the ready, to raise them as soon as the sun went in and lower them the instant it came out. In some establishments it was the boys' job, too, in the flowering season, to pollinate the inside fruit; every afternoon after the dinner break they would do the rounds with a rabbit's tail on the end of a cane.

Percy recalled hours of pot washing in the tank by the potting shed – with achingly cold water – and equally long hours with a thumb over the end of a hose, watering the wall fruit under the watchful eye of Mr Hamilton, who, although he was a kindly man, had a habit of timing the procedure (see Chapter 2). As a garden boy Percy was also the messenger between the kitchen gardens and the kitchens. An old gardener at Longleat in Wiltshire remembers making daily trips in his youth to the kitchen, one mile away, with a loaded barrow similar to a costermonger's. The route was not the same as the one used by the family – by whom no gardener was ever to be seen. It was very uneven and he had to travel agonizingly slowly to avoid bruising the fruit. The earliest memories of many gardeners involve endless sweeping and raking, so that never a leaf or speck of mud could mar a pathway. It was the apprentices' and garden boys' last job at the end of each day to ensure that not one footprint was left on the gravel paths throughout the gardens.

The hours and routines were virtually the same in all large gardens. Gardeners worked eight hours a day from Monday to Friday and four hours on Saturdays. There was a rota for the journeymen on night-time and weekend duty. This extra time, which was unpaid, involved watering, checking the hothouse temperatures and ventilators, and attending to the boilers, from noon on Saturday to last thing on Sunday, as well as banking-up the fires last thing every night (at 10 p.m.) and fuelling them first thing every morning (at 6 a.m.). If there were flued fruit walls the duty-man had to see to the little fires that heated them, as well. Holidays were literally no more than a day off on each of the annual 'holy days' – Easter, Whitsun and Christmas.

Very few young working men possessed watches in the old days, so 'Work time' and 'knocking-off time' were signalled by the ringing of a garden bell, which in some gardens hung by the visitors' entrance, so that the owner could alert the head gardener that he was there, and in others outside the office. If the stable yard was close to the kitchen garden, as was often the case, the stable clock would serve the gardeners as well as the stable lads. At mealtimes some of the men would make for the mess room, where there would be a small stove, a kettle, a kitchen table, benches and chairs. Others, including the head gardener, made for their own houses in the grounds, or the bothy by the backsheds. In Percy's day it was the boys' job to make tea for everyone, but in bigger gardens a local woman was in attendance.

THE BOTHY

Percy was lucky to be able to live at home with his family at Pylewell. Other boys, and some of the unmarried men, had to make do with the bothy – a garden lodging that might range in standards of comfort and facilities from the level of a pigsty or stable to the luxury of a small cottage.

The bothy at Pylewell is now in ruins, damp and dark, with ivy growing through the grubby, broken windows, but even when it was in good repair it could only have been described as a cabin, slightly better than a stable. It had nothing like the comfort of a married estate worker's cottage, let alone that of the head gardener's cottage. It is situated just outside the garden wall, conveniently near the smaller boiler's stoke hole, and is actually smaller than the potting shed. It consists of two tiny rooms with small windows: the bedroom had room for two

single beds and a little fireplace, an equally small living room had a small cooking range, a sink and a copper for heating water for washing. The lavatory was outside, at one end of the building and was used by all the men. If the employer was stingy with the coal allowance the inhabitants would have to supplement their meagre bed-coverings with whatever they could find; old sacking came in useful for this purpose.

An unmarried journeyman or foreman could ask for 'bothy and full attendance' as part of his wages. In the 1930s this might mean handing over 10 shillings a week out of a total pay of 25 shillings a week. To put that sum in perspective, it roughly equals today's minimum agricultural wage: at that time a packet of twenty cigarettes cost 10½d. and beer was 5d. a pint. In return, a garden boy would cook the unmarried men's breakfast (this was eaten two hours after work began, much as 'elevenses' are today). Their midday meal and supper would be cooked for them by a woman from the village, who would also wash up, clean, make the beds and do the laundry.

Alternatively, a journeyman or foreman could cater for himself. The inside foreman would subtract his 'grub score' – whatever he owed the village shops, which would send bread, meat and groceries – from his wages. In return he was allowed a limited amount of the more ordinary produce from his employer's garden, although a man could be sacked for taking as much as a bunch of carrots without permission. It was not unknown for a little barter to be done with other employees on the estate – a dairymaid could be bribed to part with a bowl of cream in exchange for a few less-than-perfect peaches, and the game-keeper might come to a similar arrangement with the odd rabbit or bird.

Old gardeners are wont to reminisce about their bothy days with affection, despite the fact that it was often a spartan life. A bothy with a bathroom was most unusual. As recently as 1950, a young man who wanted to smarten up for a special occasion would wait until everyone else had gone home, then take an unofficial bath in the rainwater tanks in the hothouses. The cold water could be pumped out and replaced with hot water drawn from the heating pipes.

THE GARDENER'S WAY OF LIFE

Apart from the squalor of some living conditions, the life of a gardener was in general a good one – plenty of fresh air, good food and exercise – and gardeners were often extraordinarily long-lived. The Rench or Wrench family of nurserymen, for example, had a farm near Parsons Green in West London, which only three generations had occupied over the course of two centuries. The first Mr Rench, born in 1630, lived to ninety-nine and had thirty-three children; his heir lived to 101 and had thirty-five children, one of whom married the incumbent of 1830, a Mr Fitch.

In 1605 the professional gardeners of London – a group that included market gardeners, florists, landscapists, implement dealers, botanists and herbalists – formed themselves into a Company. Its earliest objectives were to regulate the trade in fruit and vegetables and prevent dishonest trading. Later it extended its membership to apprentices and journeymen, ruling that no master could employ a journeyman not apprenticed to a member of the Company. The badge of trade of a professional gardener

– one who had trained with a member of the Company – was a dark blue apron. To say of a gardener that 'he has donned the blue apron' meant that he was a trained rather than an unskilled man.[4]

A dark blue apron, tied round the waist, with large pockets and wisps of bass tucked into the apron strings, continued to be the traditional garb for a gardener. He would use one of the two lower pockets for tools such as pruning knives or secateurs, and the other for rubbish such as the odd dead leaf or twig. The upper pocket held matches and the cigarettes that he was allowed to smoke only when he was head gardener. An apron was worn by all ranks, except when digging, because then it got in the way. All gardeners wore lace-up leather boots too, and the rule was that they had to be clean every morning. Rubber Wellington boots were considered an expensive luxury and were, in any case, less comfortable than leather boots to work in.

Trousers were tied with leg ties just below the knee, to stop them flapping in the mud. These came in handy for stowing a pruning knife and a 'man' - a wedge-shaped piece of wood for scraping tools clean while digging or hoeing. In winter, a shirt with collar and tie was the rule for all the men in smart gardens; high-fronted waistcoats kept the tie tucked in; if modern waistcoats were worn they allowed long ties to fall forward during work, making the wearing of a bow tie advisable.

Young German gardeners in the late eighteenth century were advised to wear gloves if they did not wish to have hands like 'bears' paws'.[5] The gardener would also wear a steel tread on his shoe when digging, to protect the sole. The only man allowed to wear a bowler hat was the head gardener. Hats and caps of all kinds – billycocks, boaters, berets and tam-o'shanters – were worn by everyone else, for shade in the summer and warmth in winter. A photograph of Mr Hamilton, taken in 1937, shows him wearing comfortable and relatively informal clothes: a tweed pork pie hat, no jacket, but a high-buttoned waistcoat, a tie, shirtsleeves rolled up, thick trousers and shiny boots.

THE GARDENER'S EDUCATION

From the 1890s, scholarships enabled the sons of people with low incomes to enjoy the luxury of a formal education in horticulture. The first horticultural college, at Swanley in Kent, was founded in 1889; it was followed by the Cheshire Horticultural College at Holmes Chapel in 1895, and Studley College in Worcestershire, which opened in 1898. The Royal Horticultural Society's General Examination in Horticulture was introduced in 1893 and incorporated into a National

Diploma in 1913. Swanley, an enlightened, independent establishment, opened a branch for young women gardeners in 1891. Its success led in 1902 to the foundation of the Glynde School for Lady Gardeners in Sussex (whose three patrons were Gertrude Jekyll, Maria Theresa [Mrs] Earle and William Robinson). Wye College, a branch of London University at Ashford in Kent, inaugurated the first degree course in horticulture in 1916.

But for most aspiring gardeners, education depended on apprenticeship. Head gardeners were, by tradition, teachers to the younger members of their staff, and strict disciplinarians to boot. The apprentices of the more distinguished head gardeners would pay their masters a premium; however, all too often most young gardeners simply worked for very low wages, gleaning what they could as they went along.

Mr Hamilton's was, perhaps, the last generation of professional gardeners to learn the trade entirely by first-hand experience. The system allowed young men to take time off if they wished, to study for one of the external horticultural diplomas that would help them to gain better jobs as they went on, but this was by no means compulsory. An apprentice might eventually decide to follow one of several branches other than that of 'the private, or serving gardener' (this description included work in public parks). If he wanted to be independent he could become a tradesman, propagating plants in a commercial nursery or working in a market garden; if he had a creative bent he might become a garden designer or landscape architect (otherwise known as 'an artist gardener'). If he were adventurous he could go on expeditions as a botanist-cum-plant collector. Whatever path he chose, a well-run private garden was acknowledged to be the best starting point for an education in horticulture, and its kitchen garden was the centre of that learning.

In Loudon's day – that is to say during the period covered by the first half of the nineteenth century – the young gardener who hoped to reach the top of his profession was expected to start his apprenticeship with a general knowledge of mathematics (including the basics of geometry and land surveying) and the ability to read and write. If he were industrious and intelligent, he would reap the benefits of a career that was not then perceived to be as lowly as it so often is today.

In the head gardener's office there would be (or should be) a library for the use of all the gardeners. According to Loudon this would contain all the newest, best available and most relevant reference books. If the head gardener were 'of a humane and kind turn of mind', he might even hold the occasional gardening seminar, assembling his workmen (and women), reading aloud and 'expounding' to them, answering questions, or encouraging them 'to read aloud to, and question one another, in such a way as to blend entertainment with instruction'. With or without this encouragement, the apprentice was expected to know enough botany and natural history to be able to 'refer any natural production to its place in the Linnæan system'; to study the weather, its seasons, chemistry and signs; to learn the uses and history of gardening implements and machines, by 'manually exercising them . . . under the direction of his master' as well as by talking to 'intelligent carpenters, millwrights, and engineers'; to learn likewise the uses of the commoner garden plants, with 'recourse to books on cooking, medicine, chemistry and farming'; to develop his memory for numbers; to jot 'everything interesting, whether professional or general' in a pocket memorandum-book; to visit neighbouring gardens to observe what was going on there; and after five years, when he had become a journeyman, to: 'move to a different part of the country . . . leisurely on foot, botanising and collecting insects and minerals, and visiting every distinguished garden on his way'.[6]

William Robinson and Joseph Paxton both started as humble garden boys and ended up with fame and riches, something that was not so very remarkable in those days. Qualities similar to those possessed by Paxton were, in fact, the very ones that the owner of any large estate in the nineteenth and early twentieth centuries would expect to find in his head gardener. Moreover, it was in the kitchen gardens and glasshouses that these qualities were most in demand.

As the hothouses, the backsheds, the very walls of kitchen gardens like this one at Pylewell gradually disappear, and the walks and orderly lines of fruit, flowers and vegetables are replaced by couch-grass, brambles and nettles (or by poly-tunnels, tennis courts, swimming pools and bungalows), it seems sad that the skills and horticultural secrets of men like Percy Gregory and W. F. Hamilton are likely to vanish with them. That probability is what prompted me to write this book, tracing as much as I could of the long history of kitchen gardening, before it was too late.

REFERENCES AND NOTES

INTRODUCTION pages 10–21
1 Victoria County History, Hampshire I, p.514
2 D.S.Stagg, *Calendar of New Forest Documents*, 15th-17th centuries, p.251: Hampshire County Record Office, 42M74.E/T2 (1617)
3 Dr L.O.J. Boynton, *Official Handbook to Appuldurcombe House*, DOE/Ministry of Public Buildings and Works, 1967, p.24 [in which the author of *Théorie et la pratique du jardinage . . .* is mistakenly named as Le Blond]
4 Edward Gibbon, *Memoirs of my Life* (Ed. Georges. A. Bonnard, Nelson, 1966, p.116)
5 *Thomas Rowlandson's Drawings for a Tour in a Post Chaise*, introduction and notes by Robert. R. Wark, The Huntingdon Library, 1963, plate 38
6 William Gilpin, *Remarks on Forest Scenery and other Woodland Views. . .* 2nd edn., 1794, p.132
7 *Weld Papers*, Dorset County Record Office, D10/E167
8 *Letters from Weld to his Steward, Wood*, D.C.R.O. D10/E170
9 *Letters to and from Weld to his Gardener, Thomas Abernathy*, D.C.R.O. D10/C168
10 D.C.R.O, D10/E176
11 W.F.Perkins, *Boldre*, 4th edn., 1935, p.4

CHAPTER ONE: LOCATION pages 22–31
1 Batty Langley, *New Principles of Gardening*, 1728, part IV, section II, p.195
2 Stephen Switzer, *The Practical Fruit-Gardener*, 1724, pp.16 and 21, and *The Practical Kitchen Gardiner*, 1727, pp.2-6
3 Humphry Repton and J.A. Repton, *Fragments on the Theory and Practice of Landscape Gardening*, 1803, ed. J. C. Loudon, 1816, fragment xxix, p.177
4 Charles M'Intosh, *The Book of the Garden*, 1853, vol. I, p.13 [I have not found any mention of this feature by Walter Nicol himself.]
5 *Memorial of Henry Wise and Joseph Carpenter to Vice-Chamberlain Coke*, 1717, Coke mss, formerly at Melbourne Hall and now in the British Library (add. mss 69942), HMC 12th report, 1889, series 23, pt III, pp.118-180
6 Stephen Switzer, *The Practical Fruit-Gardener*, 1724, pp.23-4
7 Philip Miller, *The Gardener's Dictionary*, 6th edn., 1752, no page numbers, see under 'Kitchen Garden'

CHAPTER TWO: WATER pages 32–41
1 Sources include Barry Cunliffe, *Iron-Age Communities in Britain*, 2nd edn., 1978; D.M. Dunlop, *Arabic Science in the West*, 1958; W.F. Jashemski, *The Gardens of Pompeii*, 1979; Peter Reynolds, *The Iron-Age Farm*, 1979; Peter Salway, *Roman Britain*, 1981; A.M. Watson, *Agriculture and Innovation in the Early Islamic World*, 1983; K.D.White, *Roman Farming*, 1970
2 Friar Henry Daniel, *Aaron Danielis*, Brit. Lib. Arundel ms 42, *c.*1385
3 'The Tarring fig gardens', in *The Garden*, 19 October 1901, pp.267-8
4 Jean-Baptiste de la Quintinye, *Instructions pour les Jardins Fruitiers et Potagers*, 1690 (trans. John Evelyn as *The Compleat Gard'ner*, 1693), see 'Ados' under 'A' in the Dictionary (unnumbered preliminary pages)
5 Joseph Carpenter, *The Retir'd Gardener*, 2nd edn., 1717, p.7
6 Richard Bradley, *New Improvements of Planting and Gardening*, 3rd edn., 1720, p.187
7 William Cobbett, *The English Gardener*, 1829, no page numbers, see chap. II, para.45
8 Didymus Mountain (pseudonym of Thomas Hill), *The Gardener's Labyrinth*, 1577, part I, chap.24, pp.48-54
9 John Worlidge, *Systema Horti-culturae*, 1677, p.263
10 Thomas Hitt, *A Treatise of Fruit-trees*, 2nd edn., 1757, p.270

CHAPTER THREE: WALLS FOR PROTECTION pages 42–57
1 James Anderson, *The New Practical Gardener and Modern Horticulturist*, *c.*1872, p.116
2 Prince Hermann von Pückler-Muskau, *A Tour in England, Ireland and France*, 1832, v.iii, p.190
3 James Anderson, *The New Practical Gardener . . .*, *c.*1872, p.124, and in Patrick Neill, *The Fruit, Flower and Kitchen Garden*, 1849, p.13
4 Stephen Switzer, *The Practical Fruit-Gardener*, 1724, p.294
5 Jean-Baptiste de la Quintinye, *Instructions pour les Jardins Fruitiers et Potagers*, 1690 (trans. G. London and H. Wise as *The Compleat Gard'ner*, 1699), p.80
6 Charles M'Intosh, *The Book of the Garden*, 1853, vol. I, p.13

7   William Robinson, *Gravetye Manor*, 1911 (ms in the Lindley Library, Royal Horticultural Society)
8   William Lawson, *A New Orchard and Garden*, edn. of 1683, p.12
9   Stephen Switzer, *The Practical Fruit-Gardener*, edn. of 1752, p.298
10 John Laurence, *The Fruit-garden Kalendar*, 1718, p.24
11 Stephen Switzer, *The Practical Fruit-Gardener*, 2nd edn., 1731, p.322
12 Benjamin Whitmill, *Kalendarium Universale*, 1748, pp.233-6
13 Jean O'Neill, 'Walls in half-circles and serpentine walls', in *Garden History*, vol. 8:3 (Winter 1980), pp.69-76
14 David Taylor Fish, in *Cassell's Popular Gardening*, vol. 4, *c.*1885, p.178
15 Thomas Langford, *Plain and Full Instructions to Raise all Sorts of Fruit-Trees that Prosper in England*, 1681, p.59

CHAPTER FOUR: HEATED WALLS AND OTHER EMBELLISHMENTS pages 58–67
1   Sir Hugh Platt, *Floræs Paradise*, 1608, p.42 and in *Garden of Eden*, 1625, Book I, p.21; Book II, p.3
2   John Laurence, *The Fruit-garden Kalendar*, 1718, p.22
3   Thomas Moore and Maxwell Masters, *Epitome of Gardening*, 1881, p.66
4   The author in conversation with the gardener at Fonthill, 1983
5   Elisabeth Hall, 'Hot walls. An investigation of their construction in some northern kitchen gardens', in *Garden History*, vol.17:1 (Spring 1989), pp.95-105
6   Walter Nicol, *The Gardener's Kalendar*, 1814, p.379
7   John Laurence, *The Gentleman's Recreation*, 1716, pp. 75-83
8   Samuel Collins, *Paradise Retriev'd*, 1717, p.71
9   Letter from Philip Miller in Richard Bradley's *A Treatise on Husbandry and Gardening*, vol. 2, 1724, p.174
10 John Laurence, *A New System of Agriculture and Gardening*, 1726, pp.343-4
11 Stephen Switzer, *The Practical Fruit-Gardener*, 2nd edn., 1731, p.291
12 J.C. Loudon, *Encyclopædia of Gardening*, 1834 edn., p.559
13 Walter Nicol, *The Gardener's Kalendar*, 1814, p.220
14 Stephen Switzer, *The Practical Fruit-Gardener*, 1731, p.291
15 William Jones, *The Gardeners' Receipt Book*, 1858, p.65
16 J.C. Loudon, *Encyclopædia of Gardening*, 3rd edn., 1825, p.297
17 William Robinson, *Gleanings from French Gardens*, 1868, p.257

CHAPTER FIVE: WALLS FOR FRUIT pages 68–77
1   Leviticus 19: 19
2   Sir Hugh Platt, *Floræs Paradise*, 1608, pp.62-3
3   Prudence Leith-Ross, *The John Tradescants*, 1984, pp. 29-35
4   Thomas Langford, *Plain and Full Instructions to Raise all Sorts of Fruit-trees that Prosper in England*, 2nd edn., 1696, p.69
5   *Ibid.* 1696, p.78
6   Ralph Thoresby, *Diary* (16 March 1702), quoted by Patrick Neill, *Fruit, Flower and Kitchen Garden*, 1849, p.24
7   George Bunyard and Owen Thomas, *The Fruit Garden*, 1904, p.107
8   William Cobbett, *The English Gardener*, 1829, no page numbers, see ch.VI, para.259
9   Thomas Rivers, 'Upon the Advantages of Root Pruning in Pear Trees', *Trans. Hort.*, 2nd series II, pp.471-9, read 7 April 1840
10 John Scott, *Scott's Orchardist*, 2nd edn., 1872, pp.8-9
11 Sir Hugh Platt, *Floræs Paradise*, 1608, pp.174-5
12 Stephen Switzer, *The Practical Fruit-Gardener*, 1724, p.11
13 Thomas Hitt, *A Treatise of Fruit-trees*, 2nd edn., 1757, p.38

CHAPTER SIX: THE LAYOUT OF BEDS, BORDERS AND PATHS pages 78–95
1   Virgil, *Georgics IV*, 1st century BC
2   Ernest Horn and Walter Born, *The Plan of St Gall*, 1979, Vol. II, p.203
3   Didymus Mountain (pseudonym of Thomas Hill), *The Gardener's Labyrinth*, 1577, part I, chap.13, pp.25-6
4   *Ibid.*, part I, chap.12, p.22
5   John Parkinson, *Paradisi in Sole Paradisus Terrestris*, 1629, p.461
6   John Reid, *The Scots Gard'ner*, 1683, part I, chap.5, p.23 (facsimile edn. Mainstream Publishing, 1988)
7   François Gentil, *Le Jardinier Solitaire*, 1704 (trans. G. London and H. Wise as *The Retir'd Gard'ner*, 1706, p.62)
8   John Reid, *The Scots Gard'ner*, 1683, part 2, chap.6, p.103
9   Leonard Meager, *The English Gardener*, 1670, pp.161-2
10 John Reid, *The Scots Gard'ner*, 1683, part 1, chap 4, p.21
11 *Ibid.* part I, chap 5, p.25
12 Charles M'Intosh, *The New and Improved Practical Gardener*, 1847, p.793
13 Stephen Switzer, *The Practical Kitchen Gardiner*, 2nd edn., 1727, p.10

14 William Cobbett, *The English Gardener*, 1829, no page numbers, chap.II, para.16

15 Letter, dated 19 October 1828, from Harriet, Countess of Granville (Castle Howard ms. J/18/38)

16 Inventory, taken for the purposes of a lease, which describes in detail the kitchen garden at Henry Drummond's estate, The Grange, Northington, Hampshire, 19 October 1795 (Royal Archive Deeds 6/172, Windsor Castle)

17 Charles M'Intosh, *The Book of the Garden*, 1853, vol.I, p.61

18 Claude Mollet, *Théâtre des Plans et Jardinages*, 1652, p.141

19 François Carvallo, 'Le jardin potager d'ornement de Villandry', in *La Gazette Illustrée des Amateurs des Jardins*, 1955-6 (quoted by K. Woodbridge in 'Doctor Carvallo and the Absolute', *Garden History*, vol. 6:2, p.65)

CHAPTER SEVEN: NEW VEGETABLES, OLD TECHNIQUES pages 96–117

1 A.B. Bartlett, 'Beaulieu Monks at Work, Production and Labour in the Account Book of Beaulieu Abbey, 1269-70', *c.*1978, unpaginated typescript in the Beaulieu Archives, Beaulieu, Hants

2 *Ibid.*

3 For details of sources, see John Harvey, *Mediaeval Gardens*, 1981

4 Letter from John Harvey to author, 23 January 1989

5 *Abbot of Westminster's Accounts for the Manor of La Neyte*, 1275-76 (Westminster Abbey Muniments, 26850)

6 All mentioned by Friar Henry Daniel (*fl.*1379): see John Harvey, *Mediaeval Gardens*, 1981, appendix 2, pp.159-162

7 Pietro de' Crescenzi, *Liber Ruralium Commodorum*, *c.*1304, book VI, pp. 55 and 103

8 Pliny the Elder, *Natural History*, 1st century AD, XXI. lv, 93 (Loeb Classical Library, 1969, vol.VI, p.229)

9 Didymus Mountain (pseudonym of Thomas Hill), *The Gardener's Labyrinth*, 1577, part II, chap.15, pp.65-6

10 *Ibid*, part I, chap.26, p.58

11 John Parkinson, *Paradisi in Sole Paradisus Terrestris*, 1629, p.462

12 Leonard Meager, *The English Gardener*, 1670, p.207

13 Robert Sharrock, *The History of the Propagation & Improvement of Vegetables by the Concurrence of Art and Nature*, 1660, p.127

14 *Le Ménagier de Paris*, *c.*1393 (ed. and trans. Eileen Power as *The Goodman of Paris*, 1928, pp.199-200)

15 John Evelyn, *Directions for the Gardener at Sayes Court*, 1686 (ed. Geoffrey Keynes, 1932, p.18)

16 John Reid, *The Scots Gard'ner*, 1683, part II, chap.6, p.108

17 William Lawson, *The Country Housewife*, 1617 (*The Country House-wife's Garden*, published by Breslich and Foss 1983, from the 3rd edn., p.34)

18 Celia Fiennes, *The Illustrated Journeys of Celia Fiennes*, 1685-*c.*1712 (ed. Christopher Morris, 1982, p.117)

19 J.C. Loudon, *Encyclopædia of Gardening*, 3rd edn., 1825, p.453, para.2371

20 William Harrison, *Description of England*, in Holinshed's *Chronicles*, 1587 (quoted by John Harvey in *Early Nurserymen*, 1974, pp.23-4)

21 John Harvey, 'Vegetables in the Middle Ages', in *Garden History*, vol.12:2, 1984, pp.89-99

22 Didymus Mountain (pseudonym of Thomas Hill), *The Gardener's Labyrinth*, 1577, part I, chap.18, p.35

23 William Turner, *The Names of Herbes*, 1548 (ed. James Britten, 1881, p.17)

24 John Reid, *The Scots Gard'ner*, 1683, part II, chap.1, p.57

25 William Early on simultaneous cropping, in *Cassell's Popular Gardening*, ed. D.T. Fish, 1893, vol.II, pp.185-8

26 Thomas Tusser, *Five Hundred Points of Good Husbandry*, 1580 (Tregaskis edn., intro. Geoffrey Grigson, 1984, p.74)

27 John Gerard, *Herball*, 1597, p.1042

28 John Worlidge, *Systema Horti-culturae*, 1677, p. 203

29 William Lucas's *Catalogue*, *c.*1677, in John Harvey's *Early Gardening Catalogues*, 1972, p.71

30 François Gentil, *Le Jardinier Solitaire*, 1704 (the 1706 translation by G. London and H. Wise, published as *The Retir'd Gardiner*, 2nd edn., revis'd by Joseph Carpenter, 1717, p.561)

31 Philip Miller, *The Gardener's Dictionary*, 7th edn., 1756, no page numbers, see under 'Phaseolus'

32 William Curtis, *Directions for Cultivating the Crambe maritima, or Sea Kale, for the Use of the Table, etc.*, 1799, pp.17-18.

33 Peter Collinson, letter to John Bartram, 2 September 1739, in William Darlington's, *Memorials of John Bartram and Humphrey Marshall*, 1849 (facsimile of 1849 edn., 1967, p.134)

34 John Evelyn, *Acetaria*, 1699; transcript edited by Christopher Driver, Prospect Books, 1996, p.99

35 John Parkinson, *Paradisi in Sole Paradisus Terrestris*, 1629, p.379

36 Timothy Nourse, *Campania Fælix*, 1700, pp.323-4

37 John Forster, *England's Happiness Increased, or a Sure and Easie Remedy against all Succeeding Dear Years; by a Plantation of the Roots Called Potatoes*, . . .1664, see title page, which continues in full as: 'whereof (with the Addition of Wheat Flower) excellent, good and wholesome Bread may be made, every Year, eight or nine Months together, for half the Charge as formerly. *ALSO* By the Planting of these Roots, Ten Thousand Men in *ENGLAND* and *WALES*, who

know not how to Live, or what to do to get a Maintenance for their Families, may of One Acre of Ground, make Thirty Pounds *per Annum. Invented and Published for the Good of the Poorer Sort, By* JOHN FORSTER *Gent.* 1664'

38 Timothy Nourse, *Campania Fælix*, 1700, p.324

39 *Ibid*, p.325

CHAPTER EIGHT: THE FRAMEYARD
pages 118–139

1 Walafrid Strabo, *Hortulus*, *c.*840 (trans. R.S. Lambert, The Stanton Press, 1923, p.21

2 Alphonse de Candolle, *The Origin of Cultivated Plants*, 1882, p.262

3 Lambeth Palace Library, *Account Roll for the Manor of Lambeth*, 1321-1322, ED 545, Forinsece

4 Didymus Mountain (pseudonym of Thomas Hill), *The Gardener's Labyrinth*, 1577, part II, chap.29, pp.135-6

5 Pliny the Elder, *Natural History*, lst century AD, Book XIX, xxiii, 67 and XIX, xxiv, 70 (Loeb Classical Library, vol.V, 1971, pp.465 and 467)

6 *Le Livre de l'Agriculture d'Ibn-al-Awam (Kitabh al-filaha) traduit de l'arabe par J.J.Clement-Mullet*, Paris 1864-66, vol. II, part ii, pp.64-6

7 Anon, *Le Calendrier de Cordoue*, 961 (ed. C.Marinescu, J.M. Millás-Vallicrosa and H. Monés, and trans. C. Pellat, E.J. Brill, Leiden, 1961, pp.76 and 186)

8 Ibn Bassal, *Kitabh al-filaha*, *c.*1085 (ed. and trans. J.M. Millás-Vallicrosa and M. Aziman, 1955), p.169

9 Aristotle, *History of Animals*, 6.2, 4th century BC, quoted in Darby, Ghalionghini and Grivetti, *Food, the Gift of Osiris*, 1977, vol.1, p.330

10 *Ibid*, vol.1, p.330

11 Pliny the Elder, *Natural History*, lst century AD, XIX. xxiii, 64 (Loeb Classical Library,1971, vol.V, p.463) and Columella, *On Agriculture*, XI, iii, 51 (Loeb Classical Library,1979, vol.III, pp.161-3)

12 Pietro de' Crescenzi, *Liber Ruralium Commodorum*, *c.*1304 (quote taken from Florentine edn. of 1605, Book VI, chap.xx, p.305)

13 Anon, but possibly Thomas Aquinas, *De Essentiis*, mid-13th century, quoted in Singer's *History of Medicine*, vol.III, p.136

14 Didymus Mountain (pseudonym of Thomas Hill), *The Gardener's Labyrinth*, 1577, part I, chap.14 (erroneously printed as ch.24), p.28

15 John Parkinson, *Paradisi in Sole Paradisus Terrestris*, 1629, p.466

16 *Ibid*. p.465

17 *Ibid*. p.463

18 Samuel Collins, *Paradise Retriev'd*, 1717, p.106

19 Philip Miller, *The Gardener's Dictionary*, 4th edn. of the *Abridgement*, 1754, no page numbers, see under 'Melonry or Melon Ground'

20 Didymus Mountain (pseudonym of Thomas Hill), *The Gardener's Labyrinth*, 1577, part II, chap.29, p.134

21 Olivier de Serres, *Le Théâtre d'Agriculture*, edn. of 1663, p.497

22 John Parkinson, *Paradisi in Sole Paradisus Terrestris*, 1629, p.466

23 John Evelyn, *Directions for the Gardener at Sayes Court*, 1686 (ed. Geoffrey Keynes, 1932, p.16)

24 John Evelyn, *Kalendarium Hortense*, 8th edn., 1691, p.84

25 Nicolas de Bonnefons, *Le Jardinier François*, 1651 (trans. J. Evelyn as *The French Gardiner*, 1675, p.143)

26 John Worlidge, Systema Horti-culturæ, 1677, p.215

27 John Evelyn, *Directions for the Gardener at Sayes Court*, 1686 (ed. Geoffrey Keynes, 1932, pp.106-7)

28 Leonard Meager, *The English Gardener*, 1670, p.51

29 Nicolas de Bonnefons, *Le Jardinier François*, 1651 (trans. John Evelyn as *The French Gardiner*, 1672, pp.139-40)

30 John Evelyn, *Kalendarium Hortense*, 5th edn., 1673, p.39 and *Directions for the Gardener at Sayes Court*, 1686 (ed. Geoffrey Keynes, 1932, p.62)

31 John Reid, *The Scots Gard'ner*, 1683, p. 33

32 John Evelyn, *Kalendarium Hortense*, 6th edn, 1676, pp.146-8

33 Gilbert White, *Garden Kalendar*, 1751-68, Feb 23-5, March 11, 18 and 25,1758 (facsimile, Scolar Press, 1975, p.55 *verso* – p.58 *verso*)

34 Paper read by Alexander Keith on 10 June 1817, in *Memoirs of the Caledonian Horticultural Society*, vol. III, 1825, pp.185-7

35 Gilbert White, *Garden Kalendar*, 1751-68, 24 April 1754 and 14 Feb. 1757 (facsimile, Scolar Press, 1975, pp.16, 39 *verso*)

36 William Forsyth, *A Treatise on the Culture and Management of Fruit Trees*, 4th edn., 1806, p.323

37 Batty Langley, *New Principles of Gardening*, 1728, part VII, section xiv, p.38

38 Richard Bradley, *New Improvements of Planting and Gardening*, 4th edn., 1720, part 3, pp.110-1

39 P.R. Enslin and S. Rehm, 'The distribution and biogenesis of curcurbitacins in relation to the taxonomy of the *curcurbitaceae*', in *Proc. Linn. Soc. Lond.*, 1956-7,169(3), pp.230-8

40 Richard Bradley, *New Improvements of Planting and Gardening*, 3rd edn., 1719, part I, p.14

41 Experiment described in a letter dated 6 October 1721, from Philip Miller to Richard Bradley, in Bradley's *A General Treatise of Husbandry and Gardening*, 1726, but not published by Miller until 1752 in *The Gardener's Dictionary*, no page numbering, see under 'Generation'

42 Columella, *De Re Rustica*, 1st century AD, IX iv, 4-6 (Loeb Classical Library, *On Agriculture*, 1979, vol. II, p.437)

43 James Macky, *A Journey through England*, 1728, vol.II, p.10

44 James M'Phail, *Treatise on the Culture of the Cucumber*, 1794, pp.50-88, also described in J.C. Loudon, *Encyclopædia of Gardening*, 3rd edn., 1825, para. 1551, p.302

45 Samuel Wood, *The Forcing Garden*, 1881, p.57

CHAPTER NINE: THE COMPOST YARD
pages 140–147

1   E.J. Russell, *Soils and Manures*, 1921, p.187

2   John Evelyn, *Directions for the Gardener at Sayes Court*, 1686 (ed. Geoffrey Keynes, 1932, p.20)

3   Theophrastus, *Historia Plantarum* [*Enquiry into Plants*], 4th-3rd centuries BC, II,ii,11 (Loeb Classical Library, 1968, p.117)

4   John Parkinson, *Paradisi in Sole Paradisus Terrestris*, 1629, p.461

5   John Laurence, *The Gentleman's Recreation*, 1716, pp.85-6

6   Timothy Nourse, *Campania Fælix*, 1700, p.325

7   Florentinus, *Geoponika; Agricultural Pursuits*, AD218, II.22 (trans. Rev. T. Owen, 1805, vol.I, book ii, sect xxii, pp.69-70)

8   *Le Livre de l'Agriculture d'Ibn-al-Awam (Kitabh al-filaha) traduit de l'arabe par J.J.Clément-Mullet*, Paris, 1864-66, vol.1, p.112

9   Varro, *De Re Rustica*, 1st century BC, I, xxxviii (Loeb Classical Library, *On Agriculture*,1979, p.265)

10 Pliny the Elder, *Naturalis Historia*, 1st century AD, XVII. vi, 51 (Loeb Classical Library, *Natural History*,1971, vol. V, p.37)

11 Columella, *De re Rustica*, 1st century AD, II xiv, 1-9 (Loeb Classical Library, *On Agriculture*, 1977, pp.195-201)

12 Sir Hugh Platt, *Floræs Paradise*, 1608, pp.1-6 and 43

13 A.G.Morton, quoting Robert Boyle's *The Sceptical Chymiste*, 1661, in *History of Botanical Science*, 1981, n.15, p.224

14 A.G.Morton, on the *Experiments* of Johann Adam Külbel (published in Dresden in Latin, 1740, and in Bordeaux in French, 1741), in *History of Botanical Science*, 1981, pp.254-5

15 Nicolas-Théodore de Saussure, *Recherches Chimiques sur la Végétation*, 1804, summarized by A.G.Morton, in his *History of Botanical Science*, 1981, pp.337-42

16 Justus von Liebig, *Die organische Chemie in ihrer Anwendung auf Agricultur und Physiologie*, 1840, summarized by A.G.Morton in his *History of Botanical Science*, 1981, pp.393-4

CHAPTER TEN: GLASS AND HEAT
pages 148–155

1   Martial, *Epigrams*, *c.*AD 93, VII lxvii

2   John Parkinson, *Paradisi in Sole Paradisus Terrestris*, 1629, p.586

3   J. Gibson, *A Short Account of Several Gardens near London. . .*,1691, in *Archaeologia*, 1796, vol XII, pp.181-92

4   John Evelyn, *Kalendarium Hortense*, 8th edn., 1691, p.62

5   John Evelyn, *Directions for the gardener at Sayes Court*, 1686 (ed. Geoffrey Keynes, 1932, pp.51-2)

6   Johannes Baptista Ferrari, *Hesperides*, 1635, Book II, chap.17, p.143

7   John Evelyn, *Kalendarium Hortense*, 8th edn., 1691, pp.150-162

CHAPTER ELEVEN: THE PINERY
pages 156–171

1   The author in conversation with the late Countess Michaelowsky

2   Gonzalo Fernandez de Oviedo y Valdes, *Historia General y Natural de las Indias*, 1535: Oviedo 1520, ms HM117 in The Huntingdon Library, California, USA and J. L. Collins, *The Pineapple*, 1960, p.13

3   D.O. Wijnands, 'Hortus auriaci: the gardens of Orange and their place in late l7th-century botany and horticulture', in *The Anglo-Dutch Garden in the Age of William and Mary, Journal of Garden History*, 1988, vol.8: nos.2 and 3, pp.61-86

4   Philotheos Physiologus, *Friendly Advice to the Gentlemen Planters of the East and West Indies*, 1684, p.4

5   *The Anglo-Dutch Garden in the Age of William and Mary, Journal of Garden History*, 1988, vol.8: nos.2 and 3, Catalogue, Vijverhof, portrait of Agnes Block, p.121

6   Captain Charles Hatton, *Correspondence of the Family of Hatton* (ed. E.M. Thompson), Camden Society, N.S., xxiii

7   Letter to the Duchess of Beaufort from Mr Bale, 1692, Brit. Lib. Sloane ms. 4062, fol. 246

8   Letter from Tilleman Bobart, Curator of the Oxford Botanic Garden, to Dr Edward Lloyd, 2nd Keeper of the Ashmolean Museum, 14 October 1693 (Bodleian Library, ms. Eng. Hist. C.11)

9   Richard Bradley, *A General Treatise of Husbandry and Gardening*, edn. of 1724, vol.1, p.206

10 Richard Weston, *Tracts on Practical Agriculture and Gardening*, 1769, p.64

11 Leonard Meager, Supplement to *The Compleat English Gardener*, 1704, p.137

12 John Evelyn, *Directions for the Gardener at Sayes Court*, 1686 (ed. Geoffrey Keynes, 1932, p.49)

13 Philip Miller, *The Gardener's Dictionary*, 6th edn., 1752, no page numbers, see under 'Tan or Tanner's Bark'

14 Richard Bradley, *A General Treatise of Husbandry and Gardening*, 1724, vol.1, July 1721, p.210
15 *Ibid.*, 1724, vol. III, January 1722/3, p.146
16 John Cowell, *The Curious and Profitable Gardener*, 1730, pp.27-8
17 J.C. Loudon, *Encyclopædia of Gardening*, 3rd edn., 1825, p.313, para.1597
18 Philip Miller, *The Gardener's Dictionary*, 6th edn., 1752, no page numbers, see under 'Green-house or Conservatory'
19 *Ibid.*, see under 'Ananas'
20 William Speechly, *A Treatise on the Culture of the Pine Apple. . .*, 2nd edn., 1779, pp.xiv-xv and 132-140
21 Philip Miller, *The Gardener's Dictionary*, 8th edn., 1768, no page numbers, see under 'Ananas'
22 John Abercrombie, *The Hot-House Gardener on the General Culture of the Pine-apple. . .*, 1789, pp.21-2
23 *Kalm's account of his visit to England on his way to America*, 1748, translated by Joseph Lucas, 1892, p.93
24 Philip Miller, *The Gardener's Dictionary*, 6th edn., 1752, no page numbers, see under 'Stoves'
25 Richard Bradley, *A General Treatise of Husbandry and Gardening*, 1724: vol.I, entry for June 1721, pp.162-3
26 John Abercrombie, writing as 'Mr Mawe', *Every Man his Own Gardener*, 1767, p.421
27 William Speechly, *A Treatise on the Culture of the Pine Apple. . .*, 1779, pp.69-71
28 Henry Phillips, *Pomarium Britannicum*, 1820, p.300

CHAPTER TWELVE: THE VINERY
pages 172–185
1 John Abercrombie, writing as 'Mr Mawe', *Every Man his Own Gardener*, 6th edn.1779, pp.479-80
2 Richard Bradley, *Gentleman and Gardeners Kalendar*, 4th edn. l724, pp.54-93
3 John Abercrombie, *The Hot-house Gardener. . .*, 1789, see title page and contents list
4 Philip Miller, *Gardeners Dictionary*, 6th edn. 1752, no page numbers, see under 'Walls'
5 Walter Nicol, *The Forcing, Fruit and Kitchen Gardener*, 3rd edn., 1802, p.103
6 William Speechly, *Treatise on the Culture of the Vine*, 1790, pp.viii-xii
7 Charles M'Intosh, *The New and Improved Practical Gardener*, 1847, p.510
8 John Harvey, *Mediaeval Gardens*, 1981, p.140
9 Leonard Meager, *The English Gardener*, 1670, p.66
10 John Parkinson, *Paradisi in Sole Paradisus Terrestris*, 1629, p.566
11 *Ibid.*, pp.563-4
12 Sir William Temple, *Upon the Gardens of Epicurus*, 1685, p.184
13 Stephen Switzer, *The Practical Fruit-Gardener*, 1724, pp.159-165

14 *Ibid.*, pp.301-3
15 Thomas Hitt, *A Treatise of Fruit-trees*, 2nd edn., 1757, pp.210-211
16 John Abercrombie, *The Complete Forcing Gardener*, 1781, p.10
17 William Speechly, *A Treatise on the Culture of the Vine*, 1790, pp.141-3
18 Thomas Moore and Maxwell Masters, *Epitome of Gardening*, l881, p.75
19 H.R.Tuffin, *Grapes, Peaches and Nectarines*, 1957, pp.246-7
20 Richard Arkwright, 'On a Method of Retarding the Ripening of Grapes in Hot Houses so as to obtain a Supply of fruit in the Winter Season', *Transactions of the Horticultural Society*,1820, III, pp.95-7
21 J.C. Loudon, *Encyclopædia of Gardening*, 3rd edn., 1825, p.750, para.4796
22 Charles M'Intosh, *The New and Improved Practical Gardener*, 1847, p.510
23 John Mearns, 'Account of a Method of Managing Vines in a Common Grapery', *Transactions of the Horticultural Society*, 1822, IV, pp.246-7
24 Charles M'Intosh, *The New and Improved Practical Gardener*, 1847, pp.476-8, 483-4 and 516-18
25 Charles M'Intosh, *The Book of the Garden*, 1853, vol.I, p.322 quoting Mr Marnock in *The United Gardeners' Journal*
26 John Mearns, 'Account of a Method of Managing Vines in a Common Grapery', *Transactions of the Horticultural Society*, 1822, IV, pp.246-7
27 Thomas Hitt's diary manuscripts, revised etc. by James Meader as *The Modern Gardener*, 1771, p.500

CHAPTER THIRTEEN:
THE NINETEENTH-CENTURY
GLASSHOUSE RANGE pages 186–197
1 Stephen Hales, *Vegetable Staticks*, 1727, p.375
2 John Lindley, in the *Gardeners' Chronicle* of 1846, quoted by Charles M'Intosh, *The Book of the Garden*, 1853, vol.I, pp.272-3
3 Walter Nicol, quoted by Charles M'Intosh, *The Book of the Garden*, 1853, vol.I, pp.291-2
4 J.C. Loudon, *The Greenhouse Companion*, 1824, section IV, p.22
5 Charles M'Intosh, *The Greenhouse, Hothouse and Stove*, 1838, p.9
6 Sir George Mackenzie, 'The Form which the Glass of a Forcing-House ought to have, in order to receive the greatest possible quantity of Rays from the Sun', in *Transactions of the Horticultural Society*, 1815, pp.171-7
7 Thomas Andrew Knight, 'On the Culture of the Pineapple', in *Transactions of the Horticultural Society*, vol.IV, 1820, pp.72-8; 1821, p.543-50 and *Trans. Hort.* vol.V, 1822, pp.142-5

8   J.C. Loudon, *Treatise on several Improvements recently made in Hot-houses*, 1805, p.192 and plates viii and ix
9   Joseph Paxton, in *Paxton's Magazine of Botany*, 1835, vol.2, p.81
10 Samuel Orchart Beeton, *Beeton's Book of Garden Management*, c.1870, pp.375-8
11 J.C. Loudon, *Encyclopædia of Gardening*, 3rd edn., 1825, p.311, para.1589
12 Samuel Orchart Beeton, *Beeton's New Book of Garden Management*, c.1870, pp.422-3
13 Charles M'Intosh, *The Practical Gardener*, 1832, p.540
14 George Anderson, 'An Account of a Method of Forcing Vines and Nectarines', in *Transactions of the Horticultural Society*, II, 1 October 1818, pp. 245-9
15 Anon, *A New System of Practical Domestic Economy*, 1823, pp.335-6
16 'A Cow Vinery', *Cottage Gardener*, vol.7, 8 Jan.1852, p.221, and 25 March 1852, pp. 393-4

CHAPTER FOURTEEN:
THE POTTING SHED pages 198–211
1   C.W.Shaw, *Market and Kitchen Gardening*, 1894, p.34
2   John Evelyn, *Directions for the Gardener at Sayes Court*, 1686 (ed. Geoffrey Keynes, 1932, pp.105-8)
3   Charles M'Intosh, *The Practical Gardener*, 1832, vol.ii, pp.1083-5
4   J.C.Loudon, *The Suburban Horticulturist*, 1842, p.142
5   Ray Palmer and W.Percival Westell, *Pests of the Garden and Orchard, Farm and Forest*, 1922, p.322

CHAPTER FIFTEEN:
PESTS AND DISEASES pages 212–225
1   Didymus Mountain (pseudonym of Thomas Hill), *The Gardener's Labyrinth*, 1577, part I, chap.27, pp.60-64
2   John Evelyn, *Kalendarium Hortense*, 4th edn., 1671, p.78
3   James M'phail, *The Gardener's Remembrancer throughout the Year*, 1794, p.131
4   Ray Palmer and W. Percival Westell, *Pests of the Garden and Orchard, Farm and Forest*, 1922, pp.338-9
5   William Forsyth, *A Treatise on the Culture and Management of Fruit-trees*, 1802, p.358
6   J. C. Loudon, *Encyclopædia of Gardening*, 3rd edn., 1825, p.437, para. 2286
7   Charles M'Intosh, *The Practical Gardener*, vol. 2, 1832, p.964
8   J. C. Loudon, *Encyclopædia of Gardening*, 3rd edn., 1825, p.436, para. 2279
9   Didymus Mountain (pseudonym of Thomas Hill), *The Gardener's Labyrinth*, 1577, part I, chap.27, p.64
10 *Kalm's account of his visit to England on his way to America*, 1748, trans. Joseph Lucas, 1892, pp.163, 259 and 376-7
11 William Jones, *The Gardener's Receipt Book*, 1858, p.78

12 John Evelyn, *Kalendarium Hortense*, 8th edn., 1691, p.84
13 John Evelyn, *Directions for the Gardener at Sayes Court*, 1686 (ed. Geoffrey Keynes, 1932, pp.82 and 108)
14 William Jones, *The Gardener's Receipt Book*, 1858, p.75
15 Columella, *On Agriculture*, 1st century AD, XII, xlvi, 2 (Loeb Classical Library, vol.III, 1979, p.283)
16 John Evelyn, *Directions for the Gardener at Sayes Court*, 1686 (ed. Geoffrey Keynes, 1932, p.106)
17 Robert Laneham, *Letters*, 1575 (ed. E.J.Furnivall, 1907, pp.50-51)
18 Charles M'Intosh, *The Practical Gardener*, 1832, vol.1, p.413
19 Raymond Bush, *A Fruit-Grower's Diary*, 1950, p.96
20 Jane Grigson, *The Mushroom Feast*, 1978, pp. xiv-v
21 Letter to the author from John Harvey, 8 October 1996
22 *Garden-Companion, for Gentlemen and Ladies*, 7th edn., 1795, p.79, item 35

CHAPTER SIXTEEN:
THE MUSHROOM HOUSE pages 226–235
1   G.C.Ainsworth, *Introduction to the History of Mycology*, 1976, pp.82-3
2   George London and Henry Wise, *The Retir'd Gardener*, 1706, vol. I, pp.102-3
3   William Robinson, *The Parks, Promenades and Gardens of Paris*, 1869, p.477
4   Peter Blackburne-Maze, 'Fungal Feast', in *The Garden*, December 1992, vol.117, pt. 12, pp.590-92
5   G.C.Ainsworth, *Introduction to the History of Mycology*, 1976, p.84
6   Richard Bradley, *New Improvements of Planting and Gardening*, 1720, pt.III, p.123
7   Richard Bradley, *A General Treatise on Husbandry and Gardening*, III, 1724, pp.103-8
8   Rymsdyk, 'A description of the mushroom stone at the British Museum', in *Museum Britannicum*, 2nd edn., 1791, p.39
9   Theophrastus, *Enquiry into Plants*, 4th-3rd centuries BC, IV. vii. 2 (Loeb Classical Library, 1968, vol.I, p.339)
10 Giacomo Castelvetro, *A Brief Account of the Fruit, Herbs and Vegetables of Italy*, 1614 (trans. and intro. Gillian Riley, 1989, p.130 and p.158)
11 Stephen Switzer, *Ichnographia Rustica: Or, the Nobleman, Gentleman, and Gardener's Recreation*, vol.3, 1742, in the *Appendix*, pp.90-93
12 J. Ramsbottom, 'The Fungus-stone, *Polyporus tuberaster*', *Proc. Linn. Soc.*, 1931-2, 76-79; and Sir John Hill, in *Botanical Tracts by Dr. Hill*, 1762; *Account of the Mushroom Stone*, 1758, pp.3-34
13 Isabella Beeton, *Household Management*, 1880, n. to para.1171, p.589

CHAPTER SEVENTEEN:
THE SEED ROOM pages 236–245

1 John Harvey, *Mediaeval Gardens*, 1981, p.78
2 John Parkinson, *Paradisi in Sole Paradisus Terrestris*, 1629, pp.463-4
3 Leonard Meager, *The English Gardener*, 1670, p.208
4 John Harvey, *Early Nurserymen*, 1974, p.5
5 John Evelyn's 'Advertisement' for George London and Henry Wise's abridgement of his translation of de la Quintinye's *Instructions pour les Jardins Fruitiers et Potagers*, 1690, pub. as *The Compleat Gard'ner*, 1699, inserted between pp.xiv and xv
6 J.C. Loudon, *Encylopædia of Gardening*, 3rd edn., 1825, p.1052, para.7454
7 John Middleton, *A General View of the Agriculture of Middlesex*, 1798, pp.262-7
8 John Parkinson, *Paradisi in Sole Paradisus Terrestris*, 1629, p.503
9 J.C. Loudon, *Encyclopædia of Gardening*, 3rd edn., 1825, p.612, para.3537
10 John Mortimer, *The Whole Art of Husbandry*, 1707, p.153
11 John Parkinson, *Paradisi in Sole Paradisus Terrestris*, 1629, p.464
12 Theophrastus, *Enquiry into Plants*, 4th-3rd centuries BC, VII.v.5 and VIII.xi.5 (Loeb Classical Library, *Enquiry into Plants*, 1980, vol.II, pp.97 and 209)
13 Philip Miller, *The Gardener's Dictionary*, 3rd edn., 1739, vol. II, no page numbering, see under 'Seed'
14 James Anderson, *The New Practical Gardener . . .*, *c*.1872, p.288

CHAPTER EIGHTEEN: PICKING,
PACKING AND STORING pages 246–261

1 Jean-Baptiste de la Quintinye, *Instructions pour les Jardins Fruitiers et Potagers*, l690 (abridged by G. London and H. Wise as *The Compleat Gard'ner*, 1699, p.152)
2 *Thompson's Gardener's Assistant* (ed.W. Watson, 1909, vol.5, p.381)
3 William Forsyth, *A Treatise on the Culture and Management of Fruit-Trees*, 1806, pp.335-7
4 *Ibid.*, p.339
5 J.C. Loudon, *Encyclopædia of Gardening*, 1825, p.440, para.2304
6 George Lindley, *A Guide to the Orchard and Kitchen Garden*, 1831, p.517
7 Benjamin Whitmill, *Kalendarium Universale*, 1748, p.198
8 J.C. Loudon, *Encyclopædia of Gardening*, 1850, p.530, para.1771
9 Charles M'Intosh, quoting Robert Thompson in *The Book of the Garden*, vol.I, 1853, p.487
10 *Ibid.*, vol.I, p.495

11 *The Gardener's Chronicle*, 22 November 1884, p.650
12 *A New System of Domestic Economy*, 3rd edn., 1823, p.223
13 George Lindley, *A Guide to the Orchard and Kitchen Garden*, 1831, p.517
14 Columella, *On Agriculture*, 1st century AD, XII.iv,5 (Loeb Classical Library, 1979, vol.III, p.197)
15 Sir Hugh Platt, *Delightes for Ladies*, 1602, no page numbering, para. a.64
16 John Parkinson, *Paradisi in Sole Paradisus Terrestris*, 1629, p.554
17 *A New System of Domestic Economy*, 3rd edn., 1823, p.222

CHAPTER NINETEEN: THE GARDENERS
pages 262–273

1 J.C. Loudon, *Encyclopædia of Gardening*, 3rd edn., 1825, p.1049, para.7444
2 Jean-Baptiste de la Quintinye, *Instructions pour les Jardins Fruitiers et Potagers* (trans. John Evelyn as *The Compleat Gard'ner*, 1693, pp.12-14)
3 John Harvey, *Early Nurserymen*, 1974, p.83
4 William Thomas Crosweller, *The Gardeners' Company*, 1908, p.19 and Charles Welch, *The Gardeners' Company*, 1900, p.21
5 Traugott Schwamstapper, *Bermerken über die Gartenkunst*, 1796 (quoted in J.C. Loudon, *Encyclopædia of Gardening*, 3rd edn., 1825, p.53, para.2371)
6 J.C. Loudon, *Encyclopædia of Gardening*, 3rd edn., 1825, pp.1136-1141, paras 7724-59

BIBLIOGRAPHY

Abercrombie, John, writing as 'Mr Mawe', *Every Man his own Gardener*, 1766

— —-   *Complete Kitchen Gardener*, 1789

al-'Awwam, Ibn, *Kitabh al-filaha*, *c.*1180 (ed. and trans. J.A.Banqueri as *Libro de Agricultura . . . (de) ebn el Awam*, 1802; and ed. and trans. J.J.Clément-Mullet as *Le Livre d'Agriculture*, 1864-7)

Anon, *Le Calendrier de Cordoue*, 1961 (ed. C. Marinescu, J.M. Millás-Vallicrosa and H. Monés, with an annotated French translation by C. Pellat, 1961)

Bassal, Ibn, *Kitabh al-filaha*, *c.*1085 (ed. and trans. J.M. Millás -Vallicrosa and M. Aziman as *Libro de Agricultura*, 1955

Beeton, Samuel Orchart, *New Book of Garden Management*, 1880

Bonnefons, Nicolas de, *Le Jardinier François*, 1651 (trans. J. Evelyn as *The French Gardiner*, 1658)

Bower, F.O., *Plants and Man*, 1925

Bradley, Richard, *New Improvements of Planting and Gardening*, 1720

— —-   *A General Treatise on Husbandry and Gardening*, 1721-6

Bunyard, George and Owen, Thomas, *The Fruit Garden*, 1904

Campbell, Susan, *A Calendar of Gardeners' Lore*, 1983

— —- *Cottesbrooke, an English Kitchen Garden*, 1987

Candolle, Alphonse de, *The Origin of Cultivated Plants*, 1882

Cassell's Popular Gardening, ed. D.J. Fish, 1885 and 1893

Cato, *De Re Rustica*, 2nd century BC (trans. W.D. Hooper as *On Agriculture*, 1934)

Cobbett, William, *The English Gardener*, 1829

Evelyn, John, *The French Gardiner*, 1658 (his translation of de Bonnefons' *Le Jardinier François*, 1651)

— —-   *Kalendarium Hortense . . .*, 1664 and 1666

— —- *Directions for the Gardener at Sayes Court*, 1686 (ed. Geoffrey Keynes, 1932)

— —-   *The Compleat Gard'ner*, 1693 (his translation of de la Quintinye's *Instructions pour les Jardins Fruitiers et Potagers*, 1690)

Gentil, François, *Le Jardinier Solitaire*, 1704 (trans. London and Wise as *The Retir'd Gardiner*, 1706)

Gerard, John, *The Herball, or Generall Historie of Plantes*, edn of 1633

Gimpel, Jean, *The Medieval Machine*, 2nd edn, 1988

Grieve, M.A., *A Modern Herbal* (ed. and intro. C.F. Leyel), 1931 and 1983

Griggs, Barbara, *Green Pharmacy*, 1981

Grigson, Geoffrey, *A Dictionary of English Plant Names*, 1974

Hadfield, Miles, *A History of British Gardening*, 1985

Hadfield, M., Harling, R., Highton, L., *British Gardeners, A Biographical Dictionary* 1980

Hartley, Dorothy, *Food in England*, 1954

— —-   *The Land of England*, 1979

Harvey, John, *Early Gardening Catalogues*, 1972

— —-   *Early Nurserymen*, 1974

— —-   *Mediaeval Gardens*, 1981

Hendrik, U.P. (ed.), *Sturtevant's Notes on Edible Plants*, 1919

Henrey, Blanche, *British Botanical and Horticultural Literature before 1800*, 1975

Hill, Thomas (pseudonym Didymus Mountain), *The Gardener's Labyrinth*, 1577

Hills, Lawrence. D., *Organic Gardening*, 1980

Hitt, Thomas, *A Treatise of Fruit-trees*, 1757

Hix, John, *The Glass House*, 1974

Horn, Ernest and Born, Walter, *The Plan of St Gall*, 3 vols, 1979

Landsberg, Sylvia, *The Medieval Garden*, 1995

Langford, Thomas, *Plain and Full Instructions to Raise all Sorts of Fruit-trees that Prosper in England*, 1681

Langley, Batty, *New Principles of Gardening*, 1728

Laurence, John, *The Clergyman's Recreation*, 1714

— —-   *The Gentleman's Recreation*, 1716

— —-   *The Fruit-Garden Kalendar*, 1718

— —-   *A New System of Agriculture*, 1726

Lawson, William, *The Country Housewife . . . with A New Orchard and Garden*, 1618

Lemmon, Kenneth, *The Covered Garden*, 1972

Le Rougetel, Hazel, *The Chelsea Gardener: Philip Miller, 1691-1771*, 1980

London, George and Wise, Henry, *The Compleat Gard'ner*, 1699 (their edited and abridged version of John Evelyn's translation of de la Quintinye's *Instructions pour les Jardins Fruitiers et Potagers*, 1690)

— —-   *The Retir'd Gardiner*, 1706 (their translation of Gentil's *Le Jardinier Solitaire*, 1704)

Loudon, John Claudius, *Encyclopædia of Gardening*, 1822

— —-   *The Greenhouse Companion*, 1824

Lovelock, Yann, *The Vegetable Book*, 1972

Macphail, J., *A Treatise on the Cultivation of the Cucumber*, 1794

Masefield, G.B., Wallis, M., Harrison, S.G., and Nicholson, B.E., *Oxford Book of Food Plants*, 1969

Mawson, Thomas H., *The Art and Craft of Garden Making*, 5th edn, 1926

Meader, James, *The Modern Gardener*, 1771 (a revision of Thomas Hitt's diary and manuscripts)

Meager, Leonard, *The English Gard'ner*, 1670

Medieval Gardens: papers given at a colloquium, Harvard University, Dumbarton Oaks, Washington D.C., 1986

Mellanby, Kenneth, *Pesticides and Pollution*, 2nd edn, 1970

Le Ménagier de Paris, c.1393 (ed. and trans. Eileen Power as *The Goodman of Paris*, 1928)

Miller, Philip, *The Gardener's Dictionary*, enlarged edn, 1731

M'Intosh, Charles, *The Practical Gardener*, vol 1, 1828; vol. 2, 1832

— —-   *The Greenhouse, Hothouse and Stove*, 1838

— —-   *The Book of the Garden*, 1853

Moore, Thomas and Master, Maxwell, *Epitome of Gardening*, 1881

Morgan, Joan and Richards, Alison, *A Paradise out of a Common Field*, 1990

— —-   *The Book of Apples*, 1992

Mortimer, John, *The Whole Art of Husbandry*, 1707

Morton, A.H., *History of Botanical Science*, 1981

Mountain, Didymus (pseudonym of Thomas Hill), *The Gardener's Labyrinth*, 1577

Neill, Patrick, *The Gardener's Kalendar*, 1814

— —-   *The Fruit, Flower and Kitchen Garden*, 1849

Nourse, Timothy, *Campania Fælix*, 1700

Palladius, *De Re Rustica*, AD 380-395 (trans. as a medieval poem, *On Husbandrie*, ed. B.Lodge, Early English Text Society, 1873-9)

Parkinson, John, *Paradisi in Sole Paradisus Terrestris*, 1629

Phillips, Henry, *History of Plants*, 1823

Platt, Sir Hugh, *Floræ Paradise. . .*, 1608 and later edns, pub. as *The Garden of Eden*, 1653-75

Piny the Elder, *Naturalis Historia*, lst century AD (trans. H. Rackham and W.H.S. Jones as *Natural History*, 1949; 2nd edn.1980). An encyclopædia in 37 books, of which Book XIX deals with kitchen gardens.

Quintinye, Jean-Baptiste de la, *Instructions pour les Jardins Fruitiers et Potagers*, 1690 (see Evelyn, and London and Wise)

Reid, John, *The Scots Gard'ner*, 1683

Rivers, Thomas, *The Miniature Fruit Garden*, 1850

Robinson, William, *Gleanings from French Gardens*, 1868

— —- *Gravetye Manor*, 1911 (ms. in Lindley Library, RHS, London)

Salisbury, E.J., *The Living Garden*, 1935

Scott, John, *Scott's Orchardist*, 2nd edn., 1872

Sharrock, Robert, *The History of the Propagation & Improvement of Vegetables by the Concurrence of Art and Nature*, 1660

Shaw, C.W., *Market and Kitchen Gardening*, 1894

Simmonds, N.W. (ed.), *Evolution of Crop Plants*, 1976

Speechly, William, *A Treatise on the Culture of the Vine*, 1790

— —- *A Treatise on the Culture of the Pine Apple*, 1796

Switzer, Stephen, *Ichnographia Rustica*, 1718

— —-*The Practical Fruit-Gardener*, 1724

— —-*The Practical Kitchen Gardiner*, 1727

Theophrastus, *Historia Plantarum*, *c.*300 BC (trans. A.F. Hort as *An Enquiry into Plants*, 1916)

— —-De Causis Plantarum, *c.*300 BC (trans. Benedict Einarson and George K.K. Link as *On the Causes of Plants*, 1975)

Thirsk, Joan (ed.), *The Agrarian History of England and Wales*, 1985

Thompson, Robert, *Thompson's Gardener's Assistant*, 1878; also edns of 1909 and 1925 (ed. W. Walton)

Turner, William, *The Names of Herbes*, 1548 (ed. James Britten, 1881)

Tusser, Thomas, *Five Hundred Points of Good Husbandry*, 1573

Varro, *De Re Rustica*, lst century BC (trans. William Davis Hooper as *On Agriculture*, 1934)

Vilmorin-Andrieux, Messrs., *The Vegetable Garden* (pub. William Robinson), 1905

White, Gilbert, *Garden Kalendar*, 1751-68 (reproduced in facsimile by the Scolar Press, 1975)

Whitmill, Benjamin, *Kalendarium Universale*, 4th edn 1748

Wilson, C. Anne, *Food and Drink in Britain*, 1973

Wood, Samuel, *The Forcing Garden*, 1881

GLOSSARY AND BIOGRAPHIES

Abercrombie, John (1726-1806): Scottish horticulturalist, who came south to work at Kew, then established his own nursery and kitchen garden. Author of many works on gardening, including (under the alias of Thomas Mawe, 1766) *Every Man his own Gardener*, the 25th edition appearing in 1848. Subsequent editions appeared as *The Complete Gardener*.

ados: beds made in the form of sloping banks, sometimes in pairs, for raising early crops (from the French *à dos* or *adosser*, meaning back-to-back).

amurca: an extremely bitter, toxic by-product of olive oil, known scientifically as oleuropin and found in the watery fluid removed with each pressing. Used by the Romans as a herbicide, pesticide, insecticide, wood preservative and copper polish.

Atkinson, William (?1773-1839): architect, chemist, geologist and botanist. Born in County Durham, he trained as a carpenter, becoming a pupil of the architect James Wyatt. Designer in 1822 of one of the first glasshouses to be heated by hot water.

barilla: a form of sodium carbonate obtained by burning kelp or *Salsola kali*, a maritime plant found in Spain, Sicily and the Canary Islands. It is used to make soda, soap and glass and was used in gardens to kill slugs.

basic slag: a waste by-product of the stainless steel industry, being the phosphoric impurities or 'slag' which rise as scum when pig-iron is melted and purified by the Bessemer process. Crushed, it is a valuable long-term fertilizer. First marketed in Germany in 1886, reaching Britain in 1894.

bass/bast: a fibrous material derived from the piassava plant of Brazil, Madagascar and West Africa. It was used to make brooms, mats, cords and plant ties.

Bentinck, Hans Willem, 1st Earl of Portland (1649-1709): former page to William III; at his estate at Zorgvliet in Holland he had a noted garden. Following his king to England, in 1689 he added plants from his own collection of exotics, including pineapples, to William and Mary's collection at Hampton Court. Bentinck was Superintendent of the Royal Gardens in England from 1689 to 1700, with George London (*q.v.*) under him as Master Gardener and Deputy Superintendent.

Boerhaave, Hermann (1668-1738): director of the Leiden Botanic Garden 1709-30. He determined, among other things, the best angle for the slope of the glass roof of a greenhouse.

Bordeaux mixture: originally made in Bordeaux in 1885 by Professor Pierre-Marie-Alexis Millardet as a fungicide for vines, the mixture (also known as *'bouillie bordelaise'*) became the first universal fungicide. It was made by dissolving 8 kilogrammes of copper sulphate in 100 litres of water in one vessel; 17 kilogrammes of quicklime were slaked with 30 litres of water in another, then poured on to the copper sulphate solution.

Boyle, Robert, F.R.S. (1627-91): Irish physicist and chemist, a director of the East India Company and one of the founders of the Royal Society. His researches into air, combustion and respiration were of great practical use to botanists.

Bradley, Richard, F.R.S. (?1686-1732): first Professor of Botany at Cambridge in 1724, horticulturalist, and author, between 1713 and 1732, of almost thirty books on gardening, botany and agriculture. He travelled in Holland in 1714 and France in 1719, and was the first to describe the cultivation of pineapples in England.

Brown, Lancelot ('Capability') (1716-83): landscape designer. Born in Northumberland, he came south in 1739. While head gardener at Stowe, he resited the kitchen gardens there (*c*.1742); he also resited those at Longleat, Tottenham Park, Claremont, Old Wardour, Broadlands and Syon. He was appointed Master Gardener at Hampton Court in 1764, where it is said he planted the Great Vine in 1768.

Brydges, James (1st Duke of Chandos) (1673-1744): a keen gardener. Richard Bradley (*q.v.*) supplied him in 1718 with plants for his great garden at Cannons, where Tilleman Bobart was head gardener.

budding: a type of grafting in the propagation of fruit trees and roses, using a suitable bud from the scion (*q.v.*) with a portion of bark.

Carew, Sir Francis (1530-1611): gardener and Elizabethan courtier, connected by marriage to Sir Walter Raleigh (*q.v.*), from whom he obtained the orange pips that grew into the trees of his famous orangery at Beddington, near Croydon.

Carpenter, Joseph (*fl*. 1700-43): nurseryman and seedsman; partner, from 1714-43, in Brompton Park Nurseries. He was responsible for the abridged edition of *The Retir'd Gardener* (1717), first published in 1706 by George London and Henry Wise as a translation of François Gentil's *Le Jardinier Solitaire* (1704).

Cecil, William, 1st Baron Burghley (1520-98): Chief Secretary of State and Principal Advisor to Queen Elizabeth I. Builder of Burghley House in Lincolnshire and Theobalds in Hertfordshire. One of the first to grow orange trees in England.

Cheshunt compound: an inorganic soil drench based on copper sulphate and ammonium carbonate, invented in 1921.

Cobbett, William (1776-1835): political reformer, farmer, nurseryman and gardener; MP for Oldham, best known for his *Rural Rides* but also the author of several books on gardening, including *The English Gardener*, 1829.

Collinson, Peter, F.R.S. (1694-1768): Quaker haberdasher and linen draper; a prolific correspondent on horticultural and botanical matters, and patron of several notable North American and Far Eastern plant collectors.

Columella, Lucius Junius Moderatus (*fl*. AD 60): born in Cadiz, southern Spain, he spent most of his life in Italy, farming and writing treatises on agriculture, animal husbandry, viticulture and gardening, *De Re Rustica* and *De Arboribus*.

Curtis, William (1746-99): botanist, entomologist, apothecary, author and publisher of *The Botanical Magazine* (1787-present day), and Gilbert White's *Natural History of Selborne* (1789). He used his botanic garden at Brompton, London for agricultural experiments, including the growing of seakale.

Daniel, Henry (1315 or 1320-*c*.1385): Dominican friar, physician, herbalist, botanist and gardener in Stepney, London. He translated medical treatises into English and is the author of a herbal and a significant gardening treatise (both mss in the British Library).

Decker, Sir Matthew (1679-1749): born of Flemish parents in Amsterdam, he came to England in 1702, made a fortune as a director of the East India Company, and was known in royal circles. He settled in Richmond, Surrey, where he had an extensive garden. It was here that the pineapple was first successfully cultivated in England.

De' Crescenzi, Pietro (1230-1320): Bolognese lawyer, author, in 1305, of *Liber Ruralium Commodorum*, an enormously popular compendium on husbandry, much translated and republished over the fifteenth and sixteenth centuries.

De la Quintinye, Jean-Baptiste (1624-88): originally trained as a lawyer, he took up garden design after a trip to Italy, eventually becoming head gardener at Versailles under Louis XIV. He laid out *Le Potager du Roy* there in 1687 and wrote his *Instructions pour les Jardins Fruitiers et Potagers* in 1690. This was translated by Evelyn as *The Compleat Gard'ner* (1693).

derris dust: an insecticide, especially against pests such as beetles, weevils and caterpillars, made from the powdered root of an East Asian climber; originally used as a poison to kill fish.

De Saussure, Nicolas-Théodore (1767-1845): Swiss naturalist and chemist, he advanced the discoveries of his predecessors regarding photosynthesis, the effects of light and air on germination and the absorption by plants of nitrogen.

Dioscorides, Pedianos (*fl. c.* AD 60): author of *Materia Medica*, until the Renaissance the standard work on pharmacology, three-fifths of the drugs described being based on plants.

double grafting: the first scion, with one set of desired characteristics, is grafted low down on the rootstock; a second scion, with a different set, is later grafted higher up on the first scion when it has taken.

espaliers: fruit trees trained along metal or wooden supports to form a narrow fence or hedge, against a wall, or free-standing as a border to walks or borders, in which case they are termed contre-espaliers.

Evelyn, John, F.R.S. (1620-1706): diarist and horticulturalist; a Royalist, he left England for the Continent in 1641, returning in 1652 to live quietly under the Lord Protector, making a garden at his father-in-law's house, Sayes Court, in Deptford. With the Restoration, he served on many public committees and was prominent in the rebuilding of St Paul's Cathedral. He translated de Bonnefons' *Le Jardinier François* as *The French Gardiner* in 1658 and de la Quintinye's *Instructions pour les Jardins Fruitiers et Potagers* as *The Compleat Gard'ner* in 1693. His *Acetaria*, the chapter on salads from his unpublished *Elysium Britannicum*, appeared in 1699. In 1662 he delivered a paper to the Commissioners of the Navy on oak trees, which later became *Sylva* (1664). To it was appended *Kalendarum Hortense*, the first gardening programme of work to be published in England.

Faccio de Duillier, Nicolas, F.R.S. (1664-1753): a Swiss mathematician and religious fanatic, he came to England in 1687, becoming tutor to Lord Russell's son and later, the author of *Fruit-walls Improved* (1699).

Fish, David Taylor (1824-1901): Scottish horticultural journalist. Editor of *Cassell's Popular Gardening* until 1866.

Forsyth, William (1737-1804): royal gardener, founder member of the Horticultural (later Royal) Society and the inventor of a curative plaster for cankered trees which, when found to be useless, caused his disgrace. Forsythia is named after him.

free stocks: rootstocks raised from seedlings.

Gentil, François (*fl.* 1704): a Carthusian lay-brother, and for over thirty years gardener to the Charterhouse in Paris. Author of *Le Jardinier Solitaire* (1704) which, with Liger's *Le Jardinier Fleuriste*, was translated by London and Wise as *The Retir'd Gard'ner* in 1706.

Gerard, John (1545-1612): barber-surgeon and botanist, superintendent of Lord Burghley's (*q.v.*) gardens, curator of the College of Physicians' garden, author of the *Herball* of 1597 and a *Catalogue* of the plants in his own London garden (1596).

grass plat: a flat area of plain grass, sometimes ornamental in shape and bounded by paths of sand or gravel.

green manure: where animal manure was unavailable, Roman farmers ploughed-in green crops of vetch, lupines and beans, unaware of their nitrogenous content or the value of humus, but conscious of the good they did.

guano: the droppings of seabirds. (The word is derived from the Spanish *huano* - dung.) Rich in nitrogen and phosphate, it was first brought to Europe by Humboldt in 1804 from the offshore islands of Peru as a fertilizer, and was first imported to England by Lord Derby, at Liverpool, in 1840.

Hales, the Revd Stephen, F.R.S. (1677-1761): plant physiologist and chemist; a protégé of Bradley (*q.v.*) at Cambridge and a friend of Gilbert White's family. His experiments on plants resulted in *Vegetable Staticks* (1727).

hellebore powder/ground hellebore: the ground rhizomes of white and green hellebores (*Veratrum album and V. viride*). A dangerous poison, especially if inhaled, it was used as a dust or a spray against sawfly caterpillars. As exposure to air renders it harmless, it had to be used while still fresh, but this meant that it could be safely used on fruit trees.

Hill, Thomas (*c.*1528-75/6): author of several popular scientific books, including the earliest work in English on gardening in general, *A Most Briefe and Plesaunte Treatise* (*c.*1556), which was enlarged to become *The Proffitable Arte of Gardening* (1563 and 1568). His second gardening book, *The Gardener's Labyrinth*, appeared under the pseudonym of Didymus Mountain in 1577, and contains the first reference in an English gardening book to the making of hotbeds.

Hitt, Thomas (d. 1770): gardener and nurseryman, apprenticed in the gardens of the Duke of Rutland at Belvoir Castle. He specialized in fruit trees and published his *Treatise of Fruit-trees* in 1755.

humours (the four): the four elements and their natural properties; water (cold and wet), earth (cold and dry), air (hot and wet) and fire (hot and dry). The ancient, classical doctrine held that healthy plants, like the human body, were dependent on a perfect balance between these four elements.

Ibn al-'Awwam (d. *c.* 1200): Moorish author of a treatise on husbandry; he was also a gardener in Seville.

Ibn Bassal (d. 1105): a widely travelled botanist, the author of a treatise on agriculture and gardening, and until 1085 gardener to the sultan of Toledo.

intercropping (also known as intersowing): the practice of growing early or rapidly-maturing crops (such as lettuces or onions) between later or slower crops (such as celery or potatoes), in order to make the maximum use of the ground. Not to be confused with mixed planting (*q.v.*).

Justice, James, F.R.S. (1698-1763): Scottish horticulturist, Dutch bulb importer and author, who first brought pineapples to Scotland; he described his own achievements in *The Scots Gardiners Director* (1754).

kainit: discovered in the 1840s (*kainos* is Greek for 'new'). Basically a mixture of common salt, potassium chloride and magnesium chloride, it was originally found as a natural deposit in Stassfurt, Germany, so it is arguably a natural fertilizer rather than an artificial one. Its impurities have reduced its usefulness except in fruit orchards as an autumn- or winter-dressing.

Kalm, Peter (1716-79): Swedish naturalist and traveller, a student of Carl Linnaeus. His *Travels in England* (1753) are full of information for the garden historian.

Knight, Thomas Andrew, F.R.S. (1759-1838): President of the Horticultural Society from 1811 to 1838, the author of numerous treatises on fruit-growing, plant-breeding and the design and heating of hothouses.

knot: an intricate, often interlacing design, formed by low, clipped shrubs, coloured earths or gravel, and flowers. Popular in sixteenth- and seventeenth-century gardens.

Langley, Batty (1696-1751): architect, landscape designer and surveyor, draughtsman, gardener. Born in Twickenham, Middlesex, the son of a gardener. He opposed the stiff formal designs of London and Wise (*q.v.*), being an admirer of the new natural style and a follower of William Kent. An avant-garde designer of the follies and temples later to become so popular. His *New Principles of Gardening* (1728) is full of practical, first-hand advice for the kitchen gardener.

Lawes, Sir John Bennet (1814-1900): from 1834 owner of Rothamsted Manor and the inventor, in 1840, of superphosphate, which made him a millionaire. In 1843 he set up a research station on his farm, where agricultural experiments continue to this day.

Lawson, William (1554-1635): a church minister and Yorkshire gardener with almost fifty years' experience; he wrote the first gardening book for ladies, *The Country Housewife's Garden*, in 1617 and *A New Orchard and Garden* the following year.

London, George (*fl.*1673-d.1713-14): apprenticed to the royal gardener John Rose at St James's Park; in charge of Bishop Henry Compton's collection of rare plants at Fulham Palace and assistant to Bentinck (*q.v.*) at Hampton Court, he was also a founder (in 1681) of Brompton Park Nurseries. With Henry Wise (*q.v.*) as partner, he advised on many of the most prominent gardens of the day. He visited Leiden in 1685 and Versailles and other great French gardens from 1697-8. With Wise, he translated Gentil's *Le Jardinier Solitaire* as *The Retir'd Gard'ner* (1706) and abridged, also with Wise, Evelyn's translation of de la Quintinye's *Compleat Gardner* in 1699.

Loudon, John Claudius (1783-1843): son of a Scottish farmer, interested as a boy in science, and apprenticed at fourteen to an Edinburgh nurseryman; he came to London in 1803 as a landscape gardener. He was also a farmer, a journalist, a traveller with a thirst for knowledge and an indefatigable worker. His publications include works on public squares and parks, villa gardens, hothouses, crematoria and arboreta as well as his magnificent *Encylopaedia of Gardening* (1822) and *The Gardener's Magazine*, which he founded in 1826 and edited until his death.

marl: a naturally-occurring mixture of clay and chalk, originally used by the Romans to improve poor, dry soils.

Meager, Leonard (*fl.*1670-97): gardener and author of one of the most popular gardening books of his time, *The English Gardener* (1670), full of practical advice and first-hand information. Also the author of *The Mystery of Husbandry* (1697) and *The New Art of Gardening* (1697).

metaldehyde: invented in the Second World War as fuel for army camp-stoves; used mixed with bran as a poison bait for slugs and snails.

Miller, Philip, F.R.S. (1691-1771): gardener and author, the son of a Scot, for whom he first worked, gardening in Deptford near London. He set up

thereafter as a florist, nurseryman and garden designer in his own right. From 1722 until his death he was curator of the Apothecaries' Garden in Chelsea; under him the garden gained international renown. Miller was secretary, from 1730, of the Society of Gardeners, a group of some twenty London nurserymen who met monthly in Chelsea. His *Gardener's Dictionary*, first published in 1731, went into nine editions.

M'Intosh, Charles (1794-1864): Scottish gardener and author, he gardened first in Scotland, then worked in two notable gardens in England, Sir Thomas Baring's at Stratton Park and Prince Leopold's at Claremont, before returning to Scotland as gardener to the Duke of Buccleuch at Dalkeith, where he remained for twenty years. The vast experience he gained there was incorporated in several books, among them *The Practical Gardener* (1828-9) and *The Greenhouse, Hothouse and Stove* (1838). His two-volume *The Book of the Garden* appeared in 1853.

M'Phail, James (1754-1805): a peasant's son from Aberdeenshire, Scotland; by 1785 he was head gardener to Lord Hawkesbury (later Lord Liverpool) at Addiscombe Place, near Croydon, where he remained for twenty years. A noted grower of cucumbers, melons and pineapples, he wrote in 1794 his *Treatise on the Culture of the Cucumber*, with designs for a new type of pit which did much to tidy up the appearance of the frameyard and increase its productivity.

mixed planting: an ancient practice in which a mixture of seeds of fast-maturing and slower-maturing crops is sown randomly on the same bed. As the earlier crops are harvested first, the later crops grow on in the spaces left vacant. Not to be confused with intercropping (*q.v.*).

Mollet, Claude (d. *c.*1613): French gardener, *Jardinier-en-chef* to Henri IV and Louis XIII at Fontainebleau and the Tuileries; his brother Gabriel and two nephews, Gabriel and André, all worked in England in the royal gardens for Charles II.

Nicol, Walter (d.1811): Scottish horticultural architect and author; head gardener to the lst Marquess of Townshend at Raynham Hall, Norfolk and head gardener at Wemyss Castle, Fifeshire. He left in 1797 to become a horticultural architect in Edinburgh. He published four works on gardening between 1798 and 1810.

nicotine: a volatile poison derived from tobacco, used in gardening as an insecticide; in its pure state it is highly toxic to humans and animals.

orangery: in the seventeenth century frequently an integral structure, later a separate garden building in which orange trees could be sheltered during the winter.

Palladius, Rutilius (*fl. c.* AD 380): author of *De Agricultura*, a guide to husbandry in the form of a calendar, translated into English verse in the late fourteenth century; much of it is based on the works of Varro, Martial, Columella and Pliny and was itself frequently quoted thereafter.

palliasses/paillassons: straw, grass or reed mats (from the French *paillasse*) used to protect seedlings, fruit blossom, glass bells and frames from extreme heat, wet or frost. An early example of their use occurred in twelfth-century Seville, where Arab gardeners protected young plants on hotbeds, and oranges and other fruit trees with straw mats and hangings.

Parkinson, John (1567-1650): English apothecary, with a garden in London in which he grew his 'rarities'; a friend of the collector John Tradescant the Elder (*q.v.*). Herbalist to James I and Royal Botanist to Charles I, following the publication in 1629 of *Paradisi in Sole Paradisus Terrestris*, an important and beautifully illustrated treatise on horticulture. After de l'Obel's death in 1616 Parkinson acquired his notes and incorporated them in his *Theatrum Botanicum* (1640).

Paxton, Sir Joseph (1803-65): the son of an English farmer, by the age of twenty-three he was the Duke of Devonshire's head gardener at Chatsworth. Here he improved the gardens, including the kitchen gardens, and designed new greenhouses, culminating with the Great Stove at Chatsworth and the 1851 Crystal Palace in Hyde Park, London, for which he was knighted. He became an architect, an MP, a railway millionaire, an author and the editor of a botanical magazine. He was co-founder of *The Gardener's Chronicle*, still going strong.

Platt, Sir Hugh (*c.*1552-1608): the son of a wealthy brewer who devoted his life to the study of husbandry and was knighted in 1605 for his services to science. The first part of his book *The Garden of Eden* appeared posthumously in 1608, as *Floræs Paradise*; it was subsequently given its English title in 1653. The second part of *The Garden of Eden* was added in 1660. Here, as well as enquiring into the possibilty of heated walls, Platt suggested a way of heating plant-houses with steam piped from boiling vats or cauldrons. He also described in detail the making of hotbeds, and gave methods for retarding the ripening of fruit, advancing the maturity of peas and watering by capillary action.

Pliny the Elder (Gaius Plinius Secundus, AD 23-79): Roman cavalry officer, lawyer and friend of the Emperor Vespasian, he completed his *Historia Naturalis* just before he died. The sections devoted to gardening and medicinal herbs provide important references for Roman kitchen gardening.

pyrethrum powder: an insecticide made from the ground flowerheads of several Caucasian and south-eastern European species of pyrethrum, including *Chrysanthemum cinerariifolium*. The powder, which is non-toxic to humans, can be used as a dust, mixed with water as a spray, or burnt as a fumigant.

quassia chips/wash: the chips or shavings of the wood of *Picrasma excelsa*, a West Indian tree. The wood contains a bitter insecticidal substance (quassin, also found in *Quassia amara*) which was extracted by boiling the chips in water. Soft soap was dissolved in the solution, which was used as a wash against aphids.

quincunx: a planting pattern, usually of fruit trees, with four trees marking the corners of a square and a fifth marking the centre.

Raleigh, Sir Walter (1552-1618): English courtier, navigator and author, not best known for his connections with horticulture, but he was instrumental in introducing the potato to Ireland, and orange trees to England. Gerard (*q.v.*) dedicated the second Catalogue of his plants to Raleigh in 1599.

rampions/rampion bellflower (*Campanula rapanculus*): a European native plant, naturalized in Britain, cultivated in sixteenth and seventeenth-century gardens. Its white, fleshy roots were eaten raw or cooked and the leaves made winter salads.

Reid, John (1655-1723): son and grandson of Scottish gardeners, himself a gardener until 1683, when he published his *Scots Gard'ner* and went to America to become Surveyor-General of New Jersey. He never returned.

Repton, Humphry (1752-1818): English landscape designer. He disliked banishing kitchen gardens to a distance, and designed them both for recreation and use, incorporating pleasant walks from the house and screens of shrubs and trees to hide the walls. Best known for his 'Red Books', illustrated with 'before and after' watercolours of the gardens he was designing.

Rivers, Thomas, III (1798-1877): born into a family of Suffolk nurserymen, he worked first with roses, and then with fruit trees, pioneering dwarfing varieties. He also invented the orchard house.

Robinson, William (1838-1935): landscape gardener, author and editor; born in Ireland, he worked there as a gardener until 1861, when he came to the Royal Botanic Gardens in Regents Park, London, to work under Robert Marnock (1800-89). He became horticultural correspondent of *The Times* in 1867 and published many works on gardening between 1868 and 1903, including *The English Flower Garden* (1883) and *The Wild Garden* (1870). He met his protégée Gertrude Jekyll in 1875 and she worked with him on his magazine *The Garden*.

rocambole (*Allium scorodoprasum jajlae*): similar to garlic, but milder and more delicate in flavour, especially when in its green state. Also known as the sand leek and tree onion.

service tree/sorb apple (*Sorbus domestica*): native of Central and Southern Europe and possibly of Britain as it grows both wild and in gardens here. It is a tree with clusters of berry-sized fruits. These are gathered unripe and left in a warm place to ripen completely, then used dried, or to make verjuice (*q.v.*).

smallage/small-ache: an old name for celery, derived from the Latin *selinum* and *apium*. Wild celery (*Apium graveolens)* is native to Britain, and was used as a purifying herb and flavouring for pottage.

soft soap: mainly used for its spreading and smothering properties, but also mildly insecticidal. Dissolved in boiling rainwater or soft water, it is used as a spray or wash, either on its own or in combination with other insecticides such as carbolic acid, hellebore powder, derris dust or quassia (*q.v.*). Made by saponifying vegetable oils with potash.

span roof: usually refers to the roof of a glasshouse with two sides meeting at the apex; may also be used of a frame, when it is called a double-span roof. A single or half-span roof has only one side, like a lean-to roof; a three-quarter span has one full side and one half side.

Speechly, William (?1734-1819): gardener to the 3rd Duke of Portland at Welbeck from 1767 to 1804, he was sent to Holland in 1771 by his employer, a descendant of Bentinck (*q.v.*), to learn what he could of Dutch gardening. He rebuilt both the pinery and the vinery on his return and published *A Treatise on the Culture of the Pine Apple* in 1779, followed by *A Treatise on the Culture of the Vine* in 1790.

sport/rogue: mutant of a plant variety, often with variegated leaves or flowers of a different colour.

Switzer, Stephen (1682-1745): landscape gardener, draughtsman and writer, apprenticed to London and Wise (*q.v.*) and possibly a kitchen gardener at St James's Palace. Books include *The Practical Fruit-Gardener* (1724) and *The Practical Kitchen Gardiner*

(1727). While a champion of the new, natural gardens of his contemporaries, his designs for fruit and kitchen gardens were formal and elaborate.

tallies: flat sticks used as plant labels. Derived from the notched tallies used by employers to record stints of work, and hence their debts.

Theophrastus (*c.*370-*c.*285 BC): Greek philosopher, pupil and friend of Aristotle, whose books and garden he inherited. His description of 450 species of plants led Linnaeus to call him 'the father of botany'.

tobacco/tobacco refuse (*see also* **nicotine**): the stems left after processing tobacco for smoking in pipes or as snuff, etc. Tobacco was first used in English gardens in the seventeenth century, and made into infusions and powders for use as a herbicide and earthworm killer. It was not used as a fumigant until the eighteenth century.

Tradescant, John (the Elder) (*c.*1570-1638): botanist and curio collector; gardener at Hatfield House to the Cecil family, who sent him to Europe to collect plants. He introduced many new varieties of fruit and vegetables and was a friend of Parkinson (*q.v.*). Appointed Keeper of the King's Gardens at Oatlands.

Tradescant, John (the Younger) (1608-62): at first assisted, then succeeded his father (*q.v.*) at Oatlands and made plant-collecting trips to Virginia.

Turner, William (1510-68): physician, botanist and belligerent Protestant, often in exile abroad. Known as 'the father of English botany', his major work is *The New Herball* (1551).

Varro, Marcus Terentius (116-27 BC): Roman scholar and prolific author; his work on husbandry, *De Re Rustica* (37 BC), includes much on agriculture and viticulture, but nothing on horticulture. However, there is a section on gourmet foods.

verjuice: sour, fermented liquid made from the juice of unripe grapes, service fruit, gooseberries or crab apples, used in cooking as vinegar.

Walsingham, Sir Francis (*c.*1530-90): English statesman and spy. Sent on embassies to France (1570-73) and the Netherlands (1578). Towards the end of his life he became a religious recluse, able to devote time to his garden but dying in poverty and debt.

White, Gilbert (1720-93): clergyman and naturalist, best known for his *Natural History of Selborne* (1789), but also a keen gardener. He was acquainted with Miller (*q.v.*), Curtis (*q.v.*) and Hales (*q.v.*) and kept a meticulous record, from 1751 to 1768, of his own gardening activities, published as *Garden Kalendar*.

Whitmill, Benjamin (*fl.* 1722-30): nurseryman and member of the Society of Gardeners (*see* Miller), he compiled their *Catalogues Plantarum* (1730). A skilled and experimental fruit grower, he also wrote a gardening calendar, *Kalendarium Universale* (1748).

Wise, Henry (1653-1738): apprenticed to, then partner with George London (*q.v.*) at Brompton Nurseries from *c.*1687. Appointed Royal Gardener 1702 until his retirement in 1727. After London's death Wise took first Joseph Carpenter (*q.v.*) as his partner at Brompton and then James Bridgeman. Translated, with London, Gentil's *Le Jardinier Solitaire* as *The Retir'd Gard'ner* (1706) and abridged, with London, Evelyn's translation of de la Quintinye's *Instructions pour les Jardins Fruitiers et Potagers* as *The Compleat Gard'ner* (1699).

Worlidge, John (*c.*1630-1693): English writer on gardening; later editions of his *Systema Agriculturae* (1669) contain a gardener's calendar.

ACKNOWLEDGEMENTS

Some of the acknowledgements for help with writing the first edition of this book, which was published nine years ago as *Charleston Kedding*, are repeated here. But I would like to emphasise the extra special help given to me with this new edition by Lady Jean O'Neill and Penelope Whitaker, sisters of the late Billy Whitaker, and aunts of Lord Teynham, the present owner of 'Charleston Kedding' which is here given its true name of Pylewell Park. I am very grateful to him for allowing me to reveal Pylewell's true identity. I would also like to thank Mr and Mrs Maurice Thomas for their memories of war-time Pylewell.

For both editions I owe thanks to numerous friends in the Hampshire Gardens Trust, and the Garden History Society, for directing me to particular kitchen gardens, archives and books. Chief among these guides, without question, were the late Dr John Harvey and Dr Sylvia Landsberg, whose expertise included, besides their knowledge of medieval gardens, the arts of research and encouragement.

For information on Dutch kitchen gardening I am indebted to Dr Jan Woudstra and Ar Koppens (who also translated lengthy Dutch texts). Other translations for which I am grateful were made from the Spanish by the late Frances Partridge and Robin Campbell (my late husband); from medieval Italian by Chlöe Chard; from Latin by Jenny Gowing and Scarlet Buckley. I also frequented numerous libraries, but none so constantly as the Royal Horticultural Society's Lindley Library, where the knowledge and unfailing helpfulness of the librarian, Dr Brent Elliott, made every visit fruitful.

This would only be half a book however, without the spoken reminiscences and horticultural advice of several professional gardeners. Top of this list must come Doug Brereton, Fred Nutbeam and Arthur Hopkins, late of Cottesbrooke Hall, Buckingham Palace and Chatsworth respectively. I should also like to thank the owners of all the kitchen gardens I have visited over the last twenty-five years – some 450 in all, both public and private – with special thanks to those who allowed me to make drawings, notes and photographs.

I would like to thank, warmly, all the friends who gave me moral support while I was at work on both editions of this book, with special thanks to those who took me to see kitchen gardens in their own parts of the country. On the production side of this new edition I would like to thank Jane Crawley for her patient editing and Becky Clarke for the book's design.

SOURCES FOR DRAWINGS

The full-page composite drawings in this book are based on a variety of sources – photographs, maps, interpretations of contemporary descriptions in manuscripts and books, or sketches made by the author on site. Where there is space I have given the source on the drawing itself; some of the others, for which there was no space, are listed below.

p.10: Plan of Pylewell's kitchen garden from 1st edn. Ordnance Survey map

p.10: Plan of Queen Victoria's kitchen garden at Windsor from Charles M'Intosh's *Book of the Garden*, 1853, vol. I, plate 10

p.22: View of Pylewell from an anonymous print, *circa* 1700 and an engraving in *Vitruvius Britannicus*, 1739

p.22: Plan of Melbourne Hall from a plan in Derbyshire Record Office

p.22: Plan of Herriard Park from a plan in Hampshire Record Office

p.42: Plan of Chatsworth's kitchen gardens from Ordnance Survey map, 1929

p.42: Hott Wall *circa* 1790, from a drawing by Sir John Soane, Soane Museum, London

p.42: Sloped Wall from a plate in Stephen Switzer's *The Practical Fruit -gardener*, 1731

p.42: Arched Foundations from Thomas Hitt's *Treatise of Fruit-trees*, 1757, plate II

p.42: Raised Walk from woodcuts of gardens in Thomas Hyll's *The Gardeners Labyrinth*, 1577

p.42: Wall in Half-rounds from a description in Thomas Langford's *Plain and Full Instructions . . .*, 1681

p.42: Wooden Wall heated by Dung from a description in Benjamin Whitmill's *Kalendarium Universale*, 1748

p.42: Beard's Glass Walls from a line engraving in Anderson's *The New Practical Gardener*, *c.*1872

p.42: Buttress to deflect the Wind seen at Constable Burton, Yorkshire

p.58: Horizontal Shelters from a description in Stephen Switzer's *Practical Fruit Gardener*, 1731 and John Laurence's *The Gentleman's Recreation*, 1716, fig.3

p.58: Glass Coping with Portable Fronts from Beeton's *Garden Management*, *c.*1870

p.58: Rendle's Patent Protector from Rendle & Co.'s *Catalogue*, *c.*1870

p.58: Foxley's Patent Brick from *Journal of Horticulture and Cottage Gardening*, 1864

p.58: Caleb Hitch's Bricks, from illustrations in Richard A. Storey's paper in *East Hertfordshire Industrial Archaeology*, i. 1971

p.78: Garden Plan 1 from *Macdonald's Dictionary of Gardening*, 1807, plate F, vol.3

p.78: Garden Plan 2 from Thomas Hitt's *Treatise of Fruit-trees*, 1757, plate I

p.96: St Gall Plan from Ernest Horn and Walter Born's *The Plan of St Gall*, 1979

p.96: A Gentleman's Garden from a woodcut in Thomas Hyll's *The Gardeners Labyrinth*, 1577

p.148: A Dutch Orangery from Jan van der Groen's *Jardinier du Pays-bas*, 1572

p.148: Construction and Cross-section of an Orangery from Pieter de la Court's *Landhuren, Lusthaven, Plantagien*, 1691

p.148: John Evelyn's Greenhouse from *Kalendarium Hortense*, 1691

p.157: Hampton Court Stove from a drawing in the *Fort Album Historic Survey* at Hampton Court, *c.*1701

p.157: Speechly's Pine and Grape Stove from William

INDEX

page numbers for illustrations are in *italic*